Confucian Image Politics

Confucian Image Politics

MASCULINE MORALITY IN SEVENTEENTH-CENTURY CHINA

Ying Zhang

UNIVERSITY OF WASHINGTON PRESS *Seattle and London*

the modern language initiative

THIS BOOK IS MADE POSSIBLE BY A COLLABORATIVE GRANT FROM THE ANDREW W. MELLON FOUNDATION.

Illuminating the Ming

This publication also was made possible by a grant from the James P. Geiss Foundation, a private nonprofit operating foundation that sponsors research on China's Ming dynasty (1368–1644).

The publisher also gratefully acknowledges the contributions to this publication by the Department of History and the Arts and Humanities Division of the College of Arts and Sciences at Ohio State University.

Printed and bound in the United States of America

20 19 18 17 16 5 4 3 2 1

University of Washington Press
www.washington.edu/uwpress

Library of Congress Cataloging-in-Publication Data

Names: Zhang, Ying (History teacher) author.
Title: Confucian image politics : masculine morality in seventeenth-century China / Ying Zhang.
Other titles: Masculine morality in seventeenth-century China
Description: 1st edition. | Seattle : University of Washington Press, 2016. | Includes bibliographical references and index.
Identifiers: LCCN 2016009721 | ISBN 9780295998534 (hardcover : alk. paper)
Subjects: LCSH: Political ethics—China—History—17th century. | Confucian ethics—China—History—17th century. | China—Officials and employees—Conduct of life—History—17th century.
Classification: LCC JQ1509.5.E8 Z4375 2016 | DDC 172.0951/09032—dc23
LC record available at http://lccn.loc.gov/2016009721

The paper used in this publication is acid-free and meets the minimum requirements of American National Standard for Information Sciences—Permanence of Paper for Printed Library Materials, ANSI Z39.48–1984. ∞

Dedicated to my laoshi and shimu,
Chun-shu Chang and Shelley Hsueh-lun Chang

CONTENTS

PREFACE AND ACKNOWLEDGMENTS

In 2009, I was excited to learn that the Changchun Temple still existed in Beijing. Built in the 1590s by the mother of the Ming Wanli emperor, the temple was patronized throughout the seventeenth century by emperors and prominent officials, from the late Ming to the early Qing dynasty. Its famous female donor in the early Qing, a courtesan-turned-concubine named Gu Mei, changed the temple landscape by having a beautiful pavilion built on a hill. I had been studying Gu Mei and her turncoat husband for some time but was struggling with the polarized images of this couple in historical sources and scholarship. To unpack these images as a historian, I felt I needed to build a personal connection with the couple. So I went to visit the temple, accompanied by an old friend who was also fascinated by the deep connection between Beijing temples and imperial political history.

When we got there, the temple complex looked so new and neat that I doubted whether I would find the inspiration I had been looking for. The staff there, mostly government employees, confirmed that much of the complex had been reconstructed recently, although a few objects were originals. My greatest disappointment was that the whole area had been leveled in the past hundred years; the pavilion and the hill where it had stood were long gone. My friend asked the staff whether they had heard of the pavilion. One of them pointed to a high building afar: "Look! That's the Xuanwu People's Hospital. It was built where the pavilion used to be."

As I set my eyes on that hospital, my mind's eye immediately saw Gu Mei's Buddhist devotion and philanthropy, her amazing artistic talents, her personal experiences in a time of war and political change, and her generous support for literati friends, many of whom were

Ming loyalists who refused to serve the next dynasty, the Qing. Sud denly, I realized that modern hospital had become the bridge between me and the subjects of my study, or what the great Chinese historian Chen Yinke called the "historical sympathy" (*lishi zhi tongqing*)—a historian's delicate connection with the past. Had I been able to see the actual pavilion, I might have focused on its face value as a "real" and "relevant" source. But the sight of the hospital, oddly, worked the magic. It compelled me to reach out, on the emotive level, to the historical subjects and then trust the impressions I received from "feeling" the sources written by and about Gu Mei and her husband, Gong Dingzi.

The process of historical research and writing is full of interesting—and even mysterious—moments like this. This study of the political history of the dynastic change from the Ming to the Qing had been a challenging project. I struggled with the images of seventeenth-century figures, which were greatly polarized as a result of the moral-political division among the elite, whose writings constitute the majority of our sources. Ming loyalism, Confucian historiographical tradition, Qing state literary censorship, and modern Chinese nationalism all left deep marks on seventeenth-century archives. Eventually, I chose to make the competing moral images of officials like Gong Dingzi the focus of this book.

This book is not about political figures' moral images per se but about the social, cultural, and political conditions that generated and perpetuated them. I relied on my own interpretation of many personal writings to reconstruct these political figures' experiences at the intersection of their public and private lives. The moral images of political actors were such high-stake matters during this eventful century that I had to constantly debate, in my mind, with my sources and their authors about the meanings and implications of their words, art, and actions. My project was transformed from one about "restoring the truth" to one juxtaposing and making sense of competing claims about one's performance as official, father, son, husband, and friend.

The process of transforming this project was a process of intellectual and personal transformation for me. I hope this book will generate new scholarly conversations. The imperfections are mine, but they should not prevent me from expressing deep gratitude toward my mentors, colleagues, and friends. Without their generous, patient, and kind guidance and support, I would not have been able to build those meaningful connections with my historical subjects and publish my findings.

Chun-Shu Chang, my mentor, not only nurtured my intellectual growth at the University of Michigan but also influenced my understanding of a Chinese historian's mission and a scholar's lifelong pursuit of self-cultivation. His erudition, kindness, compassion, and tolerance made it possible for me to become a professional historian and complete this ambitious book.

Over the years during my research and writing, I was extremely fortunate to have had these teachers: Wang Zheng, Dorothy Ko, Hitomi Tonomura, and Dena Goodman. Their passion for feminist scholarship, intellectual sharpness and breadth, and insightful answers to my questions shaped my work and provided consistent, invaluable support in many aspects. The best way for me to express my gratitude toward them is to continue on this path and make meaningful contributions to critical gender history.

I am grateful for the generosity of many colleagues who kindly shared with me their scholarly findings and insights. The comments and suggestions I received from these colleagues on the manuscript during its various stages were immensely helpful: Michael Chang, Siyen Fei, Rivi Handler-Spitzer, Susan Hartmann, Clayton Howard, Martin Huang, Ari D. Levine, Weijing Lu, Toby Meyer-Fong, Harry Miller, Geoffrey Parker, Maria Franca Sibau, Janet Theiss, and Jiang Wu. Steven Conn, Yongtao Du, Andrea Goldman, and Julia Strauss read a long early draft patiently and offered great advice on streamlining it. Cynthia Brokaw, Patricia Sieber, Zhange Ni, and Christopher Reed carefully read the last draft of the manuscript. Their insightful questions and words of encouragement made the final revision an extremely rewarding and productive experience for me. I was also fortunate to have received excellent suggestions from the following scholars when I encountered difficult moments in research and writing: Kai-wing Chow, Beverly Bossler, Miaw-fen Lu, Sato Masayuki, Shang Wei, and Yang Haiying.

During the course of research, many institutions and individuals provided generous assistance: the rare book department at the National Library of China (in particular Dr. Cui Hongming), Shanghai Library, Library of Congress, Harvard-Yenching Library, Anhui Provincial Library, UCLA Library, University of Michigan Library, and The Ohio State University Library; Professor Zhou Zhiyuan at Anhui University, Professor Zhang Sheng at Beijing Normal

University, and Dr. Yang Haiying and Dr. Zhuang Xiaoxia at the Chinese Academy of Social Sciences.

I am grateful for the immense support from the Department of History at The Ohio State University (OSU) and my colleagues here. This project would not have come to fruition without the resources made available by the Department of History, Office of International Affairs, and the Coca-Cola Critical Difference for Women Grants for Research on Women, Gender, and Gender Equity at OSU. During 2012–13, a fellowship opportunity at the UCLA Center for 17th- and 18th-Century Studies and William Andrews Clark Memorial Library introduced me to the wonderful colleagues there. Stimulating conversations with Andrea Goldman, R. Bin Wong, Richard von Glahn, and other historians at UCLA gave me important ideas when I was conceptualizing this book.

Various parts of this research have been presented at the "Moralism and the Rhetoric of Decline in Eurasia, 1600–1900" workshop at the UCLA Center for 17th- and 18th-Century Studies (2012 and 2015), "History of Filial Piety" workshop (organized by Ellen Cong Zhang) at the University of Virginia, "Li Zhi and 16th-Century China" workshop at the University of Chicago, Association for Asian Studies, Institute of Chinese Studies at OSU, and the Pre-modernist Workshop at OSU. Feedback from fellow participants and audience at these events helped me improve the project immensely. In particular, Greg Anderson, Phil Brown, John Brooke, and Tina Sessa at the OSU Pre-modernist Workshop made it a wonderful space for my intellectual growth. Part of chapter 3 was published as "The Politics and Practice of Moral Rectitude" in *Late Imperial China*. I am thankful for Toby Meyer-Fong and Janet Theiss for helping me rethink the piece and revise it for publication.

I owe special thanks to Patricia Ebrey. I benefited from her groundbreaking scholarship and her participation in the workshop on the history of filial piety at the University of Virginia. She kindly introduced me to the amazing editorial staff at the University of Washington Press. There, Lorri Hagman's guidance, advice, and encouragement made this book possible. The two anonymous readers shared extremely helpful comments and suggestions on the manuscript.

I indulged in the love and support of many friends while I was completing the book. Although I cannot mention all of them, I am forever grateful. The Chans embraced me as a family member; the Sieber-Reano family brought me much joy; Theodora Dragostinova took great care of me. Terre Fisher has been my most reliable copy editor. Zhange Ni, an amazing scholar and poet, was always there with her excellent ideas and generous heart. Art, my source of intellectual inspiration and emotional comfort, would not have occupied such an important place in my life without Cindy Davis, my printmaking mentor.

Finally, I hope to thank my parents for supporting my intellectual pursuits with endless love and encouragement. My sister Wei shared my passion as a scholar and commitment to improving this world with our research. To my *laoshi* Chun-Shu Chang and *shimu* Shelley Hsueh-lun Chang I dedicate this book. They have influenced and nurtured me no less than my parents.

MING-QING REIGN PERIODS

MING DYNASTY

Hongwu/Taizu 1368–98
Jianwen/Huidi 1399–1402
Yongle/Chengzu 1403–24
Hongxi/Renzong 1425
Xuande/Xuanzong 1426–35
Zhengtong/Yingzong 1436–49
Jingtai/Daizong 1450–56
Tianshun/Yingzong 1457–64
Chenghua/Xianzong 1465–87
Hongzhi/Xiaozong 1488–1505
Zhengde/Wuzong 1506–21
Jiajing/Shizong 1522–66
Longqing/Muzong 1567–72
Wanli/Shenzong 1573–1619
Taichang/Guangzong 1620
Tianqi/Xizong 1621–27
Chongzhen/Sizong 1628–44

QING DYNASTY (TO 1850)

Taizu/Tianming 1616–26
Taizong/Tiancong, Chongde 1627–43
Shunzhi/Shizu 1644–61

Kangxi/Shengzu 1662–1722
Yongzheng/Shizong 1723–35
Qianlong/Gaozong 1736–95
Jiaqing/Renzong 1596–1820
Daoguang/Xuanzong 1821–50

Confucian Image Politics

Introduction

In 1620 (the forty-eighth year of the Ming Wanli reign), the literatus Feng Menglong (1574–1646) published a large collection of amusing stories titled *Jokes from History and the Present Day* (Gujin xiao).[1] In the very first chapter, Feng presents an anecdote about an encounter between courtesans and the Cheng brothers, two Neo-Confucian thinkers and officials of the Song dynasty (960–1279): "The Cheng brothers went to a banquet hosted by a literatus. Courtesans were called upon to entertain the guests. Cheng Yi's face changed and he left in anger, while Cheng Hao stayed on and had a good time. The next day, Cheng Yi visited Cheng Hao's studio and was still complaining about the banquet. Cheng Hao said: 'Yesterday there were courtesans at the banquet, but I did not have courtesans on my mind. Today there are no courtesans in my studio, yet you have courtesans on your mind!' Cheng Yi had to admit his brother was the superior."[2] This story had been invented and circulated among the literati in the sixteenth century, when the Yangming school of Neo-Confucianism dominated intellectual circles and its flirtation with Chan Buddhism became a fad.[3] It was said that Wang Yangming (1472–1529) himself particularly liked this story and often referred to it.[4] Feng Menglong, whose intellectual trajectory had been tremendously influenced by the stress on human intuition by Yangming-school followers, in particular the radical thinker Li Zhi (1527–1602), claimed that he did not publish this story to slander or encourage social deviance. Rather, it was meant to question dogmatic understandings of moral cultivation and the images of moral superiority based on such understandings.[5]

As Feng himself points out in the preface to the collection, reading such anecdotes as amusing allows the reader to "recognize the genuine" (*renzhen*) instead of "taking things to heart" (the common meaning of *renzhen*) so excessively that one loses the ability to see the truth.[6]

This anecdote also appeared in *Daily Compilations at the Zuofei Studio* (Zuofei'an ri zuan), published by the official Zheng Xuan (*jinshi* 1631) in the 1630s–40s. Stylistically, *Daily Compilations* manifested the late-Ming literati passion for *xiaopin*-style literature, or jottings that engage topics, emotions, and aesthetics outside the realm of classical and political studies.[7] In Zheng's book, the anecdote about the Cheng brothers appears in the chapter on the importance of tolerance and transcendence.[8] It exemplifies Zheng's interest in the philosophy of living a good life shared by many *xiaopin* authors, who often also shared a belief in the syncretism of Confucianism, Buddhism, and Daoism.

The success of Feng's book of "jokes" and Zheng's leisurely collection on living a good life reflect the seventeenth century's "confusions of pleasure."[9] But these books, their authors, and their enthusiastic readers represent only one side of the story of this period, a time of flourishing print culture, thriving entertainment, and a reconfiguration of the Neo-Confucian moral economy and ontological order as China worked through the upheavals of a dynastic transition from the Ming (1368–1644) to the Qing (1644–1911).[10] In some people's eyes, the popularity of this anecdote about the Cheng brothers was symptomatic of serious moral confusion among the literati, many of whom abandoned self-discipline and justified their indulgence in sensual pleasures by invoking the language of "no courtesans on my mind."[11]

The anecdote entered didactic texts. Liu Zongzhou (1578–1645), a scholarly giant and accomplished official, included it in his work on literati self-cultivation, *Manual for Man* (Renpu). Liu had presented the notion of "watchfulness over the solitary self" (*shendu*) as the correct method of moral self-cultivation, which represented a critical inheritance of the Yangming legacy. In the "Ledgers Recording Transgressions" (Jiguo ge) section of *Manual for Man*, Liu explicitly lists "mingling with courtesans" as one of the "miscellaneous transgressions" of which one should beware.[12] In the collection of anecdotes he compiled to further illustrate such transgressions, Liu not only placed the story about the Cheng brothers among "warnings against mingling with courtesans"[13] but also introduced a section on the harms of jokes and jest.

The intellectual and cultural shift exemplified by Liu's deployment of this anecdote intersected with the deepening political crisis of the Ming dynasty: factionalism, social unrest, and Manchu threats were cracking the illusion of a "floating world." The intellectual turn and the emergent factional infighting clearly showed in *Random Notes Taken in Retirement* (Linju manlu; hereafter *Random Notes*) by the official Wu Yuancui (*jinshi* 1577), a collection of stories and thoughts on Ming politics. Wu claims the anecdote about the Cheng brothers to have been a fabrication by Cheng Yi's political enemies in Song factionalism, a fabrication disseminated by figures of the Yangming school in the Ming and conveniently embraced by morally corrupt literati.[14] Wu denounces not only the Chan Buddhist flavor of the anecdote but also the very idea that Cheng Hao ever mingled with courtesans. He urges the reader instead to adhere strictly to male-female separation, a central doctrine of the Confucian gender system.[15]

Wu invoked the history of Song factionalism to question the authenticity of the anecdote, but he does not seem to have anticipated a factionalist attack on his own publication. After his book came out, his former colleague He Canran (*jinshi* 1595) published a book-length commentary in which he offered the following words on Wu's reference to the anecdote: "Pretty courtesans and alluring boys are both uncontrollable. [Wu Yuancui] has confessed that he loves boys. Therefore, if he is seated at a banquet with a courtesan, he might imagine her as a boy and still refrain from getting intimate with her. That would be fine as well."[16] When He Canran published his comments on Wu's book in Wanli 40 (1612), officials were engrossed in intensifying factional struggles in the government over a host of important policy issues. Bitter sentiments and hostility spilled over into their social world. He's tactic here is personal but representative: he took revenge for Wu's political attacks by publicly discrediting Wu's book and questioning his self-presentation as a moral exemplar and his authority as an objective political insider.[17] In response, Wu published a counter-commentary, accusing He of ignoring "public opinion" (*gonglun*) and misrepresenting his views.[18]

These intellectual, cultural, and political adventures and tensions were signs of the fundamental transformations and challenges that seventeenth-century Chinese elites were experiencing, a kind of "authenticity crisis" that affected all spheres of life.[19] Before these men could work out a solution to that crisis, rebellions and the Manchu invasions put an end to the Ming dynasty. When the rebels stormed the Ming capital of Beijing in the spring of 1644, the Ming emperor's suicide prompted the surviving elites to establish a Southern Ming court in Nanjing, the Ming's secondary capital. Within a year that region was conquered by the Qing, too.

The Qing conquest and its aggressive sociopolitical agenda ushered in the decline of the legendary Nanjing pleasure quarters, a staple of late-Ming literati culture. In the early Qing, the Ming loyalist Yu Huai (1616–1696) published *Miscellaneous Records of the Plank Bridge* (Banqiao zaji), a work on the Nanjing courtesans and their literati lovers, as an alternative means of recording Ming glory and expressing anti-Qing sentiments.[20] At his request, one of his non-loyalist friends, the Qing official You Tong (1618–1704), contributed a preface, in which he invoked the anecdote about the Cheng brothers.

> Someone said: "When Yu Huai was young he indulged in frequenting courtesans. Now this old man still enjoys writing about them. You have determined to purify your mind and pursue the Way. Why do you bother to read this stuff?" I smiled: "In history, Cheng Hao 'did not have courtesans on his mind even through there were courtesans in front of him,' while Cheng Yi 'had courtesans on his mind even though there were no courtesans around.' Clearly one is superior to the other. Now, there are courtesans in Yu Huai's writing; therefore I do not have courtesans in my work. Why not compose a preface for him?"[21]

As Yu's book, You's preface, and their literary allusions demonstrate, in the early Qing, writing about officials' moral performance was a means by which Han elites negotiated between romantic nostalgia and critical self-reflection, between Ming loyalism and the reality of Manchu conquest.

All these print references to the invented anecdote about the Cheng brothers throw light on the various dynamics that pulled the moral image of officials to the center of politics during the Ming-Qing transition (1570s–1680s), when the intersecting issues of intellectual shifts, literary publicity, factionalism, and dynastic change jointly shaped elite men's political concerns, actions, and experiences in particular gendered ways. These dynamics gave rise to seventeenth-century Chinese image politics, which unfolded in the many stories about officials' personal lives that circulated in gossip and anecdotes, in print and theater, and in social and political spectacles.[22] The tales about officials as fathers, sons, and husbands exemplified how political actors employed Confucian ethics as a language of communication in their efforts to negotiate, adapt, and survive.

SEEING THE MING-QING TRANSITION IN THE MIRROR

To explore the multiple, intertwining changes and continuities in this crucial era in Chinese history, "the seventeenth century" and the "Ming-Qing dynastic transition" are used as interchangeable chronological frameworks. This helps us go beyond simplifying binaries, such as "decline and revival" and "conservatism and progress," that permeate both the sources and the historiography of this time period.

In Confucian historical narrative, the late Ming and early Qing constitute a typical transition in the dynastic cycle, a political change that delivered the empire from a morally defective regime to a new benevolent government that would carry forward the Mandate of Heaven.[23] Late-Ming literati complained profusely about the deteriorating moral standards in society and in government. Faced with a highly commercialized economy, the rise of the merchant class, tensions between landowners and tenants, and urbanization, elites employed Confucian moral rhetoric to articulate their understanding of changing socioeconomic dynamics and to propose ways of restoring order and maintaining their relative privileges.[24] After the Ming was overthrown by domestic rebels and then replaced by the Manchu Qing, many argued that the erosion of literati moral standards, partly brought about through the popularity of the Yangming school and the radicalization of some of its number, had contributed to the moral deterioration of officials in general. In the late Ming, they had engaged in chronic factionalism, shamelessly allied themselves with evil eunuchs in the pursuit of their own self-interest, and failed to honorably commit suicide when the Ming fell.[25] After the dynastic change, the Qing rulers' moral condemnation of the fallen Ming and their posturing as a legitimate civilizing force surprisingly struck many of the same notes as had the literati criticisms.[26]

The grand narrative of this period produced by modern historians also delineates a picture of decline and revival, though it disputes the validity of the "dynastic cycle" theory. From the mid-sixteenth century, the Ming empire felt the combined effects of novel environmental, socioeconomic, cultural, and political developments. In its last seventy years, it was overwhelmed by poor harvests, natural disasters, social instability, rebellions, and factional infighting in the government. Moral crisis was manifested in, and contributed to, its political decline.[27] The "seventeenth-century global crisis" framework also describes the Ming-Qing transition as part of a global phenomenon in a time of climate change. Interestingly, the timing of decline and revival posed in this narrative does not deviate much from the one recorded in the Chinese moral-meteorological narrative.[28]

Another dominant narrative in the historiography of this period evaluates social, cultural, intellectual, and political developments in the framework of "progress versus conservatism." Evidence of political "progress" seemingly identical to the early modern European experience is found in the flourishing print culture and a host of related socioeconomic, cultural, and political changes. Lack of institutional control over late-Ming publishers resulted in the proliferation of a wide range of nonorthodox interpretations of the Confucian classics, some of which could even be considered dissenting or outlandish.[29] Most such publications did not explicitly or fundamentally challenge the imperial court or the Confucian system. Rather, they diffused the authority of the previous or established scholars of the classics. They accomplished this partly by redefining "heterodoxy" (*yiduan*) and introducing unconventional reference genres in their expository uses. Buddhist texts, unofficial histories, and even novels all entered the expositional vocabulary.[30] Literary authority shifted from the court to the reading public, and the "literary public sphere" expanded well beyond kinship networks and the official examination system, as seen in the proliferation of literary societies.[31] Print culture changed the sociopolitical landscape. Information flew in and between urban centers, weaving an increasingly complex and dense web of media representations. It was an important open domain for literati who could access and participate in it, either as readers or producers of work, from pamphlets and treatises to vernacular novels and plays.[32] Although literati could not use print to disseminate seditious language, they could employ it to shape public sentiment, promote their own agendas, and take limited but often effective action against their rivals.[33]

Did this flourishing print culture result in the emergence of a "public sphere" in the Habermasian sense in the late Ming? Scholars have not reached a consensus.[34] But some see democratic tendencies in the new types of literati associations and some of their political influences.[35] It has been implied that the joint forces of the Ming-Qing monarchal autocracy, self-destructive factional infighting, and the dogmatic application of moral norms in Confucian society repressed signs of "progress." For instance, in the late Ming, the literati cultivated more effective and egalitarian networking, some seeing friendship as parallel to the fraternal relationship in the Confucian Five Cardinal Relations (Wulun) and therefore compatible with that order.[36] But literati interests in friendship, which ranged from intellectual companionship to homosexual love, from idealistic devotion to hard-nosed networking, also faced pushback from conservative Confucians and from the paranoid Manchu court, which saw the elevation of friendship as potentially weakening familial bonds, contributing to factionalism, and fomenting seditious sentiments and actions.[37] In other words, according to this perspective, Confucian conservatism and the Qing conquest prevented the country from transforming its political system in meaningful ways.

Both of these narratives depict in different ways a system resistant to political change. Can we build a more nuanced analysis of seventeenth-century Chinese political culture based on critical but also sympathetic engagement with these established historical frameworks? Historians have begun to contextualize the narrative of decline and revival, a common self-expression of the literati, to illustrate the specific intellectual, social, and cultural strategies they undertook so as to adapt to and even implement changes.[38] Recent scholarship has also moved away from "public sphere" to "public spaces" in seventeenth- and eighteenth-century urban history.[39] Similarly, in the sphere of official politics, paying close attention to the lived experiences and emotions of officials—the most important group of political subjects—helps raise productive questions. This book asks: During this time, when a large amount of moral tales about officials were created in and circulated between the court and literati society, what kinds of political negotiations were taking place, and how did this process reconfigure the political spaces?

To answer these questions, one has to accommodate some particular problems with the primary sources that have long bedeviled scholars of the Ming-Qing transition.[40] Rebellions and dynastic change not only eliminated a huge portion of the population but also led to multiple layers of censorship imposed by the state, by literati communities, and even by individuals themselves. Meanwhile, the flourishing print culture and a well-integrated empirewide communication network generated an unprecedented amount of material in and about this period. Hence, the sources are abundant but replete with stereotypical images of the "gentlemen" and "small men."

The problem with the sources was further complicated in the high Qing. To meet the needs of its particular moral-political agenda, the court sponsored historical projects that combed through the archives and generated new accounts about the Han and Manchus of the seventeenth century. They typically eulogized the narrowly defined moral exemplars.[41] Then in the nineteenth and early twentieth centuries, driven by modern intellectuals' "national salvation" programs, large-scale efforts to discover, compile, and reprint seventeenth-century materials mushroomed. In these historical processes, Chinese elites, men and women, kept revisiting the Ming-Qing transition and the many metaphors, tales, and images from that eventful era, but especially those that fit into modern, nationalist categories.[42] Albeit with slightly different categories, they nonetheless further consolidated the contrast between the moral and the immoral. Hence, as images of the Ming-Qing transition are continuously multiplied by repeated reflection around familiar moral-political binaries, the lived experiences of our historical subjects grow ever more elusive.

This "image problem" of seventeenth-century sources and historiography reveals the "image trouble" of the most important political actors of the period, the officials, on both individual and collective levels. Late-Ming officials and their literati associates have been conventionally cast in morally contrasting stereotypes: the gentlemen's camp (the Donglin faction and the Fushe literary society) versus the evil men (the eunuch faction and rivals of the Donglin-Fushe communities). For the early Qing, the moral contrast has been drawn between Han officials who surrendered to the Qing (*erchen*) and Ming loyalists (*yimin*). These stereotypes are not merely an invention of modern historians. They were a means and result of political struggles in the seventeenth century. Making images in a large variety of genres and forms significantly transformed the political spaces and political processes of the late Ming and early Qing. Image was politics. The production, circulation, and effects of officials' competing moral images—as fathers, sons, husbands, and friends—serve as an excellent entry point into this matrix.

POLITICKING WITH CONFUCIAN VIRTUES

Across the dynastic divide, in factional infighting, political organizing, war mobilization, and postwar recovery, officials and their literati associates used fictional and nonfictional writing, art, rituals, and public spectacles to deliver and repel attacks, express opinions and emotions, and rally support. Changes in the intensity and media of political communication during this period led to not only the reconfiguration of political spaces but also interesting development in the ways Confucian ethics were employed in power struggles.

Mediated and Mediatized Political Spaces

In the seventeenth century, officially sanctioned political spaces were sites of political communication that took the form of court audiences, memorials, and negotiations among officials as well as their interactions with literati communities. Within and around these political spaces, important changes were taking place. Many factors and dynamics contributed to these changes.

In the late Ming, as people, goods, and books became more mobile, the circulation of political information gained extraordinary vigor and unprecedented complexity. The elite became experienced producers and consumers of highly mediated political information. Court politics, literary production, cultural consumption, and literati "public opinion" formed a circuit of mediated—and to a certain degree, mediatized—political realities.[43]

One of the main sources of political information at the time was the official gazetteer (*dibao*) published by the government and circulated in both official and private copies. Highly developed networks of transportation and print facilitated wider and faster circulation of the official gazetteer. Catering to the reading public's thirst for interesting information, writers and publishers often channeled material from the official gazetteer into popular literature, where it was re-presented to local and regional audiences in a more sensational manner.[44] Politics became a form of cultural consumption. In turn, literary trends also influenced the mode and mood of political communication.

The employment of literary publications for political purposes played an important role in reshaping political spaces. In imperial China, gossip and anecdote were recognized as "unruly" literary-political forces, but they had nonetheless always had a place in official historiography and power negotiations.[45] If gossip and anecdote embodied "tensions between public and private knowledge, between reliable and unreliable sources of information,"[46] then seventeenth-century print culture and political volatility only enhanced such tensions. Precisely due to readers' enhanced access to information and the diversification of information channels and genres, spreading myths, rumors, and half-baked assertions about an official's personal life in the forms of anecdote collections, commentaries, and even vernacular novels could have serious political consequences.

Vernacular novels were so widely and enthusiastically consumed by the literati that the Qing scholar Qian Daxin emphasized that the "teaching of novels" (*xiaoshuo jiao*) had transformative power and the potential for disseminating heterodox views.[47] The term *xiaoshuo* could refer to a range of literature, including fiction and petty discourse that originated in miscellaneous, unverifiable sources.[48] Many officials, as well as their literati supporters and opponents, fell under the sway of the "teaching of novels." As readers, they perceived their world through "sensational stories and intriguing dramas."[49] As political actors, they made efforts to use literature to influence negotiations with the emperor and between factions, rendering the already porous boundary between fact and fiction considerably more penetrable but politically more consequential.

Hence, using print intelligently to create a positive moral image, to paint a negative picture of enemies, and to avoid having the medium turned on oneself became an important skill for political actors. It was common for officials to resort to print and literature in order to cope with the increasing political uncertainty and volatility of their era. They published materials explicitly publicizing their moral-political accomplishments, refuting attacks, or circulating insider information about court politics. Although in some cases, a dearth of evidence prevents us from accurately gauging the outcomes of publishing endeavors, clearly, much of the published material found its way into memorials and court discussions.

One important genre of unofficial political publication was pamphlets. These allowed officials to present their views and positions, influence opinion, and garner sympathy and support, especially when they encountered difficult situations in their political lives. Increasingly, political pamphlets were printed and disseminated as a means of boosting individual or collective political reach and effectiveness.[50]

Officials also published books to communicate with the emperor, their colleagues, and the literati reading public. The contents of these books might include many genres, ranging from documentary to autobiography. For example, in late Chongzhen 11 (1638), Sun Chuanting (1593–1643), an accomplished official-general, published a book titled *Records of My Endeavors* (Jianlao lu), in which he meticulously documented battles, strategies, memorials, and the imperial edicts that conveyed recognition of his career accomplishments. Sun published this book to express his gratitude to the emperor for trusting him despite some officials' criticism, and he hoped that it would prove his loyalty.[51] The next year, Sun was impeached by a factional rival, Yang Sichang (1588–1641), and imprisoned by the emperor. From prison, Sun had his book reprinted with a new postscript that pleaded with the emperor to consider his loyalty and correct the wrongs done to him by the factionalists.[52] Although it is not completely clear to what extent this reprint contributed to Sun's release, it nonetheless affirms that officials, even while in prison, might resort to printing books to publicize their virtues and make a case for themselves.

In addition to their use of print materials, seventeenth-century literati enthusiastically pursued an interest in religious rituals and social spectacles, which also affected the outlook of political spaces. Literati in particular paid a great deal of attention to ritual in their efforts to restore social order and promote Confucian ethics. The rise of Confucian ritualism amounted to a cultural reform movement.[53] The Ming-Qing dynastic transition also gave rise to a culture that craved novelty and extremity.[54] Dramatic and even violent displays of moral heroism and devotion—often with the aid of religious and ritual tropes—filled not only the books of the period but also public spaces such as the court, theater, gatherings, and so on.[55] All these trends helped turn political spaces into platforms on which political figures could perform and authenticate moral exemplariness.

The transformation of political spaces was complex because, in the seventeenth century, tendencies toward fragmentation and integration in the cultural-political spheres coexisted. Since the late sixteenth century, all major political developments—debates over policies and reforms, the eunuch faction's persecution of literati-officials, chronic factionalism, war and violence, and the change of regime—affected large numbers of officials and their families and friends. Their stories frequently traveled with them between the political centers and local communities. In local power struggles in which officials and literati groups used literature, theater, and social spectacle to influence public attitudes, such tactics could quickly assume state-level significance. All over the empire, with unprecedented speed and breadth, printed pages, theatrical performances, and travelers circulated news and opinions about controversial thinkers, fashionable writers, notorious politicians, and unpredictable emperors. The formation of an empirewide political theater also contributed to the prevalence of competing—and often polarizing—images of prominent public figures, a situation in which controlling one's public image became increasingly difficult (see chap. 1).

Confucian Family Tales

Texts, arts, and rituals, written or performed, served as means of intensive image-making efforts and key media of seventeenth-century political spaces. I treat them as "Confucian family tales" in this study. Although not all were completely new, they were deployed in political struggles more widely and more substantially in this period.

The Confucian family tales examined here fall mainly into three categories. The first group of family tales includes biographies, pamphlets, and anecdotes about officials, genres that might impress readers as relatively reliable presentations of fact. Instead, these materials not only echoed and recycled ideas and messages that appeared in fiction but also played the most important part in channeling details of officials' personal lives into various political spaces, often providing raw material for the production of sensationalized moral images in other genres. In fact, biographies are known for their preoccupation with moral lessons, and even gossip and anecdote constitute "the acknowledged building blocks" for constructing official histories and images of public figures.[56] In premodern China, "fictionality" was not a central theoretical concern.[57] This particular literary tradition played an intriguing role in shaping image politics.

Second, the frequent employment of extant popular literature such as *Water Margin* (Shuihu zhuan) in late-Ming politics helped circulate polarized moral images of political actors. The effectiveness of such a technique was predicated on readers' familiarity with the characteristics of well-known fictional characters.[58] In turn, associating an official with a famous fictional figure could easily mold his public image into a moral archetype. Although this method did not always draw the audience's attention to the official's performance of any specific ethical expectations, it nonetheless helped frame and sensationalize political battles as moral contests.

The third category of Confucian family tales relevant to this study also involves fictional narratives, but these were vernacular novels and dramas composed specifically to represent current political events, caricature factional opponents, or glorify someone as a moral paragon and loyal official.[59] These stories can be read as family romance (*jiazu xiaoshuo*).[60] Novels of this genre depict the experiences of many characters of the same family, household, or clan against some significant historical background. They were multigenerational and engaged the ethical ideals patterned on the Five Cardinal Relations. The genre of family romance boomed in the seventeenth century as a result of people's amplified interest in politics, the negotiation of Confucian values, and the immense popularity of historical novels, crime-case fiction (*gong 'an xiaoshuo*), and gods-and-demons fiction (*shenmo xiaoshuo*).[61] When deployed as political narratives, their portrayals of elite men and women as patriarchs and matriarchs, sons and daughters, also reflected the gendered and gendering nature of Confucian ethics as a language of political negotiations in and beyond the court.

Political Processes as Image-Making Efforts

Integrating the developments in print culture, cultural trends, and political changes into the analysis of seventeenth-century political communication not only sheds new light on changes in political spaces but also generates a more nuanced account of how the elites experimented with political processes in order to adapt to new conditions. An in-depth investigation of two critical problems in seventeenth-century politics—factionalism and the Qing conquest—from the perspective of image politics allows us to describe changes in the Confucian moral-political system in its own terms.

Factionalism (*dangzheng*) appears repeatedly in Chinese imperial history. A faction was not defined simply by economic, political, or ideological interests. Rather, the bases on which factions were formed were complicated and included "family connections, common origins, patronage relationships, and simple instances of friendship and enmity."[62] The term *faction* did not always correspond to groups with a clear sense of identity, a coherent agenda or set of interests. Oftentimes, officials were labeled as factionalist simply to undermine their political credibility at court. Within a group of officials perceived as a single faction, some might embrace the label and insist that theirs was a "faction of superior men," a notion made famous in the Song dynasty by some seeking to justify the alliance among righteous officials.[63] Others might not actively associate themselves with a factional label, assuming the more traditional posture that denounced all forms of factionalism.

Did seventeenth-century factionalism significantly differ from that of the earlier dynasties? It has been argued that, like Song factionalism, the late-Ming variety adopted a court-centered approach.[64] Factions all claimed to be collectives of loyal ministers devoted to serving the public good; they did not contest imperial authority.[65] New developments in the social sphere, in particular late-Ming "public opinion," instead of facilitating a real "public sphere" or fundamental changes in government mechanism, only exacerbated factionalism.[66] In addition, moral issues had always mattered. For instance, in the Song dynasty, factional attacks were often dealt out in impeachment of officials for their association with courtesans.[67]

Meaningful changes did take place in the seventeenth century, however. In spite of the seeming similarities in the techniques of factionalism across time, the particular conditions of this era turned factional activities into much-mediated, multi-centered processes.[68] Seventeenth-century sociocultural developments significantly complicated factionalism. The intellectual problems of "authenticity" and "sincerity" became real political issues on their own account (see chap. 2). The question of how to best present and digest "facts" in print material assumed unprecedented urgency and significance in power competition. As political struggles were mediated through literary production and consumption among rivals, friends, and families, factionalism existed as and operated in the Confucian family tales; it was narrated and fought in various media and spaces. The production and circulation of officials' images as fathers, sons, husbands, and friends in novels, plays, anecdotes, and social spectacles simultaneously targeted three audiences: the court, the literati reading public, and each official's personal social base. While the issue of loyalty remained central, the factional narratives themselves ceased to be court-centered. Thus, the ruling elite did not haplessly fall into an inevitable recurrence of factionalism; they actively engaged factionalism as not only a moral rhetoric but also an evolving cultural phenomenon at a time of historic change.

By the time of the Ming-Qing transition, imperial history had accumulated many examples of factionalism. The troubling, unsettled history of factionalism, especially from the Song dynasty, fed the Ming-Qing rulers' strong fear of deception by factionalist officials—who were by definition disloyal—and caused them to overreact. Meanwhile, these rulers themselves learned to employ factionalism as rhetoric and as a tactic in their efforts to control and manage their officials. Historical memory and emperors' interventionism, in combination with print culture and intellectual shifts, made debates about the authenticity of officials' moral images a central trope in factional negotiations. The multiple, competing images of the Donglin official, the Fushe scholar, and the Han "turncoat"[69] in factional battles across the dynastic divide best illustrate the many kinds of measures undertaken by elites in their efforts to cope with change.

Examining factionalism as a forum for image battles also deepens our understanding of political experiments in the early Qing. During the times of Regent Dorgon (1612–1650) and the Shunzhi emperor (r. 1644–61), factional ties and conflicts crisscrossed among and between Han officials and the Manchus. Violent military conquest and fierce factional struggles created an environment of uncertainty, anxiety, and suspicion. Political actors had to constantly improvise if they were to survive and adapt. Manchu rulers and turncoat officials tapped Confucian ethics creatively to achieve specific political goals. Turncoats' moral images as fathers, sons, husbands, and friends were at the heart of Manchu and Han experiments that coped with political uncertainty and established Manchu superiority. In turn, the intensive deployment of Confucian ethics as a language of communication in the early Qing facilitated changes in the political meaning of some Confucian practices and in the ruler-subject relationship. For instance, individual officials now had to negotiate hard with the emperor for opportunities to display their Confucian virtues. Interaction between emperor and officials regarding officials' filial rituals became a means of conveying trust and favor (see chap. 4).

Image politics reached an interesting point in the Qing emperors' dazzling self-fashioning. Their propaganda successes in projecting the image of imperial exemplariness have been well studied.[70] Scholarship on this topic has advanced our understanding of the nature of Qing rulership and expanded our knowledge of how different traditions and influences shaped its course of action.[71] The Qing emperors were preoccupied with their image.[72] They drew on Neo-Confucian orthodoxy to appeal to the Han but at the same time strove to maintain a Manchu identity so as to perpetuate their dominance. The Qing "ethno-dynastic rule" involved an ongoing manipulation and revision of Confucian ideas in the imperial self-image.[73]

The historical developments described above did not necessarily result in the breakdown of the loyalty–filial piety unity, as previous scholarship has suggested.[74] Neither do they fit neatly in the framework of "sinicization" that took a simple conservative turn.[75] Rather, early Qing political culture resulted from a series of complicated political negotiations and experiments among various parties. In addition, as the Qing emperors gradually consolidated Manchu supremacy by personally embodying moral exemplariness, the moral-political division of labor among the ruling elites underwent a reconfiguration, which paralleled other innovations in Qing governance, such as placing less emphasis on Han officials' personal moral reputation than on other ministerial qualities.[76] Even though these changes would remain hidden behind a facade of continuity, the Qing conquest was indeed an image conquest (see chap. 4).

THE CONTINUUM OF CONFUCIAN MORALISM

Approaching seventeenth-century Chinese political culture as image politics does not suggest that the elite's moral performances were all superficial and hypocritical. On the contrary, the notion of image politics is sensitive to the reality that officials' moral endeavors not only constantly moved along the continuum of Confucian moralism but also succumbed to differing interpretations by a diverse reading public and by political competitors in an increasingly complex sociocultural environment. Further, the lens of image politics demands that we denaturalize the separation of political negotiation and moral debate—and subsequently denaturalize our assumption that the former has to be privileged over the latter to conduct good governance.

Confucian ethical ideals, in particular filial piety and gender propriety, had a long history of being employed by emperors and officials as a political weapon; moral image had always been important for the ruling elite. To better understand the relationship between politics and morality in the seventeenth century, it is necessary to look into the structure of Confucian moralism and trace how its various discursive components interacted with the above-mentioned broader political, cultural, and social environment.

Within the Confucian template of the Five Cardinal Relations, loyalty, filial piety, gender propriety, and friendship form a web of virtues centered on *zhongxiao* (lit., "loyalty and filial piety"); they continuously give one another political relevance. The history of seventeenth-century Confucian moralism shows how this web of virtues operated as a whole, and how the discursive connections among these masculine virtues were invoked and reinscribed. Of central concern are two questions, which point to the two dimensions of the continuum of Confucian moralism: In the seventeenth century, which Confucian masculine virtues could help "authenticate" an official's loyalty? How and why did political actors debate whether an official's moral performance was sincere and proper? Answers to these questions can be found in Confucian didactic texts and intellectual works. They also emerged in everyday negotiations among emperors, officials, and literati groups.

The Virtuous Circles of Filial Sons and Good Husbands

The ethics of *zhongxiao* encompassed the multiple meanings of the concepts of loyalty (*zhong*) and filial piety (*xiao*).[77] Around the third century BCE, the compound first appeared,[78] reflecting historical developments in culture, society, and government that demanded terminology that would theorize the relationship between these ideals—for example, how they were mutually constituted, and which one should be privileged conceptually and in practice.[79] By the Han dynasty (206 BCE–220 CE), filial piety had been extended to include loyalty to the sovereign.[80] The notion of *zhongxiao* took the practical form in the Han policy of offering government positions to filial sons. Although the elite prioritized different expressions of filial piety under different political conditions, the connection between filial performance and political success remained strong.[81] Emblematic of this development in the changing environment of the Han dynasty was the political ascendance of the *Classic of Filial Piety* (Xiaojing), which would later be designated a Confucian classic by the state.[82]

The *zhongxiao* discourse gained momentum in the late Ming and profoundly shaped officials' self-understanding, self-expression, and behaviors in the seventeenth century.[83] The principle of "governing with filial piety" (*xiaozhi*) had been enthusiastically embraced by Ming rulers. Although the notion of *zhongxiao* was prominent in the popular mentality and vernacular literature,[84] it had a particular impact on an official's career and life, caused by certain status-specific expectations such as that an official should resign from office to mourn a deceased parent for twenty-seven months. We cannot understand seventeenth-century Chinese political culture without carefully examining how officials' images of *zhongxiao* were produced, circulated, and contested.

My use of the term *zhongxiao* in this book reflects its multivalence and diverse meanings in seventeenth-century China. I use it as an analytical category when examining political negotiations around officials' images as (un)filial sons. In most places throughout the book, it is the transliteration of the word *zhongxiao* that our historical subjects used in the sources. It is important to remember that, depending on the specific context, this word could be used to refer to the unity of loyalty and filial piety, to praise a man's moral exemplariness, or to mean Confucian moral principles in general.

The diverse ways our historical subjects employed *zhongxiao* as a term, an ideal, and an intellectual problem expose the fallacies of a central motif of the dominant narrative of the Ming-Qing transition: namely, its narrow understanding of loyalty as Ming loyalism. This narrow understanding did indeed help mobilize Ming resistance. It inspired many officials to commit suicide after a military defeat or at the death of the Ming emperor and compelled some literati to withdraw from public service in the Qing. It also shaped Qing policies not only toward the Han population but also toward those who had fought as or for the Manchus.[85] However, loyalty in practice was a much more complicated phenomenon.

Examining multiple definitions of loyalty in connection with other Confucian virtues complicates our understandings of late-Ming political struggles as well as early Qing recovery. For instance, in the seventeenth century, across the dynastic divide, political actors negotiated "permeable categories and fluid boundaries" in their search for creative ways to adapt and survive.[86] Multiple Confucian ethical ideals were employed by the turncoats and their families to unite the two conflicting loyalties, loyalty to the Ming and loyalty to the Qing. The turncoats' complicated images as sons, husbands, fathers, and friends—produced by Manchu rulers, by their factional enemies, and by the turncoats themselves—reveal the most fascinating and complex ways Confucian moralism generated interlocking narratives of loyalty, filial piety, manly self-discipline, and friendship and thereby mediated and transformed political and social reality.

The continuum of Confucian moralism that centers on *zhongxiao* fundamentally shaped literati masculinity. The *Classic of Filial Piety* not only reiterates the compatibility of loyalty and filial piety but also affirms the connection between the *zhongxiao* ideal and elite men's other gendered roles and responsibilities.[87] These discursive connections would be invoked and elaborated upon in political negotiations and experiments. There are ample instances of this in officials' lives during the Ming-Qing dynastic change.

In the Five Cardinal Relations, the only ethics that explicitly deals with the regulation of a man's gender and sexual behaviors is the proper relationship between husband and wife (*fufu*), or gendered distinction (*bie*).[88] The applicability of this ethics to an increasingly complicated society was predicated on its strong but subtle connection with other ethical expectations for elite men. In everyday politics, this concept could imply and be used to discuss a wide range of gendered expectations, such as fulfilling responsibilities as a husband, maintaining proper order and sexual separation within the household, and resisting sexual distractions, as well as advocating women's chastity and commitment to domestic harmony.

Looking at officials *as men* complements the insights of women's historians regarding the resilience of the Confucian gender system in late imperial China.[89] Under the Confucian gender system, elite men faced a distinct set of issues in times of change and crisis.[90] The seventeenth century witnessed the emergence of alternative intellectual, spiritual, and career choices. In this more thoroughly commercialized society, elite men's access to women, like their access to luxury goods and entertainment, had grown significantly. Meanwhile, educated women in elite households and pleasure quarters played an increasingly prominent role in men's social and cultural lives.[91] These developments had sharpened the tension between the discourse on literati self-discipline and the culture of pleasure and leisure. As a result, the notion of self-restraint itself became a matter to be intensely contested and negotiated.

Elite men's lived experiences in this period cannot be reduced to an ideological struggle. Political actors' invocations of gender norms in power negotiations gave these norms specific meanings and reinscribed them. As official politics in the late Ming and early Qing turned into intense battles over personal image, officials struggled to display gendered virtues properly and intelligently, learning to walk a fine line when publicizing their masculine qualities and virtues. Their relationships with wives, concubines, and entertainers were subjected to a greater degree of scrutiny, as the flourishing print culture and reconfiguration of political power increased the exposure of officials' personal lives to public critique and expanded the circulation of competing interpretations of their behavior. Failure to fulfill one's duties as a husband, indulgence in sexual pleasures, and messy domestic arrangements all could be cited as lack of filial piety and loyalty. Conversely, an official's display of self-discipline and his spouse's feminine virtues helped to affirm his *zhongxiao* commitment. The web of masculine virtues centered on *zhongxiao*, constituting the first dimension of the continuum of Confucian moralism, determined how political struggles tangled Confucian family tales.

Sincerity and Authenticity in Moral Cultivation

The other dimension of the continuum of Confucian moralism concerns the political usefulness of the binary understanding of moral performance as either sincere or hypocritical. Across the dynastic divide, as scandalous and exemplary images of officials mushroomed inside and beyond the court, investigating and explaining discrepancies between their political reputations and moral actions became a significant part of political processes.

This development was closely related to contemporaneous intellectual and religious trends. During this time of widespread social upheaval and political corruption, the elite vehemently debated, and creatively explored, the question of how to produce worthy officials through moral cultivation. However, not only was no consensus reached, but diversity and contentiousness increased.[92] Seventeenth-century literati devoted much attention to the issue of authentic expression and sincere pursuit of Confucian virtues in the intellectual and literary realms.[93] Their critical reflections on the Yangming school, the rise of ritualism, and the trend toward syncretism all engaged these concerns.[94]

Questions of sincerity and authenticity operated as tropes in political negotiations. Officials made efforts to differentiate "sincere" from "perfunctory" moral endeavors. To communicate with the emperor, defeat political rivals, and assemble what could be presented at court as "public opinion," they extensively employed print, social spectacles, and rituals to display their sincere moral commitments.

Meanwhile, political actors' practice of Confucian ethics far exceeded the simple dichotomy of sincerity versus pragmatism. Simultaneously addressing audiences in governmental, societal, and familial spheres, a political actor could invoke Confucian ethical values for complex reasons that might combine religious belief, familial obligation, and political convenience (see chap. 3). Political experience also informed the new ways officials understood and theorized the sincere and proper pursuit of Confucian masculine virtues to fulfill *both* political and familial duties (see chap. 2).

Because friends and the ideal of friendship played indispensable roles in authenticating "sincerity," the success and effectiveness of officials' image-making relied heavily on the support of their social networks. Hence the ethics of friendship is particularly important to our investigation of seventeenth-century image politics. First, on a discursive level, the notion of friendship was legitimized and promoted by officials' shared commitment to loyalty, filial piety, and gender propriety. As a language of political communication, friendship in association with other sanctioned ethical values helped create a positive, politically meaningful narrative of moral exemplariness. Second, on a practical level, the literati published writings and commented on the poetry and art made by friends, thereby not only publicizing one another's moral performance but also expounding on the meaning of sincere and proper moral pursuits. In the Confucian family tales jointly created by officials and their friends, one's loyalty was authenticated by one's image as a filial son, trustworthy friend, and good husband. For many, this display of Confucian ethics was no less authentic than other forms (see chap. 5).

Confucian moralism thus includes a wide range of views, emotions, actions, and dynamics communicated in the language of ethical values. It also encompasses varied inspirations and rationales that cannot be neatly defined as either purely moral pursuits or instrumentalism. Its operation defies evaluations framed in terms of "progress," "stagnation," or "dysfunction." When we look at moralism from today's point of view, we are tempted to emphasize its normative aspect and regulating functions. This tendency suffers from a particularly modern preoccupation with the question of sincerity.[95] If we recognize Confucian moralism as a continuum that allowed flexible options and creative experiments, many officials begin to look considerably different from the stereotypical images that have been imposed on them by seventeenth-century loyalist literature, eighteenth-century court propaganda, and twentieth-century nationalistic narrative.

PART I

The Late Ming

CHAPTER 1

Lists, Literature, and the Imagined Community of Factionalists

The Donglin

In the Ming Wanli reign (1573–1620), an era defined by escalating factionalism in politics and a publishing boom in society, politics and print culture were profoundly entangled.[1] This was the cultural environment in which the so-called Donglin faction, the centerpiece of the late-Ming factional saga, emerged. The name "Donglin" derived from the Donglin Academy in Wuxi (in modern-day Jiangsu), where some officials lectured on Neo-Confucianism. In addition to its nod to the Donglin Academy, the term *Donglin* was known primarily among officials, the literati, and even commoners as a political faction and identity. Clear connections between Donglin intellectual endeavors and political programs in the late Ming have been identified in the following areas: Donglin opposition to the authoritarian grand secretary Zhang Juzheng (1525–1582), the fight against the abuse of power by the so-called eunuch faction (*yandang*), criticisms of incompetent and indifferent emperors, and gentry local activism.[2] Since the late Ming, much has been written about the Donglin and the several generations of officials who were, in one way or another, seen as Donglin members by their contemporaries. But one crucial question remains unresolved: Just who were the Donglin?

To avoid appearing factionalist, many Donglin-identified officials did not call themselves Donglin associates but acquiesced to the label when it was used in a positive manner. The Donglin label was applied by official and nonofficial literati readers and writers, quite loosely and arbitrarily, to those whom they merely believed to have been Donglin members. In most cases it was the political rivals or supporters of Donglin-identified officials who attached this label to certain officials and substantiated the labeling by representing those officials in particular ways.

The lack of a clear definition of its membership in the seventeenth century has posed problems for the study of the Donglin's history. However, we can turn this problem into a productive analytical angle by looking into this history as a type of identity formation. How and why did the Donglin come to be seen as a community of moral exemplars whose reputation constituted a stark contrast to the image of contemporary social deviants and "evil officials?"[3] In the meantime, why were some of the Donglin-identified officials portrayed as "fake" Donglin or anti-Donglin?[4] How did the meaning and image of the Donglin change? How do we explain the similarities in method adopted by Donglin-identified officials and their rivals in the moral tales they produced for political purposes? A cultural-historical approach to the history of the Donglin will demonstrate that the ambiguity and malleability of the image of the Donglin man were both means toward and consequences of seventeenth-century factionalism. The multiple meanings of the term *Donglin* during the 1590s–1640s and controversies around the image of the Donglin man as a moral exemplar constituted a significant part of late Ming politics.

I use "Donglin-identified officials" to refer to men whose contemporaries classified them as Donglin members and to indicate the instability of that identification. The three officials from whose perspectives I will explore the history of the Donglin never occupied top government positions, nor did they play any role at the famed Donglin Academy. Nonetheless, the ways their lives and reputation were shaped by the intersection of factionalism and print culture throw much light on the increasing importance of officials' moral images in political processes and help explain the rise of the Donglin man as a moral paragon.

The first of these men, Wu Yuancui (*jinshi* 1577), whom we encountered in the introduction to this book, was a native of Suzhou.[5] As he gradually lost his eyesight and phased out his bureaucratic career in the mid-Wanli reign, Wu wrote and published much on politics and fellow officials. Not clearly identified with any faction, he claimed to have formed strong friendships with prominent Donglin figures, in particular Gu Xiancheng (1550–1612), a founder of the Donglin group. However, Wu was critical of some Donglin-identified figures, and his publications were cited by some officials at court against the Donglin group over the course of fierce factional fighting. Wu's publishing controversies stand as a good illustration of how print culture and intensifying factionalism facilitated the circulation of political information in diverse genres, complicated officials' political claims, and destabilized the boundaries between truth and perception in political processes. The emergence of the Donglin faction and the power struggles surrounding its meaning and image must be understood in this context.

The greater roles played by various forms of literary production in factionalism of the Tianqi (1621–27) and Chongzhen (1628–44) reigns are revealed by the experiences of the other two officials, Zheng Zhenxian (1572–1628) and Zheng Man (1594–1639), father and son. Admired by some as Donglin vanguards but condemned by others as "fake" Donglin, their ups and downs reflected the unfolding contention over who the Donglin were and what they stood for. The unstable, contested moral images of the Zhengs, produced and circulated in the forms of blacklists, biographies, anecdotal writings, gossip, pamphlets, and vernacular novels, illustrate how the sensational turn of political narratives pulled individual officials' personal lives to the center of political processes. By the time the son, after years of imprisonment for the unverifiable charges of beating his mother and sexual immorality, was executed, his reputation had been manipulated by multiple parties to help sharpen the image of the "real" Donglin man, the emblem of filial piety and self-discipline.

During the forty years between Wu Yuancui's publishing ventures and Zheng Man's efforts to publicize his self-defense from prison, factionalism had spread well beyond the court. It had turned into a transgenerational problem and permeated local politics, complicated regional social networks, crept into the competitive publishing industry, and became the subject of a wide variety of literary production. In other words, factionalism had become, simultaneously, a social, cultural, and literary phenomenon. The moral image of officials produced in these spaces traveled to the court and became a vital part of political processes.

PRINTING POLITICS

The late-Ming literati's strong demand for political information was met by their increased access to the officially printed gazetteer (*dibao*) and to privately printed news that went beyond the carefully worded governmental publications.[6] The enhanced availability of popular literature also profoundly changed the circulation and reception of political information. The interpenetration of politics and literature, in format and content, created both opportunities and confusion for officials. Wu Yuancui's publishing adventure gives us a glimpse of this development.

Between Wanli 37 and 39 (1609–11), Wu printed and reprinted a collection of anecdotes and notes on contemporary politics in his *Random Notes* (discussed in the introduction). *Random Notes* grew out of a small project but quickly expanded and assumed its current title.[7] The first volume, appearing in Wanli 37 (1609), sparked some interest among official and literati readers. Encouraged by the positive reactions, Wu published additional volumes.[8] He sent the books to former colleagues for comments. Many people borrowed copies from one another to get a glimpse.[9] The work got so much attention that soon it went into another printing, with some revisions.

In Wanli 40 (1622), the official He Canran (*jinshi* 1595) published *Critical Commentary on Random Notes* (Manlu pingzheng; hereafter *Critical Commentary*). He claimed he was annoyed by Wu's first volume but became deeply disturbed by Wu's further publications. Eventually, after the reprint of *Random Notes* came out, He decided he must publish a response pointing out Wu's misleading documentation and problematic comments. Outraged by He's criticisms, Wu published a rebuttal, *Counter-Commentary on Critical Commentary on Random Notes* (Bo Manlu pingzheng; hereafter *Counter-Commentary*). Wu also disseminated copies of a short summary of his *Counter-Commentary* among officials, which triggered his rival's decision to publish a new book, *Counter-Counter-Commentary on Critical Commentary on Random Notes* (Bo Bo Manlu pingzheng; hereafter *Counter-Counter-Commentary*).[10] In the course of a single year, these two officials exchanged several rounds of fire in print. Readers' enthusiasm, together with Wu's and He's own interest in self-promotion and self-defense, surely drove them to roll out their exchanges with such speed.

He Canran's *Critical Commentary* adopted a format that was common in literary commentaries (fig. 1.1).[11] The page was divided into two registers, the upper section for marginal comments (*meipi*) and the lower section for the main text.

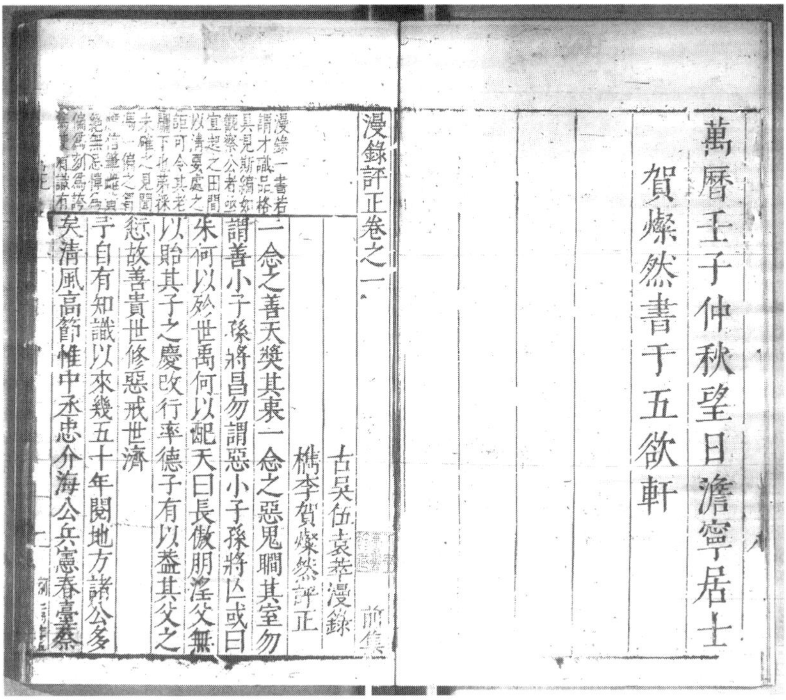
萬曆壬子仲秋望日澹寧居士
賀燦然書于五欲軒

漫錄評正卷之一
古吳伍袁萃漫錄 前集
檇李賀燦然評正
一念之善天奬其衷一念之惡鬼瞯其室勿
謂善小子孫將昌勿謂惡小子孫將亾或曰
朱何以殄世禹何以配天曰長傲朋淫父無
以貽其子之慶改行率德子有以蓋其父之
愆故善貴世修惡戒世濟
予自有知識以來幾五十年閱地方諸公多
矣清風高節惟中丞忠介海公兵憲春臺蔡

Figure 1.1. Page from He Canran's *Critical Commentary on Random Notes* (*Manlu pingzheng*). Wanli period.

In the third round of their exchange, He's commentary appeared in the form of both marginal comments and double-column interlineal comments (*shuang hang jiapi*) in the text itself (fig. 1.2).

Scholars of the history of books, scholarly publication, and vernacular novels have examined how commentary formats enhanced commentators' ability to convey their views persuasively and enriched the reading experience of their audience.[12] When this format was employed in political publications, it not only satisfied the debaters' need to pointedly present their arguments and evidence but also delivered detailed information to readers who, at the height of the factional infighting in the Wanli reign, craved political news. These two authors—Wu and He—now used this format to retort, clarify, and offer additional evidence by which to establish their own authority and discredit their rival.

As publishing became easier and more available, political reporting, personal attacks, literary views, and intellectual debates blended

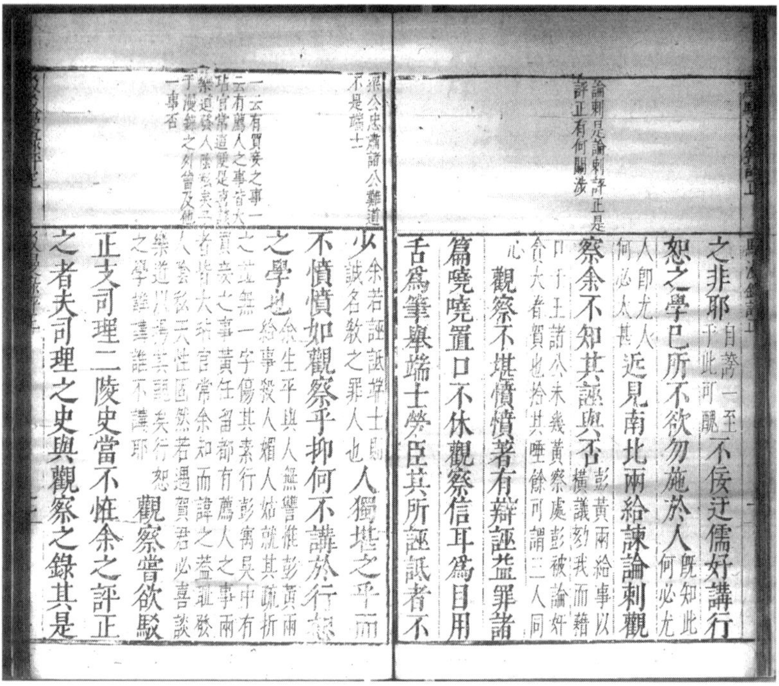

Figure 1.2. Page from He Canran's *Counter-Counter-Commentary on Random Notes* (*Bo Bo Manlu pingzheng*). Wanli period.

further. For instance, Wu published copiously on a major political controversy of the time: the factional fight over the corruption case of Governor Li Sancai (d. 1623).[13] Li was a strong ally of prominent Donglin figures such as Gu Xiancheng. But in Wanli 37 (1609), allegations of his corruption erupted so forcefully that some Donglin-identified officials had to decide whether to defend him and on what grounds a defense could be formulated. Many, including Gu Xiancheng, did stand behind Li. Amid the fierce factional debate, Wu Yuancui presented himself as an objective observer and politically neutral official. But in *Random Notes*, partially published in that same year, he attacked the two censors who had criticized his position on the governor's case, which immediately drew fierce attacks from the pro-Li side. In the next few years, the political division caused by Li's case grew more and more complex, as shown in the publications by Wu Yuancui and He Canran in Wanli 40–41 (1612–13). In *Critical Commentary* (1612), which appeared soon after Wu printed and advertised the second edition of

Random Notes, on Wu's criticism of the above-mentioned two censors, He Canran lambastes Wu for departing from the Confucian principle of tolerating others' faults. In response, in an interlineal comment in *Counter-Commentary*, Wu retorted that he never exposed the moral defects of those two censors, even though they had committed misconduct such as buying a concubine and making official recommendations improperly. Of course, printing this response unwisely provided more evidence for He Canran's observation, in a marginal comment in *Counter-Counter-Commentary*, that Wu had just demonstrated the tendency to expose others' personal faults (see fig. 1.2).[14] Using commentary format allowed these two officials to engage questions of factional politics, moral issues, and personal reputation all at the same time. Rather than presenting a coarse mélange, this format simply reflects the reality that these conversations among officials could not be neatly compartmentalized. Printing efficiencies and the creative use of various literary formats further entwined politics and morality and discussions thereof.

The He-Wu crossfire highlights the intricate relationship among print, the explosion of political information, and competition among officials within a progressively factionalist environment. Print promised to expose truths to readers beyond the small group of insiders. In this highly factionalized environment and competitive social domain, officials made greater use of print for their interpretations of political events and their colleagues' behavior. He Canran's clever employment of the commentary to establish his own insider status and authority to his readership is compelling.

He carefully checked the two editions of Wu's *Random Notes* and painstakingly analyzed any discrepancies and errors that he considered noteworthy. He pointed to the changes Wu made in the second edition as evidence of Wu's manipulation of the facts. He also discussed discrepancies between Wu's documentation and more reliable sources—such as the official gazetteer and other officials' publications—so as to argue Wu's lack of credibility. To bolster his own credibility, He informed readers that when Wu published a new book, *Draft Work from the Yi'an Hall* (Yi'antang gao), which recycled some material from *Random Notes*, Wu quietly corrected the problems that He had pointed out even though he publicly dismissed He's criticisms.[15]

Competition for authority in print was driven by, and also contributed to, the factional battles fought at and beyond the court. Why did

He Canran so patiently—and even a bit obsessively—comb through the two editions of *Random Notes* and publish a point-by-point commentary to discredit Wu? His hostility toward Wu was ignited by a reference Wu had made to him in *Random Notes*, writing that a memorial He had submitted in Wanli 33 (1605) amid the factional disputes over the latest round of bureaucratic evaluations was the most ridiculous of all. Wu accused He of attempting to protect a fellow official from his hometown (*tongxiang*) and of trying to please the powerful grand secretary Wang Xijue (1534–1614), a pivotal figure in Wanli politics and leader of the Zhe faction (*Zhe dang*), whose key figures came from Zhejiang.[16] Wu's comment exacerbated He's frustration with factionalism. He Canran had been proud of this particular memorial and felt that precisely because it approached personnel disagreements from a neutral standpoint, he had alienated both the Zhe and Donglin factions. He not only had failed to benefit from being a Zhejiang native but instead was marginalized by all factions and suffered one demotion after another.[17] In response to Wu's assertions, He took advantage of the ease of access to publishing and effectively attacked *Random Notes*.

Under He's attack on his credibility, Wu mobilized "public opinion" (*gonglun*) and made it manifest in his *Counter-Commentary* by attaching a long appendix that quoted praise for *Random Notes* from more than twenty colleagues (fig. 1.3). Parading these supposedly fair and representative comments was meant to expose the biased and malicious nature of He's comments.

He Canran, however, in *Counter-Counter-Commentary*, cynically shrugged off Wu's parade of "public opinion." He questioned whether such "public opinion" was objective at all. "When the literati print their works or compose something, naturally they send them to good friends and close associates. The recipients of these publications are not there to express honest or tough-minded comments; they are certain to ring with high praise. Critical friends are rare. These comments are meaningless. Wu gathered all these [flattering comments] and printed them only to show off."[18]

The Wu-He exchange thus vividly demonstrates how print provided rival authors with opportunities to claim authority, objectivity, and popularity. As the use of print ramped up, officials had to continue exploring for even more effective means of defeating their rivals. It is therefore not surprising that Wu's and He's colleagues became interested in employing vernacular literature for such purposes. As

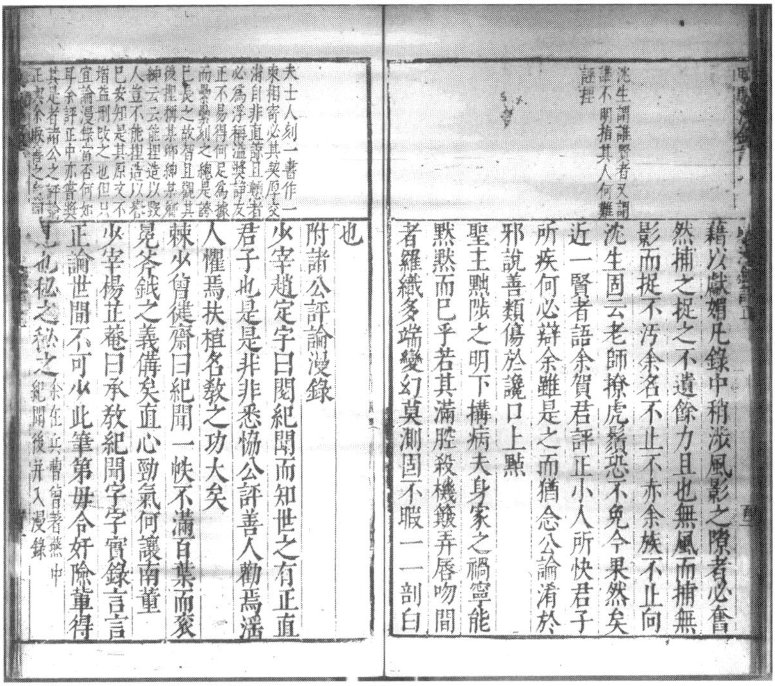
藉以獻媚凡錄中稍涉風影之際者必奮
然捕之捉之不遺餘力且也無風而捕無
影而捉不汚余名不止不赤余族不止向
沈生固云老師撩虎鬚恐不免今果然矣
近一賢者語余賀君評正小人所快君子
所疾何必辯余雖是之而猶念公論淆於
邪說善類傷於讒口上黙
聖主黜陟之明下搆病夫身家之禍寧能
黙黙而已乎若其滿腔殺機簸弄唇吻間
者羅織多端變幻莫測固不暇一一剖白

也
附諸公評論漫錄
少宰趙定宇曰閔紀聞而知世之有正直
君子也是是非非悉協公評善人勸焉滛
人懼焉扶植名教之功大矣
棘少曾徤齋曰紀聞一帙不滿百葉而裒
晃斧鉞之義備矣直心勁氣何讓南董
少宰楊芷菴曰承教紀聞字字實錄言言
正論世間不可少此筆第毋令奸險輩得
見也秘之秘之

Figure 1.3. Page from Wu Yuancui's *Counter-Commentary on Critical Commentary on Random Notes* (*Bo Manlu pingzheng*)

print culture changed the transmission and presentation of political information, it significantly shaped the formation of, and negotiations over, factional identities. Factionalism became an increasingly complex literary phenomenon and subject of cultural consumption. It was under these conditions that competing images of the Donglin—and their increasingly personal content—emerged.

FACTIONAL IDENTITY AND PRINT

When Wu Yuancui published the first edition of *Random Notes* in Wanli 37 (1609), he did not try to align his political commentary and social activities along the dichotomy of Donglin versus anti-Donglin. His vague ties with the Donglin are reflected in the "messiness" of his publications. However, Wu did feel pressure to carve out a factional position, even though he had already retired. That pressure came from the realities of court politics.

During the Wanli reign, the word *Donglin* carried positive meanings for some, while for others, the label had only negative connotations. Rival factions, adopting Song-era factional terminology, referred to the Donglin as an "evil faction" (*xiedang*), one that consisted of officials who either promoted false teachings (*weixue*) or pursued factional interests.[19]

One of the first officials to actively publicize the Donglin as a righteous political force and delineate a positive Donglin image in print was Wu Liang (*jinshi* 1601). Around Wanli 37 (1609), Wu Liang compiled and published a well-received volume, *Memorials of the Wanli Court* (Wanli shuchao). He had very close sociopolitical ties with some of its prominent contributors, such as Gu Xiancheng, Qian Yiben (1546–1617), and Gao Panlong (1562–1626), who were considered among the founders of the Donglin. This publication for the first time presented Donglin officials as having a powerful and distinctive voice.[20] Later, in the course of the heated debate over the Donglin leaders' support for the controversial Li Sancai, Wu Liang not only defended Li but also took the extraordinary action of having Gu Xiancheng's letter of support printed and disseminated all over the capital.[21]

Wu Liang made tremendous efforts to portray the Donglin as a faction of worthy men. He had publicly mentioned three ways in which the Donglin was defined at the time, of which he endorsed only the first one: "Today, worthy men and gentlemen are definitely Donglin; the officials upon whom the Donglin rely are also Donglin."[22] He expressed strong criticism of those who considered Donglin an "evil faction."[23] This negative portrayal already had substantial support among officials.

Meanwhile, Wu Yuancui's publications reminded Wu Liang that outside the court, the meaning of the Donglin went well beyond the above-mentioned dichotomy. It was negotiated in officials' social activities and, importantly, in their publications. Individual officials often took a flexible stance. Instead of engaging the Donglin as a political faction, they tended to create a positive social connection between themselves and the most admired Donglin-identified figures, in effect turning them into celebrities. This explains Wu Yuancui's simultaneous opposition to Li Sancai and claims of friendship with Donglin leaders.

Wu Liang, a self-claimed Donglin member, strongly contested such appropriation of the Donglin fame.[24] Insisting on identifying a correct list of Donglin men, Wu Liang defied the ambiguous factional lines drawn in publications such as those by Wu Yuancui. In the memorial in which he defined the Donglin faction, Wu Liang referred to his own book *Memorials of the Wanli Court* as the standard while dismissing Wu Yuancui's *Random Notes* as an example of a politically problematic list: "No one would refer to *Random Notes* for the names of the worthy men [who are Donglin]!"[25]

But Wu Yuancui unwaveringly maintained his "third position" and put out more books to make his case. He printed a collection of memorials by officials who protested the Donglin leaders' support of Li Sancai;[26] in other publications he portrayed himself as being in the same intellectual-social camp as certain Donglin icons. For instance, in *Random Notes*, Wu Yuancui stressed that he and Gu Xiancheng had, more than once, attempted to meet for gatherings at the Donglin Academy, but for health reasons he was never able to make it to those occasions.[27] Thus, the circulation of Wu's book among officials and the literati threatened Wu Liang's efforts to claim a unified image for the Donglin.

The contentious nature of the meaning and image of the Donglin can also be detected in He Canran's response to Wu Yuancui's self-presentation in *Random Notes*. Wu Yuancui claimed:

> In Liangxi (Wuxi, where the Donglin Academy was located) there gathered a number of outstanding gentleman-scholars. Gu Xiancheng not only perfectly fulfilled filial duties but also produced deep and solid scholarship. Ye Maocai shies away from fame and mundane desires in his pursuit of self-cultivation. Gu Yuncheng, An Xifan, Gao Panlong, and Liu Yuanzhen all embrace noble ideals and demonstrate extraordinary character. Their honest criticisms contribute to making decisions about the most fundamental policies and help correct the mistakes made by His Majesty. This group of scholar-officials possessed such amazing talents. [Gu Xiancheng] invited me to meet him at the Donglin Academy. But again and again I was not able to make it due to illness. In the past people talked about making friends with men from history. I have missed meeting these Donglin gentlemen in person. Indeed our encounters [or lack of them] in this life are all predetermined. Still, friendships formed in spiritual attraction from afar are not so different from those found in face-to-face meetings.[28]

Here, besides identifying the key members of the Donglin and associating them with the particular location of the academy in Wuxi, a particular activity (lecturing there), and a particular set of qualities, Wu Yuancui extended the social contours of the group to include officials like him, who enjoyed "friendships formed in spiritual attraction" (*shenjiao*) with these Donglin figures.

But He Canran sees Wu as a fake Donglin at best. In his *Critical Commentary*, He offers the following remarks on the passage above: "In the history of our dynasty, interest in lecturing started with Wang Yangming. In this work (*Random Notes*), Wu goes all out to denounce Wang Yangming, but he attaches himself to the Donglin (*zituo yu Donglin*), as we can see in his obsession with the idea of lecturing at the Donglin Academy. Since he knows how to praise contemporary worthy men, why does he disparage a great scholar of the past?"[29] In this way, He Canran mocks Wu Yuancui's assertion of an attenuated social affiliation with the Donglin, because Wu demonstrates little intellectual affinity with the Donglin or one of its sources of inspiration, Wang Yangming. He has successfully exposed how far Wu Yuancui has to stretch to claim a connection with the Donglin.

Although Wu Liang, Wu Yuancui, and He Canran had different understandings of the Donglin, they were similar in two important ways. First, they were not fixated on identifying the ideal Donglin official with specific personal virtues. Second, the literary genres they chose—document collections and commentary—served their main purpose of recording and spreading political insiders' views and conversations. However, as factionalism became increasingly social and personal, the genres of publications employed by officials to wage factional battles multiplied and their narratives relied more on moral stereotyping. The image of the Donglin man evolved accordingly.

POLITICAL LISTS AND FACTIONS

With the Donglin gaining more and more intellectual and political influence, officials of all factions—and their respective supporters—had a real stake in shaping the meaning and image of the Donglin. They turned to print to assert competing claims about it, but no one could completely control how readers interpreted those efforts. Wu Liang's "Donglin canon" and Wu Yuancui's array of "public opinion" testimonials anticipated a convenient form of persuasion: compiling and circulating lists of worthy men. Lists, as a particular genre of political literature, would greatly complicate the image of the Donglin. When the focus of factional contention shifted to the struggles between Donglin-identified officials and the eunuch faction in the Tianqi reign (1621–27), efforts to "list the Donglin" intensified, and the project of finding innovative ways of characterizing its members took a sensationalistic turn. Political imagination and literary imagination became inseparable and, in some cases, undistinguishable in the ongoing evolution of the Donglin image.

Donglin Blacklists

The most important change in the political atmosphere in the 1620s was that the Wanli emperor's laissez-faire style of managing the officials was replaced, in the Tianqi reign, by violent competition for power between the eunuch faction and its opponents. As this was happening, political battles increasingly focused on individual officials' moral character. The showdown between moral paragons—often identified as the Donglin—and their allegedly morally corrupt counterparts who collaborated with the powerful eunuch Wei Zhongxian escalated factionalism to a whole new level.[30]

In Tianqi 4 (1624), the eunuch faction created the *List of Notorious Donglin Fighters* (Donglin dianjiang lu), mentioning a total of 108 "evil" officials based on the roster of 108 "rebel leaders" from the novel *Water Margin*. This list instantly became the definitive register of the "Donglin faction." It in turn laid the foundation for the *List of Donglin Factionalists* (Donglin dangren bang), the officially publicized list of allegedly disloyal officials whom the eunuch faction proscribed on behalf of the emperor (in Tianqi 5 [1625]). The men whose names appeared on this blacklist became targets of the eunuch faction's political vendettas. They were deprived of official titles and, if alive, were at risk of imprisonment. Those already dead lost their titles and the honors previously bestowed upon them.[31] The Donglin blacklists as a *literary-political* project did not simply serve as a tool of factional persecution. They epitomized changes in the mode and mood of political communication, moving it further toward focusing on individual officials' personal moral image.

Assigning fictional characters' sobriquets to Donglin-identified officials was a defining feature of the *List of Notorious Donglin Fighters* and significantly increased the effectiveness of blacklisting. First, at this point, it remained unclear to many people which faction would prevail as the "righteous" force. From our distance across history, we might be tempted to believe that caricatures based on a popular novel would meet with unanimous resistance from the reading public because of their vulgarity. But this seems not to have been the case. As revealed in an account by the pro-Donglin literatus Xue Cai, even before full-scale anti-Donglin persecutions broke out, in Jiangnan, some local literati already held a negative view of the Donglin-identified officials. The rise of the eunuch faction and its full-fledged, empirewide anti-Donglin campaign unleashed these literati's resentments.[32] Thus, even before the official Donglin backlist was issued empire wide, various other versions in circulation had already engaged public curiosity and even aroused support.

Second, by fictionalizing and recycling the old "Donglin" label, the foundational blacklist, the *List of Notorious Donglin Fighters*, gave it new meanings and turned factional politics into an object of cultural consumption. Several versions of this list had existed and did not match officials with the characters in the same way. The *List of Notorious Donglin Fighters* was certainly the most "sophisticated" among them.[33] In society, the *List of Notorious Donglin Fighters* was the best known among the blacklists precisely because readers were familiar with the incredibly popular novel it played off of.[34] Some literati observed that, thanks to this pairing, the reading public was quickly swayed by the portrayal of the Donglin as an evil faction (*diandao le baixing haowu*).[35]

In effect, presenting Donglin officials in this fashion made political persecution entertaining for the eunuch faction and for the literati who disliked the Donglin. The reader participated in a literary and political game; his familiarity with the novel was key to understanding contemporary factional politics.

Matching Donglin-identified officials with fictional rebel characters was intended to indicate—sometimes deliberately inaccurately—these officials' political importance, interconnections, personal characteristics, or a combination of these.[36] For example, in the *List of Notorious Donglin Fighters*, Zheng Man was assigned the name "Peculiar Star among the Stars of Earth called the White-Faced Goodman" (Diyixing Baimian Langjun), the sobriquet of the character Zheng Tianshou. This character was carefully chosen for Zheng Man—not only did they share a surname, but Zheng Tianshou also appears in the novel in a gang of three, which coincided with the well-known trio of allies Zheng Man, Wen Zhenmeng (1574–1630), and Huang Daozhou (1585–1646).[37] Zheng Man's family was known to be one of the wealthiest in his hometown. The choice of the character Zheng Tianshou also seems to reflect the perception that Zheng Man was a man who had the money and leisure to take care of his appearance, an image that would later circulate widely among the literati.[38]

Zheng's colleague and good friend Wen Zhenmeng became the "Learned Star among the Stars of Earth called the Magic Scribe" (Diwenxing Shengshou Shusheng), the sobriquet for the rebel Xiao Rang.[39] This was also a clever match. In the novel, Xiao Rang is also a famed calligrapher. Wen Zhenmeng's grandfather Wen Zhengming (1470–1559) was the most accomplished calligrapher and painter of the Ming dynasty. The younger Wen's writing and calligraphy also enjoyed fame across the empire and helped earn him first place in the civil service examinations, a status truly deserving of the sobriquet "Learned Star." Matching Zheng Man and his friends with fictional rebels indicates that the blacklist itself had become a new type of entertaining literature. These Donglin blacklists, by fictionalizing political figures, were parodies of the idealized image of the Donglin man, a self-fashioned image of moral perfection.

Vernacular novels suggested other ways of further fictionalizing the composition of such lists. For instance, *Water Margin* has many examples of brothers—easily identifiable because they share a surname—joining the rebels. When the anti-Donglin officials compiled the blacklists, they felt free to make up factional ties among officials who shared surnames or whose names sounded the same and arbitrarily included them on the lists.[40] Thus, it is not coincidental that the *List of Notorious Donglin Fighters* matches as many as eleven officials with fictional characters simply by surname. Other Donglin blacklists asserted factional connections via mentor-disciple relationships or because the men came from the same regions.[41]

In reality, Donglin networking did not neatly reflect these traditional models of faction formation. Ironically, the blacklists' representation of Donglin factionalists appeared "real" because the lists blended the socially and literarily familiar ways of imagining factional ties. Hence, among officials, these arbitrarily compiled lists deepened and complicated the factional animosities that had already become messy and confusing since the Wanli era. As they became an important index of officials' political reputations and identities, anxiety and fear levels rose. The men named on these lists worried about being persecuted as factionalists; those who did not appear on the lists were concerned that powerful Donglin officials might block their opportunities.[42] One official told others that he felt ashamed not to be included on the *List of Notorious Donglin Fighters*. Sadly, a year later, his name did appear in the official *List of Donglin Factionalists*, and he was murdered by the eunuch faction.[43]

Modern historians, like seventeenth- and eighteenth-century literati scholars, have focused their attention on whether these lists accurately documented the names of the so-called Donglin associates.[44] Clearly, however, anti-Donglin officials did not prioritize accuracy when identifying and describing their enemies. On the contrary, they sometimes deliberately included unrelated officials in order to confuse the reading public and for entertainment. Although the inclusion of non-factionalists on a factional list was a tactic earlier employed in Song factionalism,[45] drawing inspiration from vernacular literature in compiling blacklists was a new phenomenon. The Donglin man was subject to competing imaginative interpretations.

A List for a List: The Traitors' Case

The sensationalistic, literary turn of late-Ming factionalism nascent in these Donglin blacklists not only put forth a powerfully negative image of the Donglin, but more importantly, it irrevocably changed how politics was understood and communicated. This change did not stop with the fall of Wei Zhongxian after the death of the Tianqi emperor in 1627. The influence of the lists and the images they created for individual officials lingered and continued to play a role in court politics.

The Chongzhen emperor (r. 1628–44), newly enthroned, was determined to crush the eunuch faction. However, he also harbored a less-than-positive view of the Donglin. He said at the beginning of his reign: "We cannot punish an official merely because he is associated with the label 'Donglin.'"[46] This statement does not sound enthusiastic about the Donglin; it does reflect the situation at the time, that to various degrees and for different reasons, the negative image of the Donglin still had traction for many.

An early sign of the Donglin image problem in the Chongzhen reign was the emperor's involvement in an anti-Donglin moral attack. The renowned scholar Qian Qianyi (1582–1664) was accused of participating in examination fraud in Chongzhen 2 (1629). The emperor, before a court audience, roughly dismissed Qian's self-defense and called him a "bare stick" (*guanggun*), or rascal, an allusion to the perception that rootless single men gave in to uncontrolled sexual desire and behavior.[47] This term would eventually enter Qing legal discourse from vernacular fiction, but before then, literary vocabulary had penetrated into late-Ming official discourse and even the emperor's vocabulary.[48] In fact, in the *List of Notorious Donglin Fighters*, Qian Qianyi was matched with the rebel Yan Qing, "The Prodigal," a "bare stick" type of character from *Water Margin*.

It was not an easy task for the emperor and his officials to undo the effects of the Donglin blacklists and the colorful images they evoked among the reading public. The actions of the Donglin-identified official Ni Yuanlu (1592–1644) reveal the difficulty of breaking away from factional listing and labeling. In response to the emperor's call for "abandoning cliques and transforming differences to sameness,"[49] Ni stressed the necessity of recognizing the Donglin as a faction of virtuous men who represent "true Confucian Learning of Principle (Lixue), true integrity, true moral character, and true statesmanship."[50] At the same time, Ni also understood that factional lists would always provide fodder for more disputes. Therefore, he told the emperor that as long as others ceased speaking of factions, he himself would not mention the label "Donglin" again.[51]

But list making now seemed a natural recourse for political actors and continued to evolve as a political technique. Lists were easy to disseminate and quick to produce results by direct impression; they summarized politics and identity in a black-and-white manner that inevitably provoked strong reactions. Even though the status of the Donglin remained unsettled and *Donglin* had become a forbidden term at court,[52] at the urging of officials identified with the Donglin, including Ni Yuanlu, the emperor issued the famous "Traitors' Case" (Ni'an), a list of officials to be punished because of their association with Wei Zhongxian. It was printed and announced throughout the empire.

The issuance of this new list was critical because it greatly contributed to making the moral image of individual officials central to political struggles in and outside the capital. After the release of this list, officials of various camps and their literati followers competed by questioning their rivals' moral performance. In particular, they remained concerned over the perceived discrepancies between the dominant moral reputation of a faction and the moral performance of the individuals on that faction's list.[53] Though not as sensational as the Donglin blacklists concocted by the eunuch faction, the Traitors' Case undoubtedly added momentum to late-Ming image politics.

Once the Tianqi reign had ended in 1627, the suffering and sacrifices of Donglin officials were widely publicized, and this helped establish their image as a faction of Confucian moral exemplars.[54] At the same time, the Donglin claim to moral superiority had become a point of contention in the government. To gain the political upper hand, anti-Donglin officials often impeached Donglin-identified officials for violating Confucian ethical ideals such as filial piety and gender propriety. In the late 1630s, Ni Yuanlu and his close friend Zheng Man both lost their jobs after the anti-Donglin faction leveled accusations of domestic ethical violations against them.[55] Ni was impeached for being an irresponsible husband and Zheng for being an unfilial son and wicked father-in-law, a story to which I will turn shortly.

The use of lists and literature as weapons in power struggles effectively blurred the boundaries between "real" and "feigned" moral exemplars and so directed attention to the official's actual personal character. Whereas lists simplified—or falsified—an official's political position and thereby made politics more divisive and personal, vernacular literature did much the same thing by supplying sensational details and referring to specific moral stereotypes that readers of popular literature could easily recognize and relate to. The factional images of the Donglin produced by these two related methods—lists and literature—caused confusion among officials and the reading public. As a result, officials faced ever greater pressure to "authenticate" their moral images.

THE FACE OF THE DONGLIN: THE ELDER ZHENG'S IMAGES UNVEILED

The interplay between print culture and politics made officials' personal performance as fathers, sons, and husbands increasingly important in late-Ming factional configurations and the competition among factions for power at court. To further illustrate this trend in political culture, I shall now turn to the political demise of Zheng Zhenxian and the execution of his son Zheng Man. Their experiences not only illuminate the evolution of the Donglin man as a moral paragon but, more importantly, highlight the role played by Confucian family tales in shaping factional identities.

The Zheng family hailed from prosperous Wujin County (in modern-day Jiangsu). They were related by marriage to another prestigious family in the area, the Qians, whose scions included Qian Yiben, a Donglin founding figure.[56] Zheng Zhenxian became Wu Liang's brother-in-law when he married the daughter of Wu

Zhongxing (*jinshi* 1571), who had become famous in the empire for impeaching Grand Secretary Zhang Juzheng and as a consequence being severely punished by the Wanli emperor.

In Wanli 5 (1577), an imperial order of *duoqing* (cutting short an official's mourning period for a deceased parent) prevented Zhang from resigning from office to mourn properly for his deceased father. This event triggered a series of confrontations between the emperor and oppositional officials, who expressed their opposition to Zhang's administrative style by framing his "compliance" with the *duoqing* order as a violation of filial piety. The emperor's decision to have the leading protesters beaten at court turned the incident into a sensational spectacle. This was a watershed moment, setting off the late-Ming factionalism that would evolve into a greater problem.

In succeeding years, the Grand Secretariat became the target of political attacks, while the Censorate grew into a powerful political force, with censors submitting bold memorials to the court and widely circulated essays, plays, stories, and satires between Beijing and Nanjing, the auxiliary capital and political center in the south. These materials claimed to expose alleged ethical defects of powerful officials. Many censors fashioned themselves as loyal officials courageously upholding ethical ideals, but in time, censorial authority was itself eroded by abuses of power. Censors, feared by many as "hungry hawks," became instruments of political manipulation and character assassination; wielding power in the name of moral uprightness satisfied each censor's craving for personal fame and wealth.[57]

Zheng Zhenxian's image problem arose just as public suspicion regarding the impeaching officials' self-proclaimed moral superiority was mounting. Literati readers learned about Zheng through two different political images of him that circulated in the late Wanli reign. One image presented him as an upright hero battling against the abuse of power. Wu Liang's Donglin canon, *Memorials of the Wanli Court*, included Zheng's "An Honest Memorial Exposing the Most Powerful and Treacherous Officials in the Past and Present" (Zhifa gujin diyi quanjian shu) (Wanli 36 [1608]). This memorial was a perfect fit with Wu's collection and agenda, as it scathingly called out certain former and presiding grand secretaries as venomous blackguards who abused their political power.[58] Wu appropriately placed this memorial in the chapter titled "Exposing Treacherous Officials" (Fajian), a title likely inspired by that of Zheng's memorial. Zheng had singled out Grand Secretary Zhu Geng's factionalist behavior and its corrupting effect on the central government. This view was endorsed and voiced even more strongly by Wu Liang himself.[59] These attacks on Zhu Geng, leader of the Zhe faction, likely led to Zheng's political demise.[60]

Zheng Zhenxian and Wu Liang were both considered Donglin members at some point. When the above-mentioned memorial earned Zheng a demotion to a post in remote Sichuan, he received several poems from Wu, followed by another set of poems after his departure. In these poems, Wu spoke highly of Zheng's political integrity as a fearless, honest, and loyal official.[61] He also dedicated poems to Zheng's mother, praising her achievement of the ideal womanhood and portraying her Confucian motherly virtues as an inspiration for officials striving to perform diligently their political duties.[62]

The second image of Zheng Zhenxian was not so exemplary. His impeachment of top officials was considered by some to be nothing more than vicious character assassination. Some believed that Zheng's provocative memorial against Zhu Geng and his ally Li Tingji contained dishonest charges and employed exaggerated and ill-conceived rhetoric, a typical opportunist's move.[63] Zheng's true colors became a hot topic in official circles.[64]

Vernacular literature was entering official politics around this time. To enhance their own fame, the censors—siding with their respective power holders at court—portrayed targeted officials as fictional rebel characters. These colorful attacks were disseminated through the official gazetteer and its private copies. As circulation of such images widened, they became entertaining morsels swapped at officials' drinking parties. The famous official and calligrapher Dong Qichang (1555–1636) once called the situation "a real-life *Water Margin*" (*huo Shuihuzhuan*).[65] Zheng Zhenxian was dubbed the "Bai Sheng of the Donglin faction." The Bai Sheng character in *Water Margin* was a schemer who would betray his rebel friends under torture. Why this particular character? One record explained that Zheng had attacked his colleagues in order to gain an important censorial position, and in the wake of this betrayal, his friends at court felt ashamed to work with him.[66]

At first glance, this negative image of Zheng conveys the simple truth that within the community of Donglin gentlemen there lurked this morally inferior man. However, the reality was much messier. In fact, Zheng Zhenxian did not create a clear factional identity for himself. At the time, a few factional groups were named after the home regions of their respective leaders, such as the Zhe faction (Zhejiang),

Xuan faction (Xuancheng, in modern-day Anhui), Kun faction (Kunshan, in modern-day Jiangsu), and so on, many of which later joined forces with the eunuch faction.[67] Zheng, while seen as Donglin by some, maintained an extremely close relationship with the Kun faction leaders but had created enemies in the Zhe faction.[68]

Donglin-identified officials in the last decade of the Wanli reign, surrounded as they were by accusations of factional maneuvering, were unlikely to have called Zheng the "Bai Sheng" of their own faction. Even though contemporary readers loved the characters of *Water Margin* as manly heroes, likening Zheng to a sly fictional character would have served only to ridicule the Donglin itself and reinforce their image as a collective whose loyalty and character were questionable. The damage this impression would do to Zheng and to the Donglin faction suggests that it had been the work of Donglin rivals.

These early images of Zheng Zhenxian as a Donglin man in the Wanli reign had focused primarily on his political behavior. Later, however, the public revelation of a small detail in his private life in a Donglin blacklist indicated that changes were under way: factionalism became personal.

During the Tianqi reign, when Zheng's name appeared in some Donglin blacklists, he was not matched with a rebel character from *Water Margin*. Nonetheless, at this point, rumors about his personal life were brought to notice for the first time. *The Seditious Donglin Clique* (Daobing Donglin huo), a blacklist compiled in Tianqi 6 (1626), included one sentence after Zheng's name, noting that he had "shaved his head to fake insanity."[69] This seemingly trivial detail is striking because it introduced local gossip to the list. The author(s) of the list, going out of their way to inject this information here, clearly meant to project a dubious personal image of Zheng in the hope of causing greater damage to his political standing.

This editorial move was the work of former Zhe faction members who were collaborating with the eunuch faction.[70] In other words, the previous generation of Zhe factionalists contributed to the later eunuch faction by digging up dirt on Donglin-identified figures like Zheng. This literary-political project would be carried on by yet another generation of Zhe factionalists under the leadership of Grand Secretary Wen Tiren (1573–1638) during the Chongzhen reign. They would make the dubious aspects of Zheng's domestic life appear credible by writing them into vernacular novels meant to incriminate his son.

To understand how gossip became "fact" and a footnote grew into a fatal scandal as factionalism evolved transgenerationally in the form of family romance, we must look carefully into this locally generated image of Zheng Zhenxian. When the triennial bureaucratic evaluations took place in Wanli 39 (1611), Zheng had already been demoted to Sichuan. There he received a negative evaluation and another demotion.[71] In Beijing, Wu Liang was treated similarly.[72] This was an especially heavy blow for Zheng.[73] Within the span of a couple of years, Zheng and Wu both left government service and returned to Wujin County. While Wu lived a disciplined life in temporary retirement, Zheng sought refuge in Buddhism. Frustrated by factional retaliation and mistreatment, he no longer visited other officials or socialized with local elites; he would not wear Confucian headwear and did not show up at lineage gatherings. He devoted himself completely to studying Buddhism.[74]

Locally, an increasingly bizarre image of Zheng emerged. At the time, many officials admired Master Lianchi (Lianchi Dashi) (usually known as Yunqi Zhuhong [1535–1615]), a pivotal figure in the popularization of Buddhism among the late-Ming literati.[75] His wife, a pious Buddhist, also enjoyed great popularity among gentry women. Zheng Zhenxian and his wife decided to visit the couple together.[76] His son described the rumors that followed:

> On my parents' way back, Father stopped at Kunshan [where I was studying] and took me back home. As soon as we returned, we realized there were rumors flying everywhere. Some said Father had shaved his head and become a monk. Some said I also had become a monk or Mother had become a nun. There were also people who gossiped that Father was involved in a dispute over some maid. All kinds of stories were being circulated. Father and Mother laughed them off, but the rumors didn't die and continued to spread. It was probably people conspiring to take our property who spread them.[77]

Zheng Zhenxian and Wu Liang's friendship, once extremely strong, had cooled during this period. In a letter to Zheng Zhenguang (1583–1616), Zhenxian's younger brother, Wu recalled the strong friendship and mutual trust he and Zhenxian had enjoyed in the old days.[78] According to this letter, after they retired, Wu learned about Zhenxian's "desire to withdraw from the world" (*you chushi zhi xiang*). At first Wu admired Zhenxian's choices, but then he started to question them. He decided that he trusted his friend to break away soon from such distractions and that he should not participate in gossiping about Zhenxian's domestic situation. However, because certain ill-intentioned local men had circulated rumors and then directed Zhenxian's suspicions toward Wu, their friendship had suffered.[79]

What actually happened within the walls of the Zheng household remains a mystery. Zheng's friend Wu and his son Zheng Man were obliged to refrain from writing about the specifics. Popular accounts of the Zhengs in seventeenth-century publications all contain questionable information.[80] Still, it is clear that local politics, personal spiritual pursuits, and domestic relations in combination created a messy situation for the retired Zheng Zhenxian.

For some time, Zheng Zhenxian's image as an official indulging in Buddhism, as well as the sensational details associated with it, stayed mostly local and within the realms of the concerned clans. As factional struggles intensified during the Tianqi reign, however, as mentioned earlier, some vague information about his domestic life began to trickle into political media, just as the Donglin image took a sensationalistic literary turn. The face of Zheng Zhenxian as an official of the evil Donglin faction, a corrupt man, would become more clearly defined after his death, when, amid factional struggles in the Chongzhen reign, depictions of the Zhengs' domestic and religious life were exhibited in the empirewide political theater in the form of novels, biographies, and anecdotes.

THE MAKING OF A TRANSGENERATIONAL SCANDAL

The Zhengs, father and son, never served together at court. Image politics is all that connected their careers, which actually overlapped only in lists and literature: they both first appeared on the Donglin blacklists during the Tianqi reign. By the Chongzhen reign, anti-Donglin officials were weaving their stories into various forms of literature as a way of attacking the son. The father's and son's different but overlapping experiences with image politics most vividly reveal the evolution of factionalism as a literary problem. In the struggles in and around literary production, the idealized image of the Donglin man as a loyal official, filial son, and self-disciplined man gradually crystallized.

The Fall of an (Un)filial Son

When Zheng Man began his career in Beijing in Tianqi 2 (1622), Donglin-identified officials had just helped enthrone the young

Tianqi emperor. Emboldened by their sudden dominance at court and eager to restore the bureaucratic order they regarded as having been severely crippled in the Wanli reign, these officials alienated enough of their peers to cause factional discord to flare. Meanwhile, the young emperor's reliance on the eunuch Wei Zhongxian triggered fierce criticism from officials, the most vocal of whom were identified and slandered as Donglin. Wei Zhongxian gradually built alliances with officials who were either marginalized by the Donglin or sought easy promotion. Soon after Zheng Man entered the government, he submitted a memorial backing his friend Wen Zhenmeng's criticism of Wei's intrusion into government matters. This move earned him the reputation of being an upright and outspoken official at the outset of his career, but it also offended Wei. Demoted, Zheng returned home. In Beijing, Donglin-identified officials persisted in their campaign against Wei, but within a couple of years, many of them had been demoted, arrested, or even murdered. The most horrific of these cases, the torture and killing of six officials, epitomized the suppression of the Donglin at this time.

From his hometown in Jiangnan, Zheng Man had hoped to help rescue the imprisoned officials but soon learned of their deaths. Because it was said that a six-leaved yellow ganoderma (*lingzhi*) miraculously appeared upon the martyrdom of the six, Zheng composed a long poem, "Song of Yellow Ganoderma" (Huangzhi ge), to commemorate them.[81] The poem was circulated quickly to and within the capital. Several officials in the eunuch faction who had previously followed Zhu Geng, the former Zhe faction leader and grand secretary impeached by Zheng's father, took advantage of Wei Zhongxian's furious reaction to this poem. They identified Zheng Man as a Donglin leader and implicated him in the "confession" of another persecuted Donglin official. When the eunuch faction began persecuting officials with blacklists, they identified Zheng as a key member of the Donglin and included him in almost all such lists. Hearing of his pending arrest, Zheng went underground and fled to the mountains in the south.[82]

After the fall of Wei Zhongxian and the enthronement of Emperor Chongzhen in 1627, the likelihood of Zheng returning to court looked promising. The new emperor announced his dedication to promoting "governing with filial piety." During the years of terror, Zheng had proved himself a filial son and loyal official. Just as the emperor summoned him back to court along with other officials persecuted by the eunuch faction, Zheng lost both his parents. He dutifully observed two terms of mourning, establishing his *zhongxiao* credentials were known among Donglin supporters during the early Chongzhen reign.

But soon after his return to court in Chongzhen 8 (1635), events took a dramatic turn. Chief Grand Secretary Wen Tiren had become determined to best Wen Zhenmeng, Zheng's close friend and ally, in gaining imperial favor. The emperor had just promoted Wen Zhenmeng into the Grand Secretariat. Wen Tiren worried that his position could be undermined by collaboration between Wen Zhenmeng and Zheng Man. As a result of Wen Tiren's maneuvers, the emperor demoted Wen Zhenmeng. But Wen Tiren wanted more. He decided to use Zheng to dominate completely his Donglin rivals. Having heard rumors about Zheng's family issues from Wu Zongda (*jinshi* 1604), a member of Wu Liang's clan and a grand secretary, Wen Tiren submitted a memorial that included a shocking story about Zheng Man beating his mother. On the basis of this memorial, in Chongzhen 8/11 (1635), the emperor ordered Zheng Man arrested and jailed. Officials on the Board of Punishments said: "We should not prosecute a grave crime against ethics on the basis of gossip. We would like to ask officials from [Zheng]'s hometown to verify the details." But the emperor reprimanded them for protecting Zheng.[83]

Eventually, however, the emperor realized that the case against Zheng could not be substantiated. When Wen Tiren retired in Chongzhen 10 (1637), the official in charge of the case submitted a new report at the emperor's request, which explained Zheng's innocence this way: The Zheng family was known to worship a *jixian*, a "planchette spirit" that could perform fortune-telling and miraculous investigation. Gossip had it that this spirit could identify any family member who had not behaved properly and jump out to punish that person. Zheng's mother was reportedly punished by the spirit for something she did to a maid, but Zheng had nothing to do with the incident.[84]

As the emperor was trying to decide what to do with Zheng, another fierce factional struggle over filial piety erupted. In the summer of Chongzhen 11 (1638), Donglin-identified officials, led by Huang Daozhou, negotiated with the emperor over key official appointments. They vocally challenged the emperor's decision to promote Yang Sichang (1588–1641) and Chen Xinjia (d. 1642), both of whom were in the middle of observing the mourning term for a deceased parent. They cited the age-old idea that loyal officials must be found among filial men.[85] Defiant, the Chongzhen emperor challenged the motives of the oppositional Donglin officials by bringing up Zheng Man's alleged ethical violations.[86] This made the record of Zheng's moral performance of greater importance for all parties. In the end, Zheng was executed. His "death by a thousand cuts" (*lingchi*) became a sensational public spectacle.[87]

Zheng Man's case has been considered an example of the chaos caused by rigid application of moral issues in politics. However, such a reading erases the historically specific dynamics that shaped its course, such as literati religious practices, gender concerns, literati political organizing, and, most importantly, print culture. By situating the competing images of Zheng Man in such a complicated context, we come to understand how the ideal Donglin man was constructed and contested in Confucian family tales and, more broadly, how seventeenth-century factionalism was fought and conceived as image wars.

Generational Matters

The emperor saw competing images of Zheng Man presented in the two sets of testimony regarding the case. One argued for his innocence. In addition to the initial memorials submitted by officials to protest Zheng's arrest, the emperor also received the testimony of two key witnesses from Zheng's hometown, his colleagues Lu Wanxue and Wang Zhang, who confirmed that the charges were groundless. Additionally, the emperor had in hand the testimony of Zheng's kinsmen, which also cleared his reputation.[88] However, reluctant to exonerate Zheng and lose the opportunity to use his case as a means of political leverage, the emperor took keen interest in the evidence presented by a literatus named Xu Xi (fl. 1630s).

Xu and a group of Wen Tiren allies submitted evidence of Zheng's moral corruption and claimed that their position represented "public opinion." Significantly, their testimony altered the original official charges by supplementing them with information about Zheng's alleged sexual transgressions.[89] Thus, to those who defended Zheng, the emperor exclaimed, "Xu Xi and others provided clear evidence of Zheng's crimes. These staff with no bureaucratic rank understand public opinion (*gonglun*); you officials don't. Shame on you!"[90]

The so-called public opinion was substantiated by a number of sensational narratives circulated in vernacular literature, biographies, and anecdotes. Zheng Man's uncle explicitly pointed out in his formal testimony that unofficial accounts and vernacular novels (*xiaoshi xiaoshuo*) were written to prove Zheng Man's alleged immoral conduct and incriminate him.[91] In particular, Zheng's accusers concocted at least two novels, *An Unofficial Account of Zheng's Dismissal* (Fang Zheng xiaoshi; hereafter *Zheng's Dismissal*) and *A Great Hero's Story* (Da yingxiong zhuan), to incriminate him.[92] Although the full texts have not survived, we have all the chapter titles. They reveal important information about the content and use of these narratives, in particular how factional attacks found a convenient conduit in family romances and how such narratives appeared authentic with their depictions of the transgenerational transmission of factional ties and sentiments. They drew on delineations of Donglin generations that appeared in the blacklists and further elaborated them.

Zheng's Dismissal begins with Zheng Man's father, Zheng Zhenxian. It depicts him as a sly politician, a womanizer, and an unhappy retired official gone astray with Buddhism.[93] His son Zheng Man is presented as a sex maniac and predator who seduced not only his father's concubine but also his own daughter-in-law. He beat his mother because he was jealous of her love for his younger brother. The novel attributes Zheng Man's parents' deaths to his sexual immorality; his alleged sexual interest in his sister and his father's concubine was also unfilial behavior. In addition, he was depicted as a political opportunist who attached himself to respectable officials in order to advance his career.[94]

The fictional tropes employed in *Zheng's Dismissal* demonstrate that family romances played a special role in reifying generational understandings of factionalism and could influence the outcome of a power struggle. The authors' interest in transgenerational stories recalls one of the Donglin blacklists produced in the Tianqi reign, *The Seditious Donglin Clique* (Daobing Donglin huo). The authors of that list had tried to highlight the generational change and continuities of the Donglin by creating three sections that signified the group in its early stage (*Donglin chu*), at its peak (*Donglin sheng*), and in its later phase (*Donglin wan*). This categorization reflects the authors' view that Donglin factional ties were formed based on mentor-disciple relationships, examination cohort, regional identity, and family and were reproduced along these lines. Zheng Zhenxian is listed under "Donglin at its peak," while his son is part of "later Donglin." *Zheng's Dismissal* substantiates this categorization by highlighting the father's and son's similar moral defects.

The novel revisits the messy history of factionalism in the Wanli reign and takes the opportunity to trash the senior Zheng, the Zhe faction's old enemy, in order to justify its support for Grand Secretary Wen Tiren, the leader of a new generation of the Zhe faction. The novel names two current prominent Donglin figures who had been close to the Zhengs—Sun Shenxing (1565–1636) and Huang Daozhou—as ringleaders.[95] Although we cannot tell specifically how *Zheng's Dismissal* represents Donglin factionalism, the title of chapter 37, "The Grand Secretary Wen Led Efforts to Expose the Treacherous Plot," suggests that the novel explicitly presents Donglin activities as suspicious and Wen Tiren as a nonfactional official who was single-mindedly loyal to the emperor.[96] This corresponds neatly to what Wen had said repeatedly to the Chongzhen emperor—that he was the lone loyal official at court and that, because of his nonfactionalist stance, he had come under attack from the Donglin officials.[97]

Compared to the blacklists, the novels written to incriminate Zheng Man more clearly directed readers' attention to the personal character of several generations of Donglin factionalists. These were family romances (*jiating xiaoshuo*) crafted to support a specific political agenda. *Zheng's Dismissal*, for instance, recycles old rumors about the elder Zheng's political demise, spiritual pursuits, and domestic problems, setting up the Zheng household as a realm of disorder and licentiousness. The portrayal of the elder Zheng serves the crucial purpose of "explaining" the son's disregard for Confucian ethics. In turn, the son's ethical violations help to "prove" the validity of old allegations that had led to the father's demise in the Wanli reign.

As literary historians point out, in the seventeenth century, family romance as a literary genre developed distinct themes, vocabulary, and narrative structure to accommodate the complex discursive negotiations.[98] This genre provided ample space for authors to create sensational stories about officials' moral performance across multiple generations in political, social, and familial domains. The authors of the sensational novels about the Zhengs took advantage of the flexibility of family romance to describe the Zhengs' transgenerational moral corruption and, by extension, that of the Donglin.[99] Even though this negative image of the transgenerational Donglin factionalism echoed the view of only some literati, it sheds light on the common understanding that politics was a family matter. Generational continuity, a key element of the Confucian ethical system, was a trope deployed in the Confucian family tales concocted as weapons of factionalism.

The mystery around the Zhengs' domestic circumstances became ideal raw material for a transgenerational tale.

Whereas the literary representation of generational continuity in this family romance makes a specific anti-Donglin political claim, the actual production of this novel reveals the wide scope of factionalism as a social and literary phenomenon. The endeavors of the authors of these novels were clearly informed by their own generational position in late-Ming factionalism. Xu Xi, the literatus who presented sensational stories about Zheng Man to the emperor, was a descendant of Xu Guo (1521–1596), a former grand secretary. Xu Xi joined three other well-connected literati to form a strongly pro–Wen Tiren coalition in Jiangnan. Among these men, Zhu Taifan was the offspring of Zhu Geng, the aforementioned Zhe faction leader. Wang Shimin (1592–1680) was the son of Wang Xijue, another former leader of the Zhe faction. The fourth man, Yuan Shu, whose ancestor had served as a grand secretary during the Jiajing reign, also hailed from Zhejiang.[100] This Zhejiang group's position in contemporary sociopolitical competition with the Fushe (lit., Restoration Society), a literary organization associated with the Donglin, was unambiguous.[101] Seen from this perspective, Xu Xi was not just one of those "Jiangnan troublemakers good at cooking up vernacular novels."[102] His participation in Wen Tiren's political-literary projects was part of the anti–Donglin-Fushe collaboration between Wen and regional literati groups. Considering their affinity for the Zhe faction and the frequent employment of literature in inter-literati competition, their resorting to family romances to portray the Donglin as composed of several generations of morally corrupt men makes perfect sense.

Sex Sells

Family romances might also contain lurid elements that made them a form of pornography. This increased their appeal as a political tool, as seen in the second anti-Zheng novels, *A Great Hero's Story*. In the seventeenth century, many novellas were read as erotic literature regardless of their authors' claims to the contrary, including stories that, by our standards, do not much engage sexuality.[103] The multiplicity of interpretative possibilities of such narratives could both facilitate the dissemination of sensationalistic stories about factional officials and draw attention to their performance as fathers, sons, and husbands.

A Great Hero's Story presents many characters from a wide range of social strata, from monks and neighborhood rascals to gentry women and courtesans.[104] Whereas *Zheng's Dismissal* represented real people and elaborated on the official charges against Zheng Man in order to reinforce specific political messages, *A Great Hero's Story* is a vulgar work, so fantastic in its details that it was certainly meant as entertaining satire. Chapter titles alone, such as "Madame Lu Beat Up Her Lover Out of Jealousy" and "A Gentry Daughter Gets Naked to Have Her Virginity Checked," were sensational enough to feed its readers' prurience.[105] This novel focuses so much on stories of promiscuity that, at least based on the surviving chapter titles, Zheng and court politics were convenient narrative elements around which an entertaining erotic fiction could be constructed. It could be read either or both as a piece of pornography intended for pleasure and a vivid expression of political satire.

As factionalism came to be imagined, understood, and fought via the family tales of individual officials, it obviously became more difficult for those officials to control their public image. Sensationalistic representations of political figures seem to have attracted more attention from the reading public than did serious political writings. For example, the biography of Zheng Man published by the literatus Jin Risheng (fl. 1620s–30s) in his book *Documents of Heavenly Justice* (Song tian lu bi), a collection of sources that recorded the fall of the eunuch faction, highlighted Zheng's masculine virtues, in particular his filial piety. The biography was printed in Chongzhen 2 (1629), years before the case against Zheng broke.[106] Zheng's filial devotion must have made a strong impression for it to have earned a mention in this biography. The author also offers a rare account of how Zheng's career was plagued by the hostility of the Zhe faction, his father's old enemies.[107] However, the impact of Jin's thorough documentation paled in comparison to the juicy scandals depicted in novels and anecdotes.

The multiplication of literary genres for political use in this thriving print culture would further destabilize the already arbitrary distinction between "real" and "feigned" moral exemplars. The traditional lack of clear boundaries and the blurred hierarchy between formal documentation and anecdotes (discussed in the introductory chapter) meant that their competition as different genres of political information only sharpened in this period. Literary accounts, even if fictional or anecdotal, colored public views of contemporary politics and officials. Whether or not these accounts depicted Zheng truthfully was less important than the fact that they were in circulation and *suggested* the plausibility of his alleged sexual misbehavior. Once the link between Zheng and his presumed ethical violations was established in fiction, it took on a life of its own and could influence politics in a very real way. Like the eunuch faction's manipulation of *Water Margin*, the anti-Zheng novels also met the entertainment purposes of contemporary literary-political projects and effectively disseminated negative images of individual officials. Stories about Zheng beating his mother and his sexual immorality traveled everywhere in a variety of genres.[108]

The consequences of fictionalizing and sensationalizing officials' domestic lives for political purposes were devastating and alarming. When Zheng learned about the novels, he saw this development as historically unprecedented. He compared his case to the experience of Zhu Xi (1130–1200), the great Song Neo-Confucian thinker, whose career suffered under relentless factional attacks on his character: "Censor Li [Rixuan] sent me a copy of *Dao ming lu*, which contains several memorials against [Zhu Xi]. These memorials claimed that he seduced and then married two Buddhist nuns. They also accused him of allowing his son to steal cattle. This testifies to the serious nature of factional struggles at the time."[109] The notorious memorials against Zhu Xi recounted his alleged misconduct, which included a lack of filial piety, disloyalty, and sexual immorality.[110] This was a brutal and costly episode of factionalism in Song history, and officials of later generations all knew these stories. If Zheng saw many similarities between his and Zhu Xi's circumstances—even to the libelous nature of the charges—he argued that the attacks he suffered were much worse. He felt bitter and desperate because it "was unheard of" for factionalist officials to stoop so low as to produce a vernacular novel as a means of circulating charges; this was a situation that Zhu Xi had not had to face.[111]

Ming officials were all familiar with the heavy toll factionalism had taken throughout imperial history and the use of charges of sexual immorality in political attacks. However, they soon came to realize that their knowledge of factionalism in history was inadequate to coping with it in their own time. Print culture, in particular the penetration of politics by literature, invalidated the old political wisdom. Meanwhile, Ming emperors, like their officials, actively engaged the burgeoning print culture of their time. The Chongzhen emperor knew the Zhu Xi stories, but he also knew he had the power to determine which story represented "public opinion" in his own day. Eventually, he chose to embrace the one that would allow him to challenge the Donglin claim to moral perfection and keep Zheng imprisoned.[112]

The competing images of the Zhengs—and, by extension, of the Donglin—illustrate why, as print culture and factionalism became further entangled, Confucian family tales became an effective political tool. Spread in a variety of forms—long and short, outright fictional and anecdotal—they would be read as political information *and* entertaining literature. The more sensational they were, the more attention they attracted. Meanwhile, literary and political traditions complicated officials' efforts to control images. Moral-political principles, not genre, had constituted important criteria for determining "truth" and defined who was an authentic or fake moral exemplar. For instance, officials who defended Zheng Man did not challenge the emperor's decision by dismissing the novel as a less reliable genre; instead, they argued that accounts of officials' domestic issues in any form were always suspicious (see chap. 3). Hence, print culture and popularity of vernacular literature, by exposing officials' personal lives to more public attention, threatened political tradition seriously and made late-Ming politics more unstable and unpredictable.

Confucian Family Tales from Prison

Late-Ming officials understood the political power of Confucian family tales and employed print in their negotiations with the emperor and with colleagues and in their self-defense, even when they were imprisoned. Zheng Man also published from prison. A talented writer and poet, he wrote copiously while in confinement, including scholarly essays, a chronological biography of the famed Song official Su Shi (1037–1101), and his own chronological autobiography.[113] He also compiled his own poetry composed before and during the imprisonment. Some of these were published before his execution. In all his writings, Zheng Man firmly defended not only his own moral rectitude but also the exemplariness of the Zheng family.

Because Zheng Man's memorials were kept from the emperor's sight and his self-defense could not be voiced through official channels, he decided to disseminate pamphlets on his case and the trial.[114] These specifically countered the various moral charges leveled against him. For instance, one of the pamphlets documented his answers to the prosecutor's questions, in which he reflected extensively on his mother's devotion to his father, including her voluntarily acquiring a concubine in order to obtain more sons for the family. He pointed out the lack of reliability of the information provided by Grand Secretary Wu Zongda, his mother's brother, due to Wu's affiliation with the Zhe faction. He also condemned officials who recruited literati writers to concoct novels incriminating him.[115] This series of pamphlets presented Zheng's own family tale so as to convince the public that the charges against his family—such as his parents' disputes over a maid, his beating of his mother, and his sexual immorality—had been fabricated by the anti-Donglin faction.

Zheng Man also utilized other genres to combat the prolonged, serious moral attacks leveled against the Zheng family. He particularly highlighted the family's tradition of filial piety. In his chronological autobiography, for instance, Zheng set out to debunk the rumors about his parents by giving a detailed account of his father's filial actions.[116] Zheng then carefully described how, after his father died, he devoted himself to taking care of his mother. Once he had completed the prescribed three-year mourning for his father, he was scheduled to leave for Beijing and resume his government position. However, since his mother's next birthday would be her sixtieth, an important one for the Chinese, Zheng chose to remain at home longer. Then his mother fell ill and passed away. He took another three-year leave to mourn her. In the entry for Chongzhen 5 (1632), Zheng's autobiography specifically mentioned an essay he composed during the mourning term, titled "Zaiyu Asks about the Three-Year Mourning," to stress his deepened understanding of filial piety during this period.[117] Although this essay is lost to us, the title suggests that Zheng elaborated on Confucius's famous criticism in *The Analects* (Lunyu) of his disciple Zaiyu, who was reluctant to observe the full mourning period for a deceased parent.[118]

Although the initial official charge against Zheng Man was lack of filial piety, Zheng rightly realized that the literature depicting his sexual immorality had become powerful circumstantial evidence in defining his public image. Hence, his autobiography not only asserted his filial piety but also presented his filial performance in connection with literati self-discipline. Zheng recalled a promise he made as a young man to his father, before he departed for Nanjing to study:

> Father said: "Do not be distracted by courtesans. Once you get contaminated, you will suffer your whole life." I respectfully listened

> to his instruction. . . . [My classmates] from eastern Guangdong . . . got me drunk. They asked Qiu Xiaoyu, a courtesan, to take off her clothes and lie down with me. I was not aware of this until I awakened in the morning. I immediately put on my clothes and got up. Later when I traveled to Wulin, my friend Zhang Juxing ordered opera singers to serve me in bed. He said: "It is raining very hard. You can't go anywhere." I awkwardly rejected his offer. Friends circulated these stories and considered me a strange person. They do not know that I always remember Father's instruction and have never violated it.[119]

Courtesans had become an essential feature of Jiangnan literati social and cultural lives. Zheng's invocation of this particular episode in his memory of his father not only demonstrates that the Zhengs were self-disciplined men but also illuminates how filial piety contributed to his own moral cultivation.

The autobiography reinforced the main points made in the memorial Zheng had submitted to the Chongzhen emperor upon his arrest, in which he described the *zhongxiao* tradition of his family and in particular stressed the deeds of filial piety he and his father had performed. In that memorial, Zheng had praised the emperor's commitment to "governing with filial piety" and pleaded for the emperor's trust.[120] His autobiography not only reiterated the same message. It also served as a counter-narrative to the claims made in the novels created by his enemies to attack his filial piety and sexual morality. Zheng did his best to show he embodied the Confucian masculine virtues and deserved to be seen as an ideal Donglin man. However, these efforts failed to save his reputation and life.

DISTINGUISHING THE FAKE DONGLIN MAN

When the image of Zheng Man became intricately tied to the political fate of the whole group, Donglin-identified officials were confronted with the task of authenticating their collective claim to moral exemplariness. They had two options: they could defend Zheng Man's reputation and Donglin moral superiority or condemn Zheng's moral corruption and out him as a fake Donglin. Officials of all sides—and contemporary writers and readers—were divided on Zheng's case. Their debates focused on proving or challenging the assertion that the real Donglin man embodied filial piety and gender propriety. These debates again show that multiple parties participated in constructing the Donglin image and membership, under the influence of a cluster of religious, intellectual, moral, and political concerns. In this context, Zheng Man's manner of self-defense was doomed by the tricky relationship between factionalism and print. His personal image bifurcated. Anti-Donglin officials continued to invoke his alleged ethical defects in order to smear the Donglin with moral corruption and politically untrustworthiness, while some within the Donglin-Fushe community decided to portray him as a "fake" Donglin whose personal moral weakness automatically disqualified him from being one of them.

Publicizing a commitment to Confucian ethics in various media could boost a reputation, but the complexity of the readership—even within the same political camp—often crippled the effectiveness of such image-making efforts. Zheng Man's self-defense would prove inadequate. This was determined in part by his contemporaries' complicated understanding of publicity, publishing, and the proper display of literati masculine virtues.

For both intellectual and political reasons, Confucian scholars had remained ambivalent about achieving fame through lecturing and publishing.[121] Politically minded literati needed to emphasize their commitment to, and proper display of, Confucian ethical values in print. When doing so, they had to anticipate readers' differing reactions. It seriously worried the literati that print material could be used against them. For example, an official's decision to publish a collection of travel poems—even though publishing and traveling had become prevalent in late-Ming literati world—could potentially cause image problems. There is a revealing discussion of this situation in comments by the Fushe scholar Zhang Zilie (1597–1673) on a publication by Wu Shen (1589–1670), a friend and high-ranking official. In his letters, Zhang asked their mutual friends to urge Wu against publishing the poems he had written over several leisurely months' travel during Chongzhen 16 (1643). Wu had just been admonished by the emperor for failing to answer his call to lead the Ming army in a campaign to suppress rebels. Although it was said that Wu did not proceed because he was not given enough troops, his response was nonetheless disloyal.[122] As a result, he was demoted and ordered to serve in a remote garrison in Yunnan. Zhang reported to a close friend and official:

> [Wu Shen] received the edict to go to the military post. He should have speedily reported to duty. However, he spent the summer at the Wu Garden . . . [and] then went on to have a leisurely time in the

> mountains, drinking along the way and partying with literati friends. Now he is eager to publish those poems. All these actions only give others excuses to criticize him. They really do not present the model behavior of an official who had just been admonished by His Majesty. *If vicious men found an opportunity to present the poetry collection to His Majesty along with fabricated slander, as evidence of [Wu Shen]'s disrespect for His Majesty and the imperial order, how would Wu defend himself?* I hope you secretly convey my words to him and persuade him not to publish but destroy the poems.[123]

Zhang also wrote to another official to convey the same message.[124] His letters reveal the very real risks associated with publishing and the adverse attention it might bring in the politically sensitive time. His immediate concern was for Wu's image and how the publication of his poems would affect Wu's career. But clearly, worries about officials' publication derived from the intensifying factionalism and the easier access to information made possible by print.

Compared to Wu Shen's loss of imperial favor, the gravity of Zheng Man's case might make it seem too extreme to be representative. However, it is informative for us precisely because it reveals much about the tricky repercussions of publicity. Zheng had to deal with a complex audience, which included the Donglin's enemies, different groups within the Donglin clique, and Fushe scholars such as Zhang Zilie and his friends who were allied to some Donglin-identified officials.

A crucial factor that prevented all readers from appreciating Zheng's display of Confucian masculine virtues was the diverse understandings of proper performance of filial piety that had mushroomed among the literati.[125] The famous scholar and Fushe activist Huang Zongxi (1610–1695) considered Zheng a truly filial son. He pointed out that Zheng could not have explained what happened between his father, his mother, and his father's concubine to defend himself against the charges that he had beaten his mother because talking about one's deceased parents' fault itself would constitute a violation of filial piety.[126] Had Zheng disclosed his parents' domestic problems, he would likely have been criticized for it. Huang Zongxi and Zheng Man certainly represented one type of literati understanding of proper filial expression. However, there were contemporaries who believed that one could fairly prove one's own filial virtue by exposing the misdeeds of the elders in the household should that become necessary.[127] Among such people, Zheng's filial piety would not be acknowledged unless he could explain his father's domestic problems.

Another factor that complicated Zheng's battle over his image was his audience's diverse concerns and foci. Zheng's writings endeavored to portray the moral exemplariness of his family, but his candid descriptions of their domestic world were too complicated to represent the impeccable Donglin man. And they might have reinforced the impression that he lacked literati virtues. In particular, his strikingly honest accounts of the extraordinary Buddhist piety of his whole family—his parents, himself, and his wife and concubines—substantiated for many the troubled public image of the Zhengs and their questionable Donglin status.

Buddhist devotion and patronage were clearly an important part of the Zhengs' lives and identities, as was the case for many other seventeenth-century literati-officials. But the degree to which an official might wisely incorporate Buddhist piety and morality into his own public image posed a rather different question. A gendered calculation was at play. In some contrast to the situation for gentry women, whose Buddhist devotion in the domestic space could buttress claims of ideal Confucian femininity, "excessive" Buddhist pursuits could provoke the impression of a man led to commit deviant behaviors such as abandoning Confucian commitments.[128] Officials' Buddhist practices were always vulnerable to suspicion because they were often portrayed in popular discourse together with gender disorder and even sexual immorality. The sensationalistic representation of Buddhist elements in the vernacular novels that helped defame the Zhengs is a telling example.

The ideal Confucian official was expected to handle questions of Buddhism and women carefully when trying to properly display his masculine virtues in published words.[129] However, not only did Zheng Man extensively and explicitly describe the importance of Buddhism in his life, but his stories often involved multiple young women in the Zheng household. His was a complicated household, which made him vulnerable to moral attacks. Zheng had three adopted daughters by the time he turned thirty. His wife, Madam Zhou, failed to conceive in the first six years of their marriage. So his grandmother, Madam Dong, had Madam Zhou adopt a girl from the Dong family. They followed the local wisdom of "raising girls to bear boys" in fulfillment of the filial duty to continue the patriline.[130] Zheng and his wife also adopted two baby girls from remote relatives, girls who would have been drowned due to their families' poverty. The couple's Buddhist piety might have inspired these charitable adoptions.[131]

In addition, Zheng had at least two concubines. Over the years, his wife and concubines together produced six daughters and five sons.[132] Later, a girl surnamed Han, the fiancée of a Zheng son, lost her parents and moved into the Zheng household without having the official wedding ceremony. The accusation that Zheng raped his daughter-in-law, a charge presented to the emperor through the novels, apparently derived from rumors that grew from the complex domestic arrangements in the Zheng household.

In Zheng's self-presentation, he was a man of compassion and a responsible son, father, and husband. Unfortunately, his family did not look like the family of the ideal Donglin man to many literati. A comment by the literatus Zhang Xia confirms how Zheng's public image was affected by (mis)representations of his domestic situation. Arguing that it was a bad idea to have so many women of various ages and social strata (including maids) residing in the same house, Zhang surmised that Zheng's downfall originated from the fact that too many women from different backgrounds lived under the same roof and that it was impossible to find the truth in such a messy situation. Zheng himself should be the one to blame for what happened to him. It was such a pity that many considered Zheng a Donglin.[133]

Zheng's image trouble reflected not only the "purist" view of the Donglin man's filiality and gender propriety among literati readers but also the different political concerns behind such a view. While certain Donglin-identified officials persistently defended and tried to rescue Zheng, others worried pragmatically about how his dubious moral image might hurt their own standing and that of the Donglin overall. The high political stakes of the moral image of the Donglin man can be seen in the ways in which both the Donglin and anti-Donglin camps scrutinized Zheng's publications from prison.

For instance, in Chongzhen 10 (1637), a young literatus surnamed Lei, who had spent some time in the same prison, asked Zheng Man to select and comment on the examination essays of that year's newly minted *jinshi*. Zheng agreed. However, he soon discovered that his compilation had been printed and sold. Lei had a relative who ran a printing house, and this relative apparently thought he could make a profit by printing the compilation and did so without asking Zheng's permission. Later, when Lei asked Zheng to write a preface for the collection, foreseeing potential political risks, Zheng decided to use the opportunity to explain how this publication had come about without his consent. When the young man insisted that he write more on the selected essays, Zheng complied and composed a second preface to talk specifically about how to compose exam essays. It seems that the publication was not Zheng's initiative, but he decided to let it be with the two prefaces. The collection went into a second printing.[134]

The publication raised some eyebrows. Things became serious enough that Zheng Man documented the worrisome development in the Chongzhen 11 (1638) entry in his autobiography, suggesting that there had been grave repercussions. He wrote that the controversy around the publication nearly resulted in another round of attacks against him.[135] More seriously, it was not just the Donglin's enemies who paid attention. Chen Zilong (1608–1647), a famed literatus activist associated with the Donglin-Fushe community who had just passed the civil service examination that year and become an official, discovered that Zheng's preface mentioned that he and his Fushe friend Xia Yunyi (1596–1645), who also became a *jinshi* that same year, had visited Zheng in prison just before their examinations. When Chen learned about the publication of the examination essays edited by Zheng from prison, he was outraged and grew anxious.[136] According to Chen, the official in charge of Zheng's case showed him the preface in which he was mentioned and helped with arranging to have the preface removed before the manuscript went to print. Chen accused Zheng of lying: "He composed an essay in prison, praising my chivalry, talents, and willingness to help. He claimed that I always tried to offer a hand to those in trouble. He said that even when he was charged with a serious crime and few wanted to visit him, I was the only friend to stand beside him. He was lying."[137]

Chen's accusation is somewhat vague. It does not specify how Zheng's preface mischaracterized their relationship. Was he upset that Zheng fabricated his visit to prison or that Zheng had implied that they were friends? In addition, Chen's account misrepresents Zheng's preface, which only briefly mentions that Chen and Xia visited him in prison. Considering that they had passed the examinations, it was proper for Zheng to mention them in the preface to a collection of examination essays that included theirs.[138] Chen's main concern seems to have been to distance himself from Zheng. He had told Zheng's close friend and strong ally Huang Daozhou, a Donglin icon, that they must abandon Zheng in order to protect the reputation of their faction.[139]

Chen's concern vividly reflects the sense of urgency among the Donglin-Fushe camp with maintaining the purity of their moral image. Publishing complicated officials' strategies in factional struggles and enhanced their awareness of the importance of moral image. Sensational rumors about the Zheng household and Zheng himself had stoked the reading public's imagination and in that capacity entered into the factional debates. Fushe scholars, who at the time aggressively employed Confucian ethics in their own image-making, were invested in establishing a stark contrast between the moral rectitude of the exemplary Donglin-Fushe men and the moral corruption of their rivals. Given this delicate situation, who among them, if he was serious about his political future, would want to be associated with such a figure and his dubious popular image?[140] To consolidate the perfection of the Donglin man, some wanted Zheng abandoned as a fake Donglin—an unfilial son and immoral man.

By the time the executors sliced Zheng's body into a thousand pieces in Chongzhen 12 (1639), his life and moral image had already been torn apart by the factionalists and reading public. Competing political forces, rival social groups, and readers of sensational literature created, manipulated, and were entertained by his polarized images. Those images continued to be spread widely and entered more books. The only value Zheng's death had at the time might be that his allegedly fake Donglin identity, exposed by his moral defects, contributed to consolidating the connection between the ideal Donglin man and Confucian masculine virtues.

Seventeenth-century literati engaged Confucian ethics not just in treatises on behavioral norms and rituals. Much of the discursive tit for tat took place in cultural production and consumption in theater, literature, and art. Such efforts are reflected in and also affected political communications. The image of the Donglin, evolving with the mutual penetration of factionalism and print culture, sheds much light on the relationship between seventeenth-century politics and Confucian moralism.

The production, circulation, and contestation of the images of the Donglin man help explain how changing political and cultural conditions from the Wanli reign to the mid-Chongzhen reign contributed to defining the Donglin official as a filial son and self-disciplined man. The sharpening of the Donglin image reveals how the moral performance of individual officials—and debates about it—constitutes a vital part of political processes. Instead of pondering whether the Donglin was a fundamentalist Confucian movement or whether the

Donglin was in fact morally superior to its rivals, I have looked at the three officials' stories to appreciate the ways in which print culture made officials' moral images crucial in political negotiations. Print culture shaped the meaning and history of the Donglin in paradoxical ways: it contributed to creating a popular image of moral perfection for the Donglin, but it also empowered the Donglin's rivals who contested that image.

During this period, the development of factionalism—and the Donglin image— was closely related to the proliferation of print. Factional disputes and identifications spilled out of the political sphere into literary and social spaces. As print and politics became irrevocably enmeshed, many officials used print to discuss the state of factionalism, to stake out their own positions, or just to posture as political insiders, when news from the court captivated elites across the empire. Some actively employed print to advocate a particular factional cause, while others used it to circulate negative images of their enemies. As factions evolved under such conditions and became more polarized and stereotyped, centrists like Wu Yuancui—and the incoherent stances his publications represented—became increasingly obscure and even incomprehensible.[141]

The similarities and differences in the fates of the Zheng father and son should be understood in connection with the late-Ming image politics. As a result of the political chaos of the Tianqi era and the enthronement of the activist Chongzhen emperor, the extent to which factional politics was articulated in and fought through the various forms of Confucian family tales—including political lists, pamphlets, biographies, and vernacular novels—became much greater. The eunuch faction had employed political lists and popular literature to demonize enemies, a practice begun in the Wanli reign. But the practice itself continued to develop, from initially relying on existing vernacular literature to later involving entirely new fictional works fabricated to disseminate political (mis)information. Such stories harnessed the potential of stereotypical characters for manipulating the images of political actors. The genre of family romance, an exceptionally flexible literary space in which writers and readers could explore and negotiate Confucian ethics, was used to ever more destructive effect in factional struggles, which were fought and understood through political actors' images as fathers, sons, and husbands.

As a result, how to properly display Confucian masculine virtues became an increasingly difficult project for officials. First, print culture made image-making easier but also helped further blur the boundaries between "real" and "feigned" moral exemplars. Zheng Man's case also reveals the gendered dimension of this tendency. Although Buddhism and concubinage were common features in officials' lives, they had to be mindful of how to project a proper masculine image in print when they wrote about these topics. Second, as the discursive connections between loyalty and other masculine virtues were invoked by political actors in attacks and counterattacks, Confucian family tales provided a forum for connecting these virtues across generations.

The Chongzhen emperor's particular interest in promoting Confucian ethics and his attitude toward factionalism at court also contributed to the evolution of image politics. Paranoid about factionalism, he firmly believed that there was no such thing as a "good" faction. Loyalty meant, above all, nonpartisanship. Distinguishing true from feigned loyalty was a main concern in his court. The crystallization of the Donglin man as a moral exemplar took place in this context. This environment compelled officials to contemplate more deeply how to authenticate their moral commitments in multiple media. It put more emphasis on the issue of sincerity, already a key concern in the literati intellectual world, in their moral cultivation and expression.

CHAPTER 2

Displaying Sincerity

The Fushe

From the Tianqi reign (1621–27) to the Chongzhen reign (1628–44), the Fushe, an empirewide literary and social network, constituted a significant political force and played a crucial role in turning the political battlefield into an arena of moral contests. Because of their close connections with the Donglin, members of the Fushe have been seen as a "Little Donglin," one whose organization was motivated by moral considerations. Scholars who argue that the Fushe represented a departure from conventional moral conservatism have offered different understandings of the Fushe's moral performance. Some argue that, unlike the Donglin, which had formed the core of the late-Ming "moral crusade," the main concerns of the Fushe lay in social and political practices.[1] Others focus on Fushe scholars' enthusiasm for entertainment and sexual pleasures, suggesting that they justified their departure from the conventional ideal of self-discipline by redefining loyalty as a value that was compatible with and inspired by romantic love.[2] In fact, such scholarly disagreements reflect the lasting repercussions of the multiple images of the Fushe that were produced and circulated in the seventeenth century.

The Fushe was both an agent and a product of image politics. In contrast to the ambiguity of the Donglin membership, the Fushe compiled its own member rosters for communication and publicity purposes. Identifying itself chiefly as a literary organization, its image-making efforts were more self-consciously coordinated. Adept at using print and social spectacles to widen their influence and strengthen mutual support among themselves, Fushe scholars groomed their images as filial sons, true friends, and self-disciplined men in order to express their feelings, articulate their families' demands, pursue career success, and coordinate political actions.

However, as in the case of the Donglin, the Fushe's claims to be a group of moral exemplars were seriously questioned by their political rivals. Therefore, the following questions are worth pursuing: What kinds of moral images did the Fushe have? Who produced them, and why? What can we discern about the ways in which Confucian moralism shaped their struggles?

At the heart of Fushe scholars' claim to moral superiority and the challenges posed by their rivals lay the problem of sincerely pursuing Confucian ethical ideals and displaying them properly. This was a critical issue in the intellectual explorations, religious practices, and cultural production of late-Ming literati. The enhanced availability of print and the literati's diversified approaches to moral cultivation determined that the meaning of sincerity could not be separated from the actions that *displayed* the authenticity of their moral pursuits when officials engaged Confucian ethics in political communication. Examining the notion and trope of sincerity as an integral part of political negotiations deepens our understanding of the competing moral images of Fushe figures, who not only passionately pursued Confucian ideals but also abused them in their political maneuvers.

The stories of the so-called Sons of the Donglin (Donglin Zidi) and Fushe Four Gentlemen (Fushe Si Gongzi) illustrate how Confucian ethics served as a valuable means of emotive expression. The thought Fushe scholars gave to the importance of moral performance—as sons, friends, and husbands—to their personal career advancement is also a significant aspect of this politico-ethical scenario. The moral attacks and counterattacks between the Fushe and its enemies demonstrate how the Fushe employed Confucian ethics to promote its organizational agenda as well as the intertwining personal, intellectual, and political reasons behind its political enemies' claims. On each of these levels, Fushe scholars negotiated with the emperor and their rivals through the issue of sincerity in moral performance. Such endeavors were interconnected religious, social, political, and intellectual activities that enriched Confucian moralism and also enhanced the political importance of moral image.

IMAGES AND EMOTIONS

Fushe scholars socialized extensively and published copiously. Poetry, letters, theater, drinking parties, and rituals were all ways for them to express the emotions that boiled in an exciting but crisis-ridden time. In particular, expressions of filiality created a structure for their emotive lives because many of them had fathers serving in the government and struggling to survive the political turbulence. Their filial piety was heartfelt. Still, the volatile political conditions demanded that these young men prove the sincerity of such feelings. Publicizing their moral endeavors and negotiating the reception of their moral performance occupied a special place in the political spaces they inhabited.

Sons of the Donglin

The Sons of the Donglin were the younger generation of literati whose fathers had been persecuted by the eunuch faction during the Tianqi reign. The emotive dimension in their pursuit of filial piety and friendship played a significant role in perpetuating factionalism across generations and in making the Fushe a crucial link in the transformation of political culture from the Tianqi reign to the Chongzhen reign. Their fathers' suffering and the devastation inflicted on their families by the eunuch faction motivated the Sons of the Donglin to explore in depth how to pursue filial duties sincerely and properly. Being filial meant much more than announcing one's feelings and freely acting on them. Doing so was not an easy matter, as we have already seen in Zheng Man's decision not to expose his parents' domestic issues. The richness of the discourse on filial piety and the literati's diverse approaches to it demanded that a son devise the most appropriate filial expression and action in extraordinary circumstances.

Wei Dazhong (1575–1625), a native of Jiashan (in Zhejiang), was one of the Donglin martyrs murdered by the eunuch faction. Between his arrest and his death, his eldest son, Wei Xueyi (1596–1625), explored all possible avenues for securing his father's release. After arresting and throwing the senior Wei in prison, where he was tortured, Wei Zhongxian's men also maneuvered to block Xueyi's access to powerful officials and threatened to arrest him. Xueyi had to conceal his identity as he followed his father's prison wagon and sneaked into the capital.[3] Instead of resorting to dramatic measures to rescue his father, Xueyi sought help from officials covertly, because any impulsive move would jeopardize his father's life.

The filial son faced a difficult situation, as he revealed in a letter to an old friend. Anticipating doubts about his sincerity, Xueyi explained that he thought through all the legends of filial children in history but realized that, given the dangerous political condition of the time, he would endanger his father's life if he tried to emulate the legendary Tiying of the Han dynasty, a young girl who had heroically rescued her father.[4] "When I hear the stories of those loyal, filial, chaste, and heroic historical figures (*zhongxiao jie lie*), I am always inspired and moved to tears, motivated to accomplish the same. Now I have to hide myself. I cannot act fearlessly like the girl Tiying, because my pointless death would not help. I keep my life intact only to pay the debt of gratitude [to my father]!"[5]

Xueyi's filial duties also included attesting to his father's loyalty to the dynasty and safeguarding the Wei family's reputation. On the trip back from the capital, the presence of his father's coffin wagon saddened everyone along the way. Due to fatigue, stress, sorrow, and anxiety at the prospect that he still might be arrested by the eunuchs, Xueyi's health deteriorated precipitously.[6] In his last letter to the people of their hometown, he cemented his family's *zhongxiao* image and authenticated his own deep filial devotion. He thanked them for sending money to help repay what Wei Zhongxian had asserted was a bribe his father has taken, although he refused the money on the grounds that he could not violate his vow to his martyred father: "My father had someone deliver a short note from prison. . . . The note said: 'When I was taken from our hometown, people proposed to use the county fund to pay the sum imposed on me. This is unacceptable. I have been poor throughout my life and have given so little to my neighbors and countrymen. This incident had nothing to do with the public interest of our county. How could we burden them?' Alas! I have this handwritten note with me and can show it to you. How could I ignore my father's will and accept your money?"[7] Instead of accepting their money, Xueyi asked his townsmen to help sell Wei family property and attend to the needs of his mother and two younger brothers after he "went to the underworld to meet [his] deceased father."[8]

Now assured that he had preserved evidence that discredited the negative image of his father and that a sympathetic community would take care of his mother and brothers, Xueyi began a slow suicide. He stayed away from his wife and children, confining himself to deep mourning. He refused to drink water or take medicine, telling others that the sight of water and medicine only brought back the memory of his father who, when imprisoned and tortured, was deprived of these things and suffered tremendously.[9] Soon Xueyi died. Although he had not succeeded in saving his father's life, he completed a compelling filial performance with his self-inflicted psychological and bodily sufferings. His death was the most effective response to any doubts about the sincerity and impeccability of his filial devotion.

Friends swiftly resorted to print and played a crucial role in authenticating Xueyi's filiality. Immediately after the newly enthroned Chongzhen emperor crushed the eunuch faction, Qian Fen (*juren* 1642), the late Wei Dazhong's disciple and nephew of the Donglin-identified official Qian Shisheng (1575–1652), published Xueyi's writings (in Chongzhen 1/7 [1628]). Xueyi's words provided the public with detailed information about the hardships the Wei father and son had suffered and their extraordinary performance of *zhongxiao*. One of the main purposes of publication was to eliminate doubts about Xueyi's sincerity. Qian Fen shared his deceased friend's concern that some might question whether Xueyi could have done more to save his father's life. In a preface to this publication, Qian drew on some of the most moving details from Xueyi's writings and asserted that Xueyi, a truly filial son, had exhausted all possible means in his attempt to rescue his father.[10]

Wei Xuelian (1608–1644), Wei Dazhong's second son, carried on his brother's endeavors. When the Chongzhen emperor came to power, Dazhong was given a posthumous honorary title and an imperial burial ceremony. Xuelian had gone to the capital and presented a memorial written in his own blood, detailing the horrendous crimes committed against his family by the eunuch faction and requesting the highest honors for his father and brother. Thanks to this appeal, the elder brother received imperial recognition as a Filial Son, and his tablet was placed in the shrine built in honor of his father's loyalty.[11] In Chongzhen 7 (1634), Xuelian hosted his father's official burial ceremony, which attracted thousands of attendees.[12] At his request, the Donglin heavyweight Liu Zongzhou inscribed Dazhong's name on the ancestral tablet and delivered a lecture at the place where his body had rested.

In the same year, in memory of his older brother, Xuelian republished Xueyi's writings. Because brotherly love was defined as a filial duty, Xuelian's efforts to publicize Xueyi's virtues allowed him to fulfill his own filial duties as well. Furthermore, by reprinting Xueyi's work, the Wei family reclaimed "ownership" of his virtues.

Xuelian's Fushe friends also participated in authenticating his filial exemplariness. Around the time of the highly publicized burial ceremony for Dazhong and Xueyi, the Fushe had just begun to publicly take on Grand Secretary Wen Tiren. In Chongzhen 9/8 (1636), the "Donglin orphans" gathered at the Mansion of Peach Leaves (Taoyeguan) in Nanjing during the season of the civil service examinations. Almost all the Donglin martyrs' sons attended this gathering. It was Xuelian who most powerfully embodied *zhongxiao* and used it to call for the public condemnation of the former eunuch associate Ruan Dacheng (1587–1646) who was in Nanjing—and indirectly his ally, Grand Secretary Wen Tiren, then in Beijing. Xuelian himself had been actively involved in Fushe activities.[13] At this gathering, Xuelian presented to his friends a copy of the *Classic of Filial Piety*, which he had hand copied in his own blood.[14] It reiterated the strong filial emotions expressed in the "blood memorial" (*xieshu*) he had submitted to the Chongzhen emperor years before, in which he named Ruan Dacheng in particular as the primary culprit in his father's murder.[15]

The Fushe activist Fang Yizhi (1611–1671), who was present at the gathering, pointed out that the blood used to replace ink in this copy of the *Classic of Filial Piety* symbolized Xuelian's sincerity and elevated him above those who superficially performed filial deeds merely to gain fame. Xuelian's prolonged mourning in solitude as well as his assiduous study in an effort to better serve the country—acts of both loyalty and filial piety—proved his sincerity and true understanding of this Confucian classic.[16] Chen Liang, a longtime friend of the Wei brothers and a Fushe activist, summarized the Fushe friends' admiration in a poem composed on the occasion:

> The blood-writing reached the court and shook the world;
> [Xuelian's] fame soared, higher than the mountains.[17]

The Wei brothers' emotional expressions in a time of crisis were structured by some prominent intellectual and political concerns of their time. Intellectually, contemporary literati were engaged in heated debates about sincerity and self-cultivation. In the political sphere, the negative images of the Donglin conjured by anti-Donglin narratives continued to linger and influence the reading public. Moreover, remnants of the eunuch faction never completely dispersed. Thus, these young men resorted to publication, rituals, and spectacles as means of authenticating, documenting, and explaining their moral performance.

All these measures ensured that the Wei family would recover from the devastation brought upon them and survive. After Xueyi died, tremendous sympathy was showered on Xuelian. Many extended their hands. Crucial for the Wei family was the first-rate tutorship offered to Xuelian. A number of prominent scholars carefully nurtured him, including Liu Zongzhou, his mentor in the Confucian classics.[18] With such invaluable public support, Xuelian eventually passed the examinations and obtained his *jinshi* title.[19]

The Wei brothers' expression of filiality not only depended much on their friends' support in print and in public spectacles but also offered Fushe scholars occasions for articulating and demonstrating the meaning of true friendship. Before his death, Wei Xueyi had compiled a collection of his own work. To consolidate Xueyi's image as a filial exemplar, Qian Fen, who took on the task of editing the collection for publication after Xueyi's death, decided to remove poems that Xueyi had composed for leisurely occasions and added material from the period of Wei Dazhong's arrest and imprisonment.[20] In this way, a shining example of filial piety would become the overarching theme of the book. Qian argued that his editorial choices were "faithful to [Xueyi's understanding] of the Way and therefore proper." What was Xueyi's understanding of the Way? Qian asserted it was the ethics of *zhongxiao*.[21] Interestingly then, this true friend had to recalibrate the authenticity of the poetry collection in order to prove the sincerity of its late author's moral endeavors.

The Fushe Gentleman Fang Yizhi

Dynastic crises became the backdrop against which Fushe scholars displayed their various masculine virtues. In turn, their political experience in these crises informed their deepening exploration of the notion of sincerity in filial devotion. The image transformation of Fang Yizhi, a Fushe celebrity figure, sheds light on not only the emotional necessity for officials to authenticate their filial exemplariness through literary publicity and ritual performance but also the importance of integrating political experience into intellectual theorizing.

By the mid-Chongzhen reign, Fang Yizhi had become one of the famous Fushe Four Gentlemen.[22] This group occupied a special place in the Fushe. Their fathers had all been identified as victims of the eunuch faction. But these young men's appeal lay more with their Fushe personality than in their connection to the Donglin legacy. Their fame relied heavily on celebrity culture and the public's fascination with entertainment and liaisons with elite courtesans. Among the Fushe Four Gentlemen, only Fang Yizhi passed the *jinshi* examinations and became an official before 1644.

A decade after his friend Wei Xuelian presented a blood memorial at court, Fang Yizhi did so, too, petitioning for the release of his father, the official Fang Kongzhao (1590–1655). Kongzhao excelled not only in scholarship and statecraft but also in military strategy. Since his appointment as governor of Huguang (modern-day Hubei and Hunan) in Chongzhen 11 (1638), at a moment when the state struggled to suppress various rebels in multiple locations across the central and southwestern Ming territories, Kongzhao had led eight major victories of the Ming forces and proved himself an extremely capable official-general. But he disagreed with his superior, Xiong Wencan (d. 1640), a Yang Sichang protégé, over general strategies and voiced his opposition to Xiong in a memorial to the emperor. Frustrated by Xiong's repeated strategic miscalculations and astonished at the devastating consequences of Xiong's ill-conceived *zhaofu* policy (allowing the rebels to surrender peacefully), the Chongzhen emperor had Xiong arrested. According to the official history, Yang, probably in hopes of rescuing Xiong, urged the emperor to punish Kongzhao, whose subordinates suffered an embarrassing and demoralizing defeat in late Chongzhen 12 (1639).[23] At this point, the emperor was staking all his hopes on Yang's leadership in the military efforts against the rebels and the Manchus. Kongzhao was thrown into prison in Chongzhen 13/1 (1640), just before his son Yizhi scored his *jinshi* success in the metropolitan examination.[24]

Yizhi was devastated by his father's arrest. Several days before the metropolitan exam, he submitted a memorial to the emperor in which he defended his father but also expressed his willingness to receive punishment in his father's place.[25] The emperor replied that he should concentrate on the upcoming examination and stop petitioning.[26] Later, instead of celebrating the coveted success of earning a *jinshi* degree, Yizhi devoted himself to seeking ways of securing his father's release. Over the next two years, he was a model filial son: he frequented the imperial prison, knocked on powerful people's doors, and petitioned repeatedly on his father's behalf.

In fact, the filial devotion that Yizhi displayed was at once a personal commitment, a means of self-expression and self-identity, a family tradition, and a spectacle that would generate strong emotions and positive support from his contemporaries. Yizhi came from a family that had enjoyed an empirewide reputation for filial exemplariness. As studies of the seventeenth-century fad of *lumu* (lit., "residing next to a parent's tomb") demonstrate, the ascendance of the Fangs' status in their hometown Tongcheng (in modern-day Anhui) from the late sixteenth century onward was closely related to their image as pious adherents of Confucian ethical values.[27] Starting with Fang Xuejian (1540–1615), Yizhi's great-grandfather, generations of Fang men had performed *lumu*. By the time Kongzhao carried out *lumu* himself (1631–33), this ritual had become an integral part of the Fang family tradition. No less would be expected from his son Yizhi who years later indeed performed it for his deceased mother.[28]

Yizhi's emotional expression of filial piety was authenticated by his friends' efforts to publicize it. His sincere filiality crystallized in literary exchanges with friends and colleagues that were included in *Works from Manyu* (Manyu cao), a collection of works named after his Beijing residence, Manyu. During and after his father's imprisonment, a long poem, "Jichu,"[29] in which Yizhi passionately articulated filial feelings, was widely circulated and appreciated. Many officials in the capital wrote prefaces for and commented on it.

"When the father suffers so much from injustice, how can the son live!"[30] This line by the official Wei Zaode (1605–1644) communicates the image of a devoted son. In his preface to "Jichu," Wei, who had topped that year's *jinshi* cohort, emphasizes Yizhi's filial virtue by vividly describing how he withdrew from all social activities even though obtaining the *jinshi* title would normally entail innumerable celebratory gatherings and visits; instead, he stayed away from fancy food, clothes, and entertainment, splitting his time between visiting his father in prison and confining himself in the quiet residence.[31] Another friend from the same *jinshi* cohort, Tian Younian, also contributed a preface. Tian echoes Wei and recalls that when Yizhi was taking the exams in Beijing, many literati were attracted by his reputation and hoped to visit him. But he did little socializing and instead kept to his residence, aggrieved by his father's suffering.[32]

As shown in the preface composed by the official Huang Jingfang (1596–1662), Yizhi reminded people of other famous filial sons such as Feng Xingke and Qu Jia (both from the Ming Jiajing reign [1521–67]), whose acts had helped save their fathers from political disaster. The success of these exemplars' actions supposedly showed

Heaven's reward for sincere filiality.[33] However, the question of sincerity inspired these officials' more thorough reflections on the proper ways of expressing and pursuing filiality.

Their most interesting and informative discussion on this topic referenced the official Wang Shizhen (1526–1590) in contrast to Fang Yizhi. It was well known that Wang's father fell victim to factionalism during the Ming Jiajing reign, when the powerful grand secretary Yan Song (1480–1567) dominated the court. Wang tried to rescue his father and was devastated when the mission failed. But the official Yan Hun, in his preface to "Jichu," suggests that Wang was not really loyal and filial, which explains the tragedy that befell his father and the family. Yan Hun argues that the eventual execution of the elder Wang resulted largely from his son's shallow understanding of filial piety. Yan Song had hoped to recruit the junior Wang into his faction to burnish his own reputation with the latter's literary fame and popularity. Wang Shizhen not only rejected Yan's proposal but also made public his support for Yan's various political rivals. Eventually, when the elder Wang led his troops into a defeat, Yan found an opportunity to get retribution for the insult and made sure the elder Wang was severely punished. Thus, Wang Shizhen's overconfidence in his own popularity led to reckless political behavior that contributed to his father's death.[34]

Although Wang was a literary giant praised by many for his uncompromising attitude toward powerful grand secretaries such as Yan Song and Zhang Juzheng, these officials considered him an unfilial son. In doing so, they articulated some important insights, that taking pride in one's own celebrity appeal undermined filial piety and that constant self-cultivation and self-rectification at the intersection of everyday life and politics—rather than some superficial factional grudge—was the key to fulfilling true *zhongxiao* commitment.

This view was further emphasized when Yan Hun drew a stark contrast between the two men's understanding of the relationship between public service and personal moral cultivation. Yan contended that, whereas Fang Yizhi persisted in pursuing the *jingshi* (statecraft) ideal amid the family crisis, Wang Shizhen indulged in leisurely enjoyment and completely abandoned public responsibilities in his later life.[35] To Fang's friends, his actions manifested the true meaning of *zhongxiao*, whereas Wang's filiality was lost as a result of his indulgence in fame and sensual pleasures. The friends ranked Fang's filial performance higher than Wang's in order to stress that only a deep understanding of *zhongxiao* ethics, followed by its proper display, could be sincere and authentic.

These interesting discussions engaged officials' emotions, familial roles, and political experience simultaneously. Compared to others, Fushe celebrity figures such as Fang Yizhi had more opportunities to make filial performance central to their expression and identity because the deepening dynastic crisis directly affected the senior members of their families. These young men did not necessarily surpass their peers as better sons and friends. However, they had access to human and financial resources that could help publicize their moral performance. They were put in the position of not only integrating their understanding of recent political history into theorizing sincerity but also publicly negotiating the meaning of sincere filial expression.

Negotiating Sincerity and Propriety

The Fushe scholars' filial expressions and political actions, in a circulatory fashion, continuously informed and reinforced each other. The political stakes of displaying sincere moral pursuits became clearly established in the process. However, it must be noted that even in a time of extreme circumstances, one's reputation as a true moral paragon alone could not guarantee a free pass. It is more accurate to argue that such a reputation could help initiate negotiations with the emperor over the value of sincere filial expression for political communication in a specific context.

Take, for instance, the Sons of the Donglin. The Chongzhen emperor, as sympathetic as he was toward their families, voiced concerns about the "blood memorials" they had submitted. Since the beginning of his reign, these young men had presented their emotions and demands in such a powerful and unrelenting manner that they began to appear excessive and aggressive. The emperor satisfied their desire to restore the status and reputations of their fathers, but he also declared the medium of "blood memorials" to be "improper" at court.[36] In this way, the emperor not only affirmed his commitment to "governing with filial piety," but, by asserting his authority in the interpretation of the meaning of *zhongxiao* and the proper use of this language, he also implied that he would not let the Donglin community decide how to punish the eunuch faction.

Such negotiations not only delineated the discursive contours of *zhongxiao* ethics but also publicly acknowledged the legitimacy and necessity of displaying sincere filial emotions as a means of political communication in complicated situations. Officials were aware of the complexity of these negotiations, even though they—and the reading public—regularly reduced them to familiar stories about the triumph of sincerity. For instance, after almost one and a half years in prison, in Chongzhen 14/5 (1641), Fang Yizhi's father, Kongzhao, was exempted from the death penalty and sentenced to exile. It was said at the time that, because Yizhi had presented a memorial written in blood and wept outside the palace, the emperor decided it was time to acknowledge the young man's filial devotion, and with the release of Kongzhao, he recognized Yizhi as a filial paragon by following the principle of "seeking loyal officials in filial sons."[37] Sympathizers asserted that the emperor released the senior Fang mainly because he was touched by Yizhi's sincere filiality; by contrast, the emperor scolded the official Chen Biqian's son for not showing enough sorrow at court when his father suffered a military defeat and subsequent imprisonment. Although this story about the Chens seems to be false,[38] the contrast between the Fangs and the Chens drawn by sympathizers nonetheless represents the prevalent belief that proper display of sincere filiality was important for officials' political survival. This incident shows again that the Chongzhen emperor tended to negotiate with his officials in the language of *zhongxiao* rather than passively accepting their claims to moral rectitude. Such negotiations had to be conducted in nuanced ways.

IMAGE AND CAREER ADVANCEMENT

The family crises of these Fushe scholars were enmeshed in the deepening dynastic crisis of the 1630s–40s and affected their emotive lives, identities, and public images. The particularly tumultuous conditions during this time generated more opportunities than usual for them to explore, demonstrate, and negotiate with the emperor and other officials through the performance of Confucian virtues. Their focus on the question of sincerity sharpened in this time of political volatility but was also as a result of contemporary literati religious, intellectual, and social trends. Precisely because of the importance of sincerity at the intersection of everyday life and politics, Fushe scholars' paid much attention among themselves to displays of moral exemplariness in the interest of career advancement, as did some of their rivals.

It has been argued that Fushe scholars were split over their proper goal: Should they pursue moral integrity or seek political patronage?[39] But this question obscures how these two aspects were seen as intimately connected. An individual literatus's image as a moral paragon might well facilitate senior officials' patronage. Fushe scholars understood the importance of moral image for career success. At the same time, the concern with sincerity loomed large, and it demanded constant proofs of authenticity.

Fang Yizhi's image transformation into a man of *zhongxiao* resulted from the shift in his personal and career priorities, something his friend-colleagues recognized and encouraged. During Chongzhen 7–12 (1634–39), he lived mainly in Nanjing but shuttled between Nanjing and his hometown Tongcheng, a region rocked by rebellions. He enjoyed Nanjing's urban culture, literary networking, and courtesans, especially when many friends from near and far gathered there for the civil service examinations.[40] Sensual pleasures he indulged in at such times have been politely interpreted as a sanctioned "respite from daily cares and frustrations,"[41] but at the time, he embraced them not only as part of the Fushe camaraderie but also as a lifestyle. Like many of his friends, he had a mixed public image before he passed the exams and took on his family's crisis.

The gatherings of Fushe young scholars in Nanjing increasingly drew public attention to their political and personal lives. In the years Chongzhen 11–12 (1638–39), with the widely publicized campaign against Ruan Dacheng under way via the distribution of the sensational "Proclamation against Seditious Elements in Nanjing" (Liudu fangluan gongjie) and a massive Fushe gathering planned for the time of the exams, these young men's fame reached new heights. Fang was a fixture at Fushe banquets and social events featuring elite courtesans. Enthusiasm for Fang's political prospects soared when his father led successful military campaigns against the rebels, and Fang himself participated as his father's assistant, first in Wuchang (Chongzhen 11) and then in Tongcheng (Chongzhen 12).[42] Friends gathered to show their admiration and support at his departure for Wuchang, calling his participation an act of *zhongxiao*.[43] It is not clear how much Fang actually contributed to these military victories (he was sick for some time during the first venture). Nonetheless, at a time when so many literati fantasized about martial arts and military strategizing, participation in these campaigns lent Fang the aura of genuine experience.[44] He became the Fushe's brightest star. Then, as we saw earlier, the developments in factional politics, the Fang family situation in the aftermath of his father's arrest, and his own entry into government service ushered in a dramatic change in Fang's self-understanding and identity. His social life looked different after he became an official and secured his father's release. The new focus on cultivating the public image of being a filial son and good husband corresponded neatly to his life trajectory.

The self-image of Gong Dingzi (1615–1673), a Fushe associate (rather than a formal member), further sheds light on Fushe scholars' views on the relationship between the appearance of self-discipline and career concerns. Gong was not on any Fushe lists but maintained strong friendships with many Fushe members. In the spring of Chongzhen 15 (1642), the Fushe held its last large-scale gathering in Hangzhou. It was exciting for many Fushe scholars at the gathering that junior officials, such as Fang Yizhi and Gong Dingzi, took part in order to "pass on the wisdom." Clearly, officials like Gong helped enhance the Fushe's popular appeal and were included in the Fushe circle for this reason.[45]

Since conventional history has not thoroughly treated Gong's life and career, it is necessary to introduce his pre-1644 experiences carefully. Four years younger than Fang Yizhi, Gong was something of a prodigy. He passed the highest level of the civil service examinations at the age of twenty in Chongzhen 7 (1634). After receiving the *jinshi* title, unlike most promising officials at the beginning of their political careers, Gong did not elect to wait for an opportunity to become a Hanlin Academician. Instead, he chose to serve as the magistrate of Qishui (in modern-day Hubei).[46] Gong served two successful terms as a dedicated magistrate in one of the most strategically crucial regions terribly torn by rebellions and natural disasters during the Chongzhen reign. During those years, Gong accumulated rich experience in military strategy, local administration, and law.[47] In Chongzhen 14 (1641), he received a rating of Exceptional at the triennial evaluations and was promoted to serve as a censor on the Board of War. In Chongzhen 15 (1642), freshly arrived in the capital as a new member of the metropolitan bureaucracy, Gong received special recognition from the emperor; he was given important assignments and invited to accompany his majesty on New Year's Eve. He was apparently quite motivated to fulfill his duties as a censor,[48] but with his rich military and administrative experience as well as memories of ordinary people's suffering caused by war and natural disasters, he found himself idling in the belly of the bureaucracy.

Still highly motivated and idealistic, Gong began to cultivate the reputation of a loyal official.[49] In the winter of Chongzhen 16 (1643), he submitted a memorial suggesting that the emperor summon back some of the highly competent and upright officials who had been stripped of positions and remained at home in temporary retirement.[50] This was a risky move since, in the last years of the Chongzhen reign, one could be seriously punished simply for recommending an official previously dismissed by the emperor. Furthermore, Gong memorialized against the emperor's use of imprisonment and flogging to discipline his defiant subjects.[51] An additional series of memorials from Gong against current grand secretaries had irritated the emperor so much that he had Gong and a few others thrown into prison.[52]

Just two months before Gong's arrest, in the autumn of Chongzhen 16 (1643), his beloved concubine, Gu Mei (1619–1664), arrived in Beijing, leaving behind her fame as one of the most celebrated courtesans in Nanjing. From the moment she arrived in Beijing, she became Gong's true companion. The couple underwent an image transformation together. Historians have argued that courtesans who married into literati households were expected to conform to Confucian feminine virtues.[53] The Gong-Gu image transformation reveals something deeper than mere compliance with domestic norms. A courtesan-turned-concubine could do more than demarcate "a space of *qing*" with her husband and defer to his official wife. A virtuous concubine could also help improve an official's public image and career opportunities.

Gong-Gu's correspondence with an iconic Donglin figure, Fang Zhenru (1585–1645), Fang Yizhi's uncle, is particularly revealing. Upon his release from prison in Chongzhen 17/1 (1644), still deprived of official status, Gong Dingzi inscribed and sent a painting by Gu Mei to Fang Zhenru, who was governing Guangxi, on the southwestern frontier. In the inscription, he recalled that when Gu joined his household, Fang wrote to warn him not to circulate her paintings outside their home or show off her talents.[54] Gong told the senior Fang that since Gu had joined him in the capital, they had followed Fang's advice and kept a low profile, enjoying her art and poetry only in private.[55]

Gong Dingzi had developed and cherished his strong ties with several other prominent members of the Fang family as well, including Kongzhao and Yizhi.[56] For him, Fang Zhenru was at once a Donglin senior and a kind of mentor. Earlier, in Chongzhen 11 (1638), when

Fan Jingwen (1587–1644), a popular Donglin-identified official and president of the Board of War in Nanjing, was stripped of official status and lost his job for having memorialized against the promotion of Yang Sichang, Gong composed a poem offering Fan moral support. Fang Zhenru thought so highly of this poem that he publicized it among colleagues by having it printed, which undoubtedly elevated the profile of his protégé.[57] Receiving continuous recognition and endorsement from Fang would help advance Gong's reputation and career in meaningful ways.

In his inscription on Gu Mei's painting for Fang, Gong recalls that merely fifty days after Gu's arrival in Beijing, he was arrested and imprisoned. He describes Gu's womanly virtues—her modesty, dedication, and stamina, as well as the noble spirit of her art and poetry. She stopped eating delicate foods and never complained about their financial distress. She confined herself to vegetarianism and Buddhist prayers. She displayed a strong sense of devotion and filial piety. Because she had such a noble character, Gong asked her to paint for Fang and then had the painting delivered to Guangxi. Concluding the inscription, Gong promises that after this painting, he and Gu would put away their brushes and silk so that they "would not provoke their mentor's harsh scolding."[58]

The act of sending a painting bearing such an inscription to a mentor, an inscription that invokes Fang's disapproval of circulating Gu's art but also justifies the act of sending this one painting by highlighting her conventional feminine virtues, helps authenticate Gong's commitment to Confucian masculine ideals. It brings to light the careful balance this aspiring official strove to maintain in a display of both self-discipline and passion. This image-making would not have been complete without imbuing Gu, the former elite courtesan, with Confucian womanly virtues. As Gu is transformed into a companion suitable for an official, Gong also fashions himself as a model Confucian man who displays the virtues of loyalty and self-discipline.

In fact, Gu Mei's image transformation reflected Gong's changing political standing as much as her new social identity. Months before Gong sent the painting and inscription to Fang Zhenru, ten poems he composed in prison for Gu Mei's birthday had already described her in a markedly similar way. The inscription on the painting for Fang drew on those birthday poems in several places.[59] In essence, the poems depict her as a virtuous woman. In one, he expresses gratitude toward her because, out of concern for him in the cold weather, she made a quilt and had it delivered to the prison.[60] Gong praises her courage, care, and noble mind, so extraordinary in a woman whose husband had been thrown into prison for trying to fulfill his political duties.[61]

Gong's writings served to present him as a self-disciplined man, which could help earn senior officials' patronage. The importance of this image was affirmed a few years later, in the unusually complex political environment after the fall of the Ming. Gong, now serving in the Qing government, would repeatedly return to his exchanges with Fang Zhenru regarding his concubine to make claims about his own moral standing.[62]

Many Fushe friends shared Gong Dingzi's interest in moral image as a means of career advancement. They believed that, in addition to filial piety, self-discipline remained an ideal quality for officials and that displaying masculine virtues was important for achieving a successful political career. This issue bore a sense of urgency when Fushe involvement in factionalism invited constant attacks at court and when a few Fushe stars gained notoriety due to their reputations as pleasure seekers.

Tellingly, the Fushe activist Zhang Zilie once wrote a letter, titled "To a Friend, on Staying away from Sensual Pleasures," to Sun Lin (1611–1646), Fang Yizhi's friend and brother-in-law, whose fame rose when he joined the Fang father's and son's military operations in central China.[63] The letter was a powerful treatise urging Fushe friends to stop wasting energy on sensual pleasures.[64] In his letter, Zhang mentioned several popular Fushe figures, all close friends of Sun and Fang, who had not demonstrated adequate self-discipline. He called upon all his friends to pay close attention to this issue.[65]

First, Zhang refutes the view that such activities did not compromise one's commitment to public service:

> I believe you possess such extraordinary talents that indulgence in sensual pleasures might not erode them at all. But I also think that because we are facing so many crises, no talent should be wasted on useless matters. . . . In addition, a gentleman's good judgment and resolve, if spent on unwise indulgence, will not be employed for honorable causes; if spent on entertainment, it will not be employed for difficult tasks.[66]

He further explains the political risks of lacking self-discipline:

> If you continue indulging in entertainment, the most sagacious men of our time will think that the talented men among us are self-indulgent and therefore unsuitable [for important missions], and *will not nurture these talented men and help them accomplish important things*. Meanwhile, the talented men sink deeper and

> deeper into such indulgence, and will lose energy and eventually fail to stand out.[67]

Zhang Zilie's argument builds on two premises: First, indulgence in sensual pleasures undermines literati commitment to and fulfillment of the Confucian *jingshi* ideal. Second, senior officials only nurture and mentor men they take seriously, and who demonstrate real political potential, one condition of which is self-discipline.

In particular, Zhang highlights a contemporary political factor, factionalism, to reinforce his cautionary message.

> When senior scholars hear about this, they see us as thinking too highly of our talents and having little real knowledge and little prudence. They think that we do not work hard to cultivate morality and improve our scholarship, and therefore we won't be able to fulfill our responsibilities for the country. . . . *Our political enemies will secretly celebrate and take advantage of this opportunity to accuse us of factionalism and chasing undeserved fame.* This will defeat us and make us bring shame to the Confucian tradition.[68]

Zhang's understanding of the relationship between career success and moral image was shared by others, as demonstrated by the three commentators included in the printed version of this letter. These three men were Zhang's brother, the famous Fushe activist Shen Shoumin (1607–1675), and the official Xia Yunyi. Xia, who would later become a loyalist martyr, was known among the Fushe for his strong career achievements. He was considered one of the most promising officials by the Board of Personnel.[69] In his comments on Zhang's criticism of indulgence in sensual pleasures, Xia invokes the historical example of Zhuge Liang (181–234), who married an unusually ugly but virtuous wife and became one of the most accomplished ministers in Chinese history. In contrast, Xia suggests that the last emperor of the Chen dynasty, who notoriously indulged in poetry, wine, music, and women, deserved no better than to lose his country.[70]

Similarly, Shen Shoumin makes self-discipline a key issue for officials. He cites examples of model Confucian officials of the Song dynasty:

> Staying away from sensual pleasures alone is not enough. Sima [Guang] at the age of forty had not been able to have a son. His wife took a concubine for him, but he never approached her. Cheng [Yi] was physically fragile from childhood. But because he insisted on controlling his desires, he remained strong after seventy. Liu [Anshi] stopped sexual activities when he was forty, and his self-control never

> wavered. These role models not only never took a second woman [as concubine into their households] but also strove to refrain from pleasure seeking [outside]. How can one justify giving in to sensual pleasures and not regret lacking control![71]

Their comments demonstrate that these Fushe scholars not only believed in the importance of sexual morality and self-restraint for officials as an essential Confucian teaching but also stressed that there could be serious political consequences for failing to uphold the image of moral exemplariness. Precisely because Zhang Zilie understood the significance of such consequences, he offered criticism but attempted to do so in a way that would not jeopardize his friends' career future, which is why he refrained from naming names.[72]

Zhang's letter testifies to the reality that perception carried tremendous weight in late-Ming politics. Although Zhang urges his friends to sincerely pursue moral cultivation, his emphasis on projecting the *image* of self-discipline in order to gain the patronage of senior officials almost signals surrender to the reality and endorsement of scholars' performance of Confucian masculine virtues for essentially pragmatic reasons. In other words, in real-world politics, drawing a clear moral distinction between the sincere and the pragmatic might work against his friends' careers. Zhang realized that Fushe scholars were not morally superior to their rivals. He also recognized the fluidity of the boundaries between sincerity and hypocrisy and that all parties could appropriate them.

Zhang was correct. The issue of sincerity and authenticity was not merely a personal matter; it had already become a subject of factional debate at court in the struggles surrounding the idealized image of the Donglin man. Attacks on Fushe scholars claimed that they feigned moral exemplariness as individuals and as a collective were repeatedly leveled by their rivals. To understand why the Fushe's popular image as an organization of moral paragons was vulnerable to such challenges, we should first consider how the moral performance of individual Fushe scholars was used to enhance this group's organizing power and increase its appeal.

IMAGE AND ORGANIZATIONAL DEVELOPMENT

The Fushe's political appeal relied heavily on its ability to use print and public spectacle to paint itself as an organization of moral exemplars. This reputation had really taken hold with the fall of the eunuch faction in the beginning of the Chongzhen reign. When Qian Fen published the filial paragon Wei Xueyi's posthumous collected works, it was the very first publication by any of the martyred Donglin officials or their families after the demise of Wei Zhongxian.[73] Zhang Pu (1602–1641), founder of the Fushe, argued that the posthumous publication of Wei Xueyi's writings and their wide distribution preserved evidence of the loyalty of his father. Wei Xueyi's filial piety and Qian Fen's friendship perfected the senior Wei's loyalty.[74] Later, in a commemorative essay for the highly publicized burial ceremony for the senior Wei, Zhang further highlighted the significance of *zhongxiao* to the Sons of the Donglin and to Fushe organizing.[75]

Most revealing is the preface Zhang Pu composed for Qian Fen's poetry collection, in which Zhang spent much ink describing the Qian brothers' friendship with Wei Xueyi.[76] Friendship derived from, and further manifested, the true understanding of filial piety; friends illuminated one another's virtues. Images of filial sons and devoted friends went hand in hand, helping create the impression in the early years of the Fushe that it was a collective of devoted practitioners of *zhongxiao* ethics.

Indeed, the founders and early leaders of the Fushe, Zhang Pu and Zhang Cai (1596–1648), promoted this public image of the organization. The story of Zhang Pu, the son of a weak father and a maid-turned-concubine, was frequently mentioned by Zhang himself and by Fushe members. Zhang's uncle, who had become president of the Board of Punishments, tolerated his servants' abusive treatment of Zhang Pu's father, who subsequently died of depression. It became widely known that Zhang Pu wrote in his own blood on the wall: "I do not deserve to be called a son if I don't seek revenge against the evil servants!"[77] Similarly, Zhang Cai's father had died from longtime psychological abuse inflicted by a brother born of Zhang Cai's grandfather and a favorite concubine.[78] The two Zhangs' shared experience of losing their fathers in unfortunate domestic circumstances and their filial devotion toward their widowed mothers were emphasized by Zhang Pu to show the depth of their friendship.[79] They became devoted sons not only to their own mothers but to the other's mother as well.[80] Their images as filial sons and true friends were thus mutually defined and mutually strengthened. Their highly publicized stories stressed that friendship did not pose a threat to *zhongxiao* ethics and that Fushe members were committed to the Confucian Five Cardinal Relations.

Instances of this kind abounded in Fushe activities and writings. Members organized gatherings around their parents' birthdays and funerals, thereby not only reinforcing their intertwined familial and social ties but also legitimizing these opportunities to assemble.[81] Zhang Pu's biological mother, Madam Jin, received many visits and celebratory essays from Fushe members on her sixtieth birthday, including one from the Donglin celebrity Qian Qianyi, composed at the request of Zhang Pu himself.[82] When Zhang's official mother, Madam Pan, was to be buried, her funeral also attracted a large number of visitors, followed by the Fushe's most extravagant gathering.[83]

Zhang Pu had this to say at the celebration of the birthday of the Fushe friend Wu Zeng's (d. 1655) father: "Friendship does not simply concern one person. It begins with the seniors in the family. The senior chooses friends for the son. . . . The son does not befriend someone without seeking his parents' approval; without parental approval one does not easily form a friendship. This is because one wants to befriend a worthy man to bring honor to his parents; befriending an unworthy person would bring dishonor to the parents. Many in our Fushe follow this principle when choosing friends."[84] On another occasion, celebrating the birthday of the mother of Shen Shizhu and Shen Shoumin, two brothers both active in the Fushe, Zhang wrote: "My friendship with [Shen Shizhu] is built on the Five Cardinal Relations (*yi Wulun xiang zhu*). . . . There is an old saying: 'Your mother is my mother' (*ruo mu wu mu*). We now know this is not an empty idea."[85]

Such testimonials put forth powerful images for Fushe activists as filial sons and true friends. For them, the emotive content of friendship had not been drained by Neo-Confucian doctrines.[86] Friendship and filial piety could strengthen each other on emotive, social, and political levels. Fushe individuals' embodiment and promotion of friendship and filial piety in such a manner not only highlighted the importance of Confucian ethics in their everyday lives and politics but also enriched that system in new historical circumstances.

Thus, instead of seeing these prominent themes in Fushe history as a sign of its failure to go beyond tradition, it is more accurate to argue that their efforts to claim Confucian moral exemplariness were a way for them to adapt to the new sociocultural and political conditions in which they lived. This same understanding can be applied to the Fushe's deployment of the language of filial piety in factional attacks.

The Fushe organized and coordinated protests in response to the Chongzhen emperor's promotion of Yang Sichang with a *duoqing* order in Chongzhen 11 (1638). Unlike the opposition to Zhang Juzheng's *duoqing* case in the 1570s, this campaign took shape outside the court and, to a great extent, evolved among the Donglin and Fushe networks between Beijing and Nanjing. Although the Donglin-identified official Huang Daozhou played the most prominent role in the anti-Yang campaign at court (see chap. 3), it actually started with memorials submitted by the Fushe scholar Shen Shoumin in which he harshly condemned Yang's betrayal of the *zhongxiao* ideal.

Shen had arrived in Beijing as a highly recommended imperial student and was the first person in the country to memorialize against Yang Sichang's promotion. His three memorials set the tone for the most consequential political debate of the late Chongzhen reign. These three memorials portrayed Yang as failing in both loyalty and filial piety: he had abandoned his filial duty to mourn his parents for three years when he answered the emperor's call to lead the Board of War and work on military campaigns against the rebels and Manchus. He had not succeeded in these missions and therefore should be punished for failing to fulfill the requirements of both loyalty and filial piety (*zhongxiao liang kui*).[87] More alarming was the pathetic fact, Shen argued, that few officials had taken Yang to task for his moral-political failures. When certain officials formerly associated with the eunuch faction conspired to make a political comeback, Yang made it seem as if the dynasty had to rely on those morally corrupt men for military victories.[88]

Pressure built when the emperor did not respond to Shen's criticisms. Attempting to create momentum for the campaign, in Chongzhen 11/8 (1638), Fushe scholars publicized the famous "Proclamation against Seditious Elements in Nanjing," echoing Shen's memorials and specifically targeting Ruan Dacheng. This was the Fushe's most sensational political action.[89] Shen's memorials had attracted so much public attention that by Chongzhen 11/9 (1639), Huang Daozhou in Beijing felt that he had to memorialize to condemn Yang's moral defects as well.[90] This momentum propelled Cheng Yong (*jinshi* 1625), an official in Nanjing and a Fushe supporter, to follow Shen Shoumin and Huang Daozhou in criticizing Yang's violation of filial piety, an action that quickly led to Cheng's arrest.[91]

The upshot of the Fushe's "leadership" in this campaign against unfilial sons was complex. The series of political spectacles eroded the boundaries between the political spaces of Beijing and Nanjing. The Fushe scholars' roles within and between the two capitals successfully molded the Donglin-Fushe collective images into one community of moral paragons. In a sense, it was the popular appeal of the Little Donglin that pressured Donglin-identified officials such as Huang Daozhou to clarify the moral-political mission for the Donglin faction.

In the meantime, at court, these same dynamics had made the moral standing of Zheng Man a more contentious issue and in effect had diminished his chance of release. The Fushe helped create and perpetuate a distinction between Zheng Man and the "true" moral exemplars of the Donglin-Fushe community, as evinced by Chen Zilong's public denouncement of Zheng (see chap. 1 in this book). Soon after Zheng's "death by a thousand cuts" put a sensational end to that tortured case, Zhang Zilie cautioned his Fushe friends against appearing sympathetic to that disgraced man. When some Fushe members were preparing to publish the manuscript of *Collected Works of Gaiyuan* (Gaiyuan ji), the posthumous collection by the late Fushe member Wan Shihua (1590–1639), Zhang suggested to Shen Shoumin that they leave out Wan's letter to Zheng Man because the letter contained praises for Zheng that "did not conform to the 'pure elements' judgment" (*bu he qingyi*) of Zheng's moral defects.[92] Fushe friends were heavily invested in Wan's image as a moral exemplar, as shown in their concerted efforts to secure biographies of Wan from prominent figures associated with the Donglin-Fushe camp.[93] To these friends, Wan had been the emblem of loyalty, filial piety, and friendship.[94] In print, therefore, a clear contrast of the moral images of the Fushe and Zheng Man had to be preserved by erasing the record of Wan's praise for Zheng. This, again, was a true friend's responsibility.

Zheng's personal crisis had been concurrent with and intimately connected to the moral attacks aimed at the Fushe. As shown earlier, the literati who contributed to presenting sensational charges against Zheng were especially antagonistic toward their rival, the Fushe. Chen Zilong's panic and Zhang Zilie's caution reflect the Fushe community's vigilance and determination to maintain its image of moral superiority so that the organization would survive and thrive. The sincerity and authenticity of the concerned officials' moral performance was predicated largely on political needs.

REAL AND FEIGNED MORAL PARAGONS

Whereas Fushe scholars were able to mitigate internal differences to some extent as they publicized a self-image of exemplariness for the purpose of promoting their organization, once they launched moral attacks on political enemies, their claim to moral superiority faced serious challenges. These were not necessarily battles between the gentlemen and small men. In fact, it is problematic to see the rivalry through that lens. First, the boundaries between "real" and "feigned" exemplars had already been significantly confused by "public opinion" as presented in the media and further complicated by the literati's competing views on what constituted sincere and proper expression of Confucian virtues. Second, the Fushe and its challengers employed similar techniques and acted on similar rationales. In particular, sincerity was a key shared political trope.

Blaming the Publisher, Burning the Woodblock

The Fushe's image troubles began as the organization was gaining empirewide fame. In Chongzhen 4 (1631), the Fushe sustained a blow to its reputation following the brilliant success some of its members achieved in the examinations that year. It was particularly exciting that their star, Wu Weiye (1609–1671), passed the exam as the Secundus (Second Place). His essays were immediately published. However, instead of conforming to the tradition of honoring Wu's official mentor, the chief examiner Li Mingrui (1585–1671), the publication was dedicated to the Fushe leader, Zhang Pu. On discovering this serious breach of decorum and the mentor-disciple tradition, Li vowed to denounce Wu and threw public doubt on Fushe values. This instantly became a major scandal. Eventually, another Fushe member brought Wu to personally apologize to Li. They blamed everything on the printing house and had the local authorities punish the publisher for the "mistake." Although this move helped reduce the damage to the Fushe's public image, it left Zhang Pu feeling dismayed and bitter.[95] The unpleasant fallout from this event went beyond disagreement over whether violating the mentor-disciple ritual called for such strong reactions from either side; it left the impression that the Fushe did not respect Confucian ethical ideals.

The vulnerability of the Fushe's collective image invited external attacks. In the high-profile literary scuffle over the play *The Green*

Peony (Lü mudan) in Chongzhen 6 (1633), Fushe members argued that because they had rejected the request of Wen Tiren's brother to join their organization, the latter had written the play to ridicule Fushe scholars. Portraying themselves as victims of vicious literary attacks, the young men asked the two Zhangs to intervene. The Zhangs subsequently made a special trip and garnered substantial support from a friend and sympathetic official, Li Yuankuan (*jinshi* 1628). Li "banned bookshops from selling the play, had the woodblocks destroyed, charged the author, and imprisoned someone from the Wen family," thereby completely quashing the Fushe's enemies.[96]

Often considered a triumph of the Fushe over their enemies' attempt to defame them, this event merits critical reconsideration. *The Green Peony* is a romantic comedy. It dramatizes how two pairs of beautiful ladies and talented scholars overcome obstacles to their love. In particular, it mocks appeals to feigned literary celebrity. Revisionist scholarship has tried to explain the inexplicable fact that the script does not read as the slanderous material Fushe had claimed it to be, certainly not slanderous enough to provoke such extreme reactions and measures. More recently, it has been suggested that the script we have today may not be the original; it is believed to have been rewritten, after having been banned, by the pro-Fushe official Wu Bing (*jinshi* 1619).[97] This rereading of the incident warrants further investigation, but even its possibility reminds us of the danger of presuming the Fushe's righteousness and victimization. "At the time, people all wanted to put on [the play]," one Fushe insider documented.[98] Regardless of the extant version's authenticity or the reasons behind the play's appeal, the instant popularity of the play in its day suggests that the Fushe, far from being universally respected for moral exemplariness, might have been considered an entertaining spectacle in some corners of society.

The Enemy Within

The scandals surrounding Wu Weiye's exam essays and the play *The Green Peony* involved print and theater, two political techniques that Fushe scholars mastered and used to publicize their own moral performance. But they could not monopolize these media. Nor could they determine just how the increasing emphasis on moral performance in politics would affect them and their claims to sincerity and authenticity. The long battle between the Fushe and a defector from the group, the official Zhou Zhikui (*jinshi* 1631), helps shed light on the environment in which they had to maneuver.

A former Fushe member from Fujian, Zhou enjoyed great success at the beginning of his official career after he passed the examinations in Chongzhen 4 (1631), the same year as did Zhang Pu and Wu Weiye. Zhou's first job took him to the important position of assistant administrator (*tuiguan*) in the Suzhou prefectural government. Given the rise of the Fushe and the strategic importance of Suzhou in late-Ming economic, social, cultural, and political spheres, many Donglin heavyweights such as Wen Zhenmeng (a Suzhou native himself) expressed high expectations for Zhou. However, an explosive confrontation between Zhou and the Fushe leadership in Chongzhen 5–6 (1632–33) resulted in a deep antagonism that haunted the Donglin-Fushe community for many years.

According to the established narrative, based largely on Fushe-friendly sources,[99] this was a messy fight in which a selfish individual, Zhou Zhikui, betrayed the two Zhangs and lent himself to the evil grand secretary Wen Tiren as a weapon against the righteous Donglin-Fushe collective. It was said that Zhou competed with Liu Shidou, a Fushe friend who had passed the exams in the same year as Zhou and was appointed magistrate of Taicang (in modern-day Jiangsu), Zhang Pu's hometown. It was believed that because Liu was much closer to the two Zhangs, Zhou vied with him for control of local examinations as well as the transportation and management of tax and military grain.[100] In the end, in late Chongzhen 6 (1633), Liu and another local official lost their jobs. The Fushe argued that these two officials had been wildly popular and their departure triggered widespread local protest against Zhou. In Chongzhen 8 (1635), Zhou took a sick leave and left in disgrace for his hometown in Fujian. When Wen Tiren and his clique launched attacks on the Fushe and the two Zhangs in Chongzhen 9–10 (1636–37), he enlisted various "witnesses," including Zhou, who, though in the midst of mourning the death of his official mother (his biological mother was a concubine), traveled northward to testify. These events created a string of serious problems for the Fushe and the two Zhangs.[101]

Zhou's moral charges against the Fushe have been dismissed by both the Fushe itself and modern historians on the grounds that Wen Tiren used this opportunist Zhou—and the charges he fabricated—as a factional tool against the righteous Donglin-Fushe officials. This standard account—and its clichéd moral-political contrast—overlooks how Confucian ethics was specifically employed by both sides in print and public spectacles as a language of political communication and therefore obscures how the particular cultural and intellectual conditions of the late Ming shaped factionalism.

For instance, the two Zhangs and their supporters mobilized a massive campaign against Zhou Zhikui in Jiangnan, including physical harassment. Under pressure, Zhou requested a sick leave. But his superiors told him to change it to a request for *zhongyang* leave (retiring to take care of one's parent).[102] However, when the request reached the capital, some officials on the Board of Personnel decided that, since Zhou had an elder brother, it would be against the personnel code to let him take such a leave.[103] Eventually, Zhou had to change the petition back to retirement due to illness. Zhou's official mother passed away just one day after he finally arrived home.[104] Zhou departed in such disgrace and embarrassment that he forever lost the opportunity to bring imperial honors to his deceased parents, a disappointment he deeply regretted.[105]

Zhou felt especially bitter toward the two Zhangs because, according to his recollection of his supervisors' words, they had pressed colleagues on the Board of Personnel to consider not granting him a *zhongyang* leave.[106] A later official report done by pro-Fushe officials dismissed Zhou's claim as "speculative."[107] Limited sources do not allow us to be certain whether the Zhangs had indeed influenced the Board of Personnel. It is true that the board's treatment of Zhou was justified by the code. Still, since Zhou's mother was already in her nineties and dying, the board could have followed other precedents and generously granted him a short leave so that he could claim he had left office to fulfill his filial duties. Further, even if pro-Fushe officials were correct in saying that Zhou was obsessed and paranoid about Fushe animosity and character assassination, they also admitted that Zhou's superiors had indeed voluntarily requested a *zhongyang* leave for him so as to avoid greater damage to his reputation or career prospects. This was apparently a common practice.[108] However, once the request was turned down and Zhou was made a public laughingstock, he alone bore the humiliation and devastating consequences. He had become an unfilial hypocrite with little political credibility.

When Zhou later left his home during the mourning period to testify against the two Zhangs, Fushe members spread the word that because their factional enemies had promised Zhou a promotion, he had suspended mourning and agreed to testify as a witness to expose alleged Fushe corruption.[109] This inspired widespread condemnation and eventually left him disgraced. During Zhou's brief visit to the capital, some Donglin-Fushe officials, including Huang Daozhou, chastised him and tried to kick him out of Beijing. Even after Zhou returned to Fujian, Huang continued to memorialize at court against him as a co-conspirator of the evil grand secretary.[110] This must have made Zhou's situation even trickier and scarier, because he and Huang both came from Zhangzhou, Fujian. Huang's hostility might well jeopardize Zhou's local reputation.

Not every senior Donglin-identified official endorsed the moral attacks on Zhou, however. Some prominent figures, including Qian Qianyi, Qu Shisi (1590–1650), and Xu Shirou (1587–1642), expressed sympathy for him. However, while these officials enjoyed high reputations and had much influence in local and court politics, they happened to be in deep trouble themselves during those years of 1636 and 1637.[111] To make things worse, once Wen Tiren and his followers had enlisted Zhou's testimony against the Donglin-Fushe collective, Fushe partisans accused Zhou of conspiring with "vile partisans" in their anti-Donglin, anti-Fushe slander.[112] Zhou was horrified and vehemently denied that he had conspired with those men.[113] He stumbled around in this political minefield alone. In the midst of intense factionalism at court, the above-mentioned three officials told Zhou that openly denouncing the two Zhangs would cause grave damage to the Donglin-Fushe collective. Therefore they really could not do more for him other than express sympathy. All they could do was to privately convey condolences and endorse the publication of his collected writings. Their shared friend, the literatus Mao Jin (1599–1659), a famous book collector and owner of one of the best printing houses in the country, joined in contributing prefaces to Zhou's publication.[114]

Zhou Zhikui's published anthology paints a disheartening picture of the Donglin-Fushe collective by showing that, as the Fushe was becoming a powerful ally, many Donglin officials believed that sustaining the two Zhangs' moral image, though not fair to individuals like Zhou, was the only way to avoid collateral damage to their own numbers. For instance, some of the letters to former colleagues included in Zhou's collection mention that Qian Qianyi had told him that his superiors in the Suzhou area could not risk displeasing the Zhangs on Zhou's account, although Qian lamented that Zhou had been "so terribly abused" at their hands (*cuican zhici*).[115] Zhou quotes words of sympathy from other officials as well. For example, in response to Huang Daozhou's angry message to Zhou, Zheng Sanjun (*jinshi* 1598), a close ally of Huang's and a Donglin-identified figure himself, is said to have told Zhou that although the wrongs were done by the two Zhangs, "there is simply no way to give [him] a voice" (*zhi wu wu zi kaikou chu*).[116] To some senior officials, Zhou expressed deep frustration with Huang Daozhou, whose memorials failed to provide any facts to substantiate the moral attacks on Zhou. He argued that Huang did not discuss facts because he simply wanted to stop Zhou from criticizing the Fushe and the Zhangs.[117]

While the Fushe mobilized human and material resources to condemn and ostracize Zhou Zhikui by painting him as an unfilial opportunist, Zhou conducted his own campaign to expose the moral defects of Fushe celebrity figures such as the two Zhangs and the Four Gentlemen. By circulating and publishing these letters, Zhou attempted to authenticate his own filiality and political integrity by distinguishing himself from the Zhangs' fake moral images and was able to argue that his trips to testify against the Fushe were a selfless, courageous endeavor motivated by his strong *zhongxiao* commitment. He took these opinions all the way to the court just as the Chongzhen emperor was evaluating other officials' warnings against the Fushe.

Questions around the sincerity of filial expression were again at the center of this struggle. Whereas the Fushe ridiculed Zhou's fumbled filiality, Zhou fought back by exposing the insincere and inappropriate moral manipulations of such prominent Fushe scholars as the two Zhangs and the Four Gentlemen. When the Fushe was formally established in the mid-1620s, its members held a grand gathering at Yinshan near the city of Suzhou to publicize its debut.[118] Zhou noted that on that occasion thousands of boats carried the young men to waters near the Tombs of the Five Martyrs (Wuren Mu), where five local anti-eunuch martyrs had been buried. There, the young men started a drinking party.[119] The symbolism of paying homage at this tomb site was potent, not only because it showed Fushe commitment to promoting good government, but also because a commemorative essay authored by the Fushe leader Zhang Pu, "On the Stele at the Tombs of the Five Martyrs" (Wuren mubei ji), in which he spoke on behalf of the people and Donglin survivors, had launched him into official politics.[120] Zhang and the Fushe thus became linked to the Donglin of the Tianqi reign and the Chongzhen eras. However, Zhou's description of this Fushe gathering as a drinking party and self-aggrandizing spectacle throws this image into serious doubt. The impressive gathering was not a proper display of virtues but instead revealed the Fushe as a group of hypocritical fame chasers. Furthermore, on another occasion, Zhou singled out the famous Fushe Four Gentlemen, calling them "bullies and wicked men." "Self-indulgent and undisciplined," they only dressed themselves up as "pure elements."[121] This portrayal of Fushe celebrities was drastically different from their self-image of moral righteousness.

From Zhou's perspective, the reputation of the two Zhangs and the Fushe Four Gentlemen was deceptive; letting these men define the Donglin's image could upend the Donglin tradition. Just months before Fushe-Donglin figures attacked Yang Sichang's violation of filial piety, Zhou went to see a senior official and presented him with a letter in which he called the two Zhangs "disloyal and unfilial" (*bu zhong bu xiao*).[122] He also accused the Donglin icon Huang Daozhou of associating himself with these two immoral men and thereby "corrupting the Donglin tradition" (*baihuai Donglin jiafeng*). Earlier, Zhou had expressed similar views to a number of high-ranking officials. He argued that the Donglin had its own tradition, and even though the Donglin lacked manpower at court at the moment, it should resist the temptation to join forces with the Fushe. Otherwise, the public would question the moral character of the new generation of the Donglin.[123]

In particular, Zhou warned his colleagues that Huang Daozhou might ruin the Donglin tradition if he relied on the Fushe's fake exemplariness to revive and strengthen it. He challenged Huang to tell the public exactly which Fushe members were qualified to pass on the traditions established by generations of Donglin men.[124] Zhou argued that he himself, though ostracized by the Fushe, truly understood the meaning of filial piety and practiced it sincerely and properly. *He* had inherited the Donglin spirit.

In a letter to Fan Jingwen, president of the Board of War in Nanjing, Zhou recalled that when he was newly appointed to Suzhou, he looked after the sons of the Donglin martyr Zhou Shunchang, at Fan's request. Zhou Zhikui had never met Zhou Shunchang in person even though the latter once served as an official in Fujian, Zhou Zhikui's home province. Emphasizing his sincere practice of filial piety and correct understanding of its meaning, Zhou Zhikui explained that he did not visit and introduce himself to Zhou Shunchang because, during Zhou Shunchang's term in Fujian, he had just lost a parent and was refraining from socializing. But, later, during an exam trip to Jiangnan in Tianqi 5 (1625), at the height of eunuch persecution of the Donglin, Zhou Zhikui wept at Zhou Shunchang's tomb in defiance of the eunuch faction's terror, a heroic move that had deeply touched the martyr's son.[125] Thus, in Zhou Zhikui's account, not only did he follow the true Donglin tradition; he *properly and sincerely* practiced filial piety.

In his campaign to defend his own moral standing, Zhou stood firmly behind his criticism of the moral corruption of the two Zhangs and the Fushe. He argued that the two Zhangs' very act of proving their filiality by exposing problems within their families was unfilial.[126] As seen in Zheng Man's case, the proper display of filial piety was not simple. Zheng's refusal to disclose his father's domestic troubles put his own life at risk. Just how one should correctly present himself as a moral exemplar posed an especially delicate question for officials. Fushe scholars themselves had been keen to differentiate the true moral paragons from the fake ones. Zhang Pu, expressing his concerns about the procedures of recruiting and promoting officials, had once quoted the Song official Su Shi's comment that when the state attempted to recruit talent by calling upon filial paragons, everyone started to perform extreme filial acts like *gegu* (slicing a piece of flesh from one's thigh to make healing medicine) and *lumu* (residing next to the deceased parents' tombs).[127] Still, Zhang himself was criticized by Zhou Zhikui as a moral hypocrite.

Zhou's criticisms might well not have been his alone or purely politically motivated. When Zhang Pu publicly exposed the details of his father's suffering at the hands of his uncle, it probably raised some eyebrows. For example, in the epitaph for Zhang's father composed by Ma Shiqi (*jinshi* 1631), a prominent Donglin-Fushe figure, Ma seemed to feel that he needed to justify Zhang's action: "He revealed [those domestic stories,] details that had tormented his father but that his father himself could not reveal. A brother and a son have different ethical responsibilities."[128]

Zhou's many letters to Donglin-identified officials defy the conventional narrative that reduces him to a shameless clown willing to be used by Wen Tiren in factional attacks. They suggest that his rationale was much more complicated and that he was partly motivated by his conventional understanding of *zhongxiao* ethics and a desire to fulfill his familial duties. His discussion of the feigned moral exemplariness of the Fushe and the question of who was morally qualified to be included in the Donglin was legitimate—and actually quite common—at the time.

Here, it is helpful to recall the Fushe intellectual leader Zhang Zilie's cautionary letters on the question of self-discipline, which confirm that Zhou's accusations were not mere fabrications. Zhang himself warned his friends that Fushe popularity, built on networking, empty debates about literary style, superficial talk about military strategies, and self-indulgence, was meaningless and even harmful. Accordingly, he admonished Fushe scholars to take care to properly display their pursuit of Confucian ethical ideals.[129] The Fushe and its rivals, in their efforts to place personal moral performance at the center of politics, to which the debate about sincerity and proper pursuit of Confucian ethics was central, were motivated by similar concerns and resorted to very similar image-making techniques.

The political attacks at court concluded with the emperor's decision in 1639 to be lenient with the Fushe. When the emperor closed the investigation of their alleged moral corruption, he did not take a side but instead told the Fushe that they should "pursue *zhongxiao* and do not chase fame" (*jiangtu zhongxiao wu shi biaobang*).[130] Shen Shoumin, the leader in the Fushe's ill-fated anti–Yang Sichang campaign, while still complaining that the young scholars had fallen victim to false accusations, agreed with the emperor that Fushe scholars must choose to focus on self-cultivation rather than criticizing others in order to achieve quick popularity.[131] This might have been the ultimate lesson he summarized for his Fushe friends. After all, no matter how well connected and coordinated they became, they could not control where they would end up on the spectrum between "real" and "feigned" moral exemplars.

Employment of the language of Confucian ethics in Fushe scholars' emotive expression, career advancement, organizational development, and factional strife demonstrates that, with the intensification of images politics, power relations between the emperor and officials became more complicated. Their political negotiations often took place in discussions about how to conceptualize and practice Confucian ethical ideals such as *zhongxiao* and self-discipline. This situation helped reinscribe these ideals and mark the boundaries and value of moral performance in the changing environment.

The Fushe's moral struggles examined here complicate the two leading perspectives in Fushe historiography. One tries to understand the "progressiveness" of politically minded Fushe figures and what this meant for China's (failed) advance to modernity and enlightenment. The second, more in line with traditional Confucian historiography, approaches Fushe members as tragic heroes frustrated by vicious "small men" in the Ming government and then slain by the Manchu invaders. Both frameworks oversimplify the experiences of Fushe individuals and the positions of their rivals. In fact, within the Donglin-Fushe community, there existed not only "competing loyalties" but also efforts to promote the image of moral integrity for purposes of political networking.[132] Asking why and how certain types of moral images of the Fushe emerged and operated can deepen our understanding of the connection and tension between their moral pursuits and political activities. When we evaluate the Fushe's gains and losses in its members' attempts to translate its advantages in publishing, networking, and organizing into political clout, it is especially important to set those activities in the dynamic interactions among contemporary intellectual, social, cultural and political trends.[133] The moral attacks and counterattacks surrounding the Fushe, in particular the issue of sincerity and authenticity of moral performance, reveal the complex reasons behind, and consequences of, individuals' intensive engagement with Confucian ethics as a language in political communication.

Hence, Fushe scholars' individual and collective efforts at image-making cannot be reduced to a binary of moral fundamentalism versus hypocrisy. These generalizations more fairly reflect the *effects* of late-Ming image politics. Confucian ethical ideals motivated and structured these officials' efforts to adapt to historic changes and simultaneously fulfill competing political, social, and familial responsibilities. Their contributions to making officials' moral performance central to late-Ming political processes not only demonstrated the complexity of the system of Confucian moralism but also enriched it on both theoretical and practical levels.

CHAPTER 3

A *Zhongxiao* Celebrity

Huang Daozhou (1585–1646)

Zhou Zhikui's harsh criticism of the Fushe's dreadful influence on Donglin icon Huang Daozhou did not diminish Huang's stardom. On the contrary, his reputation as a moral paragon only soared as he wrestled with the Chongzhen emperor and political rivals. And it would reach new heights with his arrest and imprisonment for alleged factional scheming in Chongzhen 13 (1640).

With Huang's rising fame, anecdotes about him captivated audiences of contemporary politics. Even news about his physical suffering carried social value and cultural appeal. Huang's health had deteriorated so much in prison that he was seen to use a walking stick when he briefly stayed in Nanjing after his release. Nanjing epitomized seventeenth-century urbanism.[1] Many literati not only aspired to visit Huang's temporary residence there; they also loved to describe the image of Huang getting around with a walking stick to those who visited the city. This was how the recently promoted young official Gong Dingzi (1615–1673) learned about it when he passed through Nanjing.[2] This image of Huang left such a deep impression on Gong that, upon arriving in Beijing, he presented a memorial requesting that the emperor stop the practice of beating officials at court. This memorial annoyed the Chongzhen emperor and contributed to Gong's own arrest, incarceration, and corporal punishment.[3] Gong's allusion to Huang's ordeal in his memorial might have been just a ploy for self-promotion. Still, it points to the role of late-Ming celebrity culture in shaping factionalism and positioning officials' moral performance at the center of political processes.

Celebrity culture had emerged as a by-product of the printing boom. In order to make profits and survive, late-Ming publishing houses needed prolific and even controversial writers. Through this medium the literati not only earned some part of their livelihood but could also created great publicity, to the point that they might even become a lucrative brand name. Li Zhi (1527–1602), Chen Jiru (1558–1639), and some of the scholars associated with the Fushe attained empirewide fame this way.[4] The late Ming possessed the economic, social, and cultural conditions from which a culture of celebrity could emerge.[5]

Celebrity culture in seventeenth-century China had unique characteristics. Although writings by figures of celebrity status were highly commoditized and their names were known by the common people, their primary audience remained the educated. That being the case, they could not afford to completely detach themselves from Confucian ethical ideals. In fact, their engagement with Confucian teachings was often a key factor in their celebrity status. For instance, polarized interpretations of Li Zhi's moral performance greatly contributed to his celebrity appeal and marketability. In Chen Jiru's case, even though his celebrity might have derived partly from his seeming indifference to controversy or activism, he nonetheless capitalized on opportunities to publicize his Confucian moral commitment as a way of demonstrating his elite status.[6] Indeed, the gradual emergence of celebrity culture in the late Ming only enhanced the importance of traditional factors—family background, moral reputation, official status, networking, and wealth—on the path to sociopolitical advancement.[7]

Celebrity culture under the particular political conditions of the late Ming contributed to the evolution of image politics. For example, the dramatic expansion of the Fushe's political influence as an organization resulted from its collective celebrity appeal and the popular reputation of its leading members.[8] Donglin-identified iconic figures experienced celebrity culture in varied ways. The famed scholar-poet Qian Qianyi (1582–1664) seems to have given up on his career after losing one battle after another to his attackers, but his controversial liaison with the courtesan Liu Rushi (1618–1664) and active involvement with Fushe youths' social and literary networking enhanced his popularity.[9] In contrast, Liu Zongzhou was universally admired for his administrative skills, scholarship, and integrity. Literati society treated him as a celebrity even though Liu maintained a low profile and disciplined lifestyle. After he was spotted wearing a simple "purple cotton" robe, that style became a hot commodity in Jiangnan among the literati.[10]

In contrast to Qian and Liu, Huang Daozhou's celebrity appeal derived from his reputation as the epitome of *zhongxiao*. The aura of this image dazzled many in the Donglin-Fushe camp and led them to assert that Huang deserved the powerful position of grand secretary. The circulation of his highly politicized art made him an idol among nonelites as well. The cultural and social capital deriving from his fame as a moral exemplar made him a particular kind of celebrity.

Huang's career trajectory and the debates and negotiations in which he participated in the 1630s and early 1640s help us understand late-Ming image politics at the juncture of factionalism, rising ritualism, and contemporary obsession with publicity and sensationalism. His engagements with the *zhongxiao* ideal—from debates over the *duoqing* practice and invocation of his own filial acts when confronting political rivals to his display of a perfect unity of loyalty, filial piety, and friendship in poetry, art, scholarship, travel, and ritual activities—defined his fame. Various parties reacted differently to Huang's emergence as a *zhongxiao* celebrity. Their political negotiations over Huang's moral image reveal how celebrity culture complicated the use of Confucian ethics as a language of political communication during this period.

ZHONGXIAO RITUALS

As a historical term used frequently—and often freely—by our seventeenth-century subjects, the word *zhongxiao* could refer to different ideas, including the unity of loyalty and filial piety, the Confucian virtues or ethical system, or moral accomplishments in general. *Zhongxiao* can thus serve as an analytical lens through which to examine the verbal, visual, and embodied articulations of officials' commitment to loyalty and filial piety and as a technique of creative engagement with the rich imperial tradition of "seeking loyal officials in filial sons." In the late Ming, the productive tensions inherent in the concept of *zhongxiao*—that loyalty and filial piety are compatible and competing virtues—made it an extremely versatile and prevalent means of political negotiation. It could be invoked as an excuse for privileging one of the two virtues, it could motivate officials to creatively overcome difficulties to achieve both, and it could operate as an effective weapon of attack and counterattack.

The filial rites that played a central role in the construction of Huang Daozhou's subjectivity and popular appeal had tremendous political significance in the seventeenth-century context. These can be collectively considered as *zhongxiao* rituals. The first is the observation of a three-year (twenty-seven-month) mourning period for a deceased parent (*shouzhi*). Officials were supposed to withdraw from office to complete this observance, but exemptions from mourning at home for a full term were not rare in Ming history, especially at those times when the empire faced imminent threats.

However, in the late Ming, protests raised against violations of this norm at the emperor's request (*duoqing*) became a common method of framing criticisms of the emperor and fellow officials. Such controversy might instantly evolve into a dramatic political showdown. The Wanli emperor's decision in the 1570s against letting Grand Secretary Zhang Juzheng resign from office to mourn his father—and opposition from officials, which earned them corporal punishments and even exile—is one example.[11] The ramifications of this event would continue to shape the political landscape until the fall of the Southern Ming Hongguang regime in 1645.

The political spectacles surrounding *duoqing* controversies significantly enhanced the literati's intellectual and spiritual interest in filial rituals as well as the public's interest in court politics in the late Ming.[12] The *duoqing* debates might have reflected the late-Ming diversification of mourning rituals. But seen from the perspective of political communication, they demonstrate officials' strong interest in employing the language of *zhongxiao* as a tool of negotiation rather than their tendency to "forget" the correct mourning criteria.[13] Huang Daozhou was the central figure in a spectacle surrounding the *duoqing* order issued to the Donglin rival Yang Sichang in the late 1630s. Contrary to the observation that these confrontations arose from officials' misunderstanding of the *duoqing* precedents, a careful comparison of how Huang and his factional rivals expressly used these precedents will demonstrate something different. Precisely because officials could freely interpret and even deliberately bend those precedents, *zhongxiao* in effect functioned as a shared language by which to make political points and negotiate.

Another filial ritual that deserves special attention is that of *shoumu* (voluntarily taking up residence near the family tombs), a sensational way of carrying out mourning. It became so popular among the literati that it has been considered tantamount to a movement in the seventeenth century.[14] Ming-era Confucian scholars increasingly emphasized moral *action*—a reaction to the "subjective" approach to moral cultivation advocated by the Yangming school.[15] This emphasis manifested itself in literati displays of not only moral accomplishments but also the very *process* of moral cultivation and the *sincerity* of moral performance in ritualized actions. Whereas the Fushe celebrity Fang Yizhi performed *shoumu* for a limited length of time before becoming an official, Huang Daozhou practiced it over many years in the course of his official career, even long after the deaths of his parents, which significantly contributed to his fame as a moral paragon. In addition, Huang's frequent mention of his *shoumu* practice in debates with the Chongzhen emperor pointedly illustrates how officials quite self-consciously performed filial rituals as a way of authenticating their moral reputation and enhancing their political standing.

The third *zhongxiao* ritual that concerns us here is the ritual use of the *Classic of Filial Piety*. One does not have to completely agree with the observation that Huang Daozhou literally followed the instructions of this Confucian classic in his life and career, but his multidimensional identification with the text is unusually strong.[16] In the seventeenth century, many literati—including Huang Daozhou—used this Confucian classic to create ritualized spaces for self-cultivation. Copying, reciting, and worshipping it turned the book into a ritual prop.[17] Like Huang's twenty-year *shoumu* saga, his hand copying of the *Classic of Filial Piety* in prison physically manifested his process of moral cultivation, affirmed his moral superiority, and pressured the emperor to heed his criticisms. It also made him a cultural icon among the nonelite.[18]

As Huang's highly publicized and ritualized embodiment of *zhongxiao* blossomed into celebrity appeal, he garnered enthusiastic support and widespread endorsement from the Donglin-Fushe community. For Huang's fans, it was a natural and convenient position to take, given the influence of the celebrity culture of which Confucian moralism was an organic part.

ZHONGXIAO ON THE ROAD

One of Huang Daozhou's disciples summarized his life and career this way: "The master's Way lies only with *zhongxiao*" (*Fuzi zhi dao zhongxiao eryi*).[19] After some initial setbacks, Huang came to embody the *zhongxiao* ideal, to the extent that it would restructure his life, career, emotions, and behavior. Once such a pattern and image was established and articulated, it came to stand for the man.

Before the fall of the Ming court in Beijing in 1644, Huang Daozhou had held only positions in branches of the metropolitan bureaucracy where his literary and scholarly skills were best put to use. Due to leaves and demotions, he constantly moved between the capital and his hometown, Zhangpu (Zhangzhou prefecture, Fujian). Such travels—and the social, cultural, and intellectual activities they allowed—took a substantial amount of time and constituted a crucial part of Huang's life as an official. They displayed the process of his moral cultivation and exposed it to a wide audience. His travels in particular embodied, and also explained, his *zhongxiao* pursuits.

In Tianqi 2 (1622), this Fujianese scholar, little known outside his home province, passed the metropolitan examinations and entered the central government. Over the next two decades, as the Ming dynasty struggled through tremendous crises that eventually led to its fall, Huang Daozhou's fame as a moral exemplar and loyal official steadily rose. This fame came at the cost of a rocky career path. He experienced four major episodes of turmoil in his career, as illustrated in figure 3.1, which delineates his travels between the court and his family tombs.

Chushan (lit., "leave the mountains") and *shoumu* were the two terms Huang often employed to describe his trips to and from the capital.[20] Framing his travels with these two terms allowed him to simplify the reasons for his departures from court, which actually ranged from illness to political frustration, and kept the focus on the central motif of his life, the unity of loyalty and filial piety. *Chusan* had long been the standard term referring to the move from a man's quiet life at home to the tumultuous world of government. In Huang's case, the metaphorical reference to "the mountains" projects a strong impression because it coincides with the fact that he indeed built and lived for many years in a rustic dwelling next to his parents' tombs deep in the mountains. When he "resided next to the parents' tombs" in Zhangpu, Huang did not completely shun public activities: he delivered lectures on Confucian classics. Still, he and his admirers consciously chose the term *shoumu* to refer to his periodic retreats so as to highlight his embodiment of *zhongxiao* ethics.

Huang's travels, as well as the ways in which he and his admirers alluded to them, thus established a conspicuously ritualized life pattern. This pattern of movement between the family tombs in Zhangpu

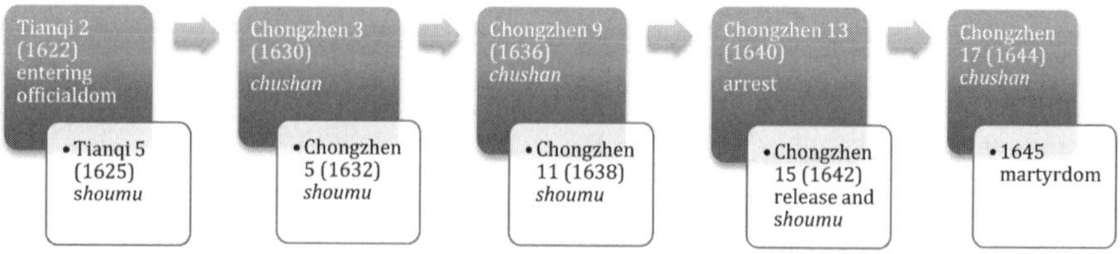

Figure 3.1. Huang Daozhou's shoumu-chushan pattern.

and the court began in Tianqi 5 (1625), precipitated by the dominance of the eunuch faction at court. In his capacity as a Hanlin compiler (*bianxiu*), Huang also had the responsibility of lecturing to the young Tianqi emperor on the Confucian classics. According to the *Ming History (Ming shi)*, Huang refused to follow the protocol of presenting texts to the emperor on his knees. The *Ming History* has interpreted this as an expression of heroic defiance toward the eunuch Wei Zhongxian. Although Wei did not move against Huang, he did feel threatened by the gesture.[21] Whether this account is accurate or not, it captures the noble image that Huang and his admirers attempted to delineate for him.

At the height of Wei Zhongxian's persecution of Donglin-identified officials, in Tianqi 5 (1625), Huang requested a leave to take care of his mother in Fujian and subsequently extended it to observe the formally mandated mourning period after she died.[22] While caring for his mother, Huang built a hut in the mountains and personally carried the dirt needed to construct a tomb for his long-deceased father. In a letter to his brother, he described with much satisfaction how he erected a stele, on which he inscribed his father's virtuous deeds, at the site. As he carved the inscription, he paused after each character and performed a kowtow. The tomb site was a long-term, carefully designed project. Huang built and arranged everything with his own hands, and it took him many years to complete. He wrote that by residing next to the tomb, he was serving his deceased father.[23] When his mother passed away the next year (Tianqi 6 [1626]), he remained in the mountains and continued to build at the site. From Tianqi 7 (1627) to Chongzhen 1 (1628), he buried or reburied his mother, grandmother, uncles, and deceased first wife in that place, some of whom had passed away long ago. He told others that fulfilling these responsibilities was his only worldly interest.[24]

Retroactively, Huang and his admirers would identify this period as the beginning of his lifelong mission to embody loyalty and filial piety perfectly and simultaneously in both his career and his personal life. His contemporary Zhang Dian (fl. 1640s–50s) observed that, from Tianqi 5 (1625), Huang "would leave this place only when going to offer criticisms to the emperor, and he would resume attending to the tombs when he returned."[25] Although we cannot exclude the possibility that Huang and his biographers left slightly exaggerated accounts of his hardships during his extended periods of residence at his family tombs, clearly he devoted considerable effort to practicing filial piety as a form of moral cultivation and self-expression.

The imagery of going back and forth between the mountains and the court thus condensed several kinds of filial rituals that characterized a particular configuration of *zhongxiao* for Huang. He not only practiced the rituals that had been prescribed in the Confucian classics, mandated by the state, and explored by Confucian scholars of his time but also ritualized his politics and life by frequently displaying the very process of cultivating *zhongxiao* in the public eye. Consequently, Huang's trips between the capital and his hometown conferred special meanings on the many spaces that he visited and where he resided during those years. In turn, these places came to delineate the contours of his *zhongxiao* commitment—the harmonious merging of his images as a filial son, loyal official, and true friend.

These images did not truly merge until Tianqi 5 (1625). Huang's first trip, which took place in Tianqi 2 (1622) immediately after he entered government service, was one whereby he had hoped to fulfill filial duties only. He traveled thousands of kilometers back to Fujian to bring his mother to the capital. But by doing so, he missed his first opportunity to prove himself a loyal official and true friend.

That was the year when Wen Zhenmeng and Zheng Man, two new officials from Huang's *jinshi* cohort, challenged the powerful eunuch Wei Zhongxian. Although Huang had promised that he would join his friends in their efforts, he hesitated because he had become more concerned about his mother. He was torn between loyalty and filial piety.[26] "I composed three memorials but burned them all because I had to bring my mother to the capital," he later recalled.[27] Not only was he unable to reconcile filial piety and loyalty, but by withdrawing from this joint effort, he also fell short of fulfilling his responsibility as a friend. Although the competing relationship between loyalty and filial piety had been a familiar one over the course of imperial history, this experience must have been a difficult first lesson to swallow for this junior official.[28]

The unified image of a filial son, trustworthy friend, and loyal official began to coalesce over the next several trips Huang took up and down the Grand Canal. A calligraphic presentation of poems produced in Chongzhen 3 (1630) illustrates his strengthened efforts to unify loyalty, filial piety, and friendship. On his trip northward to Beijing that year, Huang and his family visited Zheng Man, who was observing the three-year mourning for his father. Huang was eager to express his admiration for Zheng's political integrity and their friendship.[29] This time, he produced a calligraphy scroll for Zheng. This calligraphic work is arranged very artistically and shows a degree of formality.[30] Beginning with those poems dedicated to Zheng in Tianqi 2 (1622) and ending with new poems written during this latest reunion, it records their meetings over a nine-year period (1622–30). Huang had extended the scroll twice as his travel plans changed, adding more poems to it each time, until it came to include fifteen old and new poems.

Thus, the completed scroll consists of three sections. The first, which is the longest, highlights the moral exemplariness of the Zheng father and son. The poems are arranged in chronological order, providing a complete record of their friendship over the nine years. The first poem in this section begins by expressing admiration for Zheng Man—and their other friend Wen Zhenmeng—for having courageously stood up to abusers of power at court, a heroic action in which Huang had failed to participate.[31] It painstakingly portrays Zheng as a loyal official, suggesting that he deserved as much recognition as that given to Wen, who became a political superstar when he placed first among their cohort in the metropolitan examinations. The poem goes on to remind the audience that Zheng Man in fact came from a family of the most loyal officials—his maternal grandfather, Wu Zhongxing, won empirewide admiration for having challenged Zhang Juzheng's *duoqing* in the early Wanli reign, and his father, Zheng Zhenxian, driven by sincere loyalty, offered critical, substantial advice to the Wanli emperor but was demoted through the efforts of factionalists.[32]

Following the poem that lauds the *zhongxiao* tradition of the Zheng family, Huang presents a second poem, this one to illuminate friendship. He emotionally recalls that in Tianqi 2 (1622), upon his departure for Fujian to see his mother, Zheng Man, himself being forced out of the capital as a result of factional purge, still remembered to offer money to help Huang rent a horse.[33] It was Zheng's friendship that then helped Huang fulfill his filial duties.

After these two poems, Huang presented three more poems written three years later, in Tianqi 5 (1625), on his return to Fujian after he had offended Wei Zhongxian. During this trip, he paid a visit to the Zhengs. These poems reiterate the bond of friendship between Huang and Zheng Man as well as his admiration for the elder Zheng. Further, the poems stress the fact that the two friends shared a strong commitment to both loyalty and filial piety.[34] The poems chosen for the first section of this calligraphy scroll as a whole thus neatly erase Huang's failure to perform loyalty and friendship at the beginning of his career. Instead, they create a narrative of strong friendship built on shared *zhongxiao* beliefs.

The poems in the other two sections of the scroll were written years later, on two separate occasions in Chongzhen 3 (1630). During Huang Daozhou's trip back to the capital after years of living next to his parents' tombs, he and his family made a stop at the Zhengs in Wujin County. The Manchus had recently launched military assaults and seriously threatened northern Ming. Given the difficult situation on the road northward, Huang decided to leave his mother and wife behind with the Zhengs and headed for the capital alone. Later, after the situation had quieted, he returned to fetch them. The second section of the calligraphy scroll contains one long poem that Huang composed before departing for the capital without his family. The third section concludes with Huang's return to retrieve his mother and wife.[35] These two sections testify vividly to Huang's deepening appreciation of Zheng Man's friendship. Once again, Zheng's hospitality toward Huang's mother had allowed Huang to accomplish his own filial duties.

The scroll as a whole thus aptly demonstrates that Huang's friendship with Zheng was a central component of his *zhongxiao* image in the early stages of its formation during his travels. The message of these poems would become well known among Huang's allies as well as his opponents. Their contentions on the relationship between friendship and *zhongxiao* in Huang's case revealed the complex ways in which Confucian ethics operated as a language of political communication.

After these trips, a series of clashes erupted at court between Huang and the Chongzhen emperor. Huang began to publicly assert that his movement between the court and family tombs was an embodiment of his *zhongxiao*. When the new emperor succeeded to the throne, he called back many Donglin-identified officials, including Huang. In Chongzhen 4 (1631), Huang memorialized in defense of Grand Secretary Qian Longxi (1579–1645), who had been implicated in the Yuan Chonghuan (1584–1630) treason case and imprisoned. Huang went after Qian's enemies within the former eunuch faction, whom he believed sought revenge for Qian's involvement in the Chongzhen emperor's purge of that faction.[36] This memorial was met with strong questioning from the emperor, who pressed Huang to memorialize two more times to clarify his position and language.[37]

Huang's three memorials defending Qian are the earliest examples of his employment of the metaphor of shuttling between the court and his parents' tomb site as a way of articulating his self-identity and political criticism before the emperor. In response to the emperor's demand that he submit a second memorial explaining himself, Huang proudly wrote: "Having attended to the tombs (*shoumu*) for three years and served in the government (*chushan*) for only six years, I am just a rude man unfamiliar with the taboos."[38] Then, in the third memorial, he defended his loyalty by contrasting the silence and irresponsibility of many officials with his perfectly proper display of loyalty and filial piety: while piously residing by his parents' tombs in the mountains, he had not stopped reading government briefs; though far away from the capital, he had foreseen the danger arising from Qian's arrest.[39] Finally, immediately following this unpleasant exchange with the emperor, Huang submitted a request for leave so that he could "be close to the tombs [of his parents]."[40]

The *shoumu-chushan* metaphor that Huang Daozhou so effectively leveraged defined his image as an exemplary Confucian official and enhanced the rhetorical power of his memorials. His recourse to *zhongxiao* rhetoric helped him lay claim to an archetypal loyalty defined by honest remonstration with the throne, illuminating the mutual cultivation of filial piety and loyalty and drawing on the literati-official tradition of using one's filial duties as a legitimate excuse for withdrawing from politics as a form of passive protest.[41] Huang received permission to go home and resumed residence next to his parents' tombs until he was summoned to serve again. At this point, his pattern of practicing *zhongxiao* by alternating between the family tombs and the court had become established and known. His travels and calligraphy would continue to display and document his self-cultivation throughout his career, significantly contributing to his popularity as a moral paragon among the literati.

ZHONGXIAO IN DEBATES

At court, Huang Daozhou's *zhongxiao* pattern of travel was both reinforced and contested in his debates with the Chongzhen emperor and political rivals. Three debates about *zhongxiao* enhanced, but were also complicated by, his popular appeal. Although these debates took place in the space of the imperial court, their details would reach various corners of the empire because the literati and print media moved quickly and frequently between the capital and local communities.

As a language of communication shared by opponents, the effective deployment of *zhongxiao* was more complex than one side claiming moral rectitude in order to exert political pressure on others. Attacks and self-defense at court were delivered and negotiated through officials' competing arguments about how to sincerely and properly pursue filial piety. These competing arguments drew upon and appropriated a variety of officially sanctioned sources, such as the Confucian classics, established Confucian scholarship, and official histories. Huang's factional rivals displayed their own moral exemplariness and also effectively challenged Huang's understanding of *zhongxiao* ethics. In response, Huang's supporters had ever more incentive to draw a stark contrast between his moral perfection and his rivals' moral deficiency.

The first of these three debates took place in Chongzhen 9 (1636), just a few months after Zheng Man was arrested and imprisoned. The emperor had made their mutual friend Wen Zhenmeng a grand secretary. Huang Daozhou was on his way back to the court. Anticipating powerful challenges from these three friends, the senior grand secretary Wen Tiren took immediate action. He not only forced Wen Zhenmeng to retire; he also put forth the moral charges against Zheng Man that led to Zheng's arrest.[42]

When Huang arrived in the capital, several officials had failed in their efforts to impeach Wen Tiren for incriminating Zheng on unverifiable charges. One of them was Liu Zongzhou. Liu criticized the emperor's blind confidence in Wen Tiren, who had been relentlessly eliminating political opponents. This memorial so angered the emperor that he stripped Liu of official status.[43] Meanwhile, another political storm was rapidly forming. In early Chongzhen 9 (1636), somewhat desperate in his search for officials who could devise more effective strategies against the rebels and the Manchus, the emperor appointed Yang Sichang president of the Board of War. Yang answered the call, thereby cutting short the mourning term for his father.[44]

After some contemplation, Huang Daozhou decided to tackle Yang's appointment first. His memorial against Yang's promotion during the mourning term consisted of two parts. The first part questioned the appointment on the principle that it violated basic Confucian ideals. The second part protested Yang's proposal for new taxes to raise funds for military operations.[45] In the face of challenges from rebels and the Manchus, the Ming government needed to mobilize more resources. Whether Yang's tax proposals were practical or not, Huang's alternatives barely suggested anything new. Emphasizing that recent droughts were Heaven's negative reaction to the emperor's promotion of an unfilial son, Huang suggested that in order to ensure suppression of the rebels, the emperor needed to promote more suitable officials.[46] Huang's insistence on the *zhongxiao* principle was both a display of his strong belief in it and a tactic. This tactic had a precedent and a source of inspiration: during the Wanli reign, Zhang Juzheng's critics had succeeded in making a connection between his *duoqing* and natural disasters.[47] However, this time, the Chongzhen emperor remained unconvinced. He dismissed Huang's preaching as part of a factionalist agenda and went along with Yang Sichang's proposals.

Huang Daozhou did not pursue the protest further. Instead, he moved on to Zheng Man's case. In doing so, he was forced to contend with the various meanings of loyalty. When attacking Yang, he portrayed Yang as an unfilial man, while his defense of Zheng rested on criticizing their factional enemies' incorrect understanding of loyalty.

In two memorials, Huang carefully carved out his position. The first one, "On My Three Faults, Four Shameful Actions, and Seven Defects" (San zui si chi qi buru shu; hereafter "My Seven Defects"), lists Zheng as a worthy official deserving of important positions.[48] Unsurprisingly, the emperor reacted with fury to this memorial for its praise of Zheng. Huang then submitted a response that explicitly defended Zheng's record of loyalty and filial piety. He expressed concern that the emperor might give credence to the sensational charges that had been presented to the court as evidence of Zheng's ethical violations. He reminded everyone that true loyalty was demonstrated by officials' proper behavior in political debate:

> Han Qi, an official of the Song dynasty, held office in the Grand Council. Every time he came across memorials that exposed other officials' personal mistakes, he would cover those words with his hands. The emperor Renzong called him "a loyal official." Yan Zhenqing in the Tang dynasty once attacked Li Heji for lacking filial piety. But he later admitted that he blurted out those improper words as a result of drunkenness. Hence, discussion of others' personal problems should not happen in a good political environment. Nowadays, locals enjoy getting together and gossiping to entertain themselves. Everywhere, dishonest men fabricate smears to benefit personally.[49]

The historical reference to Han Qi (1008–1075) stresses the impropriety of bringing rumors about domestic affairs into court, suggesting that the emperor should dismiss the groundless charges against Zheng. The reference to Yan Zhenqing (709–784) implies that officials often recklessly and irresponsibly make grave but unverifiable accusations. On the basis of these examples, Huang suggests that Zheng's attackers should be condemned for disloyalty.

Huang was probably aware that his arguments in these two cases could easily be interpreted as inconsistent and factionalist. According to his logic, though, his criticism of Yang Sichang and defense of Zheng Man ultimately served the sole purpose of protecting the integrity of the Confucian ethical system and the true spirit of "governing with filial piety." His actions and his scholarship on the *Classic of Filial Piety* suggest that, like many other contemporary Confucian scholars, he understood the paradigm of "governing with filial piety" as encompassing not only the important virtues of loyalty, filial piety, and self-discipline but also mutual respect between the emperor and officials and between officials of different political positions.[50] These two actions showed his consistent belief in *zhongxiao* and determination to exalt it. It was imperative for him not only to put into practice his understanding of *zhongxiao* but also to correct others' "misunderstanding" of it.

Surprisingly, the Chongzhen emperor did not admonish Huang. After this debate, Huang's fame within the Donglin camp grew quickly. As the next debate in Chongzhen 11 (1638) shows, he had accumulated so much star power that the younger generation of officials in the Donglin-Fushe community began to lobby for his promotion.

The second debate about *zhongxiao* involved a violent factional clash and tested Huang's popular appeal. After Grand Secretary Wen Tiren was made to retire in Chongzhen 10 (1637), Donglin-identified officials felt ready to put Huang into this newly vacant position. The emperor did not feel Huang could assume the responsibility as a leader in a time of crisis. Instead, he promoted Xue Guoguan (d. 1641). Xue and Zhang Zhifa (*jinshi* 1601), another grand secretary, were seen as associates of Wen's anti-Donglin camp and a continuation of his corruption and incompetence. Huang's supporters were disappointed by the emperor's decision.

Soon afterward, in Chongzhen 11 (1638), the emperor appointed several officials as tutors for the Heir Apparent. This honor represented imperial recognition of the appointees' virtue, talent, and political potential. With the release of the name list, one of them, the Donglin-identified official Yang Tinglin (d. 1646), submitted a memorial arguing that Huang Daozhou was the most qualified for this position and expressing his willingness to concede the position to Huang Daozhou.[51] The Fushe activist and official Xiang Yu (*jinshi* 1625) wrote a similar memorial.[52]

As the Donglin-Fushe camp enthusiastically announced its intention to replace its factional rivals with its own hopeful, Huang Daozhou, officials on the other side voiced strong disagreement. They cited Huang's old memorial "My Seven Defects" to challenge his understanding of *zhongxiao* ethics. Grand Secretary Zhang Zhifa argued before the emperor: "Regarding [Zheng Man's] immoral behavior and mother beating, His Majesty's edict had made a clear judgment. Zheng does not deserve to be called a human being, but [Huang Daozhou] claims that Zheng has surpassed him. Could we let someone like Huang advise the Heir Apparent?"[53]

Zhang further questioned whether Huang had properly understood and performed loyalty, filial piety, and friendship: "[Huang]'s return to court after mourning (*chushan*) was compelled by filial devotion to his mother, who had [been helped by Zheng before, and thus he] hoped to offer a favorable testimony on Zheng's behalf. We cannot say that Huang is unfilial. But he shouldn't sacrifice the public interest just because he owed a debt of thanks to Zheng."[54]

Clearly, Zhang was familiar not only with Huang's frequent deployment of the imagery of shuttling between the court and his parents' tombs but also with how the Huang-Zheng friendship had significantly contributed to establishing this image. However, in Zhang's interpretation, although Huang's filial performance was admirable, it did not transfer to loyalty, and so Huang's return to court did not really amount to an act of *zhongxiao*. On the contrary, by defending a morally corrupt man simply because he had taken care of Huang's mother, Huang actually abused and betrayed the *zhongxiao* principle. This interpretation by Zhang called into question the authenticity of Huang's image as a paragon of *zhongxiao* and instead depicted him as a factionalist.

Huang's supporters were outraged. How dared their factional rivals challenge Huang's *zhongxiao* image and block their personnel preference! They immediately reminded the emperor that this questioning of Huang's moral accomplishments was nothing more than factionalist machinations; Huang's reputation as a filial son was an indisputable, widely acknowledged fact. One of them plainly told the emperor, "Huang Daozhou served his parents with utmost filiality. Everyone in the empire knows!"[55]

Flummoxed by this conflict between officials drawn to Huang's appeal as a *zhongxiao* exemplar and those who questioned that appeal, the emperor simply observed. He saw no need to arbitrate, since both sides were using the same language to advocate for their candidate preferences. He maintained a neutral stance, ignoring the Donglin-Fushe advocacy for Huang's promotion as well as their rivals' critiques of him. However, he began to realize that Huang had become something of a political leader thanks to his *zhongxiao* fame, as shown in the emperor's attitude in the third debate.

The third debate about *zhongxiao* almost followed on the heels of the previous one. Huang led a group of officials protesting another promotion for Yang Sichang, this time to the position of grand secretary. Upon his nomination, Yang also suggested promoting Chen Xinjia (d. 1642), an official accused by the Donglin of having been an associate of the former eunuch faction. Yang recommended that Chen be appointed to supervise the war effort in key strategic regions in the north. This proposed promotion would shorten Chen's mourning period for his deceased mother by several months.[56]

Prompted by the actions of Fushe scholars in Beijing and Nanjing, the *zhongxiao* celebrity Huang Daozhou felt he must submit protests both against Yang's appointment to the Grand Secretariat in violation of mourning norms and against Chen's return to office before completing the prescribed mourning term.[57] To buttress his stance, Huang adopted a few tactics that would create a clear moral contrast between him and his rivals.

First, Huang redefined certain *duoqing* precedents in the history of the Ming. In one memorial, he cites a group of mid-Ming officials who had to suspend mourning so that they could lead crucial military campaigns. These *duoqing* cases were considered legitimate, if undesirable, given the urgent military situation then and could be supported with reference to still older historical precedents. However, even if the question of legitimacy were put aside, Huang argued, these cases still could not be used to justify Yang's and Chen's *duoqing*, because they simply were not analogous. According to Huang, the mid-Ming official Yang Bo (d. 1574) was very close to the end of his mourning period when he was summoned back to service, and therefore this case should not be considered a legitimizing precedent for Chen Xinjia.[58] This position was merely rhetorical manipulation on Huang's part. Like Yang Bo, Chen had nearly completed his mourning duty.[59] Huang misrepresented Chen's promotion as establishing a new, dangerous precedent.

Next, Huang identified another group of *duoqing* cases in Ming history as inauspicious events. His first example was Weng Wanda (1498–1552), who was called back to court as he was mourning at his father's tomb. After the Jiajing emperor rejected Weng's petition for permission to complete his mourning, Weng rushed back to the capital from thousands of kilometers away. The impatient emperor, counseled by Weng's factional enemies, withdrew his trust and favor. Here, Huang cites Weng's political demise as a punishment from Heaven to warn the emperor that depriving officials of time to complete their filial mourning was inauspicious.[60] To reinforce this point, he invokes three additional examples of late-Ming mourning violations by high-ranking officials. "Zhang Juzheng ruined his own legacy by *duoqing*. [After that,] for the next seventy years, the literati abided by the [*zhongxiao*] principle and the frontiers remained secure. However, in the late Tianqi years, Yuan Chonghuan's [rise] and Cui Chengxiu's shameful promotion to high government positions both came with violations of mourning rules. They ended up being executed and despised!"[61] Here, Huang distorts Zhang Juzheng's case and turns it, again, into an inauspicious incident. In Huang's account, because the Wanli emperor later changed his mind and decided to punish Zhang posthumously, Heaven responded by bringing relative peace to the frontiers.

The other two *duoqing* cases Huang invokes, those of Cui Chengxiu (1584–1627) and Yuan Chonghuan, occurred when the powerful eunuch Wei Zhongxian controlled the court.[62] By invoking them, Huang raises the alarm and warns the emperor that *duoqing* orders themselves signify chaos and decline. Officials who followed *duoqing* orders were all doomed men. The religious tone of such discussion about the ethics of *zhongxiao*, resounding in Huang's frequent references to the Confucian classics—in particular the *Classic of Filial Piety* and the *Book of Change* (Zhou Yi)—in his memorials,[63] reflected the cosmological significance attached to *zhongxiao* by late-Ming Confucian scholars. It was meant to enhance the impact of his rhetoric.

Huang Daozhou's employment of *zhongxiao* language in this personnel debate was quite powerful. But he and the Donglin-Fushe camp faced a strong rival. His opponent, Yang Sichang, had proved himself to be a paragon of filiality and a loyal official. Did the competition between Huang and Yang represent two traditions of interpreting *zhongxiao*? It has been suggested that, whereas Huang's privileging of filial piety followed the thought of Confucius, Mencius, and the "Sagely Governing" (Sheng zhi) chapter of the *Classic of Filial Piety*,[64] Yang's emphasis on loyalty over filial piety drew on Xunzi, Han Feizi, and other chapters in the *Classic of Filial Piety*.[65] This interpretation is helpful to an extent but risks reducing the debate between Huang and Yang to a philosophical one. In fact, Yang had demonstrated that fulfilling his filial duty had been the very motivation behind his suspension of mourning and compliance with the emperor's order.

Yang's father, Yang He (d. 1635), had once been the emperor's most trusted official. The senior Yang's missteps in dealing with rebels had serious military consequences, and he was arrested, imprisoned, and then exiled to a remote garrison, where he eventually died of an illness.[66] He was saved from the death penalty only because his filial son Sichang begged to be allowed to die in his father's place.[67] Yang Sichang thus framed his loyalty in relation to a particular form of filial devotion, a desire to redeem the Yang family honor and repay the emperor's trust. Importantly, in addition to highlighting his own acts of *zhongxiao*, in his memorials, Yang also discussed the *duoqing* precedents in Ming history that Huang had depicted as either unsuitable for comparison or inauspicious. Although Yang acknowledged the legitimacy of these *duoqing* precedents, he repeatedly expressed his reluctance to follow them.[68]

Whose views and practices of *zhongxiao* were sincere, authentic, and proper? The Chongzhen emperor had in front of him these two self-proclaimed loyal and filial men who accused each other of "misunderstanding" and "misrepresenting" *zhongxiao* ethics. Both had demonstrated a strong sense of loyalty and filial devotion, yet each accused the other of not following these principles. They even invoked the same historical references of *duoqing* in posturing as loyal officials and filial sons, albeit with different interpretations. Their stances were nothing out of the ordinary in the long history of *zhongxiao* polemics. In the next phase of the confrontation, which took place in front of the emperor and soon circulated among the literati reading public, they engaged in a lively performance of their respective *zhongxiao* commitments.

At the public debate ordered by the emperor, Yang Sichang opened by accusing Huang of failing to understand *zhongxiao*. He cited Huang's old memorial "My Seven Defects" and suggested that Huang steer clear of talking about filial piety, since in his memorial he had claimed he was "not as good as Zheng Man" (*buru Zheng Man*), which clearly indicated poor judgment and a problematic application of the *zhongxiao* principle.[69] Huang retorted that he had attacked Yang in order to defend Confucian ethics; he had always followed the taboo against speaking of others' moral defects. Huang portrayed himself as the more authentic moral paragon: He reminded the emperor that he had fulfilled his filial duty by building his parents' tombs with his own two hands. He claimed that, as a filial son, he simply could not tolerate any failure to fulfill the mandated rituals of mourning.[70]

Building on his claim to filial exemplariness, Huang then presented a long argument about why relieving Yang of the responsibility to mourn his parents at home was dangerous. According to his logic, Yang's return to office, a new promotion, and the proposed appointment of his subordinate Chen Xinjia would set in motion a chain reaction of moral failures culminating in a potential total collapse of the moral-cosmological order of the Ming. Huang's line of argument went as follows: When the *duoqing* precedents established for dealing with urgent military situations were applied so that Yang could serve at the frontier, it was acceptable, though undesirable. But as the chief official of the Board of War, he should not have violated mourning norms. After the court struck a compromise between principle and reality in order to accommodate the need for Yang's leadership as head of the Board of War, Yang should have turned down the next promotion to the Grand Secretariat. Even if a further exception could be made for Yang's entry into the Grand Secretariat, it was absolutely unacceptable for Yang to bring in Chen Xinjia, whose promotion also violated mourning rules. All these ethical violations would amount to a horrific scenario, a "world of *duoqing*" (*duoqing shijie*).[71]

This reasoning and rhetoric lacked political, intellectual, and rhetorical consistency. It sounded crooked to the emperor and only confirmed his suspicion that the Donglin-Fushe community conspired in opposition to his personnel choices in an attempt to install their own men in key government positions. Two years earlier, when the emperor had promoted Yang via the *duoqing*, Huang did not persist in his opposition, nor did he and the Fushe publicly echo each other within and outside the capital. What had emboldened Huang so much this time? The emperor mockingly replied that factionalist officials resorted to moral preaching when they in fact lacked a deep understanding of Confucian ethics.[72]

Although the emperor did not question the extraordinary displays of filial commitment by Huang and other Donglin-Fushe figures, he still challenged Huang's self-contradiction by invoking the damaging evidence against Zheng Man. Referring to the sensational literary accounts of Zheng's ethical violations, he excoriated Zheng as "having abandoned all the Five Cardinal Relations" (*Wulun jin jue*).[73] He claimed furthermore: "Lower-level staffers understand public opinion. Officials don't know what public opinion is!"[74] By saying this, the emperor dismissed the "public opinion" raised by Huang and the Fushe-Donglin community as pure factionalist slander.

In response, Huang Daozhou quoted *The Analects* as proof that he was not driven by a factional agenda. He stated that the memorial "My Seven Defects" did not say that he was "not as good as Zheng Man." Rather, he pointed out, the original language in the memorial read that his "literary skill was not as good as Zheng Man's" (*Chen wei wenzhang buru Zheng Man*).[75] He then likened his admiration for Zheng to Confucius's praise for Zaiyu: "Confucius himself said, 'My communication skills are not as good as Zaiyu's'" (*Kongzi zi yun ciling wu buru Zaiyu*).[76]

Huang's reference to Confucius and Zaiyu turned out to be a terrible choice. Zaiyu was one of Confucius's disciples. The master may have recognized him for his communication skills,[77] but *The Analects* also contains another rather unpleasant conversation in which Confucius is annoyed by Zaiyu's rejection of the three-year mourning observance for deceased parents.[78] By this reference, Huang sounded as if he was admitting that Zheng Man, like Zaiyu, was indeed unfilial, but that he—like Confucius—still recognized the unfilial man's other talents. Further, the parallel drawn by Huang between his attitude toward Zheng and Confucius's toward Zaiyu was seen as hubristic. How could Huang liken himself to Confucius? The emperor parried Huang's reference to Confucius's recognition of Zaiyu with a reference to Confucius's decision to execute the evil official Shaozheng Mao, suggesting that he himself, as sagacious as Confucius, had made a correct moral judgment in punishing the unfilial Zheng Man.[79]

Huang failed to outshine his political rivals in either the debates or the moral contest. He also proved inadequate when negotiating with the emperor through classical references. This famous audience about *zhongxiao* ended with a new demotion for him. But, by declaring he was "returning to his parents' tombs," Huang immediately turned the demotion into another demonstration of his filial piety. During this trip home, he remained in Jiangnan for some time and lectured at a local academy, where he enjoyed the enthusiastic companionship of Fushe scholars. His posturing as a filial son appeared so triumphant that neither his humiliation in the court debates nor his demotion could shake his image as a moral paragon or his popularity.

These three court debates that took place between Chongzhen 9 and 11 (1636–38) over officials' loyalty, filial piety, and friendship demonstrate that Huang's image as a champion of *zhongxiao* had become consolidated through his persistent presentation of sincere filial pursuits, his copious references to Confucian classics, and his creative interpretation of historical precedents. More important to our purpose here, however, these debates shed light on the weakness of a Donglin-Fushe leadership based on an ineffective mix of moral claims and celebrity appeal.

As the foregoing discussion has revealed, Huang was a poor spokesman and political negotiator for the Donglin. His communication skills were inadequate and even inept. He focused too much on his own reputation as a filial paragon, a pedestal on which he continued to be placed by the Donglin-Fushe community. Still, Huang's supporters and fans in and outside the court rallied to the rhetoric of *zhongxiao* and stood behind Huang's moral stature. By suppressing defectors who challenged Huang and creating distance between Huang and the allegedly corrupt Zheng Man, they played an important part in sustaining Huang's celebrity appeal as a *zhongxiao* exemplar. Advocating for Huang's promotion to high government position was an expedient but irresponsible move on the part of the

Donglin-Fushe community. It only deepened the emperor's suspicion of their factionalism.

Meanwhile, the more Huang's political opponents challenged his understanding and practice of *zhongxiao*, the harder he strove to prove that his *zhongxiao* pursuit was sincere, profound beyond any doubt. In his next trip between the court and the family tombs, he further authenticated his image as a moral paragon, this time through his use of the *Classic of Filial Piety* as a ritual trope. By using body and brush to physically display the very process of self-cultivation and authenticate his moral accomplishment, Huang once again delivered an impeccable *zhongxiao* image, one that became well known even among the common people.

ZHONGXIAO IN INK AND BLOOD

By the time Huang Daozhou learned about Zheng Man's execution in Chongzhen 12 (1639), he had already returned home to "attend to the tombs." Before his departure from the capital, he had begun to compile the *Collection of Works on the Classic of Filial Piety* (*Xiaojing da zhuan*) in the fall of Chongzhen 11 (1638), right around the time of his last court debate.[80] This project permitted him to express his hope that the emperor would realize the true meaning of "governing with filial piety." In retirement, Huang continued working on the compilation and also lectured to his students on this classic.

In Chongzhen 13 (1640), the provincial official Xie Xuelong (1585–1645) memorialized that Huang was an outstanding official and should be called back to serve. The emperor immediately interpreted this move as factional. In response, he had Xie, Huang, and several others brought to Beijing and thrown into prison. There, Huang suffered eighty lashes.[81] That punishment nearly killed him and left him partly paralyzed. During imprisonment, Huang began to hand copy the *Classic of Filial Piety*. Since he was already famous as a calligrapher, the prison staff took copies out and sold them for good prices. It was said that he copied the classic 120 times.[82] In the physical reproduction of this Confucian classic, his embodiment of *zhongxiao* was further reinforced.

Art historians have pointed out that Huang was able to mount a highly publicized political protest with this calligraphic performance, one that showed his resolve and rallied public moral support.[83] From this act of devotion, Huang also came to realize the efficacy of calligraphy as a means of spreading Confucian teachings.[84] His choice of format and style manifested that consciousness. Whereas his calligraphic presentations on social occasions were often produced on large scrolls, a format that prioritized self-expression,[85] he produced the *Classic of Filial Piety* mainly in small pamphlets using regular script (*kaishu*), a calligraphic style that would render the text more accessible.[86]

Huang Daozhou was a renowned calligrapher and Confucian scholar, and his repeated inscriptions of this text in prison embodied the ethics of *zhongxiao* in multiple dimensions and produced the strongest possible public impression. Above all, his actions reflected contemporary ritualistic approaches to moral cultivation, which met the literati needs to promote Confucianism in their lives more effectively and creatively. Rituals had symbolic and performative advantages as a mode of communication in political and social spaces.[87] Further, reciting and copying the *Classic of Filial Piety*, as well as meditating on it, had become important forms of literati self-cultivation.[88]

Efforts to promote the ideology and practice of "governing with filial piety" reached new heights in the late sixteenth century. The revival of the *Classic of Filial Piety* in the sixteenth and seventeenth centuries, when the literati re-elevated it from the status of a moral textbook for women and children to a sophisticated work of political philosophy and a ritual trope, involved more than promotion of a virtue or mere rhetoric. The literati treated this work and the notion of "governing with filial piety" as the ultimate Confucian wisdom, a means of self-cultivation and self-expression, and "a way of communicating with a higher authority."[89] In sum, as the *Classic of Filial Piety* assumed unprecedented significance and became a focus of Confucian intellectual, didactic, and ritual practices among literati, Huang's calligraphic reproduction of this text was a wise choice.

Significantly, Huang carefully numbered many of the copies he made in prison (fig. 3.2). This numbering, or serialization, of the copies combined documentary, didactic, and ritual purposes creatively. First, a community of participants and observers of a spectacle formed and gradually expanded as these numbered copies trickled out of his prison cell into the public domain. Second, serialization allowed the public to witness this exemplar's persistent and strenuous efforts at self-cultivation as an ongoing process that engaged his mind, brushwork, and body. This process, which culminated in Huang's use of his own blood as ink to make the last of the 120 copies, was a live

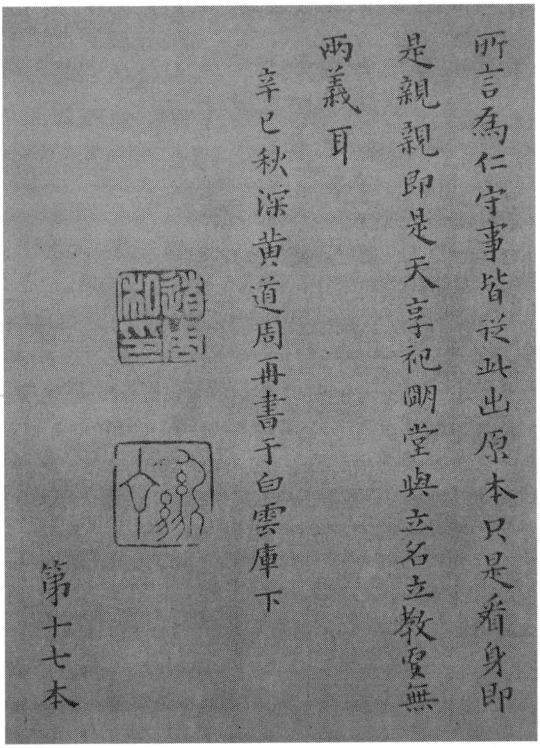

Figure 3.2. Last page of *Xiaokai Xiaojing ce*, numbered 17, made in 1641. From Zheng Wei, *Huang Daozhou moji daguan.*

performance for pursuing *zhongxiao*.[90] The use of blood for the final copy signaled the successful completion of a multidimensional ritual event and a personal journey. Huang's rich display of moral action and the very process of moral cultivation through the repeated hand copying of the classic illustrate the late-Ming cultural fascination with the novel and the extreme.[91] In fact, the power of blood writing as a ritualized program derived partly from its extreme nature.[92]

Given Huang's fame as both an erudite Confucian scholar and a calligrapher known for his immense interest in experimenting with archaic and unusual characters in order to express intellectual concerns, his audience could and would look for deep connections between his calligraphy, the meaning of the text, and his physical and mental condition during his imprisonment.[93] For instance, in one of the unnumbered copies he made in prison, Huang compared the various known editions of the classic and explains his decision to include or exclude certain words.[94] This copy itself would have been treated as a piece of scholarship on *zhongxiao*.

Huang Daozhou's efforts were replicated and thus reinforced by his wife, Cai Yuqing, an educated woman who had a demonstrated interest in politics.[95] She imitated Huang's handwriting and made and sold many copies of the *Classic of Filial Piety* in his name while he was in prison. It was said that Cai always signed her works with her husband's name, because she believed that it would not be proper to disseminate a woman's name.[96] By closely imitating Huang's calligraphy, Cai attempted not only to demonstrate her wifely virtue but also to augment Huang's political undertaking.[97] It should be stressed that by displaying a perfect combination of female talent and virtue, a main concern in seventeenth-century gender discourse,[98] Cai *completed* her husband's image as an impeccable Confucian exemplar. The fact that she not only imitated her husband's calligraphic style but also had the same interest in artistic experimentation with unusual Chinese characters testifies to their shared determination to take extreme measures to perfect Huang's public image.[99]

Huang Daozhou's celebrity appeal did deliver some political results, but again this case was not a straightforward instance of moral persuasion. In Chongzhen 15 (1642), the emperor not only pardoned Huang but also ordered his official status restored. It was said that several officials mentioned Huang's copying of the *Classic of Filial Piety* to the emperor and helped secure Huang's release.[100] This incident should not be interpreted too literally, however. At the time, the factional configuration had changed once again. In Chongzhen 14 (1641), Yang Sichang killed himself in despair over his unsuccessful campaigns against the rebels. The Donglin-Fushe community struck a deal with the former grand secretary Zhou Yanru (1593–1644) and engineered the reinstatement of this corrupt official, with whom they believed they could build a powerful alliance. Therefore, it is more accurate to view Huang's release as a compromise between the emperor and the Donglin-Fushe community, even though it was readily publicized by his fans and seen by later historians as imperial recognition of his sincere *zhongxiao* pursuits. The emperor also benefitted from endorsing this perception, of course. Huang's moral image hence served as a vehicle of negotiation for the various parties.

Fushe scholars outside the government put their own spin on Huang's release. Nanjing literati society, dominated by the Fushe, hailed Huang as a true celebrity. When news arrived that the emperor had ordered

Huang's reappointment, they gathered and wrote poems in celebration. Some of these explicitly voiced the expectation that Huang would be promoted to the position of grand secretary, even though Huang had not demonstrated any talent in administrative or military spheres.[101] Additionally, as mentioned earlier, the local literati enjoyed talking about the image of Huang getting around Nanjing with a walking stick, sharing it with visitors, and disseminating it to other parts of the empire.

Few in late-Ming politics appear to have mastered *zhongxiao* ethics more thoroughly than Huang Daozhou. He earned his celebrity status through multidimensional moral image-making at the intersection of everyday life and politics, in scholarship, policy debates, travel, art, and writing, all of which transformed his life into a *zhongxiao* spectacle and impressed his audiences in and outside the capital. Huang's significance does not lie in whether he was more filial and loyal than most of his colleagues or whether he represented moral heroism, victimization by evil men and imperial autocracy, or the seventeenth-century turn to conservatism. Rather, his story illustrates the complicated political, cultural, religious, and social factors that contributed to making officials' moral images central to political processes.

In the second half of the Chongzhen reign, Donglin-Fushe officials' need for a popular leader met literati society's fascination with the sensational. They found their candidate in Huang Daozhou. Huang's emergence as a *zhongxiao* celebrity reflects the three factors that were shaping late-Ming image politics: political volatility, print culture, and diverse approaches to Confucian moral-cultivation. However, these same conditions empowered his rivals as well. While Huang's fame as a moral exemplar soared, his rivals successfully challenged his understanding and practice of *zhongxiao*. Although he garnered enthusiastic support, that support was based less on his administrative and political acumen than on his celebrity appeal. The Donglin-Fushe community's attempt to impose its version of "public consensus" on the court and install Huang in the Grand Secretariat ultimately proved detrimental to their factional interests.

Does Huang Daozhou then prove the generalization that Confucian moralizing only encouraged hypocrisy and prevented officials from taking care of the real issues? We cannot reach a simple conclusion. In fact, Huang's deployment of *zhongxiao* rhetoric produced few political victories precisely because this rhetoric, first and foremost, was a means of negotiation. Further, our seventeenth-century subjects did not pretend that moral issues were not political issues; the separation of the two is a modern illusion. To the contrary, these debates forced them to reflect on their behavior as officials and deepen their search for better ways of fulfilling both public and familial roles. Huang could not win high position or a policy debate just by displaying his moral perfection, nor do we have evidence that had these men not spent time negotiating politics through the language of Confucian ethics, they would have found "real" solutions to the myriad problems faced by the Ming empire in the 1630s and 1640s.

What we can argue is that print culture, urbanization, expanded social networks, and celebrity culture, phenomena that historians often associate with the emergence of modernity, further tangled politics and morality in the early modern Chinese context. The language of Confucian ethics helped officials adapt and negotiate. Therefore, rather than deriving from a unitary, eternal Confucian moralism, Huang's failures—and those of the Donglin-Fushe—were the result of this community's poor strategic choices.

During the Ming-Qing transition, scholars made persistent reference to Huang Daozhao's keen interest in *zhongxiao* ethics and loyalist martyrdom, thereby further cementing his image as a Confucian exemplar. This image has indeed lingered. Since 1646, the year of his death, eulogies celebrating his rectitude have appeared in the writings of generations of historians. Huang earned the most glowing praise, posthumously, from the Qing state, the dynasty against which he fought to his death. After the Manchus had consolidated their rule, the Qianlong emperor (r. 1736–95) named Huang "a perfect man of his era" (*yidai wanren*).[102]

At the same time, some of Huang's former Ming colleagues and even some supporters, who had performed filial piety dutifully and served both the Ming and Qing courts diligently, were entered into the notorious *Biographies of Twice-Serving Officials* (*Erchen zhuan*), which was also compiled under the Qianlong emperor's patronage. Due to their failure to remain loyal to the Ming, their life experiences have been simplified or distorted, and they have been reimagined as examples of a lack of moral rectitude. Although Huang was already widely recognized as an extraordinary symbol of *zhongxiao* in the late Ming, it was the turncoat figure, the historical Other, who helped elevate him to become "a perfect man of his era."

INTERLUDE

A Moral Tale of Two Cities, 1644–1645

Beijing and Nanjing

Huang Daozhou, Yang Sichang, and the Chongzhen emperor all died for the Ming. In 1641, Yang killed himself in despair because of his unsuccessful campaigns against the rebels. In 1646, having suffered a disastrous military defeat, Huang, now grand secretary of the Longwu Southern Ming court and head of a poorly coordinated northern expedition, refused to surrender to the Qing and was executed.

In the years between Yang's suicide and Huang's martyrdom, the empire went through its most tumultuous period and changed rulers a few times. On Chongzhen 17/3/19 (April 25, 1644), rebels led by Li Zicheng (1606–1645) sacked the capital. The Chongzhen emperor hanged himself at Coal Hill. The rebels and their Shun regime were soon driven out of Beijing by the Manchus. In those months, many still imagined that the Qing might not be here to stay, while others hoped that with a Southern Ming émigré court newly established in Nanjing, the Ming could be restored or at least retain the territories in the south. But Qing troops quickly shattered Ming defenses in Jiangnan and their wishful thinking as well. The city of Nanjing surrendered in Shunzhi 2/5 (1645).

The year between the fall of Beijing and the surrender of Nanjing was particularly chaotic. A violent rupture in political chronology and everyday life, this year constitutes an interlude that is indispensable to understanding seventeenth-century image politics. Not only was attention to officials' moral images both widespread and acute, but that intensified focus generated stories with which political figures engaged the new power negotiations in the early Qing dynasty.

Friends and colleagues in Beijing were quickly split into two different worlds, one of martyrs and the other of survivors, as the political landscape swiftly changed in the north. For most officials, the decision to die by suicide and the determination to undertake it were not simply a matter of one's mental strength and loyalty to the Ming. Contingency, multiple responsibilities, and the desire to live combined to complicate the course of their actions. The struggles of those fighting factional battles in Nanjing were as intense and complex as the struggles of those trapped in Beijing. In addition, once they discovered that persecutions targeting "disloyal officials" (*nichen*) were under way everywhere, officials who had fled from Beijing to Nanjing then fled from Nanjing to somewhere else.

Until now, modern historians—following the narrative established by Qing literati—have mainly presented two opposing views regarding the moral performance of Han officials during this dynastic change. Whereas some claim that the late-Ming moral decline is manifest in the high percentage of officials who did not commit suicide, others emphasize many officials' dazzling displays of moral heroism.[1] But only when we abandon a narrowly defined notion of "loyalists" can we gain a deeper understanding of the broader struggles and trends that shaped the identities and actions of these men during this time.[2]

In order to make sense of this period of chaos in the context of seventeenth-century image politics, one has to turn a critical but sympathetic eye to the layered accounts of the moral-political performance of the disloyal official that were produced and circulated by the officials themselves, their friends, factional rivals, and contemporary observers. Precisely because Confucian ethical ideals such as loyalty and filial piety had multiple and flexible meanings, they served as a language of political communication and were used to negotiate survival or initiate persecutions. The myriad versions of the disloyal official created by the loyalists, factionalists, surviving officials, and even martyrs all served specific purposes and shaped the evolving crisis within and between the two former Ming capitals. They also reflected the political, social, and cultural dynamics, such as factionalism, literati interest in filial rituals, the culture of publicity, and sensationalism, that had conditioned officials' self-expression, behavior, and experience in the late Ming.

BEIJING: HOW NOT TO APPEAR DISLOYAL

With the situation in the north looking abysmal in the last months of the Chongzhen reign, many officials suddenly had to contemplate a real, urgent question: How could they display loyalty *and* survive in the event of a dynastic change?

In Beijing, these men had endured anxiety and fear on multiple fronts for some time. In Chongzhen 16/7 (1643), the arrival of autumn finally reined in a devastating plague that had run rampant in the capital since the beginning of the year. The plague had already wiped out a huge portion of the population and was but one of many disasters that struck that year. It significantly weakened the defense of Beijing as both rebel troops and Qing forces were rapidly devouring northern Ming territories.[3]

Around this time, a number of political earthquakes occurred, too. In particular, the political "coalition" orchestrated by the Donglin-Fushe community and the newly reinstated Grand Secretary Zhou Yanru ended with the arrest of Zhou and the Fushe power broker Wu Changshi (d. 1644) when details of their corruption came to light. Both were executed.[4] No one knew how the various political camps would realign. Natural disasters, rebellions, and the Manchu threat heaped pressure on mingled loyalties and competing interests among the ruling elite. As factional struggles had become entwined with social, economic, and personal relationships, comprehensive political reconciliation seemed as unlikely as a sudden reversal of the Little Ice Age.[5] The perfect storm had formed.

At one of the last court audiences before the fall of Beijing, the emperor tried to decide whether he should temporarily leave the capital. Factional bickering stalled the conversation. Some officials accused others of disloyalty for urging the emperor to leave and tempting him to abandon his responsibilities to the people. This rhetoric was so powerful that the emperor reluctantly gave up the idea of fleeing.[6] He was trapped, helpless and desperate.

Finally, on Chongzhen 17/3/19, upon learning that the rebels had entered Beijing and were quickly approaching the Forbidden City, the emperor, accompanied by only one eunuch, dashed out of the northern gate, climbed a hill, and hanged himself from a tree. On his white robe, the emperor wrote these lines: "My inadequate virtues and weak flesh have invited punishment from Heaven. Now treacherous rebels are invading the capital. My officials have caused all this! I must die, but I am ashamed to face my ancestors. Therefore, I take off my crown and cover my face with my hair. Rebels! You can dismember my body, but do not hurt my people."[7] Recorded at the close of the official Ming history, the Chongzhen emperor's final words show that he blamed the fall of the dynasty on his officials' incompetence and factionalism. For him, the disloyal officials were self-righteous factionalists. Later, the literati would indeed reiterate this characterization of disloyalty in their historical works.

The emperor's impeccable performance in his final moments constituted a last challenge to his officials. By his suicide, he fulfilled his role as moral example for the empire and claimed the highest moral ground. To his satisfaction, before his suicide, the empress also killed herself, and the emperor conducted some killing himself to make sure no dishonor would be brought on the imperial family:

> [His Majesty] sent for his eldest daughter. They wept together. His Majesty wanted to kill the princess but hesitated for quite a while. Then all of a sudden he jumped up and slashed her twice. The princess raised an arm to defend herself, and the arm was cut off. She fainted on the floor. Then His Majesty began to search the palaces. First he saw that the empress had already hanged herself. Then he went to the Western Palace. Imperial Consort Yuan did not seem to want to commit suicide, so His Majesty slew her with three strokes. . . . Then he sent for the other imperial consorts who had served him in bed and killed all of them.[8]

The emperor's actions were a somber reminder to officials that they would be judged by their contemporaries and literati historians. Many of those around the capital carried out killings like those in the imperial palaces. In some cases, wives and concubines killed themselves when their husbands died; in others, officials killed their women before completing their martyrdom, as their emperor had done.[9]

The arrangements made by Yang Shicong (1567–1648), an official who maintained close ties with many Donglin-Fushe figures, are revealing. Yang was captured by the rebels soon after they entered Beijing and put under house arrest. He told his wife and two concubines: "I would not have been here without His Majesty's favor. Therefore I must die. *I will follow in the steps of His Majesty, and you three the late empress.*" He threw his six-year-old daughter into a well and then swallowed poison. His wife and two concubines attempted to hang themselves. But their suicide attempts were discovered by the rebel guards. Yang and his wife were rescued. The two concubines, however, died.[10] Though not entirely successful and hard to verify, Yang nonetheless showed he was not disloyal by trying to replicate the heroic actions of the martyred emperor. Such actions, as well as accounts of them that circulated at the time, pushed officials' gendered moral performance to the center of the unfolding dynastic crisis.

The fear of projecting a disloyal image, just like the ideal of martyrdom, had been planted deep in officials' consciousness. Avoiding the appearance of disloyalty could mean different things, depending on the circumstances, even in dire moments. It shaped officials' actions in nuanced ways. Of importance here is not the degree to which these accounts describe the "true" feelings and intentions of officials who claimed to have attempted suicide, but how these actions and accounts helped officials demonstrate at the time that they were *not disloyal.*

It was difficult for the survivors to authenticate loyalty. How could one verify that a failed suicide actually took place? Stories of failed suicides would be scrutinized by others. So when Yang and his wife fled to the Southern Ming capital, like other survivor officials who managed to escape, they had to substantiate their claim that they had not betrayed the Ming. At the time, tensions ran high and local society engaged in spontaneous campaigns against the families of allegedly disloyal officials. Survivor officials who made it to the south were accused of faking loyalty as a cover for their cowardice or for secret spying missions.[11] Print material, such as proclamations, tabloid papers, and books, to which the literati reading public resorted to get quick access to the latest news about the situation in Beijing, helped disseminate information but also intensified suspicions.[12] For instance, stories about the disloyal behavior of the official Zhou Zhong (d. 1644) in Beijing were printed and spread in Nanjing.[13] Officials trapped in Beijing had anticipated this and accordingly adjusted their expectations.

Further, the officials who committed suicide and those who survived in Beijing might not have had the straightforwardly opposite understandings of disloyalty as one would assume. While some martyrs adamantly embraced a glorious death for themselves as demonstration of their loyalty, they might not have expected their colleague-friends to carry out more than the minimum. The official Meng Zhaoxiang (*jinshi* 1622) was supervising the defense of the southern city wall of Beijing when he learned that the rebels had entered the inner city. He promptly committed suicide.[14] However, he had not demanded that others do the same. Just days before, Meng's disciple, the official Xiong Wenju (1595–1668), paid him a visit and asked what he should do in the event the capital was taken. Meng replied: "No need to discuss such a topic now. We each should make our own decisions. . . . You have aged parents far away and you are not holding a key position in the government. So you have more options."[15]

Meng certainly made his own decision. Did Meng's answer help his disciple make his? It did point out an alternative path for Xiong that would not make him appear disloyal. This conversation is a vivid illustration of the moral exercises in which officials had been engaging for some time even before the capital fell. They contemplated how their moral performance could best meet their various political, familial, and personal obligations. Their ultimate actions in the moment of crisis are reflections of these ongoing ruminations.

Xiong Wenju also discussed this issue with his own disciple, Gong Dingzi. As mentioned earlier, Gong was imprisoned by the Chongzhen emperor for impeaching certain high-ranking officials. He got out of prison just two months before the rebel army captured Beijing. Gong had sustained injuries in prison, and the emperor had taken away his official status. While waiting for his wounds to heal, he had little sense of what his career prospects might be. At this point, Gong and his concubine Gu Mei's social circle consisted mostly of Fushe friends such as Fang Yizhi and, through his mentor Xiong Wenju (also a Fushe member), a few other officials originally from Jiangxi. Fang's wife, concubine, and children were with him in Beijing, while Gong and his Jiangxi friends were accompanied by their concubines.[16] As these men gathered to discuss the situation, they also had to consider its potential impact on the women in their households and their families in the south.

As it happened, when the fall of Beijing did become reality, Xiong Wenju and Gong Dingzi attempted suicide but failed. Xiong claimed that he twice tried to kill himself but was rescued. He mentioned in personal correspondence, poems, and even a public letter that a disciple and another official, who rescued and prevented Xiong from trying again, witnessed his attempts.[17] In various media, too, Gong recorded that he and Gu Mei threw themselves into a well but that their neighbors pulled them out.[18] He did not give any witness names. However, separated from his parents in Hefei (in modern-day Anhui), this pious Buddhist documented his suicide attempt in the Buddhist prayers he composed for the safety of his parents during those days of terror. The genre of prayer lends credibility to this confession despite the vagueness of the phrase "throwing ourselves into a well." It could be read as a thwarted attempt, meaning that they actually jumped into the well but were rescued, or represent many other, less heroic-looking actions. Regardless of how accurate the details of these men's stories may be, such accounts show that the officials made gestures toward suicide.

If we choose not to dismiss such survivors' accounts as formulaic narratives of feigned loyalty or retroactive self-justification,[19] we can see that their suicidal gestures were a natural course of action shaped by their intense struggle between aspiring to make a heroic display of loyalty and taking action simply to avoid appearing disloyal. These gestures—and inherent moral ambiguity in them—were invoked frequently in contemporary political negotiations and became an integral part of ongoing political processes.

Therefore, in those months in 1644, not only did martyrs have different understandings of the "disloyal official," but the survivors' gestures toward suicide and accounts of their actions also blurred the dichotomy of disloyalty and loyalty. Precisely because the term *disloyal official* did not have a stable meaning, survivors could anticipate and eventually attempt to discard the mantle of disloyalty: they did so by stressing the masculine virtues by which they could authenticate their loyalty and defy their persecutors.

Fang Yizhi succeeded in fleeing south as the rebel regime was retreating from Beijing westward, only to face the factional persecution of Donglin-Fushe figures led by Ruan Dacheng at the Southern Ming Hongguang court. He narrowly escaped Nanjing as well. As a political fugitive constantly on the run and feeling wronged, he wrote to acquaintances in defense of his loyalty. In a letter to a Fushe friend Li Wen, who remained trapped in Beijing, he complained bitterly: "A chaste woman is smeared as a licentious woman! This is like the land sinking to the bottom of the sea. How unjust!"[20] To a loyalist Fushe friend in Jiangnan, he used the same analogy: "Once Ruan Dacheng regained power, the chaste woman was slandered as licentious! This is really unjust! Unjust!"[21]

These letters revealed Fang's frustration and anxiety. When he fled Beijing, he even left behind his wife and children. In a poem composed after his flight, he emotionally recalled the painful departure:

> Wife and children knelt and wept,
> "Stay here a while together!

Heaven and earth are upside down.
Can your journey be safe?"
"My destiny is to die a thousand deaths
To avenge disgrace on the battlefield.
Once out of the tiger's lair
I'll follow the back roads."
Reunion seems so far away;
It's dusk, the sun is sinking in the west.
She cried at my leaving her,
Seizing a knife to stab herself in the heart.
"If you die, how will it help?
Look after our children!
After many changes in the world
Maybe you'll see me again, an old man."
I knew this was good-bye forever,
A wife separated from her husband.
Said only "I will miss you!"
And swallowing my sobs, I waved farewell.[22]

These lines vividly portray a model Confucian official, apparently prioritizing political duty over family, while his wife, determined to be chaste and devoted to him, contemplated committing suicide but was persuaded to give up the idea for the sake of their children. This is exactly how a morally exemplary official wanted to be perceived.

A comparison of Fang's farewell poem and Xiong Wenju's depiction of his own attempt to flee Beijing sheds further light on how a manly appearance was crucial to survivors' self-defense against accusations of disloyalty. Xiong's account describes how he, Gong Dingzi, and Tu Bihong (d. 1645), another Jiangxi native, tried to leave, and the tremendous hardships they suffered. His description gives the impression that the three officials left their women and families behind,[23] but in reality, they moved with their women and other family members. Xiong's secretary, Xu Yingfen, later specifically recalled that during their flight, Gu Mei stopped frequently to pick up dirt and splotch her beautiful face in order to avoid attracting the rebels' attention.[24]

Xiong's selective account of the escape reflects the serious concern that he and his companions would not be seen as sufficiently loyal if they revealed too many details. Strictly speaking, omission of the women from this account does not constitute a lie. Leaving out the experiences of the women who endured the terrors with them must have been painful. However, an explicit admission that they did not leave their women behind would only have reinforced the widespread accusations of their lack of loyalty—they only cared about their women. This self-conscious reflection constituted a deliberate countermeasure against the stereotypical image of the disloyal official.

Similarly, the Fushe activist Chen Mingxia (d. 1654) was not caught after the rebels entered the capital because he accompanied his concubine, a Beijing native, to her home and hid there. He attempted to hang himself upon hearing of the emperor's suicide but was rescued by the concubine's family. So he planned to flee. By accident he ran into a literatus surnamed Wang, an official in Li Zicheng's rebel government. Wang recognized Chen Mingxia, who had given him some food years before when he was poor, and tried to persuade Chen to serve the new regime. Chen begged Wang to let him go. At that time Chen learned that his in-law and colleague Song Zhisheng (1612–1669) had been captured by the rebels and tortured for money. Song claimed he was too poor to pay a ransom and enlisted Chen as a witness. Eventually, Song was released, but somehow rumor now began to circulate that Chen had collaborated with the rebels. Chen even wrote a pamphlet to deny the charges, but he dared not mention all the details, worried about the complexity of the circumstances.[25]

Such intense literary struggle involved in recounting one's escape from Beijing points to the survivor officials' acute awareness of the arbitrary nature of loyalty and disloyalty and the ways in which such awareness helped mold their actions and self-image. In fact, their experiences in the most chaotic days cannot be adequately described with the binary. For example, soon after the fall of Beijing, the rebels were hunting down Ming officials by using the official roster. Gong Dingzi thought that since he had been stripped of official status, he might be able to evade detection and sneak out of the capital. Meanwhile, the rebels tracked down Fang Yizhi and forced him to reveal Gong's whereabouts, which led directly to Gong's arrest. This pained Fang tremendously, for he had failed the ethical ideals of loyalty and friendship and turned his friend into a suspected traitor.[26] Ironically, later, Fang would be admired for being a loyal man while Gong the disloyal official.

After the Manchus defeated Li Zicheng at the Shanhai Pass, the rebels started looting before retreating westward from Beijing toward Shaanxi. With their surveillance significantly loosened, Fang found an opportunity to escape and did not hesitate to leave his family behind with a view to fulfilling the ideal of loyalty. But Gong Dingzi, Xiong Wenju, and Tu Bihong were not so lucky. Due to the extreme chaos and violence in the area, they were able to travel only four kilometers over a span of six days. Then an encounter with some militiamen in a Beijing suburb left them with severe injuries. Hungry and confused, they took shelter in a desolate Buddhist temple. There they learned from an old servant that the Manchus, with the help of Ming forces, had driven Li Zicheng out of Beijing and called upon former Ming officials to attend the Chongzhen emperor's funeral. When Gong, Xiong, and Tu returned to mourn for their martyred emperor, they found themselves trapped.[27] At this point, they had no choice but to accept appointments from the Manchus. Committing suicide now, strictly speaking, could not even be considered an expression of loyalty to the Ming.[28]

To avoid appearing disloyal was difficult for survivor officials to achieve. Indeed, their complicated personal stories and decisions were being simplified by attackers to fit the narratives produced for political persecution and war mobilization; the image of the disloyal official became increasingly clearer. Still, these officials themselves refused to accept the arbitrary labeling and grouping: their different political identities did not prevent them from maintaining their friendships and extending them to the next generation; and they persistently produced accounts of their wartime experiences, resisting the increasingly dominant narrative of the disloyal official (see part 2 in this book).

RIGHTEOUS LITERATI LEADERS IN JIANGNAN

While some survivors struggled to avoid the appearance of disloyalty in the face of the rapid political change in Beijing between the suicide of the Chongzhen emperor and the arrival of the Manchus, stories that stereotyped the "disloyal official" traveled quickly to and around the south, where it affected survivor officials' reputations and families. "Witnesses"—former colleagues who had succeeded in reaching Nanjing—reported to the court what they presented as truthful accounts of these survivor officials. How to tease apart the conflicting narratives surrounding survivor officials' moral performance soon emerged as a major issue in factional struggles.

In the explosive atmosphere of 1644–45, few in the south were seriously concerned about the ins and outs of the survivors' complicated experiences. Many were busy condemning disloyal officials as a strategy for war mobilization and factional infighting. The self-proclaimed righteous literati of Jiangnan led the effort to stigmatize officials detained in Beijing. Such actions directed public attention and anger toward officials' moral images in the moment of dynastic crisis. The accusers were themselves not necessarily motivated by strong loyalism or political insights, though. In fact, much of this posturing was little more than sensational self-aggrandizing spectacles meant to establish their "leadership."

Ten days after the emperor's suicide on Chongzhen 17/3/19, officials and commoners in the south began to hear the news. But it was not until Chongzhen 17/5/4 (June 8, 1644), nearly two months after the fall of Beijing, that the regent, the Prince of Fu, issued an empire-wide mourning order, officially confirming the fall of Beijing.[29] As gossip continued to trickle south, the public's condemnation of men who had allegedly collaborated with the rebels appeared in the form of public proclamations in many places across Jiangnan. These proclamations, written and disseminated in counties and prefectures for the purposes of war mobilization, emphasized the rebels' uncontrollable lust for treasure and women, but they went to much greater lengths to expose the moral corruption of the stranded officials, detailing their deviant lifestyles and the contemptible methods they used to please the rebel leaders. From these proclamations emerged a sharp image of the disloyal official, a figure sadly lacking in Confucian masculine virtues.

The most widely circulated proclamations presented the disloyal official as violating literati-official gender norms and connected these moral defects directly to disloyalty. The "Proclamation Rebuking Turncoat Officials," drafted by the literati in one county, denounced such men by describing their depravity before the fall of Beijing.[30] According to this proclamation, such officials cared only about networking and factionalism; they purloined the people's wealth to support their indulgence in prostitutes and concubines; they and their friends jettisoned statecraft but engaged in vulgar entertainment.[31] Their promiscuity and lack of political integrity were symptomatic of their disloyal behavior upon the fall of Beijing.

Another proclamation, circulated in Changshu County (in modern-day Jiangsu), condemned four of its native sons—Chen Biqian, Shi Min, Zhao Shijin, and Gui Qixian—all of whom held important positions in the metropolitan government in the late Ming. According to the script, these officials' debauchery before the fall of Beijing had anticipated their disloyalty. Shi Min was said to have engaged in intimacy with other men in order to obtain favors and to have exchanged and slept with his friends' wives and concubines. Chen Biqian was said to have habitually used profane language and obsessively gossiped about inner chamber matters, built personal connections through bribery, and shared his bed with both men and women.[32]

The image of the "disloyal official," built on such sensational stereotyping, was used by local literati to stir up public emotion and establish their leadership status. Chen is described in the Changshu County proclamation as "striving to attach himself to the Donglin." In fact, Chen was unmistakably a Donglin-identified figure. He had stood up against the eunuch faction in the Tianqi reign, and his name had appeared on the Donglin blacklists.[33] In the Chongzhen reign, Chen led the Ming army on a series of successful campaigns against rebels in Henan, though he was later penalized for a subordinate's defeat. Before Beijing fell to Li Zicheng, he had been appointed president of the Board of Works. It was said that the Chongzhen emperor once expressed admiration for the moral rectitude of four officials, Wen Zhenmeng, Chen Biqian, Liu Zongzhou, and Huang Daozhou.[34] Being praised together with three iconic Donglin leaders uncontestably affirms Chen's status in the Donglin community. The depiction of Chen's alleged moral corruption, in particular the sensational details presented by the proclamation in support of that image, was meant to stir up emotions and mobilize people for a trial by public opinion. It made the case that this immoral, disloyal official must *not* have been a Donglin.

The author of this piece seems to have been a supporter of the Donglin-Fushe community who assumed his audience was composed of sympathizers invested in the image of moral superiority of this community. According to Feng Menglong, who was collecting and printing information about the north during this time, people in Chen's hometown in Changshu had thought highly of him but felt extremely disappointed at his failure to commit suicide.[35] The author of the proclamation thus freely labeled Chen. The repackaging of Chen's image as that of an immoral man and hence a feigned Donglin exposes the problematic nature of the leadership of such "righteous literati." Their method was easily as damaging as that adopted by the anti-Donglin forces in the Southern Ming government, whose persecution, somewhat ironically, targeted Chen as an evil Donglin factionalist.[36]

In Songjiang County (in modern-day Jiangsu), local literati disseminated similar proclamations in which they condemned the officials

Yang Zhiqi, Zhu Ji, and Yang Rucheng. Two proclamations singled out Yang Rucheng, citing corruption and sexual promiscuity as evidence of disloyalty. They claimed he was a former eunuch factionalist and had willingly surrendered to the rebels. He and his cousin Yang Zhiqi also faced charges of sexual immorality. He was greedy and corrupt, and his whole family was smeared as sexually promiscuous.[37] These officials not only were said to have taken orders from rebel leaders but also allegedly offered their wives and concubines to the rebels. This proclamation was accordingly titled "Rebuking Turncoat Officials Who Surrendered Themselves and Offered Their Wives to the Rebels!"[38]

Alongside the figure of the immoral-disloyal official, the rebel was portrayed as a hooligan from the countryside who became a bloodthirsty rapist-bandit. The disloyal official was slandered for serving as the rebel ruler's subject, and his wife offered sexual service.[39] These statements generally claimed that the rebels spared the turncoat's life because he had offered his women, reinforcing the stereotypical images of the rebels' dangerous masculinity and the disloyal official's lack of Confucian masculine virtues. This reversal of power relations between bumpkin rebels and corrupt elites, brokered through the surrender of the elites' women, put across the menacing inversion of the social hierarchy in a most startling way. In the Confucian philosophy of politics and society, disorder and boundary crossing were considered the gravest threats. The image of the disloyal official in the fallen capital had a powerful impact precisely for this reason.

Playing on widespread fears, such sensationalistic depictions of the disloyal official and a horrifically subverted social hierarchy appeared to be a sound mobilization strategy. These tactics quickly gave rise to local antagonism toward families of the officials who remained in Beijing. Literati and commoners alike in Suzhou plundered and burned the houses of several such officials. In Changshu County, people attacked one official's residence and incinerated effigies of four coffins of three generations of his family. In Haiyan County, one turncoat's home was looted and set alight, and the casket of his deceased father was disinterred and burned. These officials had all been accused and convicted of disloyalty and promiscuity in the court of public opinion at a time of mass hysteria induced by political catastrophe.[40]

The dynastic crisis was thus, to some extent, complicated by media events. Moral attacks aimed at officials caught in Beijing were driven by certain literati's desire for publicity and self-promotion. These fame chasers enjoyed having a forum in which to flaunt their literary skills by drafting and disseminating inflammatory proclamations. The audience also went along with the colorful exaggerations in those accounts.[41]

The early Qing scholar Ji Liuqi (b. 1622), who lived through the transition and documented such events, was so disturbed by what he witnessed that he added a warning to his readers about one particularly provocative proclamation published by the literati in Jiaxing. The rhetoric of the piece was so inflammatory and ferocious that Ji wrote, "It is acceptable to overpraise others, but one should not go overboard with criticism. Such language! Young men would not miss much if they did not read this proclamation. I include it here not to endorse its relentlessness, but rather because it shows an admirable familiarity with historical references. It is a pity that the author only wanted to show off his writing skills and didn't care about the life and death of others!"[42]

This criticism recalls the worries and anxiety that had long persisted among officials in the late Ming. The literati had been manipulating the convenient communication system for their own purposes. By broadcasting irresponsible, sensational information about officials' domestic lives, they threatened their targets' careers and reputations.[43] These 1644–45 proclamations carried on a trend that would eventually lead to fatal consequences in the most chaotic and violent years of the Ming-Qing dynastic transition.

The literati's abuse of public communication at this critical moment raised the stakes of officials' moral images in the Southern Ming court. It turned resistance campaigns into schemes for public humiliation of individual officials and, more importantly, pressured officials in the Nanjing government to launch a divisive project by which to "authenticate" loyalty. Qi Biaojia (1602–1645), governor of the Wusong area and a Donglin associate, did not endorse the excited Fushe activists of Wu County in Suzhou, who crafted inflammatory public posters and mobilized the masses to attack certain officials' residences.[44] Under such inflammatory circumstances, Qi urged the court in Nanjing to take immediate measures to identify officials who most definitely had willingly surrendered to the rebels so that the local literati and commoners would not have excuses for continuing their self-proclaimed righteous campaigns against all officials stranded in Beijing.[45]

Similar abuses occurred in other parts of Ming-controlled territories. Hundreds of kilometers away, in Jiangxi, the official Xiong

Wenju's father was detained in a local prison on the charge that Xiong had collaborated with the rebels. Xiong's teenage son, Xiong Dinghua, went to protest his father's innocence and volunteered to stay in prison in his grandfather's place. The grandfather was released, but due to a chronic disease from which Dinghua suffered, the grandson's health quickly deteriorated due to lack of proper care and treatment. This eventually led to his death.[46]

This family tragedy was but one of many caused by the peculiar situation in the Southern Ming, when local literati "leadership" and the "Case of Traitors' Followers" (*Cong ni an*), a list issued by the court identifying disloyal officials, combined to create a dangerous situation. The Donglin-Fushe officials in Nanjing realized that the self-proclaimed righteous literati were not the only ones who demanded that disloyal officials be rooted out and set apart from the truly loyal ones. They faced similar pressures from their factional rivals at court.

NANJING: THE BATTLE BETWEEN THE PURE ELEMENT AND ITS ENEMIES

In 1644–45, factionalism in the Southern Ming Hongguang government contributed to making officials' moral image central to political processes. The Donglin-Fushe community and its rivals both invoked the connections between officials' (dis)loyalty and moral performance as a language of political struggle and negotiation. To understand how this happened, we must first examine how self-righteous officials tried to meddle in the imperial succession by manipulating the images of two princes.

Painting the Portrait of the Imperial Successor

Confirmation of the Chongzhen emperor's suicide required immediate action in Nanjing, the secondary capital of the Ming. However, responses were hampered as the city became mired in a host of controversies: Which prince was best qualified in terms of lineage to inherit the crown? Which officials should be honored as loyal martyrs and which punished as disloyal collaborators? Should officials formerly associated with the eunuch faction be allowed to serve in the émigré court?[47]

Unfortunately, the Heir Apparent had disappeared, and the Chongzhen emperor's other sons were being held captive in Beijing.

Officials of all camps in Jiangnan, whether in office or in retirement at this point, publicly and privately discussed whether the Prince of Fu (1607–1646) or the Prince of Lu (1608–1646) should be enthroned.[48] In terms of lineage status, the former had the stronger pedigree for inheriting the throne.[49] However, everything about him provoked anxiety among the Donglin officials. His deceased father, the elder Prince of Fu, had been the Wanli emperor's favorite son and the cause of serious discord between the emperor and his officials from the 1580s to 1610s. In the eyes of many pro-Donglin literati, that prolonged and difficult negotiation, known as the "Struggle to Defend the Principle of Imperial Succession" (Zheng Guoben), was one of the defining moments in the birth of the Donglin.[50] Although the Wanli emperor eventually gave up the idea of ignoring the succession rule and designating the Prince of Fu as his Heir Apparent, Donglin-identified officials never let down their guard until the prince died at the hands of rebels in Chongzhen 12 (1641). Now, they were suspicious of his son, the junior Prince of Fu.

Two contrasting images quickly went into circulation in Jiangnan. They depicted a morally corrupt Prince of Fu and a "worthier" Prince of Lu, who was favored by many in the Donglin-Fushe community. Champions of the Prince of Lu claimed that the other prince "had a reputation for lasciviousness, ignorance, and irresponsibility." They cited reasons why the Prince of Fu should not become ruler: greed, promiscuity, alcoholism, lack of filial piety, abuse of subjects, no interest in learning, and improper intervention in legal processes.[51] Simultaneously, these officials asserted the moral exemplariness of the Prince of Lu by whitewashing the facts of his less-than-exemplary lifestyle.[52]

These contrasting representations of the two princes were instrumental not only in the power struggle surrounding the imperial succession but also to the officials' efforts to promote an image of their own moral superiority over their rivals and gain the political upper hand in the Nanjing-based new court. Such efforts resulted in a backlash that had fatal consequences. For example, between the fall of Beijing and the establishment of the Hongguang court, the most powerful man in Jiangnan was Shi Kefa (1601–1645), president of the Board of War in Nanjing. Like his Donglin-Fushe fellows, Shi had favored the Prince of Lu on the grounds that this prince was morally more fit than the Prince of Fu. Shi's professed opposition to enthroning the Prince of Fu would inform their lukewarm relationship ever after. The prince certainly felt disgraced by the widely circulated list of moral charges against him.[53] Shi's *de facto* marginalization after the Prince of Fu was enthroned exemplified the heavy price paid by the Donglin-Fushe camp for meddling in the imperial succession by engaging in a moral smear campaign. Now these officials had to scramble to defend themselves against charges of disloyalty. The seed of their future image troubles had been planted.[54]

The Poster Boy for Disloyal Officials

In the émigré court, factions and factional intrigues returned as soon as appointments were made. The most pressing and sensitive question was whether officials who had been in the eunuch faction should be appointed to government posts. The "pure element" (*qingliu*)[55] argued that since such officials had been named in the "Traitors' Case" (Ni'an) by the late Chongzhen emperor, they therefore should not be reinstalled. Bitter confrontations over the issue meant that old factional divides were quickly revived.

Among the many disagreements, controversy over the appointment of Ruan Dacheng proved the most fatal. Grand Secretary Ma Shiying (d. 1646) had close ties with Ruan and helped him reenter politics. This revived the old animosity between the Donglin and the eunuch faction and presented Ruan with an opportunity to take personal revenge against the Donglin-Fushe members who had relentlessly harassed him in the 1630s. It was in this context that the notorious "Case of Traitors' Followers" took place.

While the "pure element" protested having Ruan as a colleague, the other party, loosely labeled as the associates of Ma-Ruan in many historical records, launched counterattacks. These attacks and counterattacks centered on individual officials' moral performance. Ruan understood that the "pure element" at court had friends and relatives stranded in Beijing who could be portrayed as disloyal. If they hesitated to punish those disloyal officials, then how could they repudiate officials incriminated in the "Traitors' Case" two decades ago? As many contemporaries keenly observed, Ruan and Ma tried to divert attention from Ruan's troublesome past by deliberately confusing the earlier "Traitors' Case" with the new "Case of Traitors' Followers" (Cong ni an). The cases sounded similar but were completely different in nature.

The strategy of highlighting Donglin-Fushe hypocrisy—by stressing the contradiction between their claim to loyalty and their opportunism—added to the already inflammatory rhetoric employed by literati loyalists in Jiangnan. Initially, Ruan stated that in response to the attacks against him based on his appearance in the "Traitors' Case," he should now propose a "Collaborators' Case" (*Shun an*).[56] The Donglin-Fushe officials found themselves in an untenable situation as they were confronted with the agonizing task of articulating a politically sensible stance vis-à-vis the figure of the disloyal-immoral collaborator, a label arguably attributed to their own number or friends. A stark contrast had to be drawn between their public image and that of the disloyal official. Accordingly, some Donglin officials expressed support for the creation of another list, which was eventually known as the "Case of Traitors' Followers."

Ma Shiying's memorial, "Execute the Traitor Officials" (Qing zhu nichen shu) (dated the sixth month of 1644), opened the "Case of Traitors' Followers" and also set the tone for subsequent purges. It pointedly condemned officials who had disguised themselves as "pure elements" in order to earn promotions in the Chongzhen era and asserted that they betrayed the martyred emperor's faith when they surrendered to the rebels. This memorial identified Gong Dingzi, an official who had abandoned loyalty to indulge himself with a concubine, as the epitome of such moral hypocrites.

Like the political rhetoric used against survivor officials in the public proclamations, this memorial reinforced an easily recognizable archetype. Ma asserted: "Many of those who had served the emperor in prestigious positions in the metropolitan bureaucracy, as administrative and censorial officials, and had always posed as upright gentlemen, surrendered to the rebels. . . . After Gong Dingzi surrendered, he always defended himself like this: 'I meant to kill myself, but my concubine would not allow me to do it.' This 'concubine' is Gu Mei, the Nanjing courtesan (*Qinhuai chang*) whom Gu had taken into his household when he was a censor."[57]

It is noteworthy that the last sentences of this passage sound so plausible that these characterizations of Gong and Gu were readily accepted and widely circulated. Gong's relationship with an elite courtesan made them natural suspects for sexual indulgence and disloyalty. Because Gong was identified by some as a Donglin-Fushe figure, Ma Shiying's choice of Gong as the poster boy for disloyal officials was a clever move. Not only would it damage Gong's reputation, but it also by implication created image trouble for the entire Donglin-Fushe collective in Nanjing, which had long prided itself on being the community of the "pure elements."[58]

Many officials became alarmed at the potential harm of such gendered image attacks. Once the court had circulated a tentative list of treacherous officials, the official Li Weiyue expressed strong concerns. He memorialized to argue that the word *ni* (disloyal) should be applied as carefully as *shijie* (unchaste) would be for a woman. "*Officials most cherish their reputations, and labels must be properly given* . . . . If they are not traitors, they should be given only the label they deserve and punished in accordance with evaluation rules. If we call all of them *ni*, we are doing something similar to calling women who have lost their homes but maintained their chastity "unchaste"! That would be most unfair."[59] The analogy of masculine loyalty and female chastity was a familiar one. Li's memorial warned that indiscriminately calling the survivor officials traitors was arbitrary and dangerous because that image was vulnerable to political manipulation. It was an irresponsible label, and officials should avoid applying it recklessly precisely because the state of one's moral image could mean life or death.

Even in the face of such serious doubts and opposition, an imperial order issued in the name of the emperor pressed the Board of Punishments to finalize the list of disloyal officials. It explained its unforgiving attitude and stressed that, "[for] those who offered their daughters and maids [to the rebels], their crimes should be punished with more than imprisonment and labor. The officials have betrayed their country to such a degree that a judgment must be delivered and shown to the people."[60] The language used in the official condemnation of allegedly disloyal officials in Beijing in this list and the negotiations over it mirrored the general political atmosphere in the south at the time. It justified harsher punishments for those who behaved in an "unmanly" fashion by asserting that such immoral-disloyal behavior among survivor officials was especially heinous, echoing the message contained in the proclamations disseminated by the "righteous literati." It is thus not surprising that factionalists on both sides also used gendered ethics to differentiate "disloyal officials" in the Hongguang court.

Differentiating the Disloyal Men in the Nanjing Government

The Nanjing government had been a Donglin-Fushe stronghold since the 1630s.[61] Much of the factional infighting in the Hongguang court naturally aimed to influence official appointments. Unhappy with the initial personnel decisions, some officials launched moral attacks on Donglin-Fushe associates, accusing them of embezzlement and consorting with courtesans. The latter charge was leveled specifically at two officials, Jiang Cai (1607–1673) and Jiang Gai (1614–1653), brothers and Fushe activists, who indeed had been enjoying the pleasures offered by Nanjing's courtesans in the legendary Qinhuai district.[62]

The Donglin-Fushe camp, too, deployed the language of Confucian ethics in its negotiations over personnel choices. In response to the four official recommendations put forth by the official-general Liu Zeqing (d. 1645?), Shi Kefa pointed out that all of the candidates had failed to demonstrate moral rectitude. Shi likely opposed the promotion of these officials because they were known to be close to the former eunuch faction. To avoid sounding factionalist, however, he chose to question their personal moral performance. This proved to be an unwise tactic. One of these officials, Liu Guangdou (1591–1652), had shown himself to be a capable bureaucrat in various positions during his career in the late Ming. In the mid-Chongzhen reign, his career had stalled due to his friendships with former members of the eunuch faction. Now at the Hongguang court, Shi Kefa accused him of indulgence in sensual pleasures.[63] By doing so, Shi provoked strong resentment from the Donglin's rivals.

The Ma-Ruan clique escalated its moral attacks on Donglin-Fushe figures. The most serious, launched by Ruan Dacheng, accused the official Lei Yanzuo (*juren* 1640) of unfiliality and disloyalty. Lei did not hold a particularly prominent status in the Donglin-Fushe community, but he proved a perfect target. First, gossip circulated, portraying him as an unfilial son, a subject to which I will return shortly. Second, he enjoyed a close relationship with Grand Secretary Jiang Yueguang (1584–1649), the most senior Donglin-identified official at the Hongguang court. Echoing Ruan, Ma Shiying instructed Zhu Tonglei, a member of the Ming imperial family, to submit a memorial specifically targeting Jiang.

In this memorial, Zhu listed Jiang's five major crimes. The first two involved issues of disloyalty and were based on rumors that he and Donglin coconspirators had plotted to control the government and the military. The third charge against Jiang was that he covered for disloyal officials in the north. The fourth was bribery, and the fifth was an accusation that he had raped his daughter-in-law.[64] Unwilling to put up with these personal insults, Jiang resigned. The accusations, however, eventually led to an imperial order that his alleged accomplice, the unfilial son Lei Yanzuo, kill himself in prison.[65]

The process of differentiating disloyal officials at the Hongguang court once again tested the validity of Donglin-Fushe claims to moral superiority. Ruan Dacheng's memorial "Condemning the Most Disloyal, Unfilial, and Treacherous Official" (Buzhong buxiao dani yuanxiong shu) accused Lei Yanzuo of ethical violations. First, Ruan maintained that in Chongzhen 8 (1635), when rebels attacked Taihu County (in modern-day Anhui), Lei's home region, Lei and his wife disguised themselves in shabby clothes but dressed his father in nice clothes so the rebels would release them and, instead, torture his father for money. In a second and related accusation, Ruan reported that Lei had plotted with Jiang Yueguang against the emperor during the period when he should have shunned political activities and concentrated on mourning his deceased mother.[66]

Even though the claim that Lei deliberately exposed his father to danger was likely groundless, accusation of Lei's violation of filial rituals was based on the impression that Lei failed to perform the role of a mourning son properly. Discrepancies in the sources prevent us from verifying or refuting the charges against Lei. According to the Taihu gazetteer, in Chongzhen 16 (1643), when his mother died, Lei firmly rejected his superior's attempt to keep him in service with a *duoqing* order. He dutifully took mourning leave, but instead of returning to Taihu, he resided in Nanjing.[67] Given that his hometown had just been sacked by rebels in a bitter battle that had led to its utter destruction and a large number of deaths, it seems understandable that Lei would choose to spend the mourning term in Nanjing.

Lei's choice of location for mourning might be justified by war and dislocation, but the accusation that he actively participated in political maneuvers during the mourning period was difficult to refute—and this behavior constituted a serious breach of *zhongxiao* ethics on several levels. It was reported that after news of Beijing's fall reached Nanjing, as Donglin-Fushe officials were plotting to intervene in the imperial succession, a certain "senior Donglin official" (i.e. Jiang Yueguang) went to talk to Lei. This would later be invoked as evidence of Lei's treason.[68] Lei's biography in the Shunzhi 10 (1653) edition of the Taihu gazetteer, a compilation in which Lei's own brother participated, emphasized his filial piety and downplayed his involvement in factional scheming around the imperial succession. This narrative clearly challenged the charges against Lei. Such editorial decisions reflect the understanding shared by many during the Ming-Qing transition that to fulfill one's filial duty, an official in mourning should avoid meddling in governmental affairs in any public fashion, let alone involving himself in conversations about manipulating the imperial succession.

However, in contrast to the record in the Taihu gazetteer, in which Lei's political activity during mourning is described as passive and minimal, Lei's friend and Fushe activist Chen Zhenhui, who was in Nanjing at the time and extremely well informed, recalled that Lei went around speaking about avenging the martyred emperor. Chen apparently saw no problem in a mourning son's highly public participation in political activities; to the contrary, such action surely testified to Lei's loyalty.[69] Whereas the biography that downplays Lei's political participation was meant to stress his victimization by the evil faction in the Hongguang court, the discrepancies between these accounts of Lei's moral performance clearly revealed the diverse contemporary understandings of *zhongxiao* that complicated factional struggles.

Once again, the Donglin-Fushe camp, like its counterparts in the Chongzhen reign, had to carve out a politically safe image. A memorial submitted by the censor Yuan Kai is revealing. He commented on the "disloyalty" of Gong Dingzi and Lei Yanzuo in order to refute Ma-Ruan's attacks on the Donglin-Fushe community. First, he argued that Ma-Ruan should not use examples such as Gong Dingzi to challenge the Donglin's moral stature: "Guang Shiheng (another survivor official in Beijing) and Gong Dingzi were new to the metropolitan government and prided themselves on making remonstrations. [By the time Beijing fell,] people had not yet been able to judge whether or not these men should be considered gentlemen with true integrity." Yuan suggested that the court should instead consider martyrs like Ni Yuanlu, whose loyal devotion had been authenticated by their suicides. These men were real representatives of the upright Donglin group.

Next, Yuan pointed out that the moral charges against Lei Yanzuo were really aimed at the Donglin image; Lei's moral performance merely gave the Donglin's rivals an easy target: "Lei Yanzuo was observing a mourning term for his deceased mother at his residence when officials were convening about the imperial succession issue. He publicly denounced the Prince of Fu for lacking filial piety, which disqualified the prince for succeeding to the throne. Ma Shiying had tried twice to use the succession controversy to implicate Shi Kefa, but to no avail. He now has to try this tactic again on Lei Yanzuo!"[70] Yuan's memorial exemplified certain officials' ambivalence toward Lei's moral performance and the understanding that had Lei strictly followed mourning rules as many colleagues did, he would not have subjected himself—and the Donglin-Fushe camp—to political attacks.

Hence, some officials explicitly suggested that they should focus their efforts on protecting the reputations of colleagues whom they considered morally impeccable. They defended their collective image with selective counterattacks, letting those with less perfect moral records—such as Lei—fight their own battles.[71]

However, the Donglin-Fushe image-making efforts were inadequate. It was naive for officials in the Donglin-Fushe camp to imagine that the Donglin-identified martyrs were beyond moral attack. In fact, the Ma-Ruan clique's efforts to undermine the Donglin-Fushe claim to moral superiority even extended to Ni Yuanlu, who had committed suicide and become a martyr upon the fall of Beijing. In the late Chongzhen reign, anti-Donglin officials had exploited Ni's domestic problems with his first wife and his failure to maintain a perfect image as a husband. This case was invoked again by the Ma-Ruan faction at the Hongguang court. Liu Kongzhao, who had put forward charges against Ni in the Chongzhen reign, now managed to have the official title of Ni's second wife, Madam Wang, revoked.[72] This ethical charge definitely influenced people's perceptions of Ni at the time,[73] making it difficult for the Donglin-Fushe community to build its collective image of moral superiority on Ni's martyrdom.

The image-making struggles surrounding the "disloyal official" in Nanjing during 1644–45, like those in Beijing and in local communities in Jiangnan, continued the trend of image politics. "Gentlemen (*junzi*) felt sorry for Ni Yuanlu because [his domestic problems] had left a stain on his admirable reputation!"[74] This comment by the literatus Tan Qian (1593–1657) affirms the importance of moral images at this time of political volatility. More importantly, it confirms that the stress on officials' moral performance in the Southern Ming was not simply a political instrument of some small men. Precisely because Confucian ethics was the shared language of political negotiation, many literati believed that maintaining an impeccable moral image in one's personal life was crucial for officials.

Various images of the "disloyal official" circulated within and between the two former Ming capitals, Beijing and Nanjing, in this critical year. The martyrs, survivors, resistance movements, and rival factions all contributed to drawing attention to individual officials' moral performance, past and present, though their efforts to define the disloyal official served different purposes and led to complex consequences.

The contested images of the disloyal official, in both Beijing and Nanjing, show that contemporary social, cultural, and political conditions jointly determined how Confucian ethics as a language of political communication operated during this most chaotic year of the dynastic transition. The so-called disloyal officials and pure elements, and their rivals in the Southern Ming, were all bound to engage the fact that moral perfection remained the ideal but was difficult to achieve in an increasingly complex society; the dynastic crisis only intensified and significantly complicated the elite's struggle to solve this problem.

When the final page of the history of a dynasty has turned, the faces of its officials suddenly look different. In volatile circumstances, individuals undeniably adopted convenient political positions and identities. It also might be true that difficult circumstances tested their moral resolve, and some failed such tests. However, the stark contrast between loyal and disloyal officials in conventional history, focusing in particular on personal moral records, is too neatly drawn. Most officials' acts cannot be easily pinned down along the continuum of Confucian moralism—between sincere moral pursuits and pragmatic employment of the rhetoric. Not only did they struggle to fulfill multiple ethical duties; the environment of image politics also pressed them hard to dispute disloyalty and authenticate their loyalty through the gendered performance of other Confucian virtues.

Investigating how the images of the "disloyal official" were created and maintained not only helps us recover some of the distorted or buried personal experiences of political actors in seventeenth-century China; it also reveals the high stakes involved for officials who had to perform Confucian ethical ideals properly in order to survive in, and adapt to, the changing political landscape.

Eventually, although the Hongguang court proceeded to issue a list of disloyal officials, after some negotiation, the names of Gong Dingzi and two dozen other officials were dropped into the minor category of "Undecided." Thus, they avoided the most damning label.[75] But many tragedies and much damage had already occurred. For many of the survivor officials, the image war would continue after the surrender of Nanjing in 1645 as they became "turncoat" officials in the next dynasty. For example, Gong's notoriety as a disloyal man who had failed to commit suicide because of his concubine would be repeated in factional infighting in the Qing Shunzhi court. Thus, officials' image-making remained an urgent task in both the unconquered and fallen regions of the empire. Indeed, it would be central to the intense factional struggles in the early Qing court and to the literati's recovery.

PART II

The Early Qing

CHAPTER 4

Moralizing, the Qing Way

After the Manchus relocated the Qing capital from Manchuria to Beijing in 1644, many officials who had been trapped there joined the new government, whether voluntarily or reluctantly. They became turncoats. Although the dynastic calendar had changed overnight, prompting literati-officials' identities also to change abruptly, their public and personal lives underwent complicated and uneven adaptations in the early Qing. The moral images of turncoat officials—produced in court spectacles, imperial propaganda, memorials, and literary and artistic works—illustrate interwoven changes and continuities in political culture across the dynastic divide.

In this new era of political trial, the dynamics of image politics seem both familiar and alien. Factionalism at court provides an excellent example. It persisted but had become more complicated: it now existed among Han officials across generations, among the Manchus, and between Han and Manchu officials. The Qing conquest complicated the dynamics of Han factionalism. After the death of Regent Dorgon in 1651, who dominated the court and ruled on behalf of the young emperor, Manchu factionalism unfolded in battles over turncoats' moral performance. Further, unlike Dorgon, who had shunned and suppressed the rhetoric of factionalism, in the post-Dorgon era, the Shunzhi emperor himself created a new discourse of factionalism and employed it as a tool for asserting Manchu moral superiority. In these circumstances, the unstable image of what I call the "loyal turncoat" mediated Manchu and Han factionalisms.

Although the moral claims made for political purposes sounded similar to those of the late Ming, early Qing image politics dealt with new complexities in political concerns and brought about nuanced changes in Confucian moralism. Manchu rulers and Han subjects now negotiated trust and favor through the gendered image of the loyal turncoat. The process of such negotiations, in turn, altered the political implications of some *zhongxiao* rituals. In addition, in both factional contests and the consolidation of the conquest, early Qing politics that played out as moral struggles helped reconfigure the moral-political division of labor among the ruling elite.

The Manchus seem to have had no clear blueprint for governing in their minds.[1] In those years of uncertainty, they improvised much—with the turncoats' assistance—as they strove to carry out the great enterprise of the Qing. The images of the "loyal turncoat" as son, father, and husband were at the heart of political experiments.

IMAGES OF HAN FACTIONALISM: THE TURNCOAT'S HAIR AND CONCUBINE

In Shunzhi 2/5 (1645), the night before the turncoat Li Wen (1608–1647) shaved his head and adopted the Qing hairstyle, he had a dream about the spirit of his hair, which called itself a "remnant subject" of the Ming. In the dream, Li's hair confronted his decision to shave his forehead. Li wept, but then replied: "Men have hair, just as plants and trees have branches and leaves. They flourish in spring and wither in autumn, not because spring is blessed and autumn is condemned. [Men have hair,] just as birds and beasts have feathers and fur. They shed in summer but grow thicker in winter, not because winter treats us better while summer does not. [Change] is beyond our control. Therefore we have to live with it."[2] Eventually, in the dream, Li convinced his hair. The next day, he shaved it off.

Dynastic cycles, like seasonal changes, follow cosmological laws. By 1644, there had been many dynastic changes in history; new dynasties, including those created by non-Han ruling houses, were retrospectively seen as legitimate. Commenting on dynastic change was a familiar exercise for literati-officials. However, actually living through one and making life-and-death decisions within this milieu was new. The Ming-Qing transition was thus a mixed experience for turncoats, both familiar and foreign.

Meanwhile, the Manchus had become familiar with the Confucian discourse before moving the capital to Beijing. They had legitimized their rule and justified aggression against the Ming by employing concepts such as the Mandate of Heaven and *zhongxiao*. Further, they also had some experience dealing with Han literati, both officials and nonofficials, in the process of state making and expansion.

Still, when they actually descended the south side of the Great Wall, they were overwhelmed by the complexity of the situation that awaited them. At court, for instance, a particularly thorny issue was the many configurations of "generations" among the turncoats, which made Han factionalism almost unfathomable.[3] Transgenerational factional sentiments were simply too strong and too deeply entrenched, and they ran through nearly the entire metropolitan bureaucracy.

The Manchu ruling elite and Han officials quickly discovered that straight talk was counterproductive. This can be seen in the discussions of policies regarding head shaving and the former eunuch faction. Turncoats in particular had complicated relationships with, and diverse attitudes toward, the Manchu rulers. Some joined the government reluctantly, wanting to wait and see how the situation developed before fully committing themselves; others wanted only to save their own skins and were always looking for opportunities to quit. Some actively sought recognition from the new rulers; certain officials tried to show their loyalty by voluntarily shaving their heads. A mandate that Han men shave their foreheads was suspended briefly after it triggered vehement anti-Manchu resistance among the literati. But some officials, such as Sun Zhixie (1591–1647) and Li Ruolin (d. 1651), had moved quickly on their own to have their heads shaved. These officials emboldened the Manchus and made life more difficult for other colleagues.[4]

Han collaborators who did not voluntarily shave their heads resisted the prospect of resuming this policy in different ways. In Shunzhi 2/5 (1645), the vocal censor Zhao Kaixin (*jinshi* 1634) submitted a most critical memorial attacking Li Ruolin. He invoked the conventional factional rhetoric that "evil officials could not serve the emperor with the Way."[5] Jin Zhijun (1593–1670), Zhao's friend, immediately submitted a memorial, appearing to praise the Manchu rulers and criticize Zhao. However, its actual intent was to defend Zhao and plead against reimposing the mandate.

> Shaving the head or keeping the hair cannot determine a man's moral character. If it is wrong to claim that only those who keep the hair are good men, then should we not label all those who have shaved as evil? After all, the empire has been unified. Both Manchu and Han

> are now Qing officials and serving Your Majesty together. Officials offer their service to the court with sincere devotion, not with their appearance. The court has employed and recognized its officials not because they have adopted a suitable outfit but because they have a sincere heart. In addition, Censor Zhao has learned about the court's unambiguous policy of permitting men to keep their hair. Why was he overly concerned about the court changing its stance simply because some colleagues advocated otherwise? The more suspicion, the more confusion. The court has issued the edict reiterating that those who do not wish to shave should not be forced to do so. We should have stronger faith that the kingly way is based on human feelings. I sincerely hope that officials of all ranks maintain a harmonious relationship and collaborate in serving this virtuous court and pursuing a government of benevolence and righteousness. Do not quarrel over head and hair![6]

Stressing the importance of sincerity over appearance, Jin's memorial urged leaving the subject unmentioned, pretending it was a nonissue. Sincerity could authenticate loyalty. As long as loyalty was associated with one's heart and not one's appearance, the court had no reason to press Han subjects to shave. Jin in fact sensed the danger in framing head shaving in political terms: Once this debate became explicitly associated with factionalism, there would be no middle ground left between shaving and not shaving. It would offer Dorgon an opportunity to instead use appearance to define loyalty and enforce head shaving among all turncoats. Indeed, Dorgon saw through Jin and explicitly dismissed his ambivalence.[7] A strict head-shaving policy ensued.

Following this round of confrontation over head shaving and its devastating outcome, more violent clashes boiled up among turncoats at court when the news of Nanjing's fall and the destruction of the Ming Hongguang regime arrived. In Shunzhi 2/7 (1645), Dorgon instructed that the Hongguang emperor and his top officials be brought to Beijing. Until this point, a month earlier, one turncoat had already memorialized against offering positions to the "evil officials of the Southern Ming government," in particular Ma Shiying and Ruan Dacheng. In response, the court announced that Southern Ming officials had been granted amnesty and their previous misconduct or crimes should not be discussed.[8] The censor Wu Da (*jinshi* 1634) persisted and memorialized against reappointing any officials who had been identified as former eunuch associates or had been responsible for ruining the Southern Ming.[9] He singled out Ruan Dacheng in this vehement warning, hinting at unusually intimate ties between Ruan and the pro-Manchu grand secretary Feng Quan (1595–1672), a former eunuch associate.[10]

In the minds of such men, their identity as loyal officials was an extension of their Ming self-image, to which opposition to the eunuch faction remained central. There arose a wave of impeachments against Feng Quan, a seemingly perfect target. In Shunzhi 2/8 (1645), the censor Du Lide (1611–1691) attacked Feng for attempting to recruit Ruan-Ma.[11] Soon, several other censors piled on against Feng. Among them, Li Senxian (*jinshi* 1640) adopted the strongest rhetoric, requesting that Feng and his son be executed.[12] So many memorials condemned Feng that the court announced that such memorials would no longer be considered or circulated.[13]

Dorgon summoned officials of the rival factions and questioned them. He decided that this was a case of slander aimed at pro-Manchu officials who had shaved their foreheads and had their families don Manchu clothes ahead of other officials. Dorgon, already well informed on Ming factionalism, questioned the censors, including Gong Dingzi, as to why they continued to indulge in Ming-style factionalism and tried to incriminate turncoats who were loyal to the Qing. Gong and his factional allies were admonished and humiliated.[14]

After these confrontations, the next round of factional attacks was aimed at individual officials' moral performance rather than a faction, and hence was less likely to provoke a collective reaction. Take the charges against Gong Dingzi as an example. Gong's father died in Shunzhi 3/4 (1646). Following the custom of requesting an official honor for the deceased parent, he submitted a memorial before taking leave to return home to mourn.[15] But a serious charge against Gong for his lack of *zhongxiao* was leveled by the censor Sun Poling (*jinshi* 1646), who demanded that Gong's request be denied:

> Gong Dingzi was a traitor to the Ming; he served as a censor in the rebel government. The Qing appointed him to the position of censor and then promoted him to the Court of the Imperial Stud. However, he does not devote himself to work in order to pay back the imperial favor. Instead, he knows only banqueting and drinking, as well as chasing entertainers. Years ago he spent a fortune to buy a courtesan, Gu Mei. He was infatuated with her and lavished gifts upon her. His infatuation made him the laughingstock of Jiangnan. He has ignored his parents, wife, and children. Even with the news of his father's death, he has not stopped carousing. Now he has the audacity

> to ask for an official honor for his father so he can show off in his hometown.[16]

This depiction of Gong as a *disloyal* turncoat simultaneously questioned his ability or intention to fulfill the roles of a loyal subject, a filial son, and a responsible husband and father. His infatuation with a concubine defined his moral defects and led him to ignore his filial and familial responsibilities, which in turn called into question his loyalty to *both* the fallen Ming and the Qing. Earning burial sacrifice from the court for one's deceased father was an important filial duty and honor for an official. On the basis of these charges, Gong, who had always been a filial son,[17] was deprived of this privilege because his sexual indulgence had led him to abandon *zhongxiao* ethics. That was not the end of the insult. Gong was also demoted two degrees in rank before he departed for his hometown to complete the three-year mourning term.

The impeachment of Gong for his lack of filial piety and indulgence in sensual pleasures shed light on the inseparability of factionalism, regional literati networks, and officials' personal lives. Censor Sun's father was the aforementioned Sun Zhixie, a longtime factional enemy of the Donglin-identified officials. Sun Poling himself had just passed the metropolitan civil service examinations in Shunzhi 3/3 (1646) and received his first official appointment just before memorializing against Gong.[18] The senior Sun fell from imperial favor due to his deplorable performance as governor of Jiangxi in Shunzhi 2–3 (1645–46). He had volunteered to lead campaigns there to suppress discontent and ensure the smooth transfer of power to the Qing, but he failed so miserably in the provincial capital of Nanchang that a censor impeached him for incompetence. Sun then reported that the thousands of former Ming royal family members residing in Nanchang should be considered a potential security concern. He suggested that the court disperse them to various counties or even to other provinces if they were disobedient.[19]

Nanchang was one of the large cities designated to provide for a prince and his household in the Ming. By the fall of the Ming, the former Ming royal family members in the greater Nanchang area, distinctively surnamed Zhu, had a history of intermarriage with locally prominent families. For example, Gong Dingzi's friend Li Yuanding (*jinshi* 1622) had married Zhu Zhongmei (fl. 1621–61), a daughter of the Ming royals.[20] The Ming loyalist Peng Shiwang (1610–1683), a good friend of Gong's and of a few others in Gong's circle, had married the daughter of the Ming Prince of Ruichang.[21] Hence, the sociocultural bonds between former royal family members and local literati in the region were significant. An assault on Zhu-surnamed families meant an assault on the local elite. Dorgon rejected Sun Zhixie's suggestions; instead Sun was summoned back to Beijing in Shunzhi 3/4 (1646) on the grounds that local institutions had been stabilized and order largely restored. This was apparently an excuse to replace him, since Jiangxi was becoming a huge headache for the court.[22] In effect, Sun's political career was buried in Jiangxi.

This complicated backstory explains the sudden personal attacks on Gong Dingzi by the junior Sun soon after the elder Sun's recall. Gong, an Anhui native whose ancestors originated in Jiangxi, had banded together with friends who hailed from that region, especially the aforementioned colleagues whose hometown was in the greater Nanchang area. The mutual detestation between this group and the Suns thus drew from several layers of sociopolitical friction and hostility: the Donglin-Fushe's history of opposition to the eunuch associates in the late Ming, grudges between turncoats with different relationships to the Manchus, and different regional identities.[23]

Factional enmity in the form of personal attack may also help explain the unusual punishment ordered for Song Yizhen (*jinshi* 1642), son of a prominent family in the greater Nanchang area. He had already been fulfilling official responsibilities as a commissioner in Hunan for more than half a year when he lost his job for having reported belatedly to his post.[24] His punishment came immediately after Gong Dingzi was attacked and demoted. The language used in the official document concerning Song's misconduct demands our attention. It specifically points out that his delay was caused by a detour to his hometown "in the company of a concubine."[25] If we compare this accusation with language used in similar documents submitted to the Board of Personnel reporting other delayed arrivals at new posts, it becomes clear that the phrase "visit his hometown in the company of a concubine" was unusual.[26] Upon hearing this very personal charge, Song immediately confined himself to his residence and refused to continue with any official duties, even though a special session of the civil service examinations in Hunan was quickly approaching and demanded his urgent attention.[27]

This series of personal attacks on Gong Dingzi and his Jiangxi friends reflects the shift in Han factional struggles from open confrontation to attacks on individual officials' moral performance. Until

Regent Dorgon's unexpected death in Shunzhi 7/12 (1651), Han factionalism appeared to have been brought under control, even though it persisted in a less confrontational, less political fashion. Soon, however, the image of the loyal turncoat would take on new significance under the Shunzhi emperor, whose first task in the post-Dorgon era was to establish his own authority.

MANCHU FACTIONALISM AND TURNCOATS' *ZHONGXIAO*

After Dorgon died, Manchu factionalism erupted openly in the form of battles over turncoats' moral performance. The ways in which the language of *zhongxiao* was deployed by the Manchu ruler and his officials defy simple generalization, however. They indicate that the Shunzhi emperor's experiments with ruling techniques went beyond mere ideological promotion of Confucian practices.

Dorgon's Dominance and Demise

The changing images of the turncoat official Huang Tu'an (*jinshi* 1637) corresponds neatly to some key moments in Manchu factional infighting. After his successful military suppression of the rebels and bandits in Yizhou near Beijing, Huang was promoted to the governorship of Gansu in Shunzhi 2/4 (1645). He attempted to turn down the promotion with the excuse that he had to take care of his aged mother, but his petition was firmly rejected. He was ordered to report immediately to his new post in the northwest where the rebels were still many and active. About a year later, Huang was made governor of Ningxia. He again petitioned to retire to take care of his mother. The Board of Personnel determined that Huang's petitions were not really motivated by filial devotion but were simply attempts to avoid challenging appointments to war-torn areas in the northwest. Lacking loyal commitment and sincere filiality, this official should expect to lose his official status. Just this occurred in Shunzhi 3 (1646), when Dorgon was consolidating his dominance over Manchu nobility rivals and also tightening his control of the Han bureaucracy, exploring ways to turn it into an obedient and efficient governing machine.

Several top officials, led by Grand Secretary Fan Wencheng (1597–1666), felt the Board of Personnel should not have so crudely dismissed Huang's request. Indeed, Huang had an eighty-one-year-old mother and his plea to retire and fulfill his filial duties was completely legitimate, Fan observed. These officials hoped to discuss the case with Dorgon but failed to find an opportunity. So they reported the case to Prince Jiagalang, Dorgon's major rival and co-regent. Jiagalang told the officials to wait and did not intervene. Nonetheless, Dorgon disciplined Fan Wencheng and his colleagues for breaching protocol and taking the matter to Jiagalang. Huang Tu'an, Jiagalang, and the officials involved with the matter all received some form of punishment.[28] Huang was judged to have faked filial piety and failed to demonstrate true loyalty.

After Dorgon passed from the scene and the Shunzhi emperor began to assert his own authority, in Shunzhi 9 (1652), with the support of Fan Wencheng, Huang's *zhongxiao* commitment earned him back his official status. Huang's political misfortune in Shunzhi 3–4 (1646–47) conveniently served as evidence of Dorgon's mishandling of the government: by punishing an official for petitioning to fulfill his filial duty, Dorgon had ignored the principle of governing with filial piety. This maneuvering allowed the emperor to justify the elimination of his political rivals.[29]

Whereas Huang's filial commitment helped earn back his career, by contrast, Grand Secretary Song Quan (1598–1652) lost his job due to an alleged lack of *zhongxiao*. Merely two months after Dorgon's death, the case against Song emerged, put forth on the same day by two different censors, Chen Diaoyuan (*jinshi* 1639) and Wang Tingjian (*jinshi* 1646). Chen leveled two charges: first, Song Quan's memorial to the Shunzhi emperor, in which he was expected to offer insightful suggestions on policies for the post-Dorgon period, was empty and vague; second, Song had violated the principle of *zhongxiao* by acceding to Dorgon's *duoqing* order and presiding over the ceremonies of the metropolitan civil service examinations when he should be mourning his mother.[30]

Wang Tingjian's memorial elaborated on the question of *zhongxiao*: "[Proper mourning over] the loss of one's parent is a matter of following the traditional rules of the Three Mainstays and Five Constant Virtues (*san'gang wuchang*). While Song Quan's service might have been needed by the government, which could justify his *duoqing*, did he really have to don celebratory garments to interview the examination candidates? He cared about cultivating the mentor-disciple bond but ignored his filial duties."[31]

Both censors concluded by urging the emperor to announce the arrival of a new political era by dismissing the unfilial, disloyal Song immediately. The court assumed the posture that it would not wrong Song. At the emperor's request, the Board of Personnel was charged with "investigating" the case and reporting the results of their discussion to the emperor. A month later, the board decided that the two censors' accusations against Song were true and recommended that he be ordered to retire immediately. The emperor "agreed" with their suggestions.[32] Song promptly left the capital and returned to his hometown in Henan, where he died of an illness one year later.

By portraying Song Quan as an unfilial son and disloyal official, these attackers took aim at the remnants of Dorgon's clique without explicitly saying so. It was Dorgon who had ordered the *duoqing* and appointed Song to preside over the examinations when he should have been in mourning. The official record shows that in Shunzhi 5/12 (1649), "the Grand Secretary Song Quan requested [leave] to observe mourning for his deceased mother. The imperial edict ordered: since the Grand Secretariat deals with a great deal of important business, [Song Quan] should continue his duties as usual but could observe mourning privately to complete his *zhongxiao* (*yi quan zhongxiao*)."[33] Never a factionalist himself, Song was implicated because Dorgon had trusted his administrative skills. Once Dorgon had been politically denounced, Song's case offered an opportunity for the Shunzhi emperor to condemn Dorgon and get rid of his former followers. Song's *duoqing* record made him a convenient case the emperor could use to press factional purges and flaunt his newly acquired authority.[34] This episode reveals the court's preference for negotiation through the language of Confucian ethics over overt purge when it could be avoided. At the same time, however, Manchu infighting unwittingly reinforced the association between the loyal turncoat and Confucian ethics.

The Shunzhi Emperor's Experimentation

The post-Dorgon court shed the regent's high-handedness but unleashed Han factionalist energies and led to new rivalries among the Manchus. The Shunzhi emperor was inconsistent in his ruling style, but his tireless adjustments and experimentation makes his reign fascinating to the historian.[35] A revealing example was how he sent political messages through the image of Song Quan. In his battles with Dorgon's faction, the emperor endorsed the censors' relentless attacks on Song's lack of *zhongxiao*. But merely a year later, upon

Song's death, the emperor rejected some officials' suggestion that the Song family should not receive an imperial condolence. He insisted on granting the Songs the most prestigious mourning allowances, such as nine imperial mourning altars, a posthumous honorary title for Song, officials to perform mourning, and an imperial edict of mourning.[36] This de facto restoration of Song Quan's moral image reveals the emperor's interest in allowing the language of Confucian ethics to play a prominent but nuanced role in politics.

The emperor's attitude toward the repeated moral attacks on another turncoat, Dorgon's reliable ally Chen Mingxia (1601–1654), offers an even more interesting example of how this ruling technique helped the emperor and the turncoats navigate the matrix of intertwining Han and Manchu factionalisms. Chen came under attack about two months after Song Quan's retirement. The assaults began with a lengthy memorial by a censor named Zhang Xuan (d. 1651), which listed ten crimes Chen had supposedly committed. The main charges included promoting Dorgon's agenda, affiliating with former eunuch associates, mishandling personnel matters as a result of factional concerns and self-interest, violating mourning norms, and so on.[37] That Zhang listed Chen's betrayal of *zhongxiao* ethics among the top charges is highly instructive. He makes the familiar connection between Chen's disloyalty—to the dynasty and to the young Shunzhi emperor himself—and his lack of filial devotion, arguing that after his father died, "[Chen] cared only about his career and showed no grief. He found excuses to take the *duoqing* order. Dorgon granted him five hundred taels of silver and a leave to return home to properly bury his father. However, he rushed back to court to secure power and Dorgon's favor, ignoring his father's burial. . . . He cares little about the emperor or his father and therefore should be condemned."[38] To stress the severity of Chen's violations, Zhang invoked Song Quan's case: "The former Grand Secretary Song Quan has been ordered to leave the government because he supervised the metropolitan examinations during the mourning period. Chen Mingxia's circumstances are ten times worse than Song's!"[39]

Chen's impeachment was followed by one unexpected turn after another. First, the all-Manchu panel of officials who delivered judgment did not refute Zhang's accusations but suggested that because Chen's *duoqing* had happened a long time before and was covered by an imperial amnesty, Chen should not be punished for it retroactively. Instead Zhang was executed shortly thereafter by the order of

Tantai, the Manchu president of the Board of Personnel and Chen's ally. Merely three months after that, things took an even more dramatic turn. The Shunzhi emperor accused Tantai of having formed a faction with the late Dorgon, claiming that Tantai had executed Zhang and dismissed the charges against Chen in order to protect factional interests. Tantai himself was then executed in Shunzhi 8/8 (1651). Still relying on Chen as a political tool, the emperor did not order severe punishment for Chen but rather used his case to strategically position himself amid the Manchu and Han factionalisms.[40]

One year later, a second complaint against Chen for lacking *zhongxiao* was lodged. The turncoat Luo Guoshi (*jinshi* 1637) had impeached Han officials on the Board of Personnel for manipulating personnel decisions for factional reasons. He presented as examples the delayed reappointments of two friends, Hao Jie (*jinshi* 1637) and Gong Dingzi, after they had fulfilled their respective mourning terms. Luo argued that manipulating personnel policy not only indicated corruption, but more seriously, demonstrated officials' neglect of the importance of *zhongxiao*. Those who had dutifully completed mourning were not being rewarded. This appeared to be criticism of the current board president, but Luo's real target was Chen Mingxia, who was given a *duoqing* and did not mourn for the full three years for his deceased father. In this memorial, he painted Chen as an enemy of *zhongxiao*.[41] Although there seemed to some consensus that Chen had indeed obstructed the reappointments of Gong and Hao,[42] the Shunzhi emperor did not act on this charge. He still needed Chen in the Grand Secretariat, and no personnel action ensued.

In the end, a damaging impeachment leveled by Grand Secretary Ning Wanwo (1593–1665) offered the emperor a timely opportunity to get rid of Chen Mingxia. Chen was executed in Shunzhi 11/3 (1654). Mysteries surrounding this case still persist. Some scholars believe that Chen was suspected of Ming loyalism,[43] while others argue that the emperor grew alarmed by signs of Chen's interference in government procedures.[44] It seems that Chen's deep involvement in both Han and Manchu factional infighting finally appeared to challenge imperial authority and provoked the emperor's suspicions. Pertinent to our investigation here is the recurring charge of Chen's violation of *zhongxiao*: Ning's memorial cites "public opinion" that Chen lacked *zhongxiao* and tolerated his son's criminal behavior.[45]

These three attacks on Chen Mingxia during Shunzhi 8–11 (1651–54) show the flexible ways in which the language of *zhongxiao* operated in political communications endorsed by the Shunzhi emperor. As the cases of Song Quan and Chen Mingxia show, it was the emperor who determined whether and when a Han turncoat could be considered a *zhongxiao* exemplar. In his efforts to manage the interlocking Manchu and Han factionalisms, the image of the loyal turncoat as filial son seems to have become his most adaptive, effective tool.

TRUST, FAVOR, AND THE RECOGNITION OF FILIAL EXEMPLARS

The pervasive, complex nature of early Qing factionalism was one of the factors that made the political environment full of uncertainty and distrust. Factional competition went beyond court intrigues and threatened the consolidation of the Qing conquest, in particular, the military and political campaigns to suppress resistance. Maneuvers around the gendered image of the loyal turncoat shed light on the many trials of the Manchu rulers and their turncoat subjects. Confucian ethics provided a language of communication by which they could negotiate trust and favor.

Building trust and displaying favor through marriage alliances had proved effective for Manchu and Mongol nobles since the beginning of the Qing empire. However, this method generated few sustainable benefits in Manchu attempts to secure loyalty from turncoats.[46] Manchu rulers considered giving a Manchu woman to a Han official an explicit gesture of trust, in conformity with certain social practices the Manchus retained even after coming to Beijing.[47] But it also provided Regent Dorgon a means of surveillance and control.[48] For example, Feng Quan's loyal service to the Qing court earned him a marriage to a Manchu woman arranged by Dorgon (*cihun Manzhou*).[49] Another turncoat, Hong Chengchou, was also accorded this honor. Both Feng and Hong were already married, but their Manchu women could not be subjected to the strict wife-concubine hierarchy. Therefore, some sort of special arrangements had to be made. The familial upheaval and breach of literati-official gender norms caused by such an "honor" were not easily managed.[50]

Han literati in general, the turncoats' social base, did not necessarily reject Manchu-Han liaisons per se, but they probably preferred arrangements that accommodated the Confucian gender order. The Manchu lady bestowed upon Feng Quan was termed not a "concubine" but a "secondary wife" (*ciqi*), in clear contradiction of

Confucian norms.[51] When she died in Shunzhi 10 (1653), she was given the posthumous title of "first-rank lady" (*Yi pin furen*). The literatus-historian Tan Qian mentioned this in his documentation of a sojourn in Beijing, suggesting that this honor was inappropriate, since Feng's Han wife had already received a title from the Ming as his official wife. When Feng's Manchu woman obtained a prestigious official title from the new government, the statuses of the women became confused.[52] As an ill-fated foot-binding ban demonstrated, interference with Confucian gender norms produced no benefits for the Manchus but only incurred higher political costs.[53] The image of the Han husband of a Manchu secondary wife was simply not compelling for the elite.

Hence, Manchu rulers had to look elsewhere for more effective ways of negotiating trust and favor with turncoats. As they became invested in communicating through the language of *zhongxiao*, the turncoats responded accordingly. This process, in turn, changed the political implications of some *zhongxiao* rituals, such as the three-year mourning term.

The Manchu rulers quite frequently issued *duoqing* orders to Han officials, preventing them from resigning so that they could mourn for the required duration. At first glance, such orders seemed to confirm some Han literati's claim that the Manchus were barbaric and morally inferior. Han literati's loyalty to the fallen Ming and implicit criticisms of the Qing came to center on mourning rituals, and especially the issue of *duoqing*, the practice of which they saw as emblematic of moral decline.[54] However, *duoqing* also operated as a crucial instrument of communication in the early Qing. The more frequent issuances of *duoqing* did not necessarily signify a disassociation between filiality and loyalty, nor did such orders in any way diminish the importance of *zhongxiao* as a general expression of morality. Rather, the focus of *zhongxiao* rituals was moving elsewhere: when the Manchu ruler issued a *duoqing* order or permission for an official to retire to take care of his parents, he was sending a signal of trust and favor (or lack of them).

We can detect a pattern of *duoqing* orders in this period. When an official's service was urgently needed or trusted, the Manchu rulers would insist on a *duoqing* order. If these political figures later lost imperial favor, accusations of violating *zhongxiao* ethics could arise and be employed as a strategy of moral-political attack. Meanwhile, returning home to fulfill one's filial duties (*zhongyang*) or briefly visiting parents (*guixing*) were negotiated privileges. Even though many Han officials continued to follow mourning rules by resigning from office to mourn for twenty-seven months, as soon as obtaining a leave to mourn or take care of one's parents had to be negotiated, it became an opportunity for officials to display publicly their *zhongxiao* and for the court to convey trust and favor. The importance of negotiating over such requests and expectations as a political tool increased accordingly. Consequently, the court now, by the very act of *contemplating* officials' requests to fulfill filial obligations, could take credit for promoting Confucian ethics even when it deprived some officials of the opportunity to complete mourning. In other words, *duoqing* was being transformed from an undesirable, controversial measure into a technique of ruling and a site of politicking. In the early Qing, turncoats' experiences exemplified how this experiment proceeded and the nuanced political effects their images as loyal turncoats now had.

Testing (Dis)Trust: The Case of Hong Chengchou

In Chongzhen 15 (1642), following a devastating defeat in the northeast, the Ming official-general Hong Chengchou (1593–1665) surrendered and began to serve the Qing after a period of imprisonment. At the time, the Ming court still believed that Hong had died in battle.[55] Hong played a major role in the Qing conquest of southern China after 1644. He was made the top official in Jiangnan. But he still had to earn the rulers' trust.

During Shunzhi 2–4 (1645–47), a critical moment in the Qing pacification of the southeast, it became clear that dissatisfaction among the collaborators and renewed appeals for resistance were roiling localities around the country. Much of this development could be blamed on oppressive Manchu control over surrendered Han civil and military officials as well as the Han population. At this moment, Hong's political life was no less unpredictable than the volatile situation in the south. Hong instinctively realized it would have been extremely risky for him to lead the campaign to "pacify" Jiangnan. Like many other turncoats, the political and social connections he had cultivated in his many years of service to the Ming could have easily implicated him in a case of sedition in this hotbed of resistance.[56]

Trust had to be mutual between Dorgon and Hong. Neither wanted to make a fatal misstep, nor would they abandon their joint enterprise unhesitatingly. In early Shunzhi 4 (1647), the exposure of a massive anti-Qing network in Jiangnan, whose main leader had been Hong's subordinate, seriously tested the relationship between Hong and Dorgon.[57] Hong's first attempt to remove himself from this dangerous situation occurred at the end of Shunzhi 4/2 (1647), when he submitted a filial son's request to observe mourning for his father, who had died five years before (in Chongzhen 16/9 [1643]). That same month, some of Hong's family members and servants from his hometown, Quanzhou in Fujian, had gone to Nanjing to join him. Hong submitted a memorial claiming that this was when he first learned of his father's death. This memorial did not go through regular channels to reach Dorgon's desk. Hong had a personal messenger deliver the memorial, which read in part:

> A servant called Chen Ying'an had come to Jiangnan with my brother and son. He was the first to arrive at my office on 2/20. I summoned him and asked about my family, and heard the shocking news that my father, due to years of illness, had passed away on the twenty-seventh day of the ninth month in the year of *guiwei* (i.e., Chongzhen 16, a Ming reign year that Hong avoided using). Upon hearing this, I was struck by deep sorrow. I recalled that in the ninth month of the year of *guiwei*, I was being taken care of by Your Majesty in [the earlier capital] Shengjing. During the years when my father was ill, I failed to serve at his side. Nor could I fulfill my mourning duty upon his death. An unfilial son is not a good man. During the transition I moved first to Beijing and then to Jiangnan. Letters from [my home in] Fujian could not reach me. Then since I was appointed to lead the campaign in Jiangnan, in the past three and half years I dared not think of personal matters. Now having learned about my father's death, I cannot stop weeping in my office. . . . Observing the three-year mourning shows a son's filial devotion and is common practice everywhere. I beg Your Majesty and Imperial Regent to allow me to return to Beijing to complete three years of mourning for my father.[58]

This image of a loyal turncoat conveyed three extremely important—and delicate—messages to Dorgon. First, Hong highlighted his loyalty to the new dynasty by invoking his days in the old Qing capital as well as his service during the pacification campaign in Jiangnan. He did not request to return to his hometown in Fujian to mourn, as dictated by mourning norms. Instead, he asked to "return to Beijing," showing that this was not an excuse to withdraw from service to the Qing and that he was not plotting against the regime. Second, he suggested that he understood many friends, former and current colleagues, and even relatives might have become involved in seditious activities, but he had isolated himself from personal connections and had dedicated himself to the Qing cause. Presumably this self-imposed isolation had prevented Hong from learning about his father's death sooner. Lastly, Hong asked for a gracious way to excuse himself from this mission and for Dorgon to appoint a trustworthy official to replace him if Dorgon so wished.

This move proved to be politically savvy, leaving room for both sides to contemplate, observe, and negotiate carefully. The subsequent months brought the arrest and killing of some high-profile Ming loyalists. Exchanges about this filial son's strong desire to mourn for his father tested the degree of Dorgon's (dis)trust. Even if Hong could not send or receive letters from home before 1644, and even if it was true that he had significantly limited the amount of personal communication with his old colleague-friends, it was unlikely that he had not learned of his father's death until Shunzhi 4 (1647). Before the arrival of the first group of family members in Nanjing, since Shunzhi 3 (1646), communication had taken place between his office and home in order to make travel arrangements, especially on the domestic front, which was significantly complicated by two problems: the presence of his Manchu bride and his mother's refusal to join her turncoat son.[59] When they communicated about these matters, the death of his father had to be one of the first things reported to him.

Would Dorgon be willing to go along with Hong's story and negotiate with him through the *zhongxiao* image Hong presented? In fact, Dorgon accepted the image Hong projected in his missive. In reply to Hong's request, the imperial order expressed sympathy for the Hong family's loss, but directed Hong—because the court relied on his talents in this campaign—to observe the mourning rituals in his official Nanjing residence, so that he could "fulfill both loyalty and filial piety" (*zhongxiao liang quan*). This short response closed with a statement that the court was weighing its options and asked Hong to wait for further instructions.[60] In other words, the court and Hong had reached a mutual understanding that he was not to be implicated in the resistance movement around him; the court trusted him to a certain degree and would not easily lose faith in him and his military and administrative capabilities.

However, as more anti-Manchu plots across Jiangnan came to light and some of Hong's former colleagues and friends were implicated, both his anxiety and Dorgon's suspicions quickly escalated. Hong renewed his request for a mourning leave in Shunzhi 4/4 (1647) and received another, similar reply. Finally, in Shunzhi 4/7, it was decided that Hong would be granted a leave to complete mourning in Beijing and the official Ma Guozhu (d. 1666) would replace him.[61] Between this time and his return to the capital, Hong insisted on including the phrase "Hong Chengchou in observance of mourning in office" (*jin shouzhi Hong Chengchou*) when referring to himself in memorials.[62]

The court collaborated in dressing up his transfer as a gesture toward governing with filial piety, noting that it should be publicized as an instance of allowing a loyal official to fulfill his filial duties. After returning to Beijing, Hong participated in a public event that promoted the Qing court's posture: he delivered a lecture to the new *jinshi* cohort on the meaning of the Confucian teaching of *zhong-xiao*.[63] A decision based on suspicion turned into a manifestation of imperial favor and a display of the court's commitment to "governing with filial piety" through its recognition of a loyal official's filial devotion.

If Dorgon's decision to let Hong resign and observe mourning rituals for his long-deceased father sent a message of trust tinged with suspicion in Shunzhi 4 (1647), then in contrast, the *duoqing* order issued by the Shunzhi emperor in Shunzhi 9/5 (1652), upon the death of Hong's mother, was crystal clear. Hong had just survived the emperor's latest round of factional persecutions aimed at Dorgon's associates and was deemed trustworthy enough to supervise the most difficult military campaigns in southern China. Hong requested a mourning leave, but the emperor refused to grant it. Instead, he told Hong to continue his service while observing mourning rituals privately.[64] Significant trust was confirmed in this *duoqing* order.

Testing Favor: The Case of Feng Quan

Hong Chengchou steadily secured imperial trust and favor with his carefully crafted image of the loyal turncoat—a simple man who concerned himself with nothing other than military campaigns and familial duties. Feng Quan, another Han grand secretary, had a rather different experience. He was a bearable choice among worse or less controllable turncoats at court, anxious about losing imperial favor. His factionalist baggage and insecurity, and the Shunzhi emperor's mixed feelings about him, colored their communication over Feng's filial performance. It intrigued contemporary literati who were paying close attention to court politics.

When Dorgon died and the Shunzhi emperor began purging Dorgon's men, Feng, widely seen as a factionalist trusted by the late regent, seemed to be desperately trying to stay relevant. In Shunzhi 8 (1651), upon Song Quan's departure, the emperor ordered Feng to retire, too,[65] but later summoned him back. In the ensuing years, imperial favor was at best inconsistent and often mixed with contempt. Between Shunzhi 10 and 13 (1653–56), the upper echelon of Han officials had to ride out dangerous instability. Of these officials, Chen Mingxia was executed, and Gong Dingzi became head of the Censorate only to be demoted to the very bottom of the metropolitan bureaucracy with astonishing speed. Feng offered his service wherever the emperor needed him. After Shunzhi 13, when he was ordered to retire, the emperor kept him nearby for some time as a consultant. He was an obedient and convenient tool.

Politically, the emperor had vacillated between demoting and promoting Feng. However, he showed favor by celebrating Feng's mother's longevity and Feng's filiality, frequently permitting Feng to take short leaves to visit his mother and having garments and portraits made for her by palace staff.[66] Feng's celebration of his mother's birthday in late Shunzhi 11 (1654) became a well-attended *zhongxiao* spectacle at which his colleagues elaborated on the significance of being granted such short leaves.[67] These arrangements benefited both the emperor and Feng. They allowed Feng to avoid a long period of absence from the court and the prospect of losing imperial patronage due to such an absence; they also earned the emperor ringing praise for his commitment to "governing with filial piety."

On Shunzhi 12/2/16 (1655), Feng once again requested leave to visit his sickly mother, whose condition had deteriorated drastically. Fearing that this short leave might be extended indefinitely by the emperor, who seemed to be less and less interested in keeping him at court, Feng obviously waited until the last minute, because his mother died before he could reach home in Zhuozhou, which neighbored Beijing.[68] Then Feng requested mourning leave. The Shunzhi emperor ordered a *duoqing*, telling him to mourn privately and continue to serve at court.[69] Feng proceeded to request imperial burial sacrifices and obtained them. By meticulously carrying out the protocols surrounding a *duoqing* order, the emperor seemed to indicate his intention to keep Feng at hand for a while longer. However, in less than a year, the emperor ordered Feng's permanent retirement.[70]

Contemporaries read the exchange between the emperor and Feng Quan over the latter's *zhongxiao* image with deep interest and extracted political messages from it. In some people's eyes, Feng's request to complete the three-year mourning term was merely a superficial gesture toward filial piety for political purposes. To these observers, the emperor was not fooled. For example, the literatus Tan Qian, who was staying with a Hanlin Academician and was well informed on court politics during this time, included in his diary a celebratory essay he composed to praise Feng's *zhongxiao* on behalf of his official patron and friends.[71] But Tan also documented and mocked Feng's superficial filiality. He recorded that Feng, by writing to the emperor about his mother's death and conveying his seemingly strong desire to observe the three-year mourning term, simply aimed to keep the communication with the emperor flowing and to secure a *duoqing*. The existence of both entries in one book shows that officials and the literati commonly communicated political messages through their *zhongxiao* image.

Tan's account provides rich information about how this sort of delicate communication proceeded between the emperor and officials:

> Qing rituals, such as those regarding mourning, all follow those of the Ming. . . . [Upon his mother's death,] Feng was just compiling a book to secure favor and a *duoqing* order (*qifu*).[72] He reported the death of his mother. The imperial edict expressed earnest condolence. However, wise men knew that Feng was using this only to shorten the mourning term. He then indeed received the imperial order of *duoqing*. Although he resisted the order twice, his language was not strong. Feng told others: "I could not do anything [about the *duoqing* order]. The Qing dynasty does not value mourning for deceased parents." One hundred days later, Feng Quan went back to office, even though the emperor did not send for him; nor did the emperor ask to see him. In the course of spending months on his book project, finally Feng Quan was able to meet with the emperor together with fellow grand secretaries. His Majesty's attitude was clear. . . . Officials today all observe proper mourning. Feng Quan alone did not want to comply with the norm. Earlier, Song Quan and Chen Mingxia had been granted *duoqing*. So Feng Quan hoped to follow suit.[73]

It is certainly inaccurate for Tan to claim that officials all completed the three-year mourning term because the Qing inherited the Ming system with regard to this practice. Nonetheless, his claims reveal the public impression that Feng tried desperately to retain imperial favor and that the Shunzhi emperor was the one who stipulated when and how a turncoat could successfully display a *zhongxiao* image.

Contemporary interpretations of Feng's loyal turncoat image, as reflected in Tan Qian's diary, demonstrate that officials and the literati read with utmost care the smallest details in the exchange between the emperor and turncoats about filial piety, even though they risked overinterpretation and misinterpretation. Tan's account also unwittingly affirms that people were aware of the subtle change in the implications of imperial decisions about officials' filial practices. The familiar association of loyalty and filial piety remained in the image of the loyal turncoat, but the focus of *zhongxiao* rituals was shifting. No longer did turncoats' fulfillment of filial duties alone demonstrate their *zhongxiao* virtue. Now the *process and effort of negotiating* over when and how that performance should take place was a crucial part of political communication. A related change in image politics brought about by the political experiments in the Shunzhi reign was the reconfiguration of the moral-political division of labor among the ruling elite.

A DISCIPLINING COURT AND MANCHU SUPERIORITY

From the very beginning of the Qing, competition for moral superiority occupied a central place in politics for both Manchu rulers and turncoats.[74] In Shunzhi 3/4 (1646), the first metropolitan civil service examinations of the Qing dynasty were held. The essay topic on policy spoke to the Manchus' early experience with Han bureaucrats and reflected a particular kind of moral-political pose. Toward the end, the essay question stated: "To accomplish the great enterprise of the empire, we must unify everyone's heart and will. *The Manchu way of successful governing (Manzhou zhi zhi) derives from prudent officials and sincere people.* Today, what should we do to make sure Manchu and Han officials, as well as the common people, share the same will and goal?"[75] The notion of *Manzhou zhi zhi*, the "Manchu way of successful governing," reversed the self-serving Han discourse of moral superiority and assigned to Manchu rulers the role of morally transforming Han officials, not vice versa.[76] The notion of "the Manchu way" cleverly appropriated Confucian vocabulary to construct Manchu superiority.[77]

This examination question foresaw the entanglement of factionalism and competition for moral superiority. As pointed out earlier, many layers of political division had become crisscrossed in the Shunzhi reign. Further complicating the situation, after reclaiming power from Regent Dorgon, the Shunzhi emperor appropriated a late-Ming factional terminology, *Nan-Bei dang* (Southerner-Northerner factional divide), and used it in a blatantly self-serving fashion against Han officials.[78] Because the Qing first conquered the north, northerners enjoyed a more prominent standing at the beginning of the new dynasty than they had in the late-Ming metropolitan bureaucracy, especially in the top echelons of government. Still, the so-called Northerner-Southerner divide did not really correspond to the sociopolitical realities of the early Qing.[79] Additionally, although the factional leaders of these two camps allied themselves with rival Manchu aristocrats,[80] the Shunzhi emperor appropriated the language of *Nan-Bei dang* to chastise Han officials for protecting Han interests against Manchu exploitation. Therefore, the idea of Southerner-Northerner factionalism proved an effective excuse for ethnic discrimination and persecution. This rhetoric allowed the Shunzhi emperor to discipline his wayward turncoat subjects.[81] Its ethnic dimension was framed in such a way that the turncoats' collective moral image would suffer the most. It was a trope in the Shunzhi emperor's image politics through which he asserted Manchu—and his personal—superiority.

The emperor's disciplining project took shape when his personal life became a target of criticism among Han officials. The young emperor's sexual life seemed to be attracting attention of all sorts and might have truly worried Han officials.[82] In Shunzhi 10 (1654), the censor Guo Yikun warned the emperor not to pursue potency-enhancing medicine and suggested that he moderate his sexual activities. Guo was scolded for "remonstrating to gain fame" (*guming*).[83] Then another censor, Ji Kaisheng (1627–1659), pleaded with the emperor to stop the practice of selecting young women from Yangzhou and fetching them to the imperial palaces.[84] Ji's criticism, whether based on rumor or not, did not exceed his responsibilities as a Confucian official.[85] But it outraged the emperor so much that he had Ji exiled and blocked him from benefiting from any amnesties issued during the emperor's lifetime.[86]

Manchu and Han officials during this period also vocally discussed another contentious matter concerning the emperor's personal life: his complete dismissal of the first empress and his attempt to replace the second within merely two years. The emperor's relationships with his imperial wives and consorts, in particular his unrestrained expressions of affection toward certain women against the expressed wishes of the dowager empress, set Han officials back on their heels. Dismissing the empress without any moral justifications, but simply because she fell out of the emperor's favor, was considered a sign of disorder at the very heart of the empire, the moral-cosmological center of human life. Han officials begged the emperor to change his mind, while the Manchu political elite, not sharing the same Confucian perspective, convened and decided they had no reason to oppose the emperor's wish. Although the emperor got his way the first time, he faced tremendous pressure and moral admonitions from Han officials—with support from the dowager empress—the second time.

Qing emperors could not ignore or dismiss Han criticisms of their performance of masculine virtues such as filial piety and gender propriety, and they often became defensive when criticized in these areas.[87] The Shunzhi emperor fought back by accusing turncoats of factionalism and questioning their loyalty. The pamphlet *On Admonishing Officials' Minds* (Yuzhi renchen jingxin lu), commissioned in Shunzhi 12 (1655) by the emperor and written by the turncoat Wang Yongji (1600–1659), can be viewed as the Shunzhi emperor's major propaganda campaign against the turncoats. This imperial publication emphasizes that officials must strive to correct themselves in mind and manner so as to earn their ruler's trust. This admonition was echoed in the emperor's harsh punishments in several high-profile cases of moral violations and factionalism among turncoats, including that of Gong Dingzi.[88] It was precisely at this moment that the emperor began to appropriate the terminology of Southerner-Northerner factionalism and use it extensively in his disciplining project.

The Shunzhi court turned into an arena of moral struggle. Accusations of lack of *zhongxiao* now frequently appeared in official memoranda. So did charges of other types of ethical defects. As a result, the collective moral image of Han officials grew tattered. In Shunzhi 12/7 (1655), the Board of Personnel reported that Yang Qi'e (*jinshi* 1642) twice took mourning leave but, instead of remaining at home, he had gone to Suzhou, the epicenter of literati self-indulgence and moral decadence. "He has completely forgotten about his deceased parents and ignored his duties as a son. This should not be tolerated." Eventually, Yang lost his position and was ordered to return home.[89]

In Shunzhi 13/10 (1656), censors submitted more impeachments, including one accusing Fa Ruozhen (1608–1691) of frivolity and another claiming that Xu Tingqing (*jinshi* 1647) had taken the daughter of a staffer as his concubine.[90] Still another accused vice president of the Board of Works Cheng Zhengkui (1604–1676) of improper behavior in his private life, such as indulging in drinking and visiting courtesans. Fearing the potentially serious repercussions of these moral attacks and hoping to depart the court with grace, Cheng requested a leave to return home to mourn the death of his stepgrandmother.[91] But it was not granted. Instead, Cheng lost his job for his lack of self-discipline.[92]

The punishment of the new *jinshi* Qian Yuanxiu in Shunzhi 15/10 (1658) shed light on the connection between the emperor's disciplining project and the court's broader campaign against literati interests in the empire. President of the Censorate Wei Yijie (1616–1686) accused Qian Yuanxiu of being unfilial because his father, Qian Kaizong (*jinshi* 1652), had been arrested and exiled for insufficient supervision as an examiner in the infamous Examination Scandal (Kechang An) in Shunzhi 14/11 (1657).[93] Wei pointed out that Qian Yuanxiu sat for his exams even though his father had been arrested and was headed for court on that same day. He suggested stripping the junior Qian of his official position. The emperor agreed.[94] Punishing Qian Yuanxiu demonstrated the court's commitment to governing with filial piety, elevating its moral image at a moment when the Examination Scandal created fear and controversy among the literati.

In fact, censor Wei Yijie had devoted close attention to scrutinizing colleagues' personal lives. He was most rigorous in emphasizing the importance of filial virtue for officials. In Shunzhi 15/5 (1658), he had already proposed to the emperor that filial sons, if their exemplary deeds could be verified, should receive county-level official positions.[95] In Shunzhi 17/4 (1660), Wei also memorialized to impeach Dai Mingyue (*jinshi* 1634) for not remaining at home during his mourning leave but spending that time in the capital area.[96]

Some scholars suggest that Wei, as well as certain other censorial officials, under pressure from the emperor, were sometimes forced to find fault with colleagues.[97] Others consider Wei's "ethical fervor" to have stemmed from "a particular sense of moral probity that characterized younger Han officials" who identified themselves with the Qing instead of the Ming.[98] It is easy to underestimate and oversimplify the Shunzhi emperor's role in the disciplining project. In fact, symptomatic of the various experiments the emperor carried out, his handling of Han officials' moral images could sometimes be nuanced but relentless at others. To confirm his moral superiority and political authority, the emperor monitored the agents of his disciplining project, such as Wei, making sure their attacks would serve only his interests. This much is clear from his reaction to Wei's impeachment of Lü Gong (1603–1664).

When Chen Mingxia fell from imperial favor, factional officials committed themselves to attacking those who were once close to him. Memorials about Lü Gong's alleged factional ties to Chen flooded the emperor's desk in Shunzhi 11/3 (1654), when it was decided that Chen would be executed. Lü, who had taken first place in the civil service examinations of Shunzhi 6 (1659), was never attracted to acquiring power through factionalism. The emperor had admired him and hesitated to let him go. Lü submitted a request to retire because of illness, in which he confessed that he had experienced kidney problems. The vagueness of his language led to the impression that he was referring to impotence. One censor complained that Lü had used "licentious language" in the memorial.[99] This response prompted Lü to request retirement again, and the emperor let him go.

Later, when Wei Yijie attacked Lü's moral performance, the emperor reacted differently. Wei accused Lü of indulging in drinking and sexual activity, supposedly the causes of his illness, and never reporting to the emperor after his departure from court.[100] At about that time, officials impeached Wei himself for negligence and nepotism. The emperor took those charges seriously and now demanded that Wei explain himself. Eventually, he exempted Wei, but the other two officials who had been implicated with him in the nepotism charge lost their jobs.[101] At the same time, however, the emperor told Wei not to be so critical of Lü and refused to act on Lü's alleged moral defects.[102] In other words, the emperor tolerated Wei to an extent, but he also stopped Wei from overexercising moral surveillance. The emperor's treatment of Wei and Lü once again reveals the complex ways he experimented with Confucian ethics in order to convey and negotiate trust and favor. It also reflects his determination to maintain moral superiority over his Han subjects.

IMAGE CONQUEST

The foregoing discussion calls into question the claim that Han officials such as Wei Yijie "assigned" the emperor some role in their "civilizing" project.[103] The emperor was not assigned a role but actively fought to claim moral superiority, using the moral image of turncoats as a tool. Viewed in retrospect, the experiments of the Shunzhi reign set in motion some important trends in the political culture, in particular the gradual shift of the locus of image politics from officials to the monarch. Such trends would crystallize in the Kangxi reign. A telling example is how, during the campaign against the rebellious Three Feudatories from Kangxi 12 to 20 (1673–81), the young Kangxi emperor established his moral stature before the whole empire.

Already by this time, the Kangxi emperor was familiar with political negotiations in the language of Confucian ethics.[104] He exhibited an extraordinary ability to engage in image politics as the leader of the campaign to suppress the rebellions. Indeed, the Qing victory involved successful imperial efforts on many fronts. Not only was it necessary to mobilize a huge amount of military and financial resources, but the court also launched broad-based and highly effective propaganda projects. The three feudatories—Wu Sangui (1612–1678), Geng Jingzhong (1644–1682), and Shang Zhixin (1636–1680)—either had joined the Qing or had ancestors in service to the dynasty before the capital was moved to Beijing. To meet the goal of reaching out to Han officials and people, the Kangxi emperor's mobilization campaign tailored an image for each of the three men's families, a delicate task to be sure.[105]

In Kangxi 12/12 (1674), an edict was issued to all the civil and military officials as well as commoners in Yunnan, Wu Sangui's power base, in which the emperor assured his subjects that he believed they were "all born with a *zhongxiao* nature." Since a government committed to promoting *zhongxiao* carried the Mandate of Heaven, the emperor argued, it should not be difficult for his subjects to understand which of these two camps—those who followed the seditious leader Wu Sangui or those who remained loyal to the Qing—was blessed, and which was doomed.[106] The emperor ordered this edict to be widely disseminated in Yunnan so the message could reach everyone.

A couple of months later, the emperor issued another edict condemning Wu. Two places in this document where he elaborated on the first edict are of special interest for our purposes. According to the emperor, the court had done its utmost to reward the Wu family and had ordered them to relocate from their power base in Yunnan so the grandfather, father, sons, and grandsons could be united. The emperor hence summarized Wu's crimes as "violating *zhongxiao* and betraying righteousness."[107]

This constituted a drastic departure from Wu's earlier public image, which had been circulated widely in literati society before the rebellion. The popularity of this earlier image of Wu is noted by the literatus Ye Mengzhu (1623–after 1692), whose private documentation of the dynastic transition very carefully describes Wu's filial and loyal sentiments.[108] This image had been spread through a number of early Qing novels that depicted Wu as a moral paragon. One of these, *Story of Zhongxiao* (Zhongxiao zhuan), explicitly suggests that Wu's surrender to the Qing and participation in the conquest of Beijing derived from his strong desire to fulfill filial duties.[109]

The dissemination of the Kangxi emperor's new message upon the outbreak of fighting helped reshape the public's impression of Wu. This shift is reflected in a later literary rendition of a phrase from the imperial edict, "violating *zhongxiao* and betraying righteousness." In a sensational scene in *The Frost of Guilin* (Guilin shuang), a play about the campaigns against the Three Feudatories composed by the Han official Jiang Shiquan (1725–1784), a loyal Qing official invokes this phrase when confronting Wu Sangui.[110]

Meanwhile, the Kangxi emperor painted a different image for another rebellious feudatory, Geng Jingzhong, in the hope that Geng would break his alliance with Wu Sangui. In an imperial edict issued in Kangxi 13/6 (1674), the emperor emphasized the Geng ancestors' loyalty to the Qing. Considering their contributions and out of concern that the severe punishment of the Geng men in Beijing would "terminate their lineage," the emperor ordered that the Geng family be treated benevolently, unlike the harsh measures he took against the Wu clan.[111] A month later, he further instructed the Board of War that even if the Qing army eliminated Geng's forces, he would still allow the Geng clan to collect and bury their ancestors' bones.[112] Such edicts confirmed the emperor's moral supremacy and publicized it as standing in stark contrast to the disloyalty of the men who had betrayed both the dynasty and the *zhongxiao* tradition of their families.

During these campaigns against the Three Feudatories, the court also set up Han bannerman-officials from the Fan lineage—in particular Fan Wencheng and his son Fan Chengmo (*jinshi* 1652)—as emblems and standards of *zhongxiao*. In the Shunzhi reign, the incorporation of Fan Wencheng as a Confucian erudite into the founding myths of the Qing had promoted a narrative of mutual attraction between the Manchu rulers and Han literati that aimed to erase the crucial historical distinction between "loyalty" (*zhong*) and the

Manchu concept of a slave's dedication to his master (*jurgan*).[113] In the Kangxi reign, during the campaigns against the Three Feudatories, Fan Chengmo, governor-general of Zhejiang and Fujian, had been imprisoned and murdered by Geng Jingzhong. Fan subsequently became *the* symbol of *zhongxiao* in the empire, and his *zhongxiao* reputation was enthusiastically publicized by the court.[114] Fan's borderland identity as a Han-bannerman gave his moral-political image a subtle ethnic dimension that made his exemplariness into a demonstration of Manchu moral superiority. Thus, during a crucial period in the Qing struggle to survive and adapt, the Fans represented a particular stage in the transformation of the Confucian moral-political system, whereby the moral-political leadership status of Han literati-officials began to decline in the shadow of the Manchu conquerors.

Between 1644 and 1682, Manchu rulers had to learn along the way how to consolidate their political authority. Survival and adaptation demanded creativity and tactfulness on the part of all political actors. The deployment of Confucian ethics as a language of communication was indispensable in this process, especially when the subject was complex and sensitive, necessitating extraordinary care and subtlety. Factionalism, favor, and trust were such matters. The creative use of Confucian ethics in the political experiments the Manchu rulers and the turncoats formulated as they strove to deal with the changing political situation affirmed the importance of *zhongxiao* in political communication.

In this process, individual turncoats as well as Han literati sensed that *zhongxiao* rituals were taking on new political implications. They realized that the court recognized and honored *zhongxiao* ethics and other Confucian ethical expectations differentially and sometimes expediently. This situation explains the Qing's seemingly contradictory tendencies in handling officials' mourning rules. On the one hand, *duoqing* cases became more frequent compared to the late Ming; on the other hand, the resign-and-mourn policy continued, and many officials completed this moral-political duty. In Shunzhi 10/4 (1653), the court went so far as to stipulate that Manchu officials in the metropolitan government should begin to follow this mourning procedure as well.[115] The seemingly contradictory attitudes toward the practice of *duoqing* actually exemplify the improvisational nature of early Qing politics rather than suggest a breakdown of the *zhongxiao* concept. For instance, *duoqing* had gone from an undesirable compromise between the *zhongxiao* ideal and practical concerns to a process of negotiation over favor and trust. In this and other filial practices, the emperor increasingly set the terms for displays of moral exemplariness. Hence, the continued importance of Confucian ethics as a language of political communication did not foreclose Confucian moralism but accommodated changes to it.

The changing image of the loyal turncoat complicates the conventional understanding of the Manchu rulers' deployment of Confucian teaching as evidence of either sinicization or instrumentalism. While Qing developments upgraded the importance of officials' moral performance in political processes, the court's agendas and intended messages were not simply ideological. Therefore, it is reductive to cast its intentions as either sincere or hypocritically expedient. It is also problematic to see its practice of Confucian moralism as fundamentally different from—and even inferior to—that of the literati.[116]

Further, the emperor was hardly a passive receiver of Han officials' efforts to wield their "gentlemanly influence."[117] While the Shunzhi emperor did not necessarily make his turncoats better sons, fathers, and husbands, his reign certainly succeeded in establishing Manchu moral superiority over their Han officials. Increasingly, Qing emperors outshone Han officials in moral image, taking the lead in propaganda campaigns against men who had failed to carry out their political responsibilities across generations and dynasties. The shift in the central locus of image politics took place gradually, subtly, and unevenly. Manchu rulers, from the beginning of the dynasty in the northeast, understood the potential of Confucian ethics as a political tool. Manchu emperors claimed "sagehood" by showing their familiarity with Confucian classics and patronizing literati scholarship.[118] In the Kangxi reign, when the emperor transformed the lectures on Confucian classics into public spectacles that displayed his superior intellectual insights, he even took over the instructor's role from his Han officials, in effect turning them into objects of his *jiaohua* (civilizing and transforming).[119]

It is important to note that the political experiments of the Shunzhi and Kangxi reigns also had a personal aspect. Confucian family tales once again came into play as the image of the loyal turncoat was intensely negotiated. This trend began with the Shunzhi emperor's struggles with Manchu and Han factionalisms and his disciplining of turncoats through his use of the language of Confucian ethics in court politics. The experiments continued into the Kangxi reign, with an emperor now deeply engaged in Confucianism on political, intellectual, religious, and cultural levels.

CHAPTER 5

Conquest, Continuity, and the Loyal Turncoat

In Shunzhi 6 (1649), Feng Quan celebrated his mother's eighty-seventh birthday. On behalf of a large group of officials, the turncoat Hu Shi'an (*jinshi* 1628) authored a congratulatory essay for this highly publicized occasion. Feng's colleagues all wanted to acknowledge his impressive *zhongxiao* achievements, a success story for the Qing policy of "governing with filial piety."[1]

The essay describes Feng willingly leaving his powerful position for some time to visit his aged mother and praises the sagacious ruler, the Shunzhi emperor—but in actuality, Regent Dorgon—for recognizing this official's *zhongxiao* commitment. Hu invokes two historical figures to highlight Feng's *zhongxiao* accomplishment. Both figures served as prime minister in the Song dynasty: Zhang Qixian (942–1014), increasingly dissatisfied with the emperor's policies, resigned, using the excuse of needing to care for his mother; Fu Bi (1004–1083) stepped down from his position of prime minister when his mother passed away.

Strictly speaking, these historical references were not proper for the occasion, as they differed from Feng Quan's circumstances in fundamental ways. However, they still served a meaningful purpose: Hu suggests that because Feng's mother had lived longer than the mothers of these two accomplished Song officials, Heaven had rewarded Feng, who had the good fortune to thrive in a better time. The same message was repeated at another major celebration of Feng Quan's mother by his colleagues, in Shunzhi 11 (1654).[2] Then, upon her death the next year, in an epitaph composed by the turncoat Jin Zhijun (*jinshi* 1619), Feng was again portrayed as a man of "noble aspirations to *zhongxiao*" (*zhongxiao dazhi*).[3]

Image-making efforts such as these remained an important way for turncoats to strengthen friendships and affirm political positions. By incorporating public and personal lives into one narrative, these efforts also, if unwittingly, burnished the Qing court's own image. In the early Qing, the turncoats' narrative of moral continuity—from the Ming to the Qing, and between loyalty and other Confucian masculine virtues—was intertwined with the Manchu claim to moral superiority. The Qing "ethno-dynastic rule" would reveal itself in the entangled Confucian family tales of the Manchu monarchs and their Han subjects.[4] While the Manchu claim to moral superiority constituted a significant part of the Qing consolidation of power, narratives of moral continuity were indispensable in rebuilding the turncoats' social lives and literati society across the empire. Through a variety of media such as visual art, literature, family genealogy, and public spectacles, the figure of the loyal turncoat, an emblem of Confucian ethical ideals pursued across the dynastic divide, conveniently became a site of sociopolitical negotiation between factionalists, between the Manchus and the Han, and between turncoats and Ming loyalists.

PORTRAITS OF THE LOYAL TURNCOAT

As Manchu rulers and Han officials sought ways of navigating the increasingly complex factional strife and unpredictable conditions outside the court in order to survive, adapt, and forestall political trouble, Han officials created the vivid figure of the "loyal turncoat." This figure embodied undisrupted commitment to loyalty, filial piety, friendship, and gender propriety from the Ming to the Qing.

Loyal Turncoats as True Friends

The turncoats' survival depended on their ability to mobilize social and cultural resources with which to improvise protective tactics amid uncertainty. They achieved this goal by helping one another articulate their experiences during the dynastic change and reiterate their collective and personal commitment to Confucian ideals. Take some of the turncoats associated with the Fushe as examples. Within this community, there emerged a strengthened sense of mutual sympathy and dedication. When Beijing fell, Chen Mingxia was captured by the rebels but eventually escaped to the south, where he found himself condemned as a disloyal official and wanted by the Southern Ming regime. So he fled again, and after months of living as a fugitive in various provinces, he returned to Beijing in late 1644.[5] Chen's Fushe friends there wholeheartedly embraced him as an old friend, expecting to strengthen their bonds in those trying times. A line from Cao Rong's (1613–1685) poem best captures the sentiment: "Homeless now, how can we afford to lose friends?"[6]

Another celebrity figure among Fushe scholars, Li Wen, composed two moving poems upon Chen's arrival. In the poems, he expressed his confidence that the turmoil would only draw out the most sincere feelings among the friends. Lamenting that so many extraordinarily talented friends had perished during the war, he voiced the expectation that Chen's arrival would rekindle hope and good spirits in their community in Beijing. By invoking a few famous historical references, Li unmistakably implied that Chen's loyalty and talents warranted imperial recognition in the new dynasty.[7]

At Chen's request, Xiong Wenju, another Fushe friend, composed a preface for his new poetry collection. That collection, which was to be printed soon thereafter, consisted of poems Chen had written during 1644, as he, like many of his Fushe friends, tried to survive the rebellions and the Manchu invasion. In his preface, Xiong emotionally described how he encountered this poetry collection: when he reunited with Chen, choking on tears, they told each other their own heartbreaking experiences upon and immediately after the fall of Beijing. It was at this moment that Chen showed Xiong the poems written during that period and requested a preface.[8]

Xiong employs in this preface the traditional language of *zhongxiao*, but he challenges some literati's selective invocation of *zhongxiao* for purposes of political persecution. He recalls Chen's accomplishments in the last year of the Ming dynasty, arguing that Chen did not commit suicide when Beijing fell but fled to the south only because he was loyal to the Ming. Now his return from the south testified to his loyalty to the new dynasty, which had taken over the Mandate of Heaven and pledged to serve the people better than the corrupt Southern Ming regime had.[9] Importantly, Xiong urges the reader to contemplate the meaning of true *zhongxiao* and rebukes the unfair treatment of officials trapped in Beijing at the hands of "literati in the south who snarl at Chen and slander his colleagues who have had similar experience": "They look on unconcerned and comment with such ease, 'This man should be executed' and 'that man should be arrested.' When the parents suffer, the sons who happen to be living with them are expected to kill themselves. Those who live far away do not assume any responsibility. They have already taken advantage of the situation. Now they criticize the brothers who have gone through hardships with their parents."[10]

Literary projects of this kind generated a positive image of the loyal turncoat as one who practices Confucian ethics in spite of dislocation and dynastic change. Sharing the personal sufferings inflicted by self-proclaimed loyalists strengthened their bond as true friends. Equally as important, turncoat friends fulfilled the role of witness and helped one another explain and authenticate their continuous commitment to Confucian ethics. As shown earlier, Chen Mingxia "became" a disloyal official by accident. However, he was too cautious to provide all the details of his escape attempts. In the meantime, many contemporaries, even though were aware that the established image of Chen might be inaccurate, still felt hesitant about disregarding the official lists of disloyal officials circulated by the Southern Ming government on which Chen appeared.[11] Given such circumstances, publishing the turncoats' writing and comments about their wartime experiences was ever more important.

Turncoats also constructed meaningful images of the loyal turncoat through visual art, as shown by two Fushe friends, Gong Dingzi and Cao Rong. Sometime after the Manchus drove the rebel army out of Beijing, Gong and Cao were appointed to the same positions they had held before the change of regime.[12] Gong was still trying to avoid accepting his appointment when Cao began to serve the Qing. One day, Cao brought Gong a scroll and had him ask Gu Mei to paint on it. The inscription, by Gong himself, is dated the summer of 1644, before Gong officially entered the Qing government.[13] The pictorial content of the painting has not survived, but from the inscription that alludes to orchid, a long-standing metaphor for the loyal subject, it seems to have been an orchid painting, for which Gu was well known.[14]

The message conveyed in Gu's painting and Gong's accompanying inscription reveals how carefully turncoats contemplated the proper way of displaying their commitment to Confucian ideals. Every minute detail is meaningful. In particular, the inscription's reference to the historical figure Yu Xin (513–581) allows the turncoats to defy being easily categorized as "disloyal."[15] They were *turncoats who nonetheless held fast to loyalty.*

This gift had a single focus: to convey deep sorrow. Its reference to Yu Xin and the sorrow motif produce a nuanced image of the loyal turncoat. Yu Xin does not, first and foremost, represent disloyalty here.[16] In fact, the power of this historical-literary reference is its allusion to the helplessness and sorrow in Yu Xin's famous poem, "The Lament for the South" (Ai Jiangnan fu), in which he proclaims his "reluctant disloyalty." Gong and Cao used this allusion quite often in the early years of the Qing because it suited their delicate situation very well. By that time, "The Lament for the South" had become a classic expression of sorrow over the loss of one's homeland. Through such references to Yu Xin, turncoats could plausibly present themselves as helpless victims of war—melancholic men, pained by the loss of their country and their martyred emperor. Because the historical figure Yu Xin made his political decision involuntarily, the imagery expressing his great sorrow helped the turncoats explain their circumstances and engage the question of loyalty in a nuanced but meaningful way.

Southerner turncoats in the early Qing often alluded to Yu Xin in their poetry.[17] The reference in the inscription on Gu Mei's painting is the earliest example of this. Interestingly, nearly all the turncoats who frequently used this imagery at the time belonged to Gong Dingzi's and Cao Rong's social circles. It is also significant that when the turncoats circulated this imagery in their poetry, some Ming loyalist friends responded positively to this device.[18] Therefore, just how Gong and Cao employed Yu Xin in art and literature to negotiate loyalty deserves careful consideration.

First, the image of the war victim defuses the stereotypical turncoat figure—traitor to Confucian ethics—by revealing the injustice of this misrepresentation applied to individuals caught in such unfortunate circumstances. At the time the painting and its inscription were made, neither Gong Dingzi nor Cao Rong had found an opportunity to return south to face charges leveled against turncoats in the anti-Qing stronghold areas. But news traveled between the conquered and unconquered regions, bringing with it reports of how the Southern Ming government and the public were persecuting survivor officials and their families.[19] Gong's inscription pleads for understanding of their complicated political choices through an imagined conversation between the turncoat and the loyalist. In their dialogue, he allows the lament of officials like himself to be challenged and even mocked by two figures from literature famous for political withdrawal, Chrysanthemum of the East Bamboo Fence (Dongli Ju) and Thornferns of the Western Mountains (Xishan Wei).[20] Here they clearly stand in for the Ming loyalists. "We lament before the grass and flowers, sobbing, sighing, and confessing. Our hearts are sorrowful; no poems are without pain. The Chrysanthemum of the East Bamboo Fence and the Thornferns of the Western Mountains must be laughing at us, and at [the orchids accompanying] these two frustrated fellows."[21] Gong's voice, representing the vulnerable turncoat, characterizes their situation as being helpless "prisoners of war" (*shen zuo fuqiu*).[22] Gu Mei's orchid painting, then, becomes a meaningful platform for Cao's and Gong's self-expression and self-representation as men who remain loyal at heart. They are turncoats with loyalty.

In interesting ways, the presence of Gu Mei in this gift as a "witness" testifies to the turncoats' unwavering commitment to Confucian ideals. Gong's inscription comments that Gu's painting is artistically marvelous but cannot be considered a truly good piece of work, due to its unrestrained expression of sorrow.[23] However, this critical comment actually strengthens their claim of loyalty, because the "excessive sorrow"—at the expense of artistic perfection—manifests the sincerity of their loyal sentiments. In other words, what has rendered Gu's painting artistically imperfect is precisely what authenticates these men's unwavering adherence to Confucian ethical ideals.

This act of gifting, the use of the cultural symbol of Yu Xin, and the virtuous concubine's testimony enabled friends to present one another as the "loyal turncoat." In turn, their friendship acquired new energy. But continuity in friendship and the image of the true friend could not be taken for granted, especially as war and chaos threatened and tested the officials' sociopolitical bonds and their different approaches to Confucian values. The times required that turncoats carefully nourish their friendships, among themselves and increasingly with loyalists, by following a shared understanding and practice of Confucian ethical ideals. Failure to do so could bring friendships to an end.

In fact, not all friendships were strengthened and enriched as turncoats engaged the discursive connection between loyalty and friendship. Take Gong Dingzi and Chen Mingxia as an example. In their service to the Qing, it became increasingly clear that Gong and Chen had adopted opposite approaches to their role as officials. Chen was eager to demonstrate his loyalty to the new rulers.[24] What most hurt the feelings of his Ming loyalist friends was that, in his eagerness to prove his loyalty to the Qing, he repeatedly recommended them to the court.[25]

In contrast, Gong sought only sympathy and forgiveness from his loyalist friends. Further, within the government, Gong tried to protect his colleague-friends whose family members participated in resistance movements in the south. For this he was impeached and disciplined.[26] Gong's willingness to explain his identity as a loyal turncoat and to prioritize his friends' feelings and needs made him a "true friend." Thus, the factional grudge between Gong and Chen was in fact a battle of competing moral images—one turncoat currying favor with the new ruler versus another who was a trustworthy friend, loyal at heart to his country. As shown earlier, in his impeachment of Chen Mingxia at court, the turncoat Luo Guoshi painted contrasting images of these former friends by highlighting Chen's neglect of *zhongxiao* versus Gong's persistent filial devotion and loyalty.

Loyal Turncoats as Filial Sons

In the early Qing, turncoat officials had to struggle constantly against the disloyal-immoral images imposed on them by both diehard loyalists and factional enemies at court. This was true even of seemingly successful turncoats at the height of their careers, men such as Song Quan. Song's untiring investment in his *zhongxiao* image in various forms from the late Ming to the early Qing reveals the political skills of an experienced, intelligent official at a time of crisis. The figure of the loyal turncoat emerging from his writings and actions is someone who pursues *zhongxiao* ethics across the dynastic divide, and whose moral performance is even strengthened by the dynastic change.

In the spring of Chongzhen 16 (1643), exactly one year before the fall of Beijing, Song compiled and printed a collection of poetry. Many of these poems had been composed in the previous year, when the Song family had to flee their hometown, Shangqiu in Henan, amid violence and massive destruction inflicted by rebels. For six months, Song escorted his mother, Madam Ding, from their devastated hometown to various locations before they settled temporarily in Nanjing. At one point, Song almost lost his nine-year-old son Song Luo (1634–1713), and his younger son disappeared on the journey to Nanjing. Song Quan was soon summoned by the Chongzhen emperor to lead defense efforts in the capital area. In Chongzhen 16/1 (1643), Song and his family arrived in Beijing. A couple of months later, Song published a poetry collection.[27]

The publication of this collection so soon after Song's arrival in the capital had particular meanings. The difficult times tried a man's determination to fulfill *zhongxiao* duties. Song's career had begun with his appointment as magistrate in Shanxi. Five years later, in the early Chongzhen reign, he served as a censor in Beijing until his memorials offended powerful officials and earned him a demotion. In protest, Song resigned from office with the excuse that he had to take care of his mother.[28] Thus, in the last years of the Ming, Song's moral-political performance matched perfectly with the traditional image of a loyal official, refusing to compromise with corrupt power and drawing on filial piety as both a rhetoric of political protest and an inspiration for his devotion to the emperor.

This *zhongxiao* image is made clear in the very title of the poetry collection, *Baihua Poems from a Time of Sojourning* (Baihua ke kuang), which contains a literary reference from the *Book of Poetry* (Shijing).[29] *Baihua* had long existed in literati vocabulary as a reference to filiality. Song begins the preface to this collection by emphasizing his filial duty toward his mother: "*Baihua* means the commitment to take care of one's parents."[30] *Ke kuang*, literally meaning residing as a guest who has lost his home, is used here by Song to describe the strong bond between him and his mother, Madam Ding, during their time of dislocation and hardship.[31] Publishing this collection at this particular moment made Song an emblem of the Confucian masculine ideal known as "transferring filial piety to loyalty" (*yi xiao zuo zhong*).[32]

If the publication of his poetry collection was a way for Song to reassert himself in court politics in the late Ming, then his self-portrayal as a loyal turncoat in the first years of the Shunzhi reign sheds light on how he anticipated and coped with that complex and volatile political situation in the new dynasty. During the Dorgon regency, Song's competence and political integrity secured steady promotions. He was appointed grand secretary in Shungzhi 3/1 (1646).[33] Song represented the successful, even model, bureaucrat that the Manchu rulers desired. He did not embrace any extremes in politics or policy. His proposals to the court aimed mainly to promote a balanced agenda that would protect the interests of ordinary Manchu and Han people. Further, he had remained unidentified with any particular faction. He possessed a charisma enhanced by genuine interest in military strategy and military skills. He became an indispensable figure in the government. Hence, in Shunzhi 5 (1648), upon Madam Ding's death, as a gesture of trust and favor, Dorgon rejected Song's request for a mourning leave, issued him a *duoqing* order, and continued to assign him important tasks.

Having gone through late-Ming factionalism, Song was alert to the political risks involved in a *duoqing* case. This awareness probably led him to invest heavily in a narrative of moral continuity. When his request for mourning leave was rejected, he did what he could to fulfill his filial duty. In the "Deeds of Madam Ding" (Ding taifuren xingshi), the official biographical account composed by Song for his deceased mother, he delineated an image for himself in which a son's filial devotion intersected with his loyalty to *both* the fallen Ming and the new Qing regime.

According to this account, three days before the fall of Beijing to the rebels, Song was promoted to governor of the Shuntian area, an administrative district that overlapped with Beijing. He diligently set out to patrol the surrounding regions. When the rebels began arresting and recruiting former Ming officials in the fallen capital, Song happened to be conducting an inspection tour nearby and therefore did not face imminent threat. However, his mother was stuck in the rebel-controlled city, Zunhua (in modern-day Hebei). Song mobilized his former subordinates and coordinated military actions to attack the rebels in Zunhua after learning about Li Zicheng's defeat by the Manchus at the Shanhai Pass. When Li retreated to Beijing and learned of Song's decisive leadership in the Zunhua insurgence, he immediately dispatched thousands of troops to retaliate. Song sent a trusted friend, General Tang Yü, to the Shanhai Pass to request help from the Manchus. Tang reached the pass and delivered the message requesting loan of their forces to avenge the late Ming emperor. After the Manchus drove Li Zicheng and his army out of Beijing, Song moved his mother safely back from her refuge in the mountains. He told Dorgon that he had fulfilled his duty toward the martyred Ming emperor and would like to retire.[34] Dorgon reinstalled him as governor of Shuntian, with his headquarters in Miyun, in the vicinity of Beijing.[35]

Song Quan claims that all his political decisions and actions during the late Ming and the changes of regime in 1644, especially his switching loyalty to the Qing, "resulted from Mother's influence" (*mu cheng zhi ye*). Indeed, his mother's biography radiates a spirit of *zhongxiao* and stresses that Song's accomplishments as a son and an official in the two dynasties were inseparable and continuous. It recalls how Madam Ding provided moral support for Song's answer to the Chongzhen emperor's call to take charge of the defense of the capital area, and how, when he led the military actions against the rebels, Madam Ding met with the soldiers and delivered encouraging words. Song asserts that his revenge on behalf of the martyred Chongzhen emperor through collaboration with the Qing authority should be attributed to his mother.[36] The shift in loyalty to the Qing is smooth and natural, testifying to and justified by the continuity of filial devotion.

Upon entering service with the Qing, according to this narrative, Song continued to deepen his understanding of the ethics of *zhongxiao*. He introduces his mother's virtuous life with a mention of his recent participation in compiling the *Veritable Records* of the Qing's founding emperor, Nurhaci.[37] Madam Ding died at the end of Shunzhi 5 (1658). Soon, in Shunzhi 6 (1659), the court issued an edict that commissioned compilation of the *Veritable Records* of Nurhaci's reign. Song assumed the official title of Grand Secretary of the Historiography Academy (Guoshiyuan Daxueshi). He states that even though he was given a *duoqing* order, having been granted the honorable task of supervising this history project has reminded him that composing a detailed account documenting his mother's virtuous deeds would allow him to be at once a filial son and a loyal official.[38]

Song's praise for imperial generosity upon his mother's death conveyed the same message. The Qing court had rewarded Song by sending the president of the Board of Rites to mourn Madam Ding, with an imperial edict recognizing Song's fulfillment of the ideal of "transferring filial piety to loyalty."[39] When expressing his gratitude to the court, Song made a special point of recognizing that the court had in this case made an exception by granting imperial sacrifice to a woman who had not received an official title. In this way, Song indicated that his understanding of *zhongxiao* actually continued to deepen with his service to the new dynasty.[40]

Song Quan's image as a "loyal turncoat" does not simply justify his shift in loyalty; it makes dynastic change one moment in an official's ongoing, diligent pursuit of moral cultivation. Once the pattern of *zhongxiao* is established this way, any political decision making could be turned into an episode of continuous moral growth. For example, three months after Madam Ding's death, the court appointed Song to preside over the metropolitan civil service examinations, a responsibility that required him to participate in celebratory ceremonies and hence violate mourning norms. Song complied, but in the written instructions to the examinees, he particularly stressed the moral significance of correct literary style: "Superb performance of *zhongxiao* derives from the correct style; tremendous evils derive from incorrect styles."[41] Although the same sentence had appeared a year before in a memorial jointly submitted by Song Quan and Feng Quan regarding the government regulation of literati publishing, employing the *zhongxiao* language at this sensitive moment seemed to serve a different purpose.[42] It was not incidental that another turncoat grand secretary, Hong Chengchou, lectured to this newly selected *jinshi* cohort on the meaning of *zhongxiao* in the course of his own efforts to survive at court (discussed in chap. 4).

TRANSGENERATIONAL FAMILY TALES AND MANCHU MORAL SUPERIORITY

The loyal turncoat as figured by Song Quan was a man unrelenting in his pursuit of moral cultivation. The success of this figure demonstrates the power of the continuum of Confucian moralism centered on *zhongxiao*. Song family tales spanned a few generations, from the late Ming to the early Qing. Conceptually, the notion of the dynastic cycle resembles that of the human life cycle, so the beginning of the new dynasty is considered to have been seeded in the last phases of the old one.[43] Similarly, the Confucian moral-political system both ensures and lives in generational continuity. In the context of a dynastic change, the new dynasty must be integrated into transgenerational Confucian family tales in order to take root. The transdynastic, transgenerational stories of Song Quan's family show how the loyal turncoat figure became a site of negotiation for turncoat families seeking an advantageous position between Ming loyalism and Manchu claims to moral superiority as the Manchu rulers and Han elite were working out the moral-political division of labor under new political conditions.

The Exemplary Patriarch

Song Quan had not been a controversial figure in early Qing politics, so the humiliations caused by the moral attacks on him amid Manchu factionalism in the mid-Shunzhi reign must have generated a deep sense of unfairness and the desire among Song's family and supporters to see his redemption. Song's images as presented by his son and friends—depicting his experience in late-Ming politics, during Li Zicheng's temporary occupation of Beijing, and in the early Qing—placed particular stress on continuity in his moral pursuits and the family's Confucian tradition.

Friends of the Song family understood the stakes of restoring Song Quan's public image after his political demise. The turncoat Liu Yuyou (d. 1653), Song's in-law, who had served as the president of three boards (Revenues, War, and Punishments) during the Shunzhi reign, wrote Song's epitaph.[44] He stressed that Song had persistently requested mourning leave upon the death of his mother and had attempted to decline the prestigious appointment to supervise the metropolitan civil service exams, though his efforts had not been successful.[45] Similarly, in the tombstone inscriptions composed for Song by his disciple, the official Tang Bin (1627–1687), the connection between the virtues of loyalty and filial piety was again highlighted.[46] These representations directly refuted the charges that had brought down Song Quan and insulted the Song family.

Song Quan's image as moral exemplar was further sharpened by his eldest son, Song Luo (1634–1714), in his depictions of his father as an exemplary patriarch in official documents, biographies, and the family genealogy. First, Song Luo made sure that his father's extraordinary *zhongxiao* performance would be reflected in official documents to erase the negative claims that caused his father's disgrace. During the early Kangxi reign, Song Luo became an assistant magistrate in Huangzhou. In Kangxi 6 (1667), he earned honorary titles for his family members from the court. Since the imperial documents issued for such matters were based on material submitted by the officials themselves, it is particularly telling that Song made *zhongxiao* a central piece of his family tradition: his father exemplified how filial piety turned into loyalty, and his grandmother manifested womanly virtues by educating filial sons to become loyal subjects.[47]

Starting in Kangxi 14 (1675), Song Luo compiled and printed a large amount of material related to his family history.[48] The reprint of his father's old poetry collection, which was published before the fall of Beijing, is particularly interesting and revealing. Song Luo changed the title from *Baihua Poems from the Time of Sojourning* to *Poems of Baihua Hall* (Baihuatang shi). In addition, this reprint included poems composed during the transfer of power in 1644. Whereas the original title and contents displayed an official's filial piety to his mother and loyalty to the Ming at a difficult time, in the reprint, Song Quan's loyalty to the Qing enters the picture and completes his image of transdynastic moral exemplariness. The sojourning experiences of the Song son and mother in 1644 became part of the family's journey to prosperity in the new dynasty. For example, one of the poems composed in those days, "In My Office at Miyun" (Miyun shu zhong), skillfully expresses the transfer of Song Quan's loyalty:

> Three years have passed since I bid farewell to the Ming;
> Twice have I come to Miyun.
> When not in office, I serve my caring mother;
> Nothing in the world can make me worry.[49]

These lines draw a vivid picture of an ideal Confucian man who had fulfilled *zhongxiao* by perfectly blending his loyal service to two dynasties with his filial devotion. Although the subject of Song Quan's filial narrative remained focused on Madam Ding, the object of his loyalty changed in 1644, from the Ming to the Qing. In four simple lines, this poem concludes an old era and opens a new page in his public career, with a strong sense of continuity in both his personal and political lives enabled by *zhongxiao* ethics. This shift in loyalty is naturalized in the reprint of this collection.

Song Luo continued with the image-making efforts initiated by his father, but he cemented them by making more extensive use of print. While his grandfather and father had begun to compile a family genealogy, it was Song Luo who not only fundamentally transformed its format but also had it published. As he circulated it among both officials and loyalist literati over the years, he collected more prefaces, which enhanced the influence of his family tales, and consolidated their transdynastic, transgenerational moral narrative.[50] In this genealogy, Song Luo positions his father as the most accomplished patriarch of the family since the mid-Ming: "[My father] had served in several official positions at court and in the provinces until he became a grand secretary. Always dedicated and attentive, he transformed filial devotion into loyalty (*yi xiao zuo zhong*), and therefore had really inherited and realized our ancestors' noble ideals."[51] The dynastic transition and Song Quan's switch in loyalty go unremarked upon. Instead, they serve as the background for the extraordinary continuity and consistency in Song Quan's filial performance and the Song family's Confucian tradition.

Revering the Matriarch

The appeal of the loyal turncoat in in the Songs' transdynastic family tale also derived from the figure of the Confucian matriarch, Madam Ding, who occupied a significant place in the family's struggle over image and politics. On a practical level, she stitched various generations of the family together. On the symbolic level, she helped connect the moral continuity of the Song family to the establishment of Manchu dominance.

A weighty character in the Song family tale, Madam Ding has an image that outshines even that of her turncoat son, Song Quan. When her grandson Song Luo edited the biography of Madam Ding for the family genealogy in the early Kangxi reign, he mostly copied his father's original but elaborated on the transgenerational and transdynastic moral exemplariness of the Songs. One anecdote details Madam Ding's participation in a public ceremony in the summer of 1644, at which Song Quan mobilized his Ming troops to suppress the rebels with the help of the Manchus. Madam Ding's presence justified and even motivated her son's shift in loyalty to the Qing and once again showed the power of his *zhongxiao* commitment.[52]

The matriarch not only provided the occasion for recording the Songs' loyalty toward both the Ming and the Qing, but more importantly, her story glorified the Manchu emperor's moral accomplishments. The Shunzhi emperor was merely seven years old when his uncle Dorgon ushered him into the imperial palaces in Beijing. That year, Song Luo, just eleven years old himself,[53] had gone through war and family losses with his father. In Shunzhi 4 (1647), when he was fourteen, the court issued an edict asking high-ranking officials to send one son to serve the young emperor, a duty that came with the title and status of Imperial Guard. Song Quan complied. From then on, every day, Song Luo rode a horse and wore a sword, entering the Forbidden City with the most prestigious princes and officials.

According to Song Luo, during that time, he regularly waited at the emperor's and dowager empress's meals and received his share afterward. He recalled that on special occasions and banquets, he often accompanied the young emperor. He fondly remembered that one day, while sitting next to the emperor at a feast, he put some delicacies into a pocket. The emperor, curious, asked him about it. Song knelt down and replied: "Your Majesty, my grandmother Madam Ding is seventy years old. I wanted to offer her what I had received from Your Majesty." The young emperor was delighted: "From today you can take home whatever you like!" Song would always take some rare delicacies back to his grandmother after the banquets. Madam Ding was very pleased and told him to serve the emperor with loyalty as his father did.[54] In this story the Manchu ruler's virtues and the Song family's adherence to Confucian ethics authenticate each other and are mutually constituted.

This narrative of the family's moral consistency projects a glowing image of the Shunzhi emperor, who had learned how to "govern with filial piety" at a very young age. Since Song Luo would go on to become a favorite official of the succeeding monarch, the Kangxi emperor, this family tale echoed and supported the imperial family tale and the emperor's image as a filial man. The Kangxi emperor's deployment of "dynastic filiality" as an instrument of Qing ethnodynastic rule invoked Manchu ancestral worship and also resonated with the Han notion of filiality.[55] The discourse of filial piety—and its many rhetorical and physical manifestations—served multiple political purposes, as "a gesture of bureaucratic propitiation and an ideological expression of ethno-dynastic triumphalism." Manchu dowager empresses, like Madam Ding as mother and grandmother, often figured prominently in these imperial filial performances.[56]

By the time the episode about his grandmother was printed in Song Luo's autobiography, the locus of image politics had shifted markedly toward the Manchu monarch. In Kangxi 20 (1681), soon after the campaign against the Three Feudatories had ended, the emperor proceeded to the Beijing suburbs, where he conducted burial ceremonies at the Imperial Mausoleums of Filiality (Xiaoling) for two deceased dowager empresses.[57] Manchu nobles and high-ranking Han officials added much luster to the event, which, in the words of Wang Shizhen (1634–1711), then director of the Imperial Academy of Learning (Guozijian), staged a grand display of imperial virtue.[58]

Song Luo, now a top official on the Board of Punishments, took part in this imperial filial spectacle and compiled a poetry collection at the end of the trip. Commenting on this collection, Wang Shizhen identifies connections among the excellent services of the Song father and son as officials, the prosperity of the Kangxi reign, and Song Luo's adherence to the poetic tradition descending from the *Book of Poetry*—"words of loyal officials and filial sons."[59] Wang's preface portrays how the Songs thrived in a prosperous empire where the Manchu emperors' accomplishments evinced its successful governing with filial piety. Interestingly, this portrayal strove more to elucidate the exemplariness of the Manchu emperor more than to praise the Songs' personal virtues, which no doubt reflected this important shift in early Qing image politics.

Song Luo and Wang Shizhen, like many of their Han colleagues, eventually entered history as competent administrators, dedicated agents of the state who effectively applied their cultural skills to serving the Qing civilizing projects, and admirers of their Manchu ruler's moral exemplariness. As the Manchu monarchs established their moral superiority and eventually came to embody it more fully, turncoat officials' concerted endeavors to publicize their own continuous moral pursuits across the dynastic divide not only testified to this shift of focus but also contributed to it.

Placing the Turncoat Generation

Indeed, reconfiguration of the moral-political division of labor between the Manchu monarch and his Han subjects occurred in part over conversations regarding the generational position of the turncoats. Ming loyalists participated in these conversations as well. The loyalist Zhang Zilie, in his preface composed for Song Luo's collection of work, completely omits mention of Song Luo's father, Song Quan. Instead, Zhang praised Song Xun (1522–1591), Song Luo's great-grandfather and a reputable Ming official, for his work on Cheng-Zhu Confucianism, and expressed his hope that Song Luo would not "ignore this family heritage."[60] This account fails to echo Song Luo's emphasis on the continuity of *zhongxiao* from his great-grandfather to his father. The conspicuous absence of Song Quan in this narrative reflects a die-hard loyalist's reluctance to tolerate turncoats. Even so, Zhang does not reject the idea that Song Luo could revive the family's tradition and moral reputation. In fact, he urges Song to make efforts to overcome the temporary rupture in that tradition.

The loyalist Wei Xi (1624–1681), however, delineates a different image for Song Quan. He sees both Song's undisrupted government service and his pursuit of *zhongxiao* as extraordinary accomplishments. In a postscript to the Song family genealogy, Wei stressed that Song was among the first to urge Manchu rulers to give the martyred Chongzhen emperor a posthumous title. In Wei's account, although Song had wanted to demur from serving a different dynasty, he eventually heeded the new ruler's insistent calls. Song's contrasting experiences in these two dynasties—frustration in the Ming and success in the Qing—confirmed one important moral-political lesson: emperors who "sought loyal officials in unfilial sons" would fail.[61] Here Wei seems to make the significant point that the Qing success demonstrated that the new dynasty had truly embraced "governing with filial piety," and if it intended to sustain its triumphs, it should continue on this path.

Publications by the Songs' loyalist friends, which disagreed on whether Song Quan represented continuity or discontinuity of the Confucian tradition in his family, shed light on how political conversations were mediated through the production of family tales. Different images of the turncoat employed the language of Confucian ethics in very specific ways and delivered measured political sentiments. How these images related to the emerging image of Manchu moral superiority was complex. Nonetheless, the varied representations of the turncoat all benefited the Qing court: it could take credit for employing a filial son to boost the imperial image; it could also capitalize on the turncoat's sense of shame and guilt to consolidate Manchu claims to moral superiority.

TRANSDYNASTIC MORAL CONTINUITY AND THE RECOVERY OF LITERATI SOCIETY

Because turncoat families relied on friends—including Ming loyalists—to contribute to their Confucian family tales and making the image of the loyal turncoat, competing representations of a turncoat's roles in his family constituted a space where political differences among literati could be articulated and negotiated along multiple generational lines—dynastic, factional, social, and familial. The Songs were but one of the many turncoat families who sought ways to enhance their moral standing after it was tarnished by Ming loyalist condemnations, in factional attacks at court, and in the Manchu claim to moral superiority. The recovery of the literati community inched forward partly through the evolving images of the turncoats. Between the capital and their hometowns, the picture of turncoats as the exemplary sons, husbands, and friends described in publications, artworks, and social spectacles not only transcended the dynastic divide but also turned the traumatic political change into a backdrop against which sincere moral pursuits had persisted and flourished. Loyalist friends did not just participate in this enterprise; they actually played an indispensable role, as we will see in the development of Gong Dingsi's image as a loyal turncoat.

Reconnecting with the Filial Son

In late Shunzhi 3 (1646), Gong Dingsi returned to his hometown, Luzhou (Hefei, in modern-day Anhui), as a son in mourning, in Gu Mei's company. Sailing south on the Grand Canal, their hearts were full of heavy emotions. Both memories of recent attacks on Gong's moral performance launched by factional enemies and worries that their degrading portrayal by the Southern Ming regime would linger and bring humiliation. This first trip back home since 1644 was thus a significant personal, familial, and social event for the couple. Gong would prove his commitment to the *zhongxiao* ethics by performing a variety of familial duties.

Gong had two younger brothers, Gong Dingsi and Gong Dingjian. During the dynastic transition, the youngest brother, Dingjian, was the only one of the three who remained in their hometown to take care of the household.[62] When Gong Dingsi and Gu Mei arrived in Luzhou and reunited with him, he asked her to make an orchid painting for Dingjian and then inscribed the painting himself.[63] Particularly interesting in this inscription is Dingzi's historical reference to Su Shi's meetings with his son and brother during his exile in the far south. Because Su Shi had suffered politically and personally from factionalist politics of the Song dynasty, this reference expressed Gong's two main concerns at the time: victimization by factionalism and commitment to one's familial bonds.

In this touching inscription, Dingzi elegantly lays out a peaceful and harmonious domestic scene: he and Dingjian stand side by side, "as intimate as various strands of the incense smoke lingering in the air," watching Gu Mei paint orchids for the younger brother.[64] Gu's painting, and especially its vivid description, proclaimed the familial bond between the Gong brothers and Gu. The painting, the inscription, and the poems together defied the insults that Gong's factional enemies had hurled since the fall of Beijing—that he had been led astray by a woman from the pleasure quarters and therefore ignored his political and family duties, an image employed by many contemporaries to portray the quintessential turncoat during the transition. Gu's painting once again provided the means by which Dingzi could reposition himself as a man with a strong sense of *zhongxiao*.

Gong's image as a loving eldest brother and filial son was integral to his claim to transdynastic moral pursuits. His self-imaging enabled friends of different communities to communicate comfortably in the language of Confucian ethics and, moreover, facilitated the rebuilding of social ties damaged by the conquest and subsequent political divisions. During the four years of Gong's mourning leave, he reconnected with former friends in the south, many of whom were Ming loyalists. In particular, his renewed friendship with the loyalist Yan Ermei (1603–1679) demonstrates the effectiveness of the language of Confucian ethics in connecting friends in opposite political camps.

Yan's *zhongxiao* exemplariness is legendary in seventeenth-century literati literature. First, he retained an impeccable political record during the Ming-Qing transition. Although he did not pursue an official career, Yan did occupy a prominent place in the Donglin-Fushe community. After the fall of Beijing, he was recruited by Grand Secretary Shi Kefa into the Hongguang government, hence joining the "righteous" side of the factional battle between the Donglin-Fushe camp and the Ruan-Ma clique. Following the Manchu conquest of Nanjing, Yan organized and participated in anti-Qing military activities. His rejection letter to the turncoat Wu Su (d. 1645) was widely circulated in the south and became famous as one of the most passionate proclamations against officials who had surrendered to the rebels.[65] Later, his adamant dismissal of his old friend Chen Mingxia's repeated invitations to serve the Qing was also often cited as exemplifying the loyalist determination to resist the Manchus and their Han agents.[66] Equally widespread was Yan's fame as a filial paragon. It was well known in and beyond the Fushe community that he and Wan Shouqi (1603–1652), another noted loyalist and Gong Dingsi's longtime friend, bolstered their strong commitment to filial piety by supporting each other in residing next to their parents' tombs for a long period of time.[67]

It was thus understandable that, on his very first trip to the south after 1644, Gong Dingzi sent poems to Yan, seeking understanding and reconnection. To Gong's relief, Yan replied with five poems, in which he expressed sympathy and understanding toward Gong and his decision to serve in the Qing government. Yan made it very clear that he himself would reject any invitation to work for the Manchus, but he suggested that their friendship should continue despite their different political positions. In affirming his willingness to maintain the friendship, Yan invoked the famous historical reference of Xu Shu

(b. 168), who had to serve a new ruler in order to fulfill his filial responsibility.[68] Yan explained that he had made this allusion because "at the time when the capital was conquered, [Gong's] parents were both still alive," suggesting that Gong had a legitimate reason, filial piety, not to commit suicide.[69] Considering that Yan's response to letters from Chen Mingxia, their mutual friend who was obsessed with recruiting Yan into government service, made no such gesture, one could argue that Yan's poetic exchange with Gong signaled a strong endorsement of the latter's image as a filial son.

Yan understood Gong's situation at that moment and provided exactly what Gong needed politically, socially, and emotionally. Such a friendly exchange would contribute to the turncoat's survival in the new dynasty. The two sides reaffirmed friendship using the language of filial piety. In turn, the image of these two men sharing a strong commitment to filial piety served as the basis for an exemplary friendship, one that could triumph despite the dynastic divide and political differences. The language of *zhongxiao* thus effectively conveyed their emotions, restarted their communication, and facilitated more socializing between their circles.

Mourning with the Virtuous Man

If the ups and downs of Gong Dingzi's career testified to the instability of early Qing politics, the steady rise of his reputation among literati friends proved the power of the notion of moral continuity. The humiliation and mistreatment Gong suffered at the hands of Dorgon and his turncoat collaborators in Shunzhi 3 (1646) placed him in the camp of anti-Dorgon officials.[70] After Dorgon's death, the Shunzhi emperor tried to tap this group to establish his own dominance. Gong returned to court in Shunzhi 8 (1651) following the completion of a term of mourning. Although his administrative talents earned him quick promotions, his pro-Han stance provoked the Shunzhi emperor's ire. The emperor accused him of engaging in factionalism and discrimination against the Manchus. After a series of demotions beginning in Shunzhi 13 (1656), Gong's official status plummeted, from the prestigious position of president of the Censorate to a low-ranking instructor at the Imperial Academy of Learning.[71] He was one of the turncoats targeted by the Shunzhi emperor's disciplining project right up to the emperor's death in Shunzhi 18 (1661).

After the Shunzhi emperor died, the four Manchu regents who ruled the Qing in the place of the young Kangxi emperor adopted a politics of pragmatism. The early 1660s was a time when Manchu rule faced serious challenges, and the regents immediately promoted capable officials like Gong to important positions. The political situation in the empire looked grim. The Temple Lament Case (Kumiao An) provoked suspicion of seditious ideas. In the Statement of Accounts Case (Zouxiao An), repressive measures enacted against Jiangnan literati quickly reached the level of terror with thousands of arrests.[72] The Qing had reached a crossroads.

Gong's stepmother died soon after the Shunzhi emperor's death, and his request for a mourning leave was not approved. He petitioned again, but to no avail.[73] The *duoqing* order, though it deprived him of the opportunity to retire and mourn his mother, was now a sign of trust and favor from the regents. In Kangxi 2/6 (1663), Gong resumed his previous position as president of the Censorate. He subsequently became the president of the Board of Punishments in Kangxi 3/11 (1664), president of the Board of War in Kangxi 5/9 (1666), and president of the Board of Rites in Kangxi 8 (1669).

During this period, Gong used his power to support loyalists and patronize Han scholars in the capital, some of whom were sons of his former Fushe friends. It was documented at the time that he even borrowed money for these purposes.[74] Most notably, he helped forestall at least two politically motivated lawsuits against his loyalist friend Yan Ermei. For Yan's second case, likely a literary persecution case, Gong, as president of the Board of Punishments, submitted a memorial on Yan's behalf. In late Kangxi 4 (1665), the case was resolved, and Yan was safe.[75] Many see the friendship between these two men as an example of the protection and patronage that turncoats extended to their loyalist friends.[76] However, such friendships—and the image politics built on them—benefited both sides. Yan and some other loyalist friends held up Gong as an exemplary figure in their community.[77]

The crucial role Yan played in Gong's image restoration in the early Qing was not accidental. Earlier we saw Yan's widely recognized loyalty and filial piety. It should also be noted that his *zhongxiao* performance was closely related to his legendary reputation as a manly hero, an image that he and many other loyalists publicized. In Shunzhi 12 (1655), when the news of Yan's arrest arrived, his wife and concubine committed double suicide. This was their second attempt at suicide together for their husband: the first had taken place in Shunzhi 9 (1652), but they were rescued, and their husband returned. After their deaths, Yan buried them side by side in the family cemetery. He justified this decision by arguing that the two women had committed suicide together as a sacrifice for their husband's loyalist cause.[78] Thanks to the actions of these two women, Yan gained the same kind of hypermasculine aura associated with Ming officials martyred upon the fall of Beijing. Yan's commemorative poems claim that their suicides made him even more exemplary than Wen Tianxiang (1236–1283), the loyal minister and martyr of the Southern Song dynasty, because Wen's wife had failed to commit suicide and was taken to the capital of the Yuan government.[79] Thus, the heroic actions of Yan's women enhanced his moral exemplariness.

This point was dramatically highlighted and widely disseminated by the loyalist Zhuo Erkan (b. 1653) in his *Yimin Poetry* (Yimin shi), a collection popular among early Qing literati.[80] In Yan's biography, Zhuo records that upon his arrest, Yan "slew his beloved concubine" (*shouren aiqie*).[81] Such gendered imagining around the loyalist figure echoed the ethos of martyrdom stories and made the loyalist the very opposite of the stereotypical disloyal turncoat. While it was unlikely that Zhuo himself came up with this sensational anecdote, the fact that he took the story seriously enough to include it in a carefully edited volume reveals the depth of the connection between loyalty and other gendered virtues.

Yan's image of masculine exemplariness made him the best qualified among the loyalist community to help restore Gong's moral reputation. Gong, remember, had been made a poster boy for disloyal turncoats in the Southern Ming and early Qing years. In Shunzhi 3 (1646), Yan had publicly recognized Gong's undisrupted filial piety and friendship across the dynastic divide. This time, twenty years later, he would labor to publicize Gong Dingzi and Gu Mei's extraordinary mutual commitment. In stark contrast to Yu Huai's famous account of literati-courtesan liaisons in the Nanjing pleasure quarters, which specifically picked out the flamboyant relationship between Gu and Gong, Yan crafted an image of conventional gender propriety for this couple, stressing how their relationship—with passion, devotion, and propriety—had contributed to making Gong an exemplary Confucian official throughout the dynastic transition. Gong's restoration would be accomplished through a variety of means, including literary production and public events after Gu Mei's death.

In the summer of Kangxi 5 (1666), though still unable to obtain an official mourning leave, Gong Dingzi did receive a three-month short leave to return home and make arrangements for his stepmother's funeral. From Beijing he traveled southward with Gu Mei's coffin. Upon his arrival in his hometown, Gong found a number of friends waiting, including four famous loyalists—Yan Ermei, Du Jun (1611–1687), Tang Yunjia (fl. 1640s–60s), and Fang Wen (1612–1669)—who had come from their different locales to take part in the burials. Like Yan Ermei, the other three were among the most respected and popular loyalists in the Jiangnan literati community, known far and wide for their unwavering loyalty and literary and artistic achievements.[82] Gong's friendship with these moral paragons no doubt elevated the turncoat's public image, especially on this occasion when a huge crowd of visitors gathered to offer condolences.[83] These loyalist friends turned the funerary ceremonies into an occasion that affirmed their transdynastic friendship and praised Gong's moral accomplishments as a filial son and committed husband.

How were they to commemorate Gu Mei properly without violating literati gender norms? After all, she was a sonless concubine. In addition, contrary to the account made popular by Yu Huai, Gu had not received an honorary title from the Qing. According to Yu, when Gong accepted his appointment in the Qing government, his wife, Madam Tong, refused to accept an official title and stated that she would concede to Gu the opportunity to receive honorable titles from the new government. Yu claimed that Gu eventually received an official title and thus was called "Madam Gu." Historians ever since have used this example to show that some gentry women—like Madam Tong—had more political integrity than the turncoats.[84] In fact, however, Gong's two official wives, including Madam Tong, both received honorary titles from the Qing, while Gu Mei did not.[85]

In the end, she was laid to rest in a quiet corner of the Gong family cemetery in Taohuacheng, thirty miles southwest of Luzhou.[86] It was Madam Tong, the official wife Gong married in the Ming, who would later be buried with Gong upon his death.[87] In the Gong family genealogy, Gu Mei would appear as "Woman Xu, whose birth and death dates are unclear."[88] Since Gu's dates of birth and death were well known, this record in the family genealogy was unambiguously meant to deprive Gu of her identity and erase her significance in Gong's life.

However, within the boundaries of gender and status propriety sanctioned by the norms of their class, the loyalist friends not only managed to create a space in which they could celebrate Gu's life but also promoted an ideal image for Gong. In the thirty poems composed for Gong during this visit, Yan Ermei details Gong's extraordinary accomplishments as a Confucian official, in particular the key role that he played in saving lives, and his political integrity.[89] Yan contrasts Gong to two famous historical figures, Xie An (320–385), who was extremely accomplished as an official but indulged himself with prostitutes, and Du Yu (222–284), who was overly concerned about himself.[90] In one of the poems, references to the Big Dipper and the famous Donglin Buddhist Temple at Mount Lushan (in modern-day Jiangxi) present Gong as an important political leader whose self-cultivation had brought enlightenment.[91] Given that the name "Donglin" would of course bring to mind the Donglin of the late Ming, Yan seems to invoke their connection with the Donglin-Fushe community and so points to Gong's transdynastic moral-political integrity.

On this highly publicized social occasion, Yan carefully chose the historical references for the poems he composed that would highlight Gong's masculine virtues. By referring to the legendary friendship between Xu Zhi (97–168) and Guo Tai (128–169), Yan posed himself as a committed friend visiting a filial son (Gong) and reaffirmed the connection through shared friendship and filial piety.[92] In addition, Yan dedicated many poems to Gong and Gu, depicting their strong and irreplaceable bond.[93] A set of eight poems titled "Elegiac Poems from the Town of the Peach Blossom" (Taohuacheng wanshi), for example, was devoted to their virtues. Their mutual devotion across the dynastic divide testified to Gong's persistent pursuit of loyalty, filial piety, and self-discipline throughout the transitional period.

Immediately after 1644, Gong was branded as the epitome of someone lacking *zhongxiao* ethics, a designation that resulted from political spin by factionalists in both the Southern Ming and the Shunzhi court. But over the succeeding two decades, friends like Yan Ermei persisted in their efforts to redraw his moral image. On the occasion of these public ceremonies that lasted for days, they resuscitated Gong's reputation and portrayed him as embodying Confucian masculine ideals. According to the testimonials, Gong was loyal to the people and the government, filially pious, and a devoted spouse, not a man interested in pursuing sensual pleasures. He embodied the Confucian moral-political tradition across the dynastic divide. As loyalist friends helped the turncoat restore his moral image, they rebuilt their social networks by affirming their shared understanding of, and commitment to, Confucian ethical ideals. These efforts at image-making not only engaged turncoat-specific moral-political concerns but also, intentionally and unintentionally, helped the literati community adapt to the ongoing political experiments of the Manchu rulers.

Gong Dingzi died in office in Kangxi 12 (1673), as the court was launching its campaign against the Three Feudatories. During his twenty years of service to the Qing, the evolving image of turncoats like him registered important developments in Qing politics: Emperor Shunzhi's disciplining mission had effectively weakened the turncoats' collective moral standing; the Manchu regents, who dominated the court from 1661 to 1669, were less concerned about promoting Confucian virtues than putting to use the most capable bureaucrats in order to consolidate Manchu supremacy; the Kangxi emperor began to implement propaganda campaigns that publicized imperial virtues. Gong could not have foreseen that, a century later, his name would be entered into the infamous *Biographies of Twice-Serving Officials* as instructed by the Qianlong emperor (r. 1736–95). But he lived in the seventeenth century, a fascinating era of crisis, change, and experiment. As the pendulum of history moved through the last moments of his life, Gong survived a damaged public image caused by dynastic change and became an epitome of Confucian moral perfection.

As the family tales of the turncoats demonstrate, early Qing political culture evolved without a blueprint, as a result of the interplay among diverse trends, impulses, and contingencies. Image politics, precisely because it operated at the dynamic intersection of the political, cultural, and social spheres, did not work to the advantage of any particular party. Rather, it permitted and even compelled political players to negotiate on multiple fronts in their efforts to reach a wide audience, through varied forms of media.

The image of the loyal turncoat, a moral exemplar whose practice of Confucian virtues persisted throughout the dynastic transition, constituted a site where multiple layers of sociopolitical relationships were negotiated. One of these layers was the relationship between turncoats and Ming loyalists. The conventional understanding of this relationship stresses moral contrast and political rupture. Although the revisionist narrative has demonstrated extensive interaction between the two groups, more attention to the turncoats' emotive life is needed.[94] Meanwhile, in spite of the differences among various definitions of *yimin*, the assumption that the loyalist was morally superior to the turncoats has persisted.[95] As we have seen, this conventional picture is misleading. Turncoats at the intersection of everyday politics and life had complicated images. In response to both Ming loyalism and the Manchu rulers' disciplining projects, with the help of their families and friends, turncoats persistently—and often successfully—claimed that they had consistently pursued loyalty, filial piety, gender propriety, and true friendship. As turncoats were continuously adjusting their positions in the new dynasty, their images defied narrow, simplified, and simplifying notions of loyalty.[96] Delicate and nuanced political negotiations among various parties took place in the production and circulation of these images between the capital and far-flung local communities, between the court and these officials' social-familial spaces.

Conscious, persistent endeavors by turncoats to demonstrate their adamant adherence to Confucian ethical ideals across the dynastic divide show how the continuum of Confucian moralism could be adapted to new types of political negotiations. The transdynastic and transgenerational narratives of turncoats' moral pursuits helped them, their families, and their friends express their emotions, negotiate political differences, deal with trauma, and rebuild their social networks. Their contribution to the Qing's success was significant. The processes by which Manchu rulers claimed moral superiority and turncoats declared their transdynastic and transgenerational moral exemplariness were tangled. After all, it took the conjoined family tales of Qing monarchs and turncoats to complete the dynastic transition. These stories, which were played out in in a wide range of forms such as ritual spectacle, imperial edicts, literary works, art, and biographies, produced the indispensable and compelling characters of a successful dynastic family romance: virtuous matriarchs and patriarchs, filial sons, good husbands, and true friends, all of which were conjoined with image politics.

Conclusion

From the Ming to the Qing, as the empire underwent significant political, social, and cultural changes, the Confucian moral-political spectrum was widened and enriched. It exhibited contradictory impulses and unexpected collusions, dynamics that spelled a new political culture for the seventeenth century. Although this period lacked the many media forms available today, the political communication processes nonetheless occurred across physical, textual, and embodied spaces.[1] The empire had become a world of image building: the literati's reputation and their efforts to publicize it played a significant role in their obtaining membership in influential social, cultural, and political circles.[2] Activities such as publishing, joining literary clubs, collecting objects, sponsoring entertainers and theatrical events, patronizing Buddhist temples, and even writing to advocate "chastity justice" for women,[3] all helped the literati bolster their image of superiority in a society with increasingly blurred social boundaries, professional competition, diffused cultural authorities, and emerging new markers of identity.[4] Image politics flourished in this fascinating world.

"Image problems" were everywhere, even in the lives of famed moral paragons. This situation means that the seventeenth century cannot simply be classified as a time of moral heroism or a return to conservatism. Some officials strove to fulfill their ethical duties in everyday life, but they appear in the historical record as morally corrupt. Some entered history as moral paragons, even though their political rivals seriously and legitimately contested their claims to exemplariness. But such nuances, discrepancies, and contestations are often lost with the development of historical stereotypes.

Attention to the image of both the "hero" and the "villain" figure can illuminate the production and circulation of officials' moral reputations as central to political processes during the Ming-Qing transition. Political actors' image-making efforts show the impact of print culture and related sociocultural dynamics in literati society. They also capture contemporary religious trends and intellectual concerns. Additionally, the seventeenth century was an era of experimentation, and political actors intensively and creatively engaged Confucian ethics as they searched for ways to express themselves, gain political advantage, and juggle competing social and political demands. Even though in many cases we cannot fully reconstruct an individual official's "actual" performance as a son or husband, by looking at why his personal life attracted public attention, assumed political significance, and generated surprising consequences, in particular at the discrepancies between his polarized images, we gain rich insights into the interactions among contemporary political, cultural, and social dynamics.

Confucian ethics was both a precarious and a highly flexible political tool. The question of how to display one's masculine virtues properly remained sensitive within the specific political and cultural dynamics of both the late Ming and early Qing. The complex work done by officials' moral images demonstrates that Confucian ethics did not automatically operate as a stabilizing factor at a time of crisis and transformation. How political actors applied and enriched them in everyday life and in politics was shaped by the changing historical conditions. In life and in politics, the elites extensively tapped into the conceptual connections among the various ethical ideals. In these processes, everyday-life relationships were given moral meaning, and moral assurance became an integral, material aspect of networking. Rather than "thinning out" moral ideals, image politics reproduced the Confucian ethical system.[5] Meanwhile, the continuum of Confucian moralism in its two dimensions did not simply discipline or co-opt; it enabled—and sometimes guided—people to cultivate empathy and make compromises even when they had before them a seemingly insurmountable political divide or agonizing uncertainties.

BETWEEN PERFECTION AND IMPERFECTION

The immense interest of the state and the literati in exploring the political and social potential of Confucian ethics coexisted with a sense of disenchantment—and even cynicism—in some corners of seventeenth-century China, especially after the change of regime. Early Qing literary representations highlighted the two extremes of Confucian moralism: purely instrumental, hypocritical appropriation of "dualistic" Confucian ritualism for self-interest, on the one side, and "ascetic" ritualism on the other. The latter, which sacrificed all mundane desires, was presented as a noble alternative approach to Confucian moral cultivation, but it nonetheless proved unsatisfactory because it had also already become institutionalized and turned into a means of gaining fame.[6] In both these practices of Confucian moralism, the differences between the genuine and the feigned were not only blurred but also widely manipulated. Similarly, parodies of legendary moral exemplars at the time questioned not only the credibility of their official historical portrayals as moral paragons but also the very possibility of sincere noninstrumentalist pursuit of Confucian loyalty, filial piety, and self-discipline.[7]

However, the lived experiences of literati-officials were much more complex than their sometimes cynical literary representations. The myriad accounts of officials' personal lives and moral behavior occupied a central place in seventeenth-century politics precisely because, in practice, Confucian moralism as a continuum allowed for and embraced possibilities, options, and creative alternatives. In the moral image-making of these political actors, sincerity and pragmatism were not mutually exclusive but were mutually configured. Literati concerns and disagreements about what constituted the sincere and proper pursuit and display of Confucian virtues were a generative mechanism of image politics during that period. The enhanced availability of print, networking, and publicity through social spectacles offered political actors more opportunities to display their moral accomplishments and also encouraged them to take extraordinary measures in order to "authenticate" their virtues for political purposes. Their authentication efforts inevitably drew on and invigorated discursive connections among the various Confucian masculine virtues.

Such a complex, broadened understanding of Confucian moralism—as processes of negotiation and adaptation—not only helps us problematize the conventional divide between "gentlemen" and "small men" in the historiography of seventeenth-century politics but also reveals that the Qing rulers' engagement with Confucianism might not have been any more instrumentalist or hypocritical than the Han elite's. Rather, one could argue that the many authentication efforts examined here were a form of "consensus-seeking," a creative approach to the early modern "authenticity crisis."[8]

Understanding the continuum of Confucian moralism in this way allows us to see that image politics did not simply stretch the relevance of the Confucian moral-political system across the dynastic divide; it fueled its development. While officials in the late Ming engaged in "image wars," it could be said that the Manchu deployment of Confucian ethics as a language of political communication in the early Qing paved the way for their "image conquest" of the Han. The Qing way did not just combine the Manchu way and the Confucian way; it transformed them both. Manchu rulers and Han officials engaged Confucian ethical ideals in adapting to the changing political situation and struggle for personal, familial, and collective survival. In the course of constant experimentation, some Confucian practices assumed new political meanings.

Qing rulers proved to be savvy and proactive in employing the language of Confucian ethics to establish Manchu moral superiority while limiting Han officials' options. In the High Qing, imperial moralizing endeavors led to the formation of a new relationship between the state and its subjects.[9] Although the Manchu ruler's civilizing role was passionately pursued with the assistance of his officials,[10] when these officials participated in the bureaucratization of rewarding moral exemplariness and punishing immorality in society, the officials carried less moral authority than bureaucratic responsibility. For instance, when the focus of the imperial civilizing mission shifted from masculine virtue to female chastity, this not only served to establish the court as moral arbiter but also seemed to express the new moral-political division of labor between the monarch and literati-officials.[11] The Shunzhi disciplining project and turncoats' transdynastic, transgenerational narratives demonstrate that the reconfiguration of elites' moral-political division of labor had already begun in the early years of the Qing.

Appreciating the "moralization of politics" with more sympathy, nuance, and precision will benefit historians tremendously.[12] When we break away from the binaries that have shaped the Ming-Qing transition historiography—conservatism versus progressivism, autocratic rulers versus liberal gentry, true paragons versus moral hypocrites, and exemplary heroes versus corrupt villains—to consider how political subjects creatively engaged Confucian institutions and changing material conditions in order to adapt, survive, and thrive, we gain more insight into the collective and personal decisions they made and Chinese early modernity itself.

THE POSSIBILITY OF COMPARING EARLY MODERNITIES

In the past two decades, many China scholars have contemplated the question of the "early modern." Explorations through lenses such as the "public sphere," "individualism and the self," and "globalization," to name a few, have significantly furthered our understanding of the dynamics of seventeenth- and eighteenth-century China. But the superficial resemblance to European counterparts masks substantive differences between the two contexts, especially the "overriding importance of family and communal ties" in the Chinese context.[13] As seen from an intellectual history perspective, the Chinese hardly abandoned "tradition" but rather reaffirmed it, a stark contrast to early modern Europe, where "flight from traditional authority" has been detected.[14]

Still, Confucian moralism in politics did not simply reaffirm tradition; tradition was reinscribed and transformed. While the dynamics of image politics were emerging in other contexts of the seventeenth-century world as well,[15] in China, ruling elites across the dynastic divide continued to engage in moral image-making efforts grounded in Confucian ethics. The rise of literacy rates, growing consumption of print and theater, and denser communication networks created more tools for elites to engage Confucian ethics creatively and deeply so as to meet specific but very diverse personal, familial, collective, and imperial needs in a time of uncertainty and volatility. Seventeenth-century elite's political experimentation via Confucian ethical ideals insistently tied the individual to the familial and communal; they explored "sincerity" and "interiority" in attempts to think about how the moral subject should pursue self-cultivation and fulfill social *and* political roles. At the same time, image politics in the Chinese context did not preclude the possibility of change. It opened up the political sphere to more complex interactions between the court and literati society, between politics and culture, and between ideals and practicality. It mirrored and contributed to the reintegration of elite men's roles and responsibilities as prescribed in the Confucian ethical template.

Take, for example, the representation and mediation of political struggles in a variety of literary genres, across generations and dynasties. Competing political forces took advantage of the booming print culture and efficient networking techniques when they publicized attacks and counterattacks in the form of Confucian family tales. These tales and their mediating and mediatizing functions differed significantly from the family model of politics analyzed by Lynn Hunt in her study of the French Revolution. While French family romances saw the murder of the tyrannical father figure preceding the actual regicide,[16] in seventeenth-century China, regicide was morally condemned and confessions of filial piety allowed political actors to articulate and negotiate their political positions, regardless of how they defined loyalty. Further, in both political and literary narratives, Confucian family tales implicate transgenerational dynamics and concerns far beyond the parameters of the nuclear family paradigm.[17] They helped families and communities deal with serious political ruptures such as a change of dynasty.

Thus, this cultural-historical approach to factionalism and dynastic change draws attention to "generation" as an important category of political historical analysis, helping illuminate the particularities of seventeenth-century Chinese image politics and its early modern conditions. Officials' moral reputations were at bottom family matters; two or three generations of officials from the same family underwent political upheavals together and had joint stakes in publicizing their role performance *as men*. Disciples and male descendants of officials of rival factions, including those who did not hold official positions, participated in producing images that they and their allies could use to attack political enemies. The family romances and biographies concocted to expose someone's lack of filial devotion or self-discipline often wove together sensational domestic stories of a whole family. These image-making enterprises could not only enhance the effectiveness of factional attacks but could also hold the interest of a reading public that increasingly craved the strange and sensational. Finally, when the badly fractured elite society strove to revive itself in the early Qing, recovery was accomplished to a large degree via transgenerational, transdynastic Confucian family tales in a variety of literary, artistic, and ritual forms. Family tales of turncoats further show how Manchu moral superiority was made persuasive by virtue of the loyal turncoat's moral continuity from the Ming to the Qing.

REIMAGINING THE SEVENTEENTH CENTURY

The conventional, narrow notion of "Confucian moralism" captures some realities but hides complicated historical processes that involved contingent cultural, social, and political activities of the state, communities, and individuals.[18] A biographical approach to the interplay of politics, culture, and Confucian ethics, by considering how the two dimensions of the continuum of Confucian moralism shaped historical subjects' emotions and actions, opens new opportunities to challenge the dominant historical images in seventeenth-century political historiography. These gendered dominant images have perpetuated certain moral assumptions about political men even as they have been transformed by modern Western historical vision and a Han nationalist framework in later periods. The conflation of these influences in the multilayered historical memories of the seventeenth century is best exemplified by the invention of the image of the ideal Donglin man.

In an inscription for *Miscellaneous Records of the Plank Bridge* (Banqiao zaji) by Yu Huai, the late Qing literatus Qin Jitang (1837–1908) writes: "Every one of [the courtesans] married a Donglin man."[19] Summarizing the poet's historical imagining of late-Ming politics and literati sexual adventures, this line has become one of the most frequently invoked references in the historiography of the Ming-Qing transition. Two images emerge from this picture: first, in the late Ming, "the righteous men"—namely, Donglin officials—devoted themselves to both political integrity and romantic love; second, late-Ming courtesans gained a high political profile from their association with these men. Two kinds of historical imagining intersect in the political identity of the Donglin official and his moral character: the morally exemplary Donglin man is partially constructed through the figure of the late-Ming courtesan, whose relationship with the Fushe scholar had symbolized passionate love and a devotion that paralleled loyalism.[20] On one level, this configuration obscures the fact that the meaning of the "Donglin man" was in fact unstable; his claim to exemplariness was constructed around *zhongxiao* and was constantly being contested. On another level, through this configuration, Qing literati and modern intellectuals who tended to romanticize late-Ming elites projected the romantic sentiments of some Fushe scholars onto the Donglin officials in order to increase the appeal of both of them.[21] The Donglin-Fushe man became the premodern predecessor of the ideal modern Chinese man.

In reality, Donglin-Fushe officials created less "romantic" images for themselves as Confucian fathers, sons, husbands, and friends and struggled to defend their *zhongxiao* claims. As these men's lives were subjected to more scrutiny and exposure in various media, they had to present carefully their domestic lives as ones that followed prescribed gender norms so as to advance their careers, promote their individual, familial, and organizational interests, and adapt to the changing political conditions. Their women, often talented in poetry and art, not only played an active role in officials' networking in "apolitical" spaces but also helped their husbands achieve images of moral exemplariness. Thus, understanding the operation of the continuum of Confucian moralism as gendered processes centered on *zhongxiao* is crucial to rescuing the seventeenth century from narratives produced by the Qing state in the eighteenth century and by modern intellectuals in the early twentieth century.

GLOSSARY

Ai Jiangnan fu 哀江南賦

Bai Sheng 白勝
Baihua ke kuang 白華客況
baihuai Donglin jiafeng 敗壞東林家風
Baihuatang shi 白華堂詩
Banqiao zaji 板橋雜記
Bian Sanyuan 卞三元
bianxiu 編修
bie 別
bieji 別集
Bo Bo Manlu pingzheng 駁駁漫録評正
Bo Manlu pingzheng 駁漫録評正
Bofu lu 剝復録
bu he qingyi 不合清議
buru Zheng Man 不如鄭鄤
buzhong buxiao 不忠不孝

Cai Yuqing 蔡玉卿
Cao Rong 曹溶
Chen Biqian 陳必謙
Chen Diaoyuan 陳調元
Chen Jiru 陳繼儒
Chen Jitai 陳際泰
Chen Liang 陳梁
Chen Longzheng 陳龍正
Chen Mingxia 陳名夏
Chen wei wenzhang buru Zheng Man 臣謂文章不如鄭鄤
Chen Xinjia 陳新甲
Chen Yan 陳演
Chen Zhenhui 陳貞慧
Chen Zilong 陳子龍
Cheng Hao 程顥
Cheng Yi 程頤
Cheng Yong 成勇
Cheng Zhengkui 程正揆
chushan 出山
Chushan shi 出山詩
cihun Manzhou 賜婚滿洲
ciqi 次妻
Cong ni an 從逆案
Cui Chengxiu 崔呈秀
cuican zhici 摧殘至此

Da yingxiong zhuan 大英雄傳
Dai Mingyue 戴明説
dangzheng 黨爭
Dao ming lu 道命錄
Daobing Donglin huo 盜柄東林夥
daowang 悼亡
diandao le baixing haowu 顛倒了百姓好惡
dibao 邸報
Diwenxing shengshou shusheng 地文星聖手書生
Diyixing baimian langjun 地異星白面郎君
Dong Qichang 董其昌
Dongli ju 東籬菊
Donglin 東林
Donglin chu 東林初
Donglin dangren bang 東林黨人榜
Donglin dianjiang lu 東林點將録
Donglin jiguan 東林籍貫
Donglin pengdang lu 東林朋黨錄
Donglin sheng 東林盛
Donglin wan 東林晚
Donglin zidi 東林子弟
Du Jun 杜濬
Du Lide 杜立德
Du Yu 杜預
duoji 多集
duoqing 奪情
duoqing shijie 奪情世界

Erchen zhuan 貳臣傳

Fa Ruozhen 法若真
fajian 發奸
Fan Chengmo 范承謨
Fan Jingwen 范景文
Fang Kongzhao 方孔炤
Fang Wen 方文
Fang Xuejian 方學漸
Fang Yizhi 方以智
Fang Zheng xiaoshi 放鄭小史
Fang Zhenru 方震孺
Feng Menglong 馮夢龍
Feng Xingke 馮行可
Feng Yuanbiao 馮元飈
Fu Bi 富弼
Fu wang 福王
fufu 夫婦
Fushe 復社
Fushe si gongzi 復社四公子
Fuzi zhi dao zhongxiao eryi 夫子之道忠孝而已

Gao Panlong 高攀龍
gegu 割股
Geng Jingzhong 耿精忠
Gong Cuisu 龔萃肅
Gong Dingjian 龔鼎玵
Gong Dingsi 龔鼎孠
Gong Dingzi 龔鼎孳
gong'an xiaoshuo公案小說
gonglun 公論
Gu Mei 顧眉
Gu Jingxing 顧景星
Gu Xiancheng 顧憲成

guanggun 光棍
Gui Qixian 歸起先
Guilin shuang 桂林霜
Gujin tan'gai 古今譚概
Gujin xiao 古今笑
guming 沽名
guixing 歸省
Guo Tai 郭泰
Guo Yikun 郭一鶚
Guoshiyuan daxueshi 國史院大學士
Guozijian 國子監

Han Feizi 韓非子
Han Qi 韓琦
Hao Jie 郝傑
He Canran 賀燦然
Hongguang 弘光
Hou Fangyu 侯方域
Hu Shi'an 胡世安
Huang Daozhou 黃道周
Huang Jingfang 黃景昉
Huang Tu'an 黃圖安
Huang Yuansu 黃願素
Huang Zongxi 黃宗羲
Huang Zunsu 黃尊素
Huangzhi ge 黃芝歌
hufa 護法
huishang 毀傷
huo *Shuihuzhuan* 活水滸傳

Ji Kaisheng 季開生
Ji Liuqi 計六奇
Jianlao lu 鑒勞錄
Jiang Cai 姜埰
Jiang Gai 姜垓
Jiang Shiquan 蔣士銓
jiangtu zhongxiao wu shi biaobang 講圖忠孝毋事標榜
Jiang Yueguang 姜曰廣
Jiangnan 江南
Jiaohua 教化
jiating xiaoshuo 家庭小說
jiazu xiaoshuo 家族小說
Jichu 激楚
jiguo ge 紀過格
jiji 畸集
Jin Risheng 金日升
jin shouzhi Hong Chengchou 今守制洪承疇
Jin Zhijun 金之俊
jingshi 經世
jinshi 進士
jixian 箕仙
junzi 君子

kaishu 楷書
Kechang an 科場案
Kongzi zi yun ciling wu buru Zaiyu 孔子自云辭令吾不如宰予
Kumiao an 哭廟案
Kun 昆

Lei Yanzuo 雷縯祚
Li Mingrui 李明睿

Li Qing 李清
Li Ruolin 李若琳
Li Sancai 李三才
Li Senxian 李森先
Li Tingji 李廷機
Li Weiyue 李維樾
Li Xinchuan 李心傳
Li Yuankuan 黎元寬
Li Yuanmei 黎元美
Li Zhi 李贄
Lianchi dashi 蓮池大師
lingchi 凌遲
Linju manlu 林居漫錄
Liu Guangdou 劉光斗
Liu Kongzhao 劉孔炤
Liu Rushi 柳如是
Liu Shidou 劉士斗
Liu Yuyou 劉餘祐
Liu Zeqing 劉澤清
Liu Zongzhou 刘宗周
Liudu fangluan gongjie 留都防亂公揭
lixue 理學
Longwu 隆武
Lü Gong 呂宮
Lü mudan 綠牡丹
Lu wang潞王
Lu Wanxue 陸完學
lumu 廬墓
Luo Guoshi 羅國士
Luo Xiujin 羅繡錦
Lüshi chunqiu 呂氏春秋

Ma Guozhu 馬國柱
Ma Shiqi 馬世奇
Ma Shiying 馬士英
Manlu pingzheng 漫録評正
Manyu cao 曼寓草
Manzhou zhi zhi 滿洲之治
Mao Jin 毛晉
Mao Xiang 冒襄
meipi 眉批
Meng Zhaoxiang 孟兆祥
mengzhu 盟主
Mu cheng zhi ye 母成之也

Nan-Bei dang 南北黨
nan/nü 男女
ni 逆
Ni Yuanlu 倪元璐
Ni'an 逆案
nichen 逆臣
Ning Wanwo 寧完我

Peng Shiwang 彭士望
pengyou 朋友

Qi Biaojia 祁彪佳
Qi Jiazhi 漆嘉祉
Qian Chengzhi 錢澄之
Qian Daxin 錢大昕
Qian Fen 錢棻
Qian Kaizong 錢開宗
Qian Longxi 錢龍錫
Qian Qianyi 錢謙益

Qian Shisheng 錢士升
Qian Shouyi 錢受益
Qian Yiben 錢一本
Qian Yuanxiu 錢元修
qianji 前集
qifu 起復
Qin Jitang 秦際唐
qing 情
Qinhuai chang 秦淮娼
Qishui 蘄水
Qu Jia 瞿甲
Qu Shisi 瞿士耜

Renpu 人譜
renzhen 認真
Ruan Dacheng 阮大鋮
ruo mu wu mu 若母吾母

San yuan biji 三垣筆記
Shang Zhixin 尚之信
Shaozheng Mao 少正卯
Shen Shizhu 沈士柱
Shen Shoumin 沈壽民
Shen Yiguan 沈一貫
shen zuo fuqiu 身作俘囚
shendu 慎独
Shengzhi 聖治
shenjiao 神交
shenmo xiaoshuo 神魔小說
Shi Kefa 史可法
Shi Min 時敏
shijie 失節
Shijing 詩經
shouren aiqie 手刃愛妾
shouzhi 守制
Shu 蜀
shuang hang jiapi 雙行夾批
Shuihu zhuan 水滸傳
Shun 順
Shun an 順案
Sima Guang 司馬光
Song Luo 宋犖
Song Quan 宋權
Song tian lu bi 頌天臚筆
Song Xun 宋纁
Song Yizhen 宋一貞
Su Shi 蘇軾
Sun Chuanting 孫傳庭
Sun Lin 孫臨
Sun Poling 孫珀齡
Sun Shenxing 孫慎行
Sun Zhixie 孫之獬

Tan Qian 談遷
Tang Bin 湯斌
Tang Yü 唐玨
Tang Yunjia 唐允甲
Tanyuan zazhi 彈園雜志
Tao Qian 陶潛
Taohuacheng 桃花城
Taoyeguan 桃葉館
Tian Younian 田有年
Tianjian wenji 田間文集
tifa 薙髮

Tiying 緹縈
Tongcheng 桐城
tongxiang 同鄉
Tu Bihong 涂必泓
tuiguan 推官

Wan Shihua 萬時華
Wan Shouqi 萬壽祺
Wang Shaohui 王紹徽
Wang Shimin 王時敏
Wang Shizhen 王世貞
Wang Shizhen 王士禎
Wang Tingjian 王廷諫
Wang Xijue 王錫爵
Wang Yangming 王陽明
Wang Yongji 王永吉
Wang Zhang 王章
Wanli shuchao 萬曆疏鈔
Wei Dazhong 魏大中
Wei Xi 魏禧
Wei Xuelian 魏學濂
Wei Xueyi 魏學洢
Wei Yijie 魏裔介
Wei Zaode 魏藻德
Wei Zhongxian 魏忠賢
weixue 偽學
Wen Tianxiang 文天祥
Wen Tiren 溫體仁
Wen Zhengming 文徵明
Wen Zhenmeng 文震孟
Weng Wanda 翁萬達
Wu Bing 吳炳
Wu Changshi 吳昌時
Wu Ganlai 吳甘來
Wu Liang 吳亮
Wu Sangui 吳三桂
Wu Shen 吳甡
Wu Su 武愫
Wu Weiye 吳偉業
Wu Yingji 吳應箕
Wu Yuancui 伍袁萃
Wu Zeng 吳翻
Wu Zhongxing 吳中行
Wu Zongda 吳宗達
wulun 五倫
wulun jin jue 五倫盡絕
Wuren mu 五人墓
Wuren mubei ji 五人墓碑記

Xia Yunyi 夏允彝
Xian bo zhi shi 先撥志始
Xiang Yu 項煜
xiao 孝
Xiao Rang 蕭讓
Xiaojing 孝經
Xiaojing da zhuan 孝經大傳
Xiaoling 孝陵
xiaopin 小品
xiaoshi xiaoshuo 小史小說
xiaoshuo jiao 小說教
xiaozhi 孝治
Xichuan zheng pu 浠川政譜
Xie An 謝安
Xie Xuelong 解學龍

xiedang 邪黨
xieshu 血書
Xinbian jiao Chuang tongsu xiaoshuo 新編剿闖通俗小說
xing 興
Xiong Dinghua 熊鼎華
Xiong Kaiyuan 熊開元
Xiong Wencan 熊文燦
Xiong Wenju 熊文舉
Xishan wei 西山薇
Xu Guo 許國
Xu Shipu 徐世溥
Xu Shirou 許士柔
Xu Shu 徐庶
Xu Tingqing 胥庭清
Xu Xi 許曦
Xu Yingfen 徐應芬
Xu Zhi 徐稺
Xuan 宣
Xue Cai 薛寀
Xue Guoguan 薛國觀
Xunzi 荀子

Yan Ermei 閻爾梅
Yan Hun 顏渾
Yan Qing 燕青
Yan Song 嚴嵩
Yan Zhenqing 顏真卿
yandang 閹黨
Yang Bo 楊博
Yang He 楊鶴
Yang Qi'e 楊棲鶚
Yang Rucheng 楊汝成
Yang Shicong 楊士聰
Yang Sichang 楊嗣昌
Yang Tinglin 楊廷麟
Yang Zhiqi 楊枝起
Yangming 陽明
Yanzhong jiwen 燕中紀聞
Ye Mengzhu 葉夢珠
Ye Xianggao 葉向高
yi quan zhongxiao 以全忠孝
yi wulun xiang zhu 以五倫相屬
Yi'antang gao 貽安堂稿
yidai wanren 一代完人
yiduan 異端
yimin 遺民
Yimin shi 遺民詩
You chushi zhi xiang 有出世之想
You Tong 尤侗
Yu Huai 余懷
Yu Xin 庾信
Yuan Chonghuan 袁崇煥
Yuan Kai 袁愷
Yuan Liangbi 袁良弼
Yuan Shu 袁樞
yuji 餘集
Yunqi Zhuhong 雲棲袾宏
Yuzhang congshu 豫章叢書
Yuzhi renchen jingxin lu 御製人臣儆心録
Yuzhi Xiaojing yanyi 御製孝經衍義

Zhang Cai 張采

Zhang Dian 張琠
Zhang Guowei 張國維
Zhang Hanru 張漢儒
Zhang Juzheng 張居正
Zhang Pu 張溥
Zhang Qixian 張齊賢
Zhang Xia 張夏
Zhang Xuan 張煊
Zhang Zhifa 張至發
Zhang Zilie 張自烈
Zhao Fuxing 趙福星
Zhao Kaixin 趙開心
Zhao Shijin 趙士錦
zhaofu 招撫
Zhe dang 浙黨
zheng guoben 爭國本
Zheng Man 鄭鄤
Zheng Sanjun 鄭三俊
Zheng Tianshou 鄭天壽
Zheng Xuan 鄭瑄
Zheng Zhenxian 鄭振先
Zheng Zhenyuan 鄭振元
Zhifa gujin diyi quanjian shu 直發古今第一權奸疏
zhi wu wu zi kaikou chu 只無吾子開口處
zhong 忠
zhongxiao dazhi 忠孝大志
zhongxiao jie lie 忠孝節烈
zhongxiao liang kui 忠孝兩潰
zhongxiao liang quan 忠孝兩全
Zhongxiao zhuan 忠孝傳
zhongyang 終養
Zhou Biao 周鑣
Zhou Lixun 周立勳
Zhou Maolan 周茂蘭
Zhou Shunchang 周順昌
Zhou Yanru 周延儒
Zhou Yi 周易
Zhou Zhikui 周之夔
Zhou Zhong 周鐘
Zhu Geng 朱賡
Zhu Ji 朱積
Zhu Taifan 朱泰藩
Zhu Tonglei 朱統
Zhu Xi 朱熹
Zhu Yile 朱議汸
Zhuge Liang 諸葛亮
Zhuo Erkan 卓爾堪
zimian 紫棉
zituo yu Donglin 自託于東林
Zouxiao an 奏銷案

ABBREVIATIONS

CMMYL	Sun Chengze 孫承澤. *Chunming meng yu lu* 春明夢餘錄. Hong Kong: Longmen Shudian, 1976.
DSTSJ	Gong Dingzi 龔鼎孳. *Dingshantang shiji* 定山堂詩集 (*SKJH*-ji 117).
DSTWJ	Gong Dingzi 龔鼎孳. *Dingshantang wenji* 定山堂文集. Gong shi Zhanluzhai 龔氏瞻麓齋, 1924.
GBXSJC	*Guben xiaoshuo jicheng* 古本小說集成. Shanghai: Shanghai Guji Chubanshe. 1994.
HSZXSWJ	Huang Daozhou 黃道周. *Huang Shizhai xiansheng wenji* 黃石齋先生文集 (*SKXX*-ji 1384)..
HZPWX	Huang Daozhou. *Huang Zhangpu wenxuan* 黃漳浦文選 (*TWWXCK* 137).
MDZJCK	Zhou Junfu 周駿富, ed. *Mingdai zhuanji congkan* 明代傳記叢刊. Taipei: Mingwen Shuju, 1991.
MQSLCB	Shen Yunlong 沈雲龍, comp. *Ming-Qing shiliao congbian* 明清史料叢編. Taipei: Wenhai Chubanshe, 1967–73.
MRWJCK	Shen Yunlong 沈雲龍 , comp. *Mingren wenji congkan* 明人文集叢刊. Taipei: Wenhai Chubanshe, 1970.
MS	Zhang Tingyu 張廷玉 et al. *Ming shi* 明史. Beijing: Zhonghua Shuju, 1974.
MYCTSJ	Zheng Man 鄭鄤. *Miyang caotang shiji* 峚陽草堂詩集 (*SKJH*-ji 126).
MYCTWJ	Zheng Man 鄭鄤. *Miyang caotang wenji* 峚陽草堂文集 (*SKJH*-ji 126).

QDDASLCB	*Qingdai dang'an shiliao congbian* 清代檔案史料叢編. Edited by Diyi Lishi Dangan Guan第一歷史檔案館. Vol. 6 (1980); vol. 7 (1981); vol. 9 (1983); vols. 10, 13 (1984).
SBBY	*Sibu beiyao* 四部備要. Shanghai: Zhonghua Shuju, 1927–36.
SBCK	*Sibu congkan* 四部叢刊. Shanghai: Shangwu Yinshuguan, Republican period.
SKCM	*Siku quanshu cunmu congshu* 四庫全書存目叢書. Jinan: Qilu Shushe, 1996.
SKJH	*Siku jinhui shu congkan* 四庫禁燬書叢刊. Beijing: Beijing Chubanshe, 2000.
SKWS	*Siku weishou shu jican* 四庫未收書輯刊. Beijing: Beijing Chubanshe, 2000.
SKXX	*Xuxiu Siku quanshu* 續修四庫全書. Shanghai: Shanghai Guji Chubanshe, 2002.
TSZXNP	Zheng Man 鄭鄤. *Tianshan zixu nianpu* 天山自敘年譜. In Zhang Man, *Miyang caotang wenji* 峚陽草堂文集 (*SKJH*-ji 126).
TWWXCK	*Taiwan wenxian congkan* 臺灣文獻叢刊. Edited by Taiwan Yinhang Jingji Yanjiushi 臺灣銀行經濟研究室. 596 vols. Taipei: Taiwan Yinhang Jingji Yanjiushi, 1959–72.
ZYYMQDA	*Zhongyang yanjiuyuan lishi yuyan yanjiusuo xiancun Qingdai neige daku yuan cang Ming-Qing dang'an* 中央研究院歷史語言研究所現存清代內閣大庫原藏明清檔案. Edited by Zhang Weiren 張偉仁. Taipei: Zhongyang Yanjiuyuan Lishi Yuyan Yanjiusuo, 1986.

NOTES

INTRODUCTION

1. In this book, years and dates are indicated in the following format: reign title and year/Chinese lunar month and day. For a long time scholars believed that *Gujin tan'gai* was the original title of this book, and that because the book did not attract enough attention, the title was changed to *Gujin xiao*. However, recent scholarship has demonstrated that the title *Gujin xiao* appeared first and then Feng also published it under the title of *Gujin tan'gai*. For a review of these various editions and titles, see Guo Jianping, "*Gujin tan'gai* xiaohua yanjiu." The edition referenced by this book is titled *Gujin tan'gai*.

2. Feng Menglong, *Gujin tan'gai*, 49. The Cheng Brothers refer to Cheng Yi (1033–1107) and Chen Hao (1032–1085).

3. I thank Maiwfen Lu for helping me investigate the references to this anecdote in Ming-Qing publications. I also thank her and Beverly Bossler for a very helpful discussion about the invention of the anecdote.

4. Wu Yuancui, *Linju manlu*, 695. In most of the extant editions, including the editions I referenced in this book, *Linju manlu* is printed together with *Manlu pingzheng*, a commentary on *Linju manlu* by He Canran, Wu's contemporary. The same editions also include Wu's counter-commentary, *Bo Manlu pingzheng*, and He's response, *Bo Bo Manlu pingzheng*. Unless otherwise noted, the edition used in all the footnotes in my analysis of Wu's *Linju manlu* and *Bo Manlu pingzheng* as well as my examination of He's *Manlu pingzheng* and *Bo Bo Manlu pingzheng* refers to the *Beijing tushuguan guji zhenben congkan* edition.

5. Feng Menglong, preface to the chapter "Yufu" 迂腐, *Gujin tan'gai*, 7.

6. Feng Menglong, "Zixu" 自敘, *Gujin tan'gai*, appendix, 7–12. The rhetoric clearly demonstrates the influence of the radical thinker Li Zhi. On Li Zhi and the ethics of genuineness, see Pauline Lee, *Li Zhi*, chap. 5.

7. Chen Jiru (1558–1639), whose commercial success and celebrity status were built on *xiaopin* writing, composed a preface for the first volume of *Zuofei'an ri zuan* and thought highly of it. For scholarship on *xiaopin* literature and Chen Jiru as a *xiaopin* writer, see Greenbaum, *Chen Jiru*, 143–50;

Chen Wanyi, *Wan Ming xiaopin*, esp. chap. 3; and Wu Chengxue, *Wan Ming xiaopin yanjiu*, 92–107.

8. Zheng Xuan, "Wangdu" 汪度, *Zuofei'an ri zuan*, 119.

9. This phrase comes from the title of Brook's monograph, *Confusions of Pleasure*.

10. Feng Menglong's *Gujin xiao* continued to be printed in different forms and with different titles. Zheng Xuan rolled out three volumes of *Zuofei'an ri zuan* within the span of a few years.

11. Wu Yuancui, *Linju manlu*, 695.

12. For discussion of Huang Zongzhou's criticism of the popular genre of "ledgers of merit and demerit" and his own ledger technique in *Renpu*, see Brokaw, *Ledgers of Merit and Demerit*, 121–25 and 128–38 (on the section that includes the evil of mingling with courtesans, see 134).

13. Liu Zongzhou, *Renpu leiji*, 5.107–8.

14. Wu Yuancui claims it must have been Su Shi 蘇軾 (1037–1101, the Shu faction) who made up the story. For a discussion about Su Shi, Cheng Yi, and Song factionalism, see Levine, *Divided by a Common Language*, chap. 5.

15. Wu Yuancui, *Linju manlu*, 695.

16. Ibid.; He Canran's comment is on the upper margin of the page, 695.

17. See chap. 1 in this book for more analysis of Wu Yuancui's publications.

18. It is important to note that the term *gonglun* can be interpreted in different ways. I translate it as "public opinion" in this book. Harry Miller, in his work on late Ming political history, has rendered it "public consensus." Miller, "Opposition to the Donglin Faction," 58.

19. Wu, conclusion of *Leaving for the Rising Sun*.

20. Ōki, "Mao Xiang and Yu Huai," 245.

21. You Tong, "Ti *Banqiao zaji*" 題板橋雜記, in Yu Huai, *Banqiao zaji*, 5.

22. I use the word *image* metaphorically here. In both premodern and modern times, moral-political images have always been transmitted in nonvisual media, including not only texts but also what scholars of political behavior call "image attributes" stimulated mentally by political materials (Shyles, "Defining Images of Presidential Candidates"). W. J. T. Mitchell offers an excellent discussion on the multiple meanings of "image," in particular the problem of dichotomizing "image" and "word," in his classic *Picture Theory*, esp. 83–110. For a literature review on image and politics, see Khatib, introduction to *Image Politics in the Middle East*.

23. On the concept of "dynastic cycles," see Shelley Hsue-lun Chang, *History and Legend*, 34.

24. See Chow, *Rise of Confucian Ritualism*; Brook, *Confusions of Pleasure*; Brokaw, *Ledgers of Merit and Demerit*.

25. Wang Fansen, "Qing chu shiren de huizui xintai yu xiaoji xingwei" 清初士人的悔罪心態與消極行為 and "Ming mo Qing chu de yi zhong daode yange zhuyi" 明末清初的一種道德嚴格主義, in *Wan Ming Qing chu sixiang shi lun*, 187–247 and 89–106.

26. Yang Nianqun, *Hechu shi Jiangnan?*, esp. chap. 2.

27. For reservations about this interpretation, see Chow, *Rise of Confucian Ritualism*, 15; Handlin-Smith, *Art of Doing Good*, 163.

28. Mark Elvin discusses the Confucian moral meteorology in *Retreat of the Elephants*, chap. 12. Frederic Wakeman, in his monumental work on the Ming-Qing transition, also situates this dynastic change in the context of climate change. See Wakeman, *Great Enterprise*, vol. 1, 7. For the latest, most comprehensive discussion of the "seventeenth-century global crisis," see Parker, *Global Crisis*. In this book, Parker offers a sophisticated account of the seventeenth-century crises resulting from both climate change and human activities related to it.

29. Chow, *Publishing, Culture, and Power*, esp. chap. 4.

30. Ibid., 175. See also Chen Baoliang, "Wan Ming rujia chuantong"; Brook, *Confusions of Pleasure*.

31. Chow, introduction to *Publishing, Culture, and Power*.

32. Wang Hung-tai, "Ming-Qing de zixun chuanbo."

33. Ibid.

34. Miller, "Opposition to the Donglin Faction." Other explorations include the special issue on the "public sphere" and "civil society" in *Modern China* (1993); Brook, introduction to *Praying for Power*. Wakeman proposed examining the boundaries between "public" and "official" in late imperial China instead of those between "public" and "private." See Wakeman, "Boundaries of the Public Sphere."

35. For example, He Zongmei, concluding chapter of *Ming mo Qing chu wenren jieshe*.

36. The Five Cardinal Relationships refer to the proper relationships between the ruler and subject, father and son, husband and wife, elder and younger brothers, and friends.

37. For a discussion on the special status of friendship in the Five Cardinal Relations, see Kutcher, "The Fifth Relationship." See, in addition, Martin Huang, "Male Friendship in Ming China" and "Male Friendship and Jiangxue"; McDermott, "Friendship and Its Friends." Stressing "syncretism," Vitiello offers an excellent analysis of how the idealization of male-male friendship informed new understandings of the ideal male-female relationship and also exposed the conflict between the ethics of *fufu* and *pengyou* in the *wulun* system. Vitiello, *Libertine's Friend*.

38. See, e.g., Chow, *Rise of Confucian Ritualism*; Weijing Lu, *True to Her Word*.

39. Fei, *Negotiating Urban Space*, 22–24. See also Goldman, *Opera and the City*, 5–8.

40. For a comprehensive and insightful review of the Ming-Qing transition sources, see Struve, *Ming-Qing Conflict*.

41. Crossley, *Translucent Mirror*.

42. In the concluding section of each chapter in *Women and National Trauma*, Wai-yee Li offers a succinct but insightful review of how particular seventeenth-century tropes and issues were remembered, reimaged, and appropriated in later periods. For a detailed case study of late-Qing imagination of the late Ming, see Qin, *Qing mo Min chu*. Harry Miller offers an excellent case study of this issue in his research on the oblivion of the late-Ming official Tang Binyin. Miller, "Opposition to the Donglin Faction."

43. Wang Hung-tai, "Ming-Qing de zixun chuanbo," 60; Han Li, introduction to "News, Public Opinions, and History." Fei, *Negotiating Urban Space*, 46–51. "Public opinion" has multiple context-specific meanings. In most cases in seventeenth-century China, it refers to views shared and voiced by the literati.

44. Han Li, introduction to "News, Public Opinions, and History."

45. Schaberg, "Word of Mouth"; Allen, "Oral Sources."

46. Chen, introduction to Chen and Schaberg, *Idle Talk*, 4.

47. Siyen Fei cites this example to emphasize the impact of "news-based vernacular novels" (*Negotiating Urban Space*, 198–99). But in the text, Qian Daxin seems to refer to novels in general.

48. Chen Longzheng 陳龍正, *Jiting wai shu* 幾亭外書, cited in Chen Wanyi, *Wan Ming xiaopin*, 38. See also Liu Yongqiang, "Xiaoshuo qiyuan wenti." "Petty discourse" is a translation by Graham Sanders in "I Read They Said He Sang What He Wrote," 91.

49. Fei, *Negotiating Urban Space*, 202.

50. Liu Zhongxing, "Jietie yu Mingdai gonggong yulun."

51. Sun Chuanting, preface to *Jianlao lu*, 193–94.

52. Ibid., 210–11.

53. Chow, *Rise of Confucian Ritualism*, 2.

54. Weijing Lu, *True to Her Word*, 36.

55. Jimmy Yu offers a number of case studies in *Sanctity and Self-Inflicted Violence*.

56. Chen, introduction to Chen and Schaberg, *Idle Talk*, 13.

57. Owen, "Postface," in Chen and Schaberg, *Idle Talk*, 218.

58. Wang Hung-tai, "Ming-Qing de zixun chuanbo," 70.

59. See some well-known examples in ibid.

60. Some Chinese scholars have named this genre *jiating xiaoshuo*. I dub it "family romance." I use "family" here to refer broadly to any of the following concepts: family, household, clan, and lineage. I thank Dorothy Ko for helping me explore this concept and translation. This translation is also inspired by Lynn Hunt's examination of power struggles before and after the French Revolution through the lens of "family romance" in *The Family Romance of the French Revolution*. For a critical review of the complicated history of Romance, see James Grantham Turner, "'Romance' and the Novel in Restoration England."

61. For a comprehensive study of this genre, see Liang Xiaoping, *Ming-Qing jiazu xiaoshuo*. A more focused analysis of familial ethics in such fictions is Duan Jiangli, *Lifa yu renqing*.

62. Struve, *Ming-Qing Conflict*, 640.

63. Levine, *Divided by a Common Language*, 2–3.

64. Ibid., chap. 7.

65. Levine, "Public Good and Partisan Gain," 875.

66. Levine, *Divided by a Common Language*, 174.

67. Bossler, *Courtesans, Concubines, and the Cult of Female Fidelity*, 42–43.

68. For a discussion on late-Ming factionalism and its connection to East Asian trade, war, and diplomacy, which had now become an

integral part of the globalized networks, see, e.g., Yang Haiying, *Yuwai Changcheng*.

69. In this book I use the term *turncoat* to refer to former Ming officials who surrendered to and/or served the Qing. The other common term applied to such officials, *erchen*, implies as much moral bias as "turncoat." I do not use the term *erchen* in this book because it would become an extremely important political tool the Qing Qianlong emperor used to rewrite seventeenth-century political history. For discussion of the Qianlong emperor and the discourse on *erchen*, see Crossley, *Translucent Mirror*.

70. See, e.g., Michael G. Chang, *A Court on Horseback*; Zito, *Of Body and Brush*; Kahn, *Monarchy in the Emperor's Eye;* and Spence, *Treason by the Book*.

71. Representative works include Rawski, *The Last Emperors*; Elliott, *The Manchu Way*; Crossley, *Translucent Mirror*; Michael G. Chang, *A Court on Horseback*; and Struve, *Qing Formation in World-Historical Time*.

72. Elliott, *The Manchu Way*, 147.

73. Michael G. Chang, *A Court on Horseback*.

74. Kutcher, *Mourning in Late Imperial China*.

75. Debates about sinicization and the Manchu Way in the past two decades have produced important insights. See, e.g., Rawski, "Presidential Address"; Ping-ti Ho, "In Defense of Sinicization"; Ding Yizhuang, "Reflections on the 'New Qing History' School"; and Yang Nianqun, introduction to *Hechu shi Jiangnan?*. Two recent anthologies have summarized and advanced this debate: Liu Fengyun, Dong and Liu Wenpeng, *Qingdai zhengzhi yu guojia rentong*; Liu Fengyun and Liu Wenpeng, *Qingchao de guojia rentong*.

76. Guy, *Qing Governors*. Miller, from the perspective of "state versus gentry," makes similar observations in *State versus Gentry in Early Qing Dynasty China*.

77. Scholars generally agree that *xiao* had appeared by the Western Zhou (1045–771 BCE), and *zhong* by the Spring and Autumn period (770–221 BCE). Questions related to their earliest forms, meanings, and implications are still being debated. Chan and Tan, introduction to *Filial Piety*, 1; Sato, *Zhongguo gudai de zhong lun yanjiu*, esp. 36–49; Wang Zijin, *"Zhong" guannian yanjiu*, chaps. 1 and 11.

78. Some scholars identify the *Han Feizi* as presenting the earliest textual appearance of the word *zhongxiao* (Nuyen, "Filial Piety as Respect for Tradition," 204). "Zhongxiao" is the title of the fifty-first section of the *Han Feizi*, but this word does not appear in the main text of the section. The complete compilation of the fifty-five sections in the *Han Feizi* existed by the first century BCE. Zhang Jue, *Han Feizi jiaoshu*, preface and chap. 20, 1261–62. It is possible that the use of the term *zhongxiao* in *Lüshi chunqiu* predates that in the *Han Feizi*. The passage in which *zhongxiao* appears is in book 4, section "Quan xue" 勸學. See Sato, *Zhongguo gudai de zhong lun yanjiu*. But some also question if *Lüshi chunqiu* was actually produced during the pre-Qin period (see, e.g., Wang Zijin, *"Zhong" guannian yanjiu*, 328).

79. Cheung Yin Lee, "Emperor Chengzu," 143; Wang Zijin, *"Zhong" guannian yanjiu*, chap. 11.

80. Holzman, "Place of Filial Piety," 192.

81. Brown, *Politics of Mourning.*

82. For a comprehensive introduction to this text and a brief account of the historical background for its emergence, see Rosemont and Ames, *The Chinese Classic of Family Reverence.*

83. Ying Zhang, "Politics and Practice of Moral Rectitude"; Lu Miaw-fen, *Xiaozhi tianxia.*

84. Wang Zijin, *"Zhong" guannian yanjiu,* chap. 10.

85. Crossley, *Translucent Mirror*; Wakeman, *Great Enterprise*, vol. 2. On the seventeenth-century literati's views on martyrdom and loyalism, see Ho Koon-piu, "Should We Die as Martyrs to the Ming Cause?"; McMorran, "The Patriot and the Partisans." For discussion on *yimin* as the emblem of Confucian tradition, see Zhao Yuan, *Ming-Qing zhiji shidafu yanjiu*, 220; Wing-ming Chan, "Early-Qing Discourse on Loyalty," 31.

86. Meyer-Fong, *Building Culture*, 23.

87. For example, chapter 14 of this classic discusses the connections between loyalty and other virtues such as filial piety, fraternal love, and gender distinction.

88. Scholars have recently explored a local term, *nan/nü*, and its analytical potentials. See Hershatter and Wang, "Chinese History"; Liu, Karl, and Ko, *Birth of Chinese Feminism.* As Lisa Raphals has shown, the nuanced but significant differences between usages of gendered binaries in Chinese history often get obscured in linguistic continuity. Raphals, *Sharing the Light.*

89. For discussion of "Confucian gender system, " see Ko, *Teachers of the Inner Chambers.*

90. For discussion of the Song period, see Davis, *Wind against the Mountain.*

91. Ko, *Teachers of the Inner Chambers.* For analysis of access to women during the Song-Yuan period, see Bossler, *Courtesans, Concubines, and the Cult of Female Fidelity*; Birge, "Women and Confucianism from Song to Ming."

92. Brokaw, *Ledgers of Merit and Demerit*, 18.

93. Pauline Lee, *Li Zhi.* On how late imperial fiction and drama engaged authenticity and sincerity, see, e.g., Epstein, *Competing Discourses*; Owen, "I Don't Want to Act as Emperor."

94. Chow, *Rise of Confucian Ritualism*; Brook, *Praying for Power*; Brokaw, *Ledgers of Merit and Demerit*; Lu Miaw-fen, *Xiaozhi tianxia*; and Wang Fansen, "Ming mo Qing chu de yi zhong yange daode zhuyi."

95. As scholars in various disciplines have pointed out, the term *moralism* is inadequately defined and theorized. When theorized in modern Western contexts, it is often discussed as the opposite of "morality"; the two concepts form a "fake" versus "genuine" binary. Coady, "Preface" and "The Moral Realism in Realism," in Coady, *What's Wrong with Moralism?*

CHAPTER 1: LISTS, LITERATURE, AND THE IMAGINED COMMUNITY OF FACTIONALISTS

1. Lucille Chia's review of the use of print in the Ming dynasty points to the significance of the Wanli reign in the history of print culture. Chia, "The Use of Print in Ming Dynasty China."

2. Brokaw, *Ledgers of Merit and Demerit*, 23–24. Historians have defined the Donglin differently in different research projects. For a summary of various usages of and approaches to "the Donglin" in extant scholarship, see Ying Zhang, "Politics and Morality," esp. 17–23. John Dardess points out that "Donglin" "stood for an ethical revitalization movement; it referred to a national Confucian moral fellowship; and it also labeled a Beijing political faction." Dardess, *Blood and History*, 1. For a careful analysis of the early stage of Donglin as an intellectual group but not a political party, see, e.g., Fan Shuzhi, "Donglin shuyuan." Ding Guoxiang argues that the Donglin was not a political party but was heavily involved in politics, whereas the Fushe was closer to becoming a "party" than the Donglin. Ding Guoxiang, *Fushe yanjiu*, esp. 17–25.

3. Hucker, in "The T'ung-lin Movement," calls the Donglin officials "moral crusaders."

4. Miller has probed a couple of cases in his "Opposition to the Donglin Faction" and "Newly Discovered Source."

5. See Wu Yuancui's short biography in Li Guangzuo, *Changzhou xianzhi*, 290, and in Liu Tenglong, *Suzhou fuzhi*, 30.35b and 65.38a–39b. Liu's edition of *Suzhou fuzhi* also lists some of his publications (45.47a).

6. Brook, *Confusions of Pleasure*, 171–72.

7. The small project was titled *Yanzhong jiwen* 燕中紀聞.

8. He Canran, postscript to *Bo Bo Manlu pingzheng*, and He's notes, 760. The first volume is called *qianji* and the rest *bieji*, *duoji*, *jiji*, *yuji*. In most of the extant editions, including the editions I referenced in this book, *Linju manlu* is printed together with *Manlu pingzheng*, a commentary on *Linju manlu* by He Canran, Wu's contemporary. The same editions also include Wu's counter-commentary, *Bo Manlu pingzheng*, and He's response, *Bo Bo Manlu pingzheng*. Unless otherwise noted, the edition used in all the footnotes in my analysis of Wu's *Linju manlu* and *Bo Manlu pingzheng* as well as my examination of He's *Manlu pingzheng* and *Bo Bo Manlu pingzheng* refers to the *Beijing tushuguan guji zhenben congkan* edition.

9. Although Wu Yuancui downplayed the fact that he gave copies of the book to prominent figures, the responses from these men clearly indicate that he was keen to seek their comments and recognition. See Wu Yuancui ,appendix ("Fu zhugong ping Manlu" 附諸公評漫録) to Wu Yuancui, *Bo Manlu pingzheng*, 756–60.

10. He Canran, postscript to *Bo Bo Manlu pingzheng*, 761–62.

11. "Literary commentaries" refers to printed commentaries for readers of the Classics (for examination purposes) and vernacular novels.

12. For a discussion of the literary commentary format and the development of commentary editions of vernacular novels since the sixteenth century, see Rolston, *How to Read the Chinese Novel.*

13. These publications include *Yi'antang gao*, which devotes many entries to clarifying Wu's position, and *Tanyuan zazhi*, a compilation of memorials on the Li Sancai controversy. For an insightful analysis of the case and the relationship between the Donglin and Li Sancai, see Miller, "Newly Discovered Source."

14. He Canran, *Bo Bo Manlu pingzheng*, and Wu Yuancui, *Bo Manlu pingzheng*, 710.

15. He Canran, postscript to *Bo Bo Manlu pingzheng*, 761. *Yi'antang gao* was also published and reprinted multiple times. The earliest preface is dated Wanli 38 (1610), and the latest Tianqi 1 (1621).

16. Wu Yuancui, *Linju manlu*, 718.

17. He Canran, preface to *Bo Bo Manlu pingzheng.*

18. He Canran, *Bo Bo Manlu pingzheng*, 756.

19. See the official Ni Yuanlu's recollection of the persecution of Donglin officials in Jin Risheng, *Song tian lu bi*, 508–9, 514.

20. Ono, *Mingji dangshe kao*, 94. The compilation seems to have been completed around Wanli 37 (1609), but it continued to be edited and augmented. The latest memorial included is dated Wangi 42 (1617).

21. Ibid. For a discussion about Li Sancai and the Donglin defense of him, see Miller, "Newly Discovered Source."

22. Wu Liang, "Huai fu bu tan qingyi zizai shu" 淮撫不貪清議自在疏, *Zhiyuan ji*, 8.35a–b.

23. Ibid.

24. Wu Liang once plainly told the emperor: "I am indeed one of the Donglin." Wu Liang, "Baobing wen yan pingxin pouli shu" 抱病聞言平心剖理疏, *Zhiyuan ji*, 8.39b.

25. Wu Liang, "Huai fu bu tan qingyi zizai shu" *Zhiyuan ji*, 8.35a. I believe the list he mentions refers to the Donglin because this sentence immediately follows his definition of the Donglin faction in the memorial.

26. Wu Yuancui, *Tanyuan zazhi.*

27. Wu Yuancui, *Linju manlu*, 584.

28. Ibid.

29. He Canran, commentary section in *Manlu pingzheng*, 584.

30. For a detailed analysis of these struggles, see Dardess, *Blood and History.*

31. Xia Xie, *Ming tongjian*, 2220. The *List of Notorious Donglin Fighters* is attributed to the official Wang Shaohui.

32. Xue Cai's comments on his friend Chen Zhenhui's essay, "Shu Jiazi huitui" 書甲子會推, in Chen Zhenhui, *Shu shi qi ze*, 1b–2a.

33. Qian Renlin, *Donglin biesheng*, 14b, 29b. Qian compares the various versions of this list, including those recorded in titles such as *Bofu lu* 剝復錄, *xian bo zhi shi* 先撥志始, and *Zhuozhong zhi yu* 酌中志餘.

34. Qian Renlin, *Donglin biesheng*, 13a and 16a–b.

35. Wuyue Caomang Chen, *Wei Zhongxian xiaoshuo chijian shu*, 165.

36. The Qing literatus Qian Renlin offered a brief analysis of how some names and sobriquets are matched in his introduction for *Donglin dianjiang lu* when he compiled it into *Donglin biesheng* (14b–16a).

37. This is in chapter 33 of the novel *Water Margin*.

38. See, e.g., Ji Liuqi, *Ming ji bei lue*, 263.

39. Wang Shaohui, *Donglin dianjiang lu*, 922. The translations of these sobriquets adopt those in Pearl S. Buck, *All Men Are Brothers*, 1266–72.

40. Qian Renlin points out that one of the lists, *Donglin pengdang lu* 東林朋黨錄, brought in Qian Shouyi and Huang Yuansu because they resembled the names of Qian Qianyi and Huang Zunsu, two Donglin-identified officials. Qian Renlin, *Donglin biesheng*, 1a.

41. For example, see *Donglin pengdang lu* and *Donglin jiguan* 東林籍貫, in Qian Renlin, *Donglin biesheng*.

42. Wuyue Caomang Chen, *Wei Zhongxian xiaoshuo chijian shu*, 163.

43. Qian Renlin, *Donglin biesheng*, 32a. This official was Zhou Shunchang, one of the famous Donglin martyrs.

44. For a comprehensive list of Donglin-identified officials who have appeared on major Donglin blacklists, see Ono, *Mingji dangshe kao*, 377–402.

45. I thank Ari D. Levine for pointing out this similarity.

46. Cited in Jin Risheng, *Song tian lu bi*, 170.

47. *CMMYL*, 272–75.

48. Sommer, *Sex, Law, and Society*, 14. See also Chen Baoliang, *Zhongguo liumang shi*, esp. 160–66.

49. Ni Yuanlu's memorial (CZ 1/2), in Jin Risheng, *Song tian lu bi*, 512.

50. Ibid., 514.

51. Ibid., 512.

52. Ibid., 256, in the record of the Chongzhen emperor's audience with his grand secretaries.

53. Its long-lasting impact on late-Ming politics is evident in another list that was compiled at the Southern Ming Hongguang court. See "Interlude" in this book.

54. See chap. 2 in this book. A literatus at the time, widely known for his pro-Donglin stance, observed that although some officials had legitimately challenged Donglin factionalism, the Donglin's suffering changed its image. See Zhang Shiwei, "Ji Jiongqing Wu Yinzhi xiansheng wen" 祭冏卿吳因之先生文, in *Zhang Yidu xiansheng Ziguangzhai ji shi liu juan fu Zhou libu jishi yi juan*, 262.

55. Ni Yuanlu was accused of illegitimately obtaining an honorary title for a concubine after he abandoned his wife in clear violation of the Five Cardinal Relations. Zheng Man certainly recognized the connection between his case and Ni's. *TSZXNP*, 493.

56. Ono, *Mingji dangshe kao*, 97. See also Ye Jun, "Zheng Man yanjiu," 84–86.

57. Jie Zhao, "A Decade of Considerable Significance." Translation by Zhao, n. 45.

58. Zheng Zhenxian, "Zhifa gujin diyi quanjian shu" 直發古今第一權奸疏, in Wu Liang, *Wanli shuchao*, 54–58.

59. Wu Liang clearly and specifically criticized Zhu Geng and his followers at court. He believed in his position so deeply that he admitted to the emperor that he was even willing to impeach some fine officials in order to "cut off the factional network surrounding Grand Secretary Zhu." Wu Liang, "Huai fu bu tan qingyi zizai shu," 8.35a–b.

60. Jin Risheng, *Song tian lu bi*, 435.

61. Wu Liang, "Song Zheng libu Taichu yanshi zuoqian" 送鄭禮部太初言事左遷 and "Zai yong qianyun shuhuai si shou" 再用前韻書懷四首, *Zhiyuan ji*, 2.21a–22b.

62. Wu Liang, "Zheng taijun shi" 鄭太君詩, *Zhiyuan ji*, 2.26b.

63. See, e.g., Ye Xianggao, *Qu bian*, 2.46–48. Grand Secretary Ye Xianggao (1559–1627) was respected for his nonpartisan stance. He included this incident in his documentation of government affairs but was careful not to explicitly discuss his own judgment; instead he puts "it is said" or "someone said to someone that . . ." before those passages about Zheng. The contemporary author Shen Defu briefly documented Zheng's case. He suggested that Zheng fabricated accusations against colleagues in order to present himself as a courageous official. Shen Defu, *Wanli ye huo bian*, 233–34.

64. Wu Yuancui documented former colleagues' conversations about Zheng in several places in his work *Yi'antang gao*, jin ji, 67b and shi ji, 59a, 65a. Although Wu Yuancui strongly disliked Wu Liang, he never endorsed the theory that Zheng, Wu's in-law and ally, faked political integrity. Rather, he was suspicious of the attacks on Zheng.

65. Shen Defu, *Wanli ye huo bian*, 234.

66. *Fulun xinshi* 扶輪信史, in Tang Juanshi, *Zheng Man shiji* 2, 2a. There are five sources, numbered 1–5, in *Zheng Man shiji*.

67. Xia Xie, *Ming tongjian*, 2074; Xie Guozhen, *Ming-Qing zhiji dangshe yundong kao*, 3–5, 10–30.

68. Fan Shuzhi, "Dangzheng xuanwo."

69. *Daobing Donglin huo* 盜柄東林夥, in Qian Renlin, *Donglin biesheng*, 39a.

70. Zheng had retired in the late Wanli reign and played no role at court in the anti-eunuch protests of the Tianqi reign. Various contemporary sources suggest this was Zhe faction's work, among them Jin Risheng's *Song tian lu bi*. On the collaboration between the eunuch faction and the other factions, see Xie Guozhen, *Ming-Qing zhiji dangshe yundong kao*, 31–47.

71. Qian Qianyi, "Feng anren Wu shi muzhiming" 封安人吳氏墓誌銘, *Chu xue ji*, 1427–29.

72. Wu Liang, "Jiaqingtu ji" 家慶圖記, *Zhiyuan ji*, 17.25b.

73. *TSZXNP*, 483.

74. Ibid.

75. Chun-fang Yu, *Renewal of Buddhism in China*.

76. For more on Yunqi Zhuhong's interactions with the gentry of the late Ming, see ibid.; Brook, *Praying for Power*. On the couple's influence among gentry men and women, see Jian Ruiyao, *Mingdai funu fojiao*.

77. *TSZXNP*, 483. Two announcements made by elders in the Zheng lineage publicly condemned the kin member who conspired with Zheng Man's accusers, confirming Zheng's own recollection. See "Zheng shi tongzu jiwen" 鄭氏通族祭文 and "Zheng shi tongzu zhu bu ti Zheng Yiqian xi" 鄭氏通族誅不〔悌〕鄭一謙檄, *MYCTWJ*, 504–7.

78. Zheng Zhenxian and Wu Liang not only formed a firm political alliance but also socialized frequently. Wu Liang, "Dianiao Zhongzhou ci Zheng Taichu yun zhibie" 典校中州次鄭太初韻志別, "Chunri tong Wu Zhiju Chen Meng'e Zheng Taichu you xijiao ji Guangtongsi ci Zhiju yun" 春日同吳之矩陳孟諤鄭太初游西郊集廣通寺次之矩韻, "Xie erbei tongyou zai he yun si Taichu" 携兒輩同遊再和韻似太初, in *Zhiyuan ji*, *juan* 2. Wu had always maintained a good relationship with Zheng Zhenxian's younger brother, Zhenguang, too. See Wu's poems "Song Zheng Mingchu nan huan yingshi" 送鄭明初南還應試 and "Wen Dong Yuting Zheng Mingchu dejuan" 聞董于廷鄭明初得雋, in *Zhiyuan ji*, 2.19a and 3.13a.

79. Wu Liang, "Yu Zheng Mingchu" 與鄭明初, *Zhiyuan ji*, 23.29b–30b.

80. For a detailed discussion of these misrepresentations in seventeenth- and eighteenth-century literati works, see Ying Zhang, "Confucian Principles."

81. Huang Zongxi, "Zheng Miyang xiansheng mubiao" 鄭峚陽先生墓表, *Nanlei wen ding*, vol. 3, 2.7b–8b.

82. Jin Risheng, *Song tian lu bi*, 435. Because this Chongzhen 2 (1629) publication appeared years before rumors about Zheng Man emerged, I consider it a more reliable source on Zheng's status in the Donglin community at the time. The other two relatively objective sources are Huang Zongxi, "Zheng Miyang xiansheng mubiao," *Nanlei wen ding*, vol. 3, 2.7b–8b.; Qian Qianyi, "Feng anren Wu shi muzhiming," *Chu xue ji*, 1427–28.

83. For an account of Zheng Man's arrest, see Xia Xie, *Ming tongjian*, 2239.

84. *TSZXNP*, 494; "Chongzhen 11 nian Jinyi Wu Mengming hui zou Zheng Man zhang mu shu" 崇禎十一年錦衣吳孟明回奏鄭鄤杖母疏, *CMMYL*, 730.

85. Xia Xie, *Ming tongjian*, 2776–78.

86. This exchange was well documented in many contemporary sources. Sun Chengze's *Chunming meng yu lu* (392–94) probably provides the most detailed account. More on this in chap. 3 in this book.

87. Ji Liuqi's documentation of the execution, though not completely accurate, nonetheless reflects the sensation caused by Zheng Man's case at the time. Ji Liuqi, *Ming ji bei lue*, 258.

88. "Zheng shi tongzu jiwen," *MYCTWJ*, 505.

89. One of Zheng Man's uncles, Zheng Zhenyuan 鄭振元, raised specific examples in his testimony, "Bian yuan jie" 辯冤揭, in Tang Xiuye, *Zheng an chuanxin lu yuangao*, no page number.

90. *CMMYL*, 394.

91. Zheng Zhenyuan, "Bianyuan jie," in Tang Xiuye, *Zheng an chuanxin lu yuangao*. Zhang Xia compiled a few such biographies in *Yuqiao hua*. The term *xiaoshuo* is translated here as "vernacular novels" for two reasons:

first, in the Zheng Man case, vernacular novels indeed appeared; second, the other meaning of this term, "petty discourses," is covered by the other term, *xiaoshi*. See the introduction to this volume for scholarship on gossip, anecdote, and related terms.

92. Sun Kaidi, *Zhongguo tongsu xiaoshuo shumu*, 85.

93. See the titles of chapters 1–11 of *Fang Zheng xiaoshi* 放鄭小史, in Tang Juanshi, *Zheng Man shiji* 4, 1a–2b.

94. *Fang Zheng xiaoshi*, in Tang Juanshi, *Zheng Man shiji* 4, titles of chaps. 18, 20, 35, 37, and 38.

95. They were given titles such as *mengzhu* and *hufa*.

96. Titles of chapters 36–38.

97. See Wen Tiren's biography in *MS*, 7931–37.

98. Liang Xiaoping, *Ming-Qing jiazu xiaoshuo*, esp. chaps. 3–5. For the meaning of the term and this genre, see the introduction to this book.

99. I use the term *authors* here because multiple sources suggest that the attacks on Zheng Man's sexual immorality put forth in these literary accounts were coauthored. For example, see Gu Yanwu, "Lu gongshi Laifu shu xi nian dai Xu sheren Xi cao shu gong Zheng Man shi" 陸貢士來復述昔年代許舍人曦草疏攻鄭鄤事, in *Tinglin shiji huizhu*, 806–10.

100. Lu Shiyi, *Fushe jilue*, 100.

101. Ibid.

102. Zheng Man, "Zheng Miyang duibu jietie" 鄭峚陽對簿揭貼, in Tang Xiuye, *Zheng an chuanxin lu yuangao*, no page number.

103. Richard Wang, *Ming Erotic Novellas*, esp. 134–44.

104. Again, the text has not survived. See chapter titles of *Da yingxiong zhuan* 大英雄傳, in Tang Juanshi, *Zheng Man shiji* 4, 3a–4b.

105. Titles of chapters 19 and 22 in *Da yingxiong zhuan*.

106. *Yujing xin tan*, one of the early Chongzhen publications on the *yandang* atrocities, named *Song tian lu bi* as one of the sources to which readers could resort for biographical details of the persecuted officials. Zhu Changzuo, *Yujing xin tan*, "Fanli" 凡例, 2.

107. Jin Risheng, *Song tian lu bi*, 435.

108. Xie Guozhen, *Ming-Qing zhiji dangshe yundong kao*, 54.

109. *TSZXNP*, 495. *Dao ming lu* was compiled by a Song scholar-official, Li Xinchuan (1166–1243). A collection of sources concerning Daoxue scholars, it reflects Li's particular understanding and representation of the history of Daoxue. On the nature, contents, and agenda of *Dao ming lu*, see Chaff, "The Historian as Critic"; Hartman, "Li Hsin-ch'uan." The latter also provides a detailed discussion of Li's representation of Zhu Xi in *Dao ming lu*, 344–49. Again, I thank Ari D. Levine for citations and for pointing out the crucial linkage between this text and Zheng's mention of it.

110. Li Xinchuan, "Shen Jizu he Huian xiansheng shu" 沈繼祖劾晦庵先生疏, *Dao ming lu*, 7.1. 67–69.

111. *TSZXNP*, 495.

112. Ying Zhang, "Politics and Practice of Moral Rectitude."

113. For a discussion of Zheng Man's identification with Su Shi as an official and a man, see Ying Zhang, "Politics and Morality," chap. 2.

114. Zheng Man, "Zheng Miyang xia shi die wu jie" 鄭崟陽下石疊誣揭, in Tang Xiuye, *Zheng an chuanxin lu yuangao*, no page number. At least two pamphlets drafted by Zheng have survived. His uncle and Huang Daozhou have also left us with at least one pamphlet each. Both can be found in Tang Xiuye, *Zheng an chuanxin lu yuangao*.

115. Zheng Man, "Zheng Miyang duibu jietie" 鄭崟陽對簿揭貼, in Tang Xiuye, *Zheng an chuanxin lu yuangao*, no page number. Wu Zongda was the disciple of Shen Yiguan 沈一貫, the former leader of the Zhe faction.

116. *TSZXNP*, 485, 490. For a discussion of this particular autobiography and Zheng's depiction of the *zhongxiao* tradition of his family, see Ying Zhang, "Confucian Principles."

117. *TSZXNP*, 491.

118. The episode can be found in "Yanghuo xia" 陽貨下 section of *The Analects*. Cheng Shude, *Lunyu jishi*, 1067–71.

119. *TSZXNP*, 482.

120. Zheng Man, "Tong li qi yuan shu" 痛瀝奇冤疏, *MYCTWJ*, 320–21.

121. Lu Miaw-fen, *Yangming xue shiren shequn*, chap. 8.

122. *MS*, 332–33, 6524.

123. Zhang Zilie, "Fu Yuan Linhou" 復袁臨侯, *Qishan wenji*, 423–24; emphasis added. Unless otherwise noted, in this book, I draw on the *SKJH* edition of *Qishan wenji*.

124. Ibid.

125. Lu Miaw-fen, *Xiaozhi tianxia*.

126. Huang Zongxi, "Zheng Miyang xiansheng mubiao," *Nanlei wen ding*, 8b. For more discussion on this question, see Ying Zhang, "Confucian Principles."

127. See chap. 2 in this book.

128. Still, women themselves had to walk a fine in pursuing Buddhism without looking un-Confucian. Zhou, "Hearth and the Temple."

129. Ying Zhang, "Li Zhi's Image Trouble."

130. *TSZXNP*, 486.

131. Ibid.

132. *TSZXNP* documents these daughters under the years of Tianqi 1 (1621), Chongzhen 3 (1630), Chongzhen 6 (1633), Chongzhen 7 (1634), and Chongzhen 9 (1636).

133. Zhang Xia, "*Yuqiao hua* Zheng Man benmo" 漁樵話鄭鄤本末, in Tang Juanshi, *Zheng Man shiji* 3, 4b. This view was quite influential before and after the fall of the Ming. For a discussion of representations of Zheng Man in the late seventeenth and eighteenth centuries, see Ying Zhang, "Confucian Principles."

134. Zheng Man, "Xuan dingchou fang zheng xu" 選丁丑房正序, *MYCTWJ*, 387–89.

135. *TSZXNP*, 494.

136. Chen Zilong, *Chen Zilong zizhuan nianpu*, 656.

137. Ibid.

138. Zheng Man, "Xuan dingchou fang zheng xu," *MYCTWJ*, 387.

139. Chen Zilong, *Chen Zilong zizhuan nianpu*, 656.

140. For the same reason, some literati writers of later periods were critical of how Zheng Man had been depicted by contemporaries such as Chen Zilong. For instance, see Quan Zuwang's postscript to Li Qing, *San yuan biji*, 251; Xiao Mu, "Ba *Chen Zhongyu zizhuan nianpu*" 跋陳龍裕自撰年譜, *Jingfu leigao*, 125.

141. A revealing example can be found in the writings of the early Qing official Wang Shizhen 王士禎, who was familiar with both Wu's publications and He Canran's criticisms. He points out that Wu Yuancui had attacked Li Sancai and praised a few officials who would later become members of the eunuch faction. But he does not acknowledge Wu's friendships with Donglin-identified officials at the time. Wang Shizhen, "Wu Ningfang zhu shu" 伍寧方著書, *Chi bei ou tan*, 189–90.

CHAPTER 2: DISPLAYING SINCERITY

1. Peterson argues that they were not motivated by moral considerations and this defined the difference between the Fushe and the Donglin. Peterson, *Bitter Gourd*, 99.
2. Wakeman, "Romantics, Stoics, and Martyrs."
3. *MS*, 6336.
4. Sima Qian, *Shiji*, 427, 2795.
5. Wei Xueyi, "Da guren shu" 答故人書, *Maozhan ji*, 8.10b.
6. Wei Xueyi, "Ji Pan Maoxian shu" 寄潘茂先書, *Maozhan ji*, 8.13b.
7. Wei Xueyi, "Ci lizhong fulao shu" 辭里中父老書, *Maozhan ji*, 8.14a–b.
8. Ibid., 8.15a.
9. Qian Fen, "Wei Xiaozi yiji xu" 魏孝子遺集序, *Xiaolin chu ji*, 50.
10. Ibid.
11. Huang Yi-nong, "Zhongxiao paifang yu shizijia," 47.
12. Zhang Pu, "Ji Wei Kuoyuan xiansheng wen" 祭魏廓園先生文, *Qiluzhai shiwen heji*, 521.
13. Wei Xuelian was listed as a Fushe member from Jiayi County. Lu Shiyi, *Fushe jilue*, 58.
14. Jimmy Yu has discussed blood writing related to the *Classic of Filial Piety*, pointing out that it shows the ultimate filial sacrifice and devotion in the Confucian sense. Yu, *Sanctity and Self-Inflicted Violence*, 38–39.
15. Fang Yizhi, "Xieshu *Xiaojing* tici" 血書孝經題辭, *Fushan wenji*, 487. For Wei Xuelian's original blood memorial, see Jin Risheng, *Song tian lu bi*, 630.
16. Fang Yizhi, "Xieshu *Xiaojing* tici," *Fushan wenji*, 487.
17. Chen Liang 陳梁, "Dahui tongnan xiongdi yu Pijiang yuguan jishi" 大會同難兄弟於辟疆寓館紀事, included in Mao Xiang, *Tongren ji*, 211. Wei Xuelian's brother, Xueyi, had been close to Chen Liang, too. See, e.g., Wei Xueyi's letters in *Maozhan ji*, 8.18b–19b.
18. *Jiaxing fuzhi* 嘉興府誌, cited in Huang Yi-nong, "Zhongxiao paifang yu shizijia," 47–48.
19. Wei Xuelian passed the examinations in Chongzhen 16 (1643).

20. Qian Fen, "Wei xiaozi yiji xu," *Maolin chu ji*, 51.

21. Ibid.

22. The other three are Hou Fangyu, Chen Zhenhui, and Mao Xiang.

23. These are recorded in the biographies of Yang Sichang and Xiong Wencan in *MS*, 6515 and 6737–38.

24. Ren, *Fang Yizhi nianpu*, 96.

25. Fang Yizhi, "Qing dai fu zui shu" 請代父罪疏, *Fushan wenji*, qian bian, 519.

26. Imperial response cited in Ren, *Fang Yizhi nianpu*, 96–97.

27. Weijing Lu, "Reviving an Ancient Filial Ideal."

28. He Ruchong 何如寵, preface to Fang Yizhi's *Jigutang chu ji* 稽古堂初集, in Fang Yizhi, *Fushan wenji*, 455; Ren, *Fang Yizhi nianpu*, 72–73.

29. The title "Jichu" is not translated here because it has multiple meanings. It is an ancient song name. Literally, the word *jichu* refers to indignant, sad sounds. In this particular case, the word *chu* also implies the Chu region where Fang Yizhi's father led the Ming army in the military campaigns against the rebels.

30. Wei Zaode, "Jichu xu" 激楚序, in Fang Yizhi, *Fushan wenji*, qian bian, 514.

31. Ibid.

32. Tian Younian, "Jichu xu" 激楚序, in Fang Yizhi, *Fushan wenji*, qian bian, 514–15.

33. Huang Jingfang, "Jichu xu" 激楚序, in Fang Yizhi, *Fushan wenji*, qian bian, 513. Jimmy Yu has analyzed Feng Xingke's filial act in *Sanctity and Self-Inflicted Violence*, 43–45.

34. Yan Hun, "Jichu xu" 激楚序, in Fang Yizhi, *Fushan wenji*, qian bian, 514. See also Huang Jingfang, "Jichu xu," in Fang Yizhi, *Fushan wenji*, qian bian, 513.

35. Yan Hun, "Jichu xu," in Fang Yizhi, *Fushan wenji*, qian bian, 514.

36. See the emperor's comment on Zhou Maolan's "blood memorial" in Jin Risheng, *Song tian lu bi*, 635. Zhou Maolan's father, Zhou Shunchang, was one of the Donglin martyrs.

37. Ren, *Fang Yizhi nianpu,* 105. Peterson (*Bitter Gourd*, 116–17) cites the emperor's response but points out that this story is likely "apocryphal" (chap. 6, n. 67).

38. Qian Chengzhi, a Ming loyalist, in his work *Tianjian wenji*, documents that the former governor-general of Henan, a certain Chen during the Chongzhen reign, was imprisoned, but his son donned his nice, scented robes to perform his duties at court as if nothing had happened. The Chongzhen emperor reportedly said: "How can I expect such an unfililal son to be loyal!" And he praised Fang Yizhi's expression of sincere filiality at the same time as a contrast. The emperor thus ordered Fang Kongzhao released from prison and Chen severely punished. See Qian Chengzhi, "Changgansi yu jiu zhongguan shu wangshi ji" 長干寺遇舊中官述往事記, cited in Ren, *Fang Yizhi nianpu*, 105. The imprisoned governor-general of Henan in this record apparently referred to Chen Biqian, who led successful campaigns against rebels in Chongzhen 8–9 in Henan, until he lost a battle and was

replaced. Chen's defeat took place more than a year before Fang Kongzhao was arrested. Later, Chen was promoted to president of the Board of Works (*MS*, 3502). All these suggest that the story about the emperor's condemnation of Chen's son is untrue.

39. Dennerline, *Chia-ting Loyalists*.

40. Peterson, *Bitter Gourd*, chap. 2.

41. Ibid., 139.

42. Ren, *Fang Yizhi nianpu*, 87–95.

43. Chen Zilong, preface to Fang Yizhi, *Liuyu cao*, cited in Ren, *Fang Yizhi nianpu*, 87–88.

44. For a military-historical analysis of the literati's interests and limitations regarding military theories and actions, see Yimin Zhang, "The Role of Literati in Military Action." On the seventeenth-century Chinese literati's debate about the need to acquire military skills and knowledge, and its gendered implications, see Martin Huang, *Negotiating Masculinities*, chap. 4.

45. Du Dengchun, *She shi shimo*, 7. A few scholars consider Gong Dingzi a Fushe member. See, e.g., Wang Enjun, *Fushe*, 182; Dennerline, *Chia-ting Loyalists*, 306.

46. Dong Qian, *Gong Zhilu nianpu*, 6.

47. Zuo Fu et al., *Hefei xianzhi*, 978. Gong Dingzi's official writings (memorials, essays, legal judgments, etc.) from this period are compiled in a volume titled *Xichuan zheng pu*. For an example of local appreciation of Gong's performance during his tenure as magistrate, see Gu Jingxing's poems "Wei Gong Duanyi qingsi Xichuan ci Zixing yun si shou" 為龔端毅請祀浠川次子星韻四首 and "Hengdu dashi ta zhi ming" 恆度大師塔誌銘, in Gu Jingxing, *Baimaotang ji*, 119 and 356.

48. Yan Zhengju, "Dazongbo Gong Duanyi gong zhuan" 大宗伯龔端毅公傳, in Gong Dingzi, *Hefei Gong Duanyi gong zoushu*, 4b–5a.

49. The late-Ming official and loyalist Li Qing has written about Gong Dingzi in his historical work, *San yuan biji*, in multiple places, quite negatively. I will discuss this source in a different work. It suffices here to point out that there are contradictions among Li's claims about his former colleagues. His apparent bias also undermines his self-proclaimed anti-factionalist objectivity. Therefore I choose not to rely too much on his portrayal of Gong in this book.

50. Yan Zhengju, "Dazongbo Gong Duanyi gong zhuan," in Gong Dingzi, *Hefei Gong Duanyi gong zoushu*, 4b–5a. Almost all the officials named by Gong were identified as Donglin-Fushe figures by their contemporaries.

51. This memorial attempted to persuade the emperor to tolerate two imprisoned officials, the most recent objects of the emperor's wrath and recipients of severe punishment for having personally provoked him. Gong Dingzi, "Qing ba zhaoyu tingzhang shu" 請罷詔獄廷杖疏, *CMMYL*, 715–16. For the controversial arrest and imprisonment of Jiang Cai and Xiong Kaiyuan, see Xia Xie, *Ming tongjian*, 2449–51.

52. There were several officials on the list of the Grand Secretariat in this year. It is very likely that he memorialized against Chen Yan.

53. Wang Hung-tai, "Qinglou mingji," esp. 118–19.

54. Gong Dingzi, "Ti hua ji Fang Haiwei zhongcheng" 題畫寄方孩未中丞, *DSTWJ*, 6.31a; Gong Dingzi, footnote to "Ku Fang Haiwei xiansheng" 哭方孩未先生, *Gong Dingzishi*, 1094.

55. Gong Dingzi, "Ti hua ji Fang Haiwei zhongcheng," *DSTWJ*, 6.31a.

56. Gong Dingzi's bond with Fang Kongzhao and Fang Yizhi was formed on the battlefield. During his tenure as magistrate of Qishui, he worked closely with Kongzhao, then governor of Huguang, in military campaigns against the rebels. Yizhi became close to Gong when he joined his father briefly in the fall campaigns of Chongzhen 12 (1639). See, e.g., Fang Yizhi, "Huai Gong Xiaosheng Qi ling" 懷龔孝升蘄令, *Fang zi liuyu cao*, 692. In addition, Gong claimed that his uncle Gong Cuisu had been a strong supporter of Fang Zhenru in the Wanli reign. Dong Qian, *Gong Zhilu nianpu*, 4. Gong Cuisu was included in the list of the Traitors' Case, for unknown reasons. Li Qing included in his work a conversation between Gong and a colleague, reporting that Gong publicly denounced his uncle Gong Cuisu for associating with the eunuchs. Li Qing, *San yuan biji*, 53–54. Because of the biased nature of Li's account, and also because there are multiple poetic exchanges in Gong's collections between Gong and his uncle, I question its reliability.

57. Gong Dingzi, footnote to "Ku Fang Haiwei xiansheng," *Gong Dingzi shi*, 1094.

58. Gong Dingzi, "Ti hua ji Fang Haiwei zhongcheng," *DSTWJ*, 6.31a–b.

59. Gong Dingzi, "Shengchen qu" 生辰曲, *Gong Dingzi shi*, 1123–25.

60. Gong Dingzi, "Han shen Shanchi jun song bei ye wo bu cheng mei kou zhan da zhi" 寒甚善持君送被夜臥不成寐口占答之, *Gong Dingzi shi*, 1125.

61. Gong Dingzi, "Shengshen qu," *Gong Dingzi shi*, 1123–25.

62. Gong Dingzi, "Ji Fang Haiwei Zhongcheng wen" 祭方孩未中丞文, *DSTWJ*, 4.46a–47b.

63. Zhang Zilie, "Yu youren lun yuan shengji shu" 與友人論遠聲伎書, *Qishan wenji*, 113–15. For a discussion of the addressee, see Luo Jizu, "Sun Lin *Siya ji*," 199–201. Peterson points out that later historians have tried to paint a "good" image of Sun Lin by interpreting Sun's indulgence in courtesans as self-consolation at a time of crisis. Peterson, *Bitter Gourd*, 142–43 (n. 85). Wai-yee Li also observes that "accounts of the late Ming courtesan as heroic loyalist" and an inspiration for loyalist literati during the Ming-Qing transition were mostly written in the twentieth century. Wai-yee Li, "Late Ming Courtesan," 70.

64. Zhang Zilie, "Yu youren lun yuan shengji shu," *Qishan wenji*, 113–15. Zhang's work was heavily edited for this particular edition, which was published in the early Qing. The *Yuzhang congshu* edition of this collection of works seems to be less censored, but it is different from other editions in many places. Xie Canglin has explained the differences between the two major versions of Zhang Zilie's collection of works, in Xie, "*Yuzhang congshu*."

65. Three of these names were excised from this publication. Those names are omitted in the most common editions of this book. The edition included in *Yuzhang congshu* (8.8b–11a), however, shows these names. They include Wu Yingji and Zhou Lixun.

66. Zhang Zilie, "Yu youren lun yuan shengji shu," *Qishan wenji*, 114. Kang-i Sun Chang has argued that the Four Gentlemen's "romantic liaisons with [elite courtesans] did not interfere with, but indeed helped cultivate, their dedication to patriotism." Chang, *Late-Ming Poet Ch'en Tzu-lung*, 17.

67. Zhang Zilie, "Yu youren lun yuan shengji shu," *Qishan wenji*, 114; emphasis added.

68. Ibid.; emphasis added.

69. Xia Yunyi died in 1645 as a martyr. Xie Canglin has pointed out that parts of Zhang's collection had already been printed and circulated around 1644. Xie Canglin, "*Yuzhang congshu*," 61. For a brief biography of Xia Yunyi, see *MS*, 7098.

70. Zhang Zilie, "Yu youren lun yuan shengji shu," *Qishan wenji*, 115.

71. Ibid., 114–15.

72. This is evident in Zhang Zilie's correspondence with many friends and is confirmed in his notes to a series of autobiographical essays. He emphasized that he deliberately omitted many details and names in the sections about Nanjing in order to comply with this Confucian principle. Zhang Zilie, notes to "Lü ji" 旅記, *Qishan wenji*, 268.

73. For an examination of the first group of printed literature on *yandang* atrocities, see H. Laura Wu, "Corpses on Display."

74. Zhang Pu, "Ji Wei Kuoyuan xiansheng wen," *Qiluzhai shiwen heji*, 523.

75. Ibid.

76. Zhang Pu, "Qian Zhongfang shi xu" 錢仲芳詩序, *Qiluzhai shiwen heji*, 687–90.

77. Zhang Pu, "Xiankao Xuyu fujun xingzhuang" 先考虛宇府君行狀, *Qiluzhai shiwen heji*, 571–95; Lu Shiyi, *Fushe jilue*, 47.

78. Zhang Pu, "Zeng Wenlinlang Zhang taiweng feng ruren Su taimu hezang muzhiming" 贈文林郎張太翁封孺人蘇太母合葬墓誌銘, *Qiluzhai shiwen heji*, 417–28.

79. Zhang Pu, "Zeng Wenlinlang Zhang taiweng feng ruren Su taimu hezang muzhiming," "Zhang bomu ying feng xu" 張伯母膺封序, and "Zhang Shouxian gao xu" 張受先稿序, *Qiluzhai shiwen heji*, 899–906 and 963–68.

80. Zhang Pu, "Ku Su taimu wen" 哭蘇太母文, *Qiluzhai shiwen heji*, 497–503.

81. Wang Enjun, "Fushe chengyuan."

82. Qian Qianyi, "Taicang Zhang shi shouyan xu" 太倉張氏壽宴序, *Chu xue ji*, 1064–66.

83. Du Dengchun, *She shi shimo*, 4.

84. Zhang Pu, "Wu Zhenpu xiansheng liu shi xu" 吳鎮樸先生六十序, *Qiluzhai shiwen heji*, 753–54. Wu Zeng was in charge of empirewide communications for the Fushe.

85. Zhang Pu, "Shen bomu wu shi xu" 沈伯母五十序, *Qiluzhai shiwen heji*, 751.

86. For a review of the interpretations of the discourse of friendship in the late Ming, see Martin Huang, "Male Friendship in Ming China."

87. During Chongzhen 11/2–5 (1638), Shen Shoumin submitted three memorials on this issue. See Shen Shoumin, "He Yang Wuling shu" 劾楊武陵疏, "Zai he Yang Wuling shu" 再劾楊武陵疏, and "San he Yang Wuling shu" 三劾楊武陵疏, *Gushan yiji*, 28–34. The original titles of the memorials could be found in the text of these memorials.

88. Shen Shoumin, "He Yang Wuling shu," *Gushan yiji*, 29.

89. Some scholars have pointed out the deep divides among Fushe activists regarding their political strategy and message in this case. See, e.g., Wang Enjun, "Shilun Fushe neibu."

90. For more on this, see chap. 3 in this book.

91. Ren, *Fang Yizhi nianpu*, 88–89.

92. Zhang Zilie, "Zai fu Shen Meisheng shu" 再復沈眉生書, *Qishan wenji*, 116–17. Wan Shihua's letter to Zheng Man and a preface he composed in the Tianqi reign for Zheng Man's collection of works do in fact appear in the edition of *Gaiyuan ji* that I have consulted. See Wan Shihua, "Dunzhai jingao xu" 遯齋近稿序 and "Shang Zheng Qianzhi taishi qi" 上鄭謙止太史啟, *Gaiyuan chu ji er juan er ji san juan*, 262 and 294.

93. The biographers included Jiang Yueguang, Xu Shipu, Zhou Biao, and Li Yuanmei. Li Yuanmei, "Ji Wan Maoxian wen" 祭萬茂先文, *Lianxuge ji*, 303.

94. Ibid., 302–4.

95. Lu Shiyi, *Fushe jilue*, 65–66.

96. Ibid.

97. The dominant revisionist view is that although Wu Bing authored the extant play, it was not necessarily meant to ridicule anyone as claimed by some sources. See Ding Guoxiang, *Fushe yanjiu*, esp. 204–6. Recently Lin Zhiying has suggested that the characters and plot of *The Green Peony* we have today might have been changed from those in the original precisely because Wu was a Fushe sympathizer and did not want to see the parody of Fushe scholars circulating in society. Lin Zhiying, "Yi ju wei ge."

98. Lu Shiyi, *Fushe jilue*, 68.

99. These authors include Lu Shiyi, who was a friend of many Fushe members but kept a distance from the Fushe because he did not appreciate its pragmatic networking. Modern historians argue that Lu's stance ensures the relative reliability and objectivity of his documentation of Fushe activities. See Ge and Wang, *Lu Shiyi pingzhuan*, 23–24. Other friendly contemporary accounts of the incident include Wu Weiye's *Fushe jishi* 復社紀事 and Du Dengchun's *She shi shimo*.

100. Lu Shiyi, *Fushe jilue*, *juan* 2. See also Miller, *State versus Gentry in Late Ming Dynasty China*, 143–45.

101. Lu Shiyi, *Fushe jilue*, *juan* 2 and 4.

102. Here, the records show contradictions. The memorial by Zhang Guowei in Chongzhen 11 (1628) included in *Fushe jilue* does not really support the account in *juan* 2 of the same book.

103. Zhou's mother was a concubine, and he was the eldest son of his father and this concubine. The "elder brother" mentioned refers to the son of his official mother, his father's wife. See Zhou Zhikui, "Shengmu Wu Ruren

xingzhuang" 生母吳孺人行狀, *Qicao shiji qi juan wenji ba juan Qicao erji* (*SKJH*-ji 113), 16–18.

104. Lu Shiyi, *Fushe jilue*, 73. Also see Zhou Zhikui's memorial to the Chongzhen emperor, cited in ibid., 103–6.

105. Zhou Zhikui, "Shang Xu Shimen laoshi shu" 上許石門老師書 and "Da libu Xu Yuqiu shu" 答吏部徐虞求書, in *Qicao shiji qi juan wenji ba juan Qicao erji* (*SKJH*-ji 113), 45 and 46. Lu Shiyi (*Fushe jilue*, 73) confirms that because Zhou Zhikui had not served long enough in office, he was disqualified from requesting the honors for his parents.

106. Zhou Zhikui, "Shang Susong anyuan Lu Haoyue gongzu shu" 上蘇淞按院路皓月公祖書 and "Shang Xu Shimen laoshi shu," *Qicao shiji qi juan wenji ba juan Qicao erji* (*SKJH*-ji 113), 37 and 45.

107. Zhang Guowei's memorial cited in Lu Shiyi, *Fushe jilue*, *juan* 4.

108. Zhou's biological mother had died many years before. He maintained a warm relationship with his official mother. Zhou once mentioned his former superiors' memorial, which cited a precedent for allowing such leave for Qi Jiazhi, a recent *jinshi*, to support their petition for Zhou. Zhou Zhikui, "Shang Xu Shimen laoshi shu" (CZ 10/1), *Qicao shiji qi juan wenji ba juan Qicao erji* (*SKJH*-ji 113), 45. Qi Jiazhi's *tongxiang* Wu Ganlai had also obtained a *zhongyang* leave in spite of the fact that he had an older brother. See Wu Ganlai's biographies in Yang Wenfeng et al., *Xinchang xianzhi*, *juan* 14 and *juan* 20.

109. Lu Shiyi, *Fushe jilue*; Zhou Zhikui, "Shang Xu Shimen laoshi shu," *Qicao shiji qi juan wenji ba juan Qicao erji* (*SKJH*-ji 113), 46.

110. Zhou Zhikui, "Shang Lin Rang'an libu shu" 上林讓菴吏部書, *Qicao shiji qi juan wenji ba juan Qicao erji* (*SKJH*-ji 113), 48.

111. Qian and Qu were attacked by a certain Zhang Hanru, arrested, and imprisoned before the charges were dropped. Xu Shirou, after standing up to Wen Tiren in court, almost lost his job but eventually left to serve in Nanjing as director of the Imperial Academy of Learning there. See Xu Shirou's biography in *MS*, 5719–21.

112. Lu Shiyi, *Fushe jilue*, 110.

113. Zhou Zhikui, "Da Zhang Shouxian shu" 答張受先書, "Shang Susong fuyuan Zhang Yusi zhongcheng di er shu" 上蘇松撫院張玉笥中丞第二書 (CZ 10/1), and "Shang Xu Shimen laoshi shu," (CZ 10/1), *Qicao shiji qi juan wenji ba juan Qicao erji* (*SKJH*-ji 113), 31, 35, and 44.

114. Mao Jin, preface to Zhou Zhikui, *Qicao shiji qi juan wenji ba juan Qicao erji* (*SKJH*-ji 112), 543.

115. Zhou Zhikui, "Shang Susong fuyuan Zhang Yusi zhongcheng di er shu" (CZ 10/1) and "Shang Xu Shimen laoshi shu" (CZ 10/1), *Qicao shiji qi juan wenji ba juan Qicao erji* (*SKJH*-ji 113), 36 and 43–45.

116. Zhou Zhikui, "Shang Lin Rang'an libu shu" (CZ 11/1), *Qicao shiji qi juan wenji ba juan Qicao erji* (*SKJH*-ji 113), 49.

117. Ibid.

118. Ding Guoxiang, *Fushe yanjiu*, chap. 1.

119. Zhou Zhikui, "Shang Chen Shengreng shiyu shu" 上陳升陾侍御書, *Qicao shiji qi juan wenji ba juan Qicao erji* (*SKJH*-ji 113), 42.

120. Jiang Yixue, *Zhang Pu nianpu*, 14–16; Zhang Xianbo, "Fushe de zhengdang hua," 424–25.

121. Zhou Zhikui, "Shang Chen Shengreng shiyu shu" (CZ 10/1), *Qicao shiji qi juan wenji ba juan Qicao erji* (*SKJH*-ji 113), 43.

122. Zhou Zhikui, "Shang Lin Rang'an libu shu," *Qicao shiji qi juan wenji ba juan Qicao erji* (*SKJH*-ji 113), 49.

123. Ibid., 48.

124. Ibid.

125. Zhou Zhikui, "Shang nan dasima Fan Zhigong shu" 上南大司馬范質公書, *Qicao shiji qi juan wenji ba juan Qicao erji* (*SKJH*-ji 113), 49.

126. Zhou Zhikui, "Shang Chen Shengreng shiyu shu," *Qicao shiji qi juan wenji ba juan Qicao erji* (*SKJH*-ji 113), 42.

127. Zhang Pu, "Jinshi shuo" 進士說, *Qiluzhai shiwen heji*, 1087. Translation of *gegu* is adopted from Jimmy Yu, *Sanctity and Self-Inflicted Violence*, 62.

128. Ma Shiqi, "Xuyu Zhang gong muzhiming" 虛宇張公墓誌銘, *Danningju wenji*, 236. Ma Shiqi was one of the Fushe scholars who came to be identified as members of the Donglin faction in the late Ming after they had passed the examinations and became officials. He has been included on both Fu She and Donglin lists. See, e.g., Wu Shanjia, *Fu She xingshi zhuanlue*, 3.16a; Gao Tingzhen et al., *Donglin shuyuan zhi*.

129. Zhang Zilie, "Yu shao jingzhao Xu gong lun jianju shu" 與少京兆徐公論薦舉書, *Qishan wenji*, 101–2.

130. Cited at the beginning of Shen Shoumin, "Guanshe xu" 觀社序, *Gushan yiji*, 121.

131. Ibid.

132. Dennerline, *Chia-ting Loyalists*. Dennerline focuses on analyzing the contradictions between Fushe scholars' pursuit of moral integrity and political networking.

133. Wang Enjun, *Fushe*, esp. chaps. 3–4.

CHAPTER 3: A *ZHONGXIAO* CELEBRITY

1. Fei, *Negotiating Urban Space*.

2. Gong Dingzi, "Qing ba zhaoyu tingzhang shu" 請罷詔獄廷杖疏, *CMMYL*, 715.

3. Ibid.

4. Chow, *Publishing, Culture, and Power*, 125–43; Greenbaum, introduction to *Chen Jiru*.

5. Greenbaum, introduction to *Chen Jiru*.

6. Ibid., 54; Chen Wanyi, *Wan Ming xiaopin*, chap. 3.

7. See, e.g., Wang Enjun, "Shilun Fushe neibu."

8. Chow, *Publishing, Culture, and Power*, esp. 227–40.

9. Chen Yinke, *Liu Rushi biezhuan*, chap. 4. In fact, it was the fall of Beijing and the establishment of the Southern Ming in Nanjing that gave Qian Qianyi an opportunity to reenter official politics.

10. Wang Shizhen, *Chi bei ou tan*, 194. "Purple cotton" cloth (*zimian*) actually looked brownish.

11. Kutcher offers detailed accounts of the best-known *duoqing* cases in the Ming in his *Mourning in Late Imperial China*, chap. 2.

12. See, e.g., Lu Miaw-fen, *Xiaozhi tianxia*, 198.

13. Kutcher, *Mourning in Late Imperial China*, 70–71.

14. Weijing Lu, "Reviving an Ancient Filial Ideal."

15. For a discussion on this question, see Chow, *Rise of Confucian Ritualism*.

16. Zheng Chenyin, "Huang Daozhou xiaoti shixing kao." Zheng's depiction of how meticulously Huang Daozhou carried out the teachings of the *Classic of Filial Piety* throughout his life is useful, but it also risks oversimplification. First, by the late Ming, many of the ideas and ideals laid out in this classic had become social and cultural norms and been articulated in other didactic texts as well. Second, many of the historical sources were produced to retrospectively represent Huang Daozhou as a *zhongxiao* exemplar. The authors might have consciously created the connections between his life trajectory and this classic.

17. Lu Miaw-fen, "Zuowei yishixing wenben de *Xiaojing*." Lu devotes one section to Huang Daozhou's hand copying of this text in prison.

18. This will be discussed later in this chapter.

19. The "master" in this preface refers specifically to Huang Daozhou. Cited in Hong Si 洪思, "Shouwen xu" 收文序, in *HSZXSWJ*, 2.

20. A good example can be seen in Huang's poem "Upon Leaving the Mountain" (Chushan shi), in Liu Zhengcheng, *Zhongguo shufa quanji*, vol. 56, 317–18.

21. *MS*, 6592–6600.

22. Zhuang Qichou, *Zhangpu Huang xiansheng nianpu*, 414–15. Huang's biography in the *Ming shi* inaccurately states that Huang returned home to mourn the death of his mother. In fact, his mother did not pass away until a year after he returned to Fujian.

23. Huang Daozhou, "Fudai yu xiong shu" 赴逮與兄書, *HSZXSWJ*, 127–28. This letter was composed in Chongzhen 13.

24. Zhuang Qichou, *Zhangpu Huang xiansheng nianpu*, 415.

25. Ibid., 414.

26. Hong Si, "Huangzi zhuan" 黃子傳, *HZPWX*, 365.

27. Zhuang Qichou, *Zhangpu Huang xiansheng nianpu*, 413.

28. For a discussion of Huang Daozhou's approach to this tension within the *zhongxiao* discourse, see Zheng Chenyin, "*Xiaojing* 'yi xiao wei zhong' shuo."

29. Huang Daozhou, "Piling jian Miyang zaijia si zhang" 毗陵見峚陽在家四章, *Huang Zhangpu ji*, 39.7a.

30. Fu Hongzhan, "Zuopin kaoshi," 298–99.

31. Liu Zhengcheng, *Zhongguo shufa quan ji*, vol. 56, 299.

32. Ibid.

33. Ibid.

34. Zheng Man documented this episode later in a poem "Huang Shizhai huanchao guofang" 黃石齋還朝過訪, *MYCTSJ*, 595.

35. Ibid.

36. *MS*, 6485–86.

37. For a detailed examination of these exchanges, see Ying Zhang, "Politics and Practice of Moral Rectitude."

38. Huang Daozhou, "Jiu Qian Longxi" 救錢龍錫 (Chongzhen 4/1/18), *HZPWX*, 4.

39. Ibid. (Chongzhen 4/1/27), *HZPWX*, 6.

40. Huang Daozhou, "Ni tai rong lan qing su du yi zu junxu shu" 擬汰冗濫清蠹以足軍需疏, *HZPWX*, 16.

41. Ho Koon-piu, "Should We Die as Martyrs?"

42. Wen Zhenmeng's diary shows a strong sense of alarm and urgency. Soon afterward, he left the capital and never returned to the court. Wen Zhenmeng, *Wen Wensu gong riji*, entries for Chongzhen 8/8–11 (1635), no page number.

43. Xia Xie, *Ming tongjian*, 2352–53; *MYCTSJ*, 632.

44. Yang Sichang's father died in Chongzhen 8 (1635); his stepmother died in Chongzhen 9 (1636). Yang Sichang, "Jing wen zhaoming feichang lixie kong ci shu" 驚聞詔命非常瀝血恐辭疏, *Yang Sichang ji*, 194.

45. Huang Daozhou, "Ni lun Yang Sichang bu ju liang sang shu" 擬論楊嗣昌不居兩喪疏, *HZPWX*, 24–28.

46. Ibid. Chen Xushan has argued that Huang's opposition to new taxes represented the popular view that the taxes would worsen peasants' poverty and increase local uprisings. But Chen points out that Huang's proposed alternative measure, reallocating funds from other battlefronts, was impractical. Chen Xushan, "Li chao wu bai tian," 249. See also Ju Mingku, *Zaihai yu Mingdai zhengzhi*, 360.

47. Ju Mingku, *Zaihai yu Mingdai zhengzhi*, chap. 5.

48. Huang Daozhou, "San zui si chi qi buru shu" 三罪四恥七不如疏, *HZPWX*, 34–35.

49. Huang Daozhou, "Gongyu Huang gong Daozhou jiu Zheng Man shu" 宮諭黃公道周救鄭鄤疏, *MYCTWJ*, 502.

50. For an example, see Huang Daozhou, *Xiaojing ji zhuan, juan* 2.

51. *CMMYL*, 389.

52. Ji Liuqi, *Ming ji bei lue*, 222.

53. *CMMYL*, 431.

54. Li Xunzhi, *Chongzhen chao jishi*, 516.

55. Ibid.; statement made by Feng Yuanbiao (d. 1644), an official identified as a Donglin partisan.

56. Chen Xinjia's biography in *MS*, 6636.

57. Huang Daozhou, "Lun Yang Sichang shu" 論楊嗣昌疏 and "Lun Chen Xinjia shu" 論陳新甲疏 *HZPWX*, 52–54 and 54–57. Yang Sichang's ties to some members of the former eunuch faction might have contributed to efforts by Huang's cohort to remove him. See Xin Deyong, "Ji Nan Ming keben *Xicao qiu si*," 75–81. The Fushe activist Huang Zongxi implies this

in "Zhijun Shen Gengyan xiansheng muzhiming" 徵君沈耕嚴先生墓誌銘, *Nanlei wen ding*, *qianbian*, *juan* 7, esp. 2b–3a.

58. Huang Daozhou, "Lun Yang Sichang shu," *HZPWX*, 52. Yang Bo mourned for twenty-six months. See "Qi qing nian biao" 七卿年表 in *MS*, 3466–67.

59. By the time Yang Sichang recommended Chen Xinjia, Chen had already mourned for twenty-five months, two months short of the required twenty-seven months. See Chen Xinjia's biography in *MS*, 6636.

60. Huang Daozhou, "Lun Yang Sichang shu," *HZPWX*, 52.

61. Ibid.

62. Cui Chengxiu, a former associate of Wei Zhongxian's, continued to serve as president of the Board of Works after his mother's death. *MS*, 7848.

63. For a discussion of Huang Daozhou's use of *Zhou Yi*, see Zheng Chenyin, "Shiguan yishi."

64. The translation of the chapter title follows Rosemont and Ames, *Chinese Classic of Family Reverence*, 109.

65. Zheng Chenyin, "*Xiaojing* 'yi xiao wei zhong' shuo," esp. 59–60.

66. See Yang He's biography in *MS*, 6725–27.

67. Yang Sichang's biography, *MS*, 6509. See earlier memorials submitted by Yang to petition for his father's life in Yang Sichang, *Yang Sichang* ji. *juan* 4.

68. Yang Sichang, "Weichen yi ru jinei shu" 微臣已入畿內疏, *Yang Sichang ji*, 197–99.

69. *CMMYL*, 392.

70. Ibid.

71. Ibid., 435.

72. Ibid., 435–36.

73. Ibid.

74. Ibid., 394.

75. In fact, this claim is not true. In "My Seven Defects," Huang Daozhou praises Zheng Man for both his literary skills and his moral character.

76. *CMMYL*, 434.

77. Cheng and Jiang, *Lunyu jishi*, 742–46.

78. Ibid., 1231–40.

79. *CMMYL*, 436. Shaozheng Mao's death is mentioned in *Xunzi*.

80. Zhuang Qichou, *Zhangpu Huang xiansheng nianpu*, 429, 439.

81. Ibid., 434.

82. Ibid., 433; see also "Zhu xian yi shi" 諸賢軼事, in Gao Tingzhen et al., *Donglin shuyuan zhi*, *juan* 22.

83. Lai Xiaoyun, "Cong Huang Daozhou shu *Xiaojing*," 25.

84. Ibid.

85. Ibid., 106.

86. Ibid., 123.

87. Kai-wing Chow provides a summary of ritual as an approach of Neo-Confucian moral cultivation and "didacticism and ritualism," in *Rise of Confucian Ritualism*, 11–14.

88. See Lu Miaw-fen's publications on this topic: "Religious Dimensions of Filial Piety," "Wan Ming shiren lun *Xiaojing* yu zhengzhi jiaohua," *Xiaozhi tianxia*, and "Zuowei yishixing wenben de *Xiaojing*."

89. Lu Miaw-fen, "Zuowei yishixing wenben de *Xiaojing*." For discussion of the spiritual connotations and religious functions of the text, see Lu's *Xiaozhi tianxia*, esp. chaps. 4 and 5, and "Religious Dimensions of Filial Piety." She discusses the revival of literati interest in the *Classic of Filial Piety* in *Xiaozhi tianxia*, chaps. 3 and 4.

90. Zheng Chenyin has argued that Huang Daozhou's metaphysical discussion of the meaning of *huishang*, the damage of one's body, in his comments on the *Classic of Filial Piety,* was inspired by his own prison experience and that Huang continued to hand copy the classic as a *zhongxiao* practice. It indicates a solution to, and transcendence of, the tension between loyalty and filial piety. Zheng Chenyin, "*Xiaojing* 'yi xiao wei zhong' shuo," 61. However, it should be noted that there had been historical precedents. Also, for a brief discussion of the significance of using blood to write for Huang in the cultural context of the late Ming, see Jimmy Yu, *Sanctity and Self-Inflicted Violence,* 60.

91. Weijing Lu discusses this phenomenon in her book *True to Her Word*.

92. Jimmy Yu, *Sanctity and Self-Inflicted Violence*, 60.

93. For a discussion of Huang Daozhou's calligraphic experiments in this broad cultural context, see, e.g., Bai Qianshen, *Fushan de shijie*, 71, 73.

94. See, e.g., Shanghai Shuhua Chubanshe, *Huang Daozhou Xiaojing.*

95. Cai Yuqing's poems show that she was well informed about contemporary politics, partly through correspondence with her husband. For example, "Shang shi" 傷時 and "Man yi tiaoliang younian wei fu tianzhu qunchen fuguo ye" 滿夷跳梁有年未伏天誅群臣負國也, in Huang Daozhou and Cai Yuqing, *Huang Shizhai kangli wei ke gao,* 35–36.

96. Lai Xiaoyun, "Cong Huang Daozhou shu *Xiaojing*."

97. It has been argued that Cai Yuqing used Huang's signature partly because she could sell such pieces and make enough money to get by. Ibid, 126; Fu Hongzhan, "Cai Yuqing jiqi xiaokai *Xiaojing.*"

98. Ko, "Pursuing Talent and Virtue."

99. Bai Qianshen, *Fu Shan de shijie*, 77.

100. *CMMYL,* 396. This well-known story has been mentioned by many scholars. See two works by Lu Miaw-fen, "Zuowei yishixing wenben de *Xiaojing*," 29–34, and *Xiaozhi tianxia*, 196–201. See also Zheng Chenyin and Tang Yunzhu, "Huang Daozhou yu *Xiaojing* de lishi yuhe"; Lai Xiaoyun, "Cong Huang Daozhou shu *Xiaojing*"; and Jimmy Yu, *Sanctity and Self-Inflicted Violence*, 60.

101. For example, Cao Rong, "Huang Shizhai xiansheng cihuan jisheng" 黃石齋先生賜環紀盛, *Jingtitang shiji*, 261; Du Jun, "Wen Huang Shizhai xiansheng cihuan tong zhuyou yong hun zi" 聞黃石齋先生賜環同諸友用魂字, *Chachun shichao* 茶村詩鈔, in *Du Jun, Bianyatang quanji*, 3.2b.

102. See the imperial edict issued on Qianlong 41/11/17 (1776), in *Wenyuange Siku quanshu*, 1.8.

INTERLUDE

1. Weijing Lu, *True to Her Word*, esp. chap. 1.

2. Dennerline, *Chia-ting Loyalists,* esp. the introductory chapter. Chen Yongming has pointed out that early Qing literature questioned the narrow concept of "blind loyalty" (*yuzhong*). They reoriented their perspectives toward a practical view of morality and instead emphasized turncoat officials' participation in stabilizing the empire. Chen Yongming, "Xiang Qing Mingchen."

3. *MS*, 333.

4. Ibid.

5. For discussion of the "seventeenth-century global crisis" and climate change, see Parker, *Global Crisis*, chap. 5; Liu Zhigang, *Tianren zhiji.*

6. Xia Xie, *Ming tongjian*, 2493.

7. *MS,* 335.

8. Gu Yanwu, *Ming ji shi lu,* 31.

9. Many sources printed and circulated in the early Qing documented such deeds by the martyrs. For a comprehensive account, see Xu Zi, *Xiaotian jinian fu kao*, 96–97.

10. Zhang Mingbi, "Zuo chunfang zuo zhongyun Fuxiu Yang gong zhuan" 左春坊左中允鳬岫楊公傳, *Yingzhi quanji*, 5.7b–8a; emphasis added.

11. See, e.g., "Jiangnan shimin gong jin xi" 江南士民公禁檄 and "Jintan shishen gongtao nichen xi" 金壇士紳公討逆臣檄, in Feng Menglong, *Zhongxing shilu*, 593 and 608.

12. Ōki, *Ming mo Jiangnan de chuban*, 79–84.

13. Zhang Mingbi, "Yunyang Sheng Zhibo zhuan" 雲陽盛止伯傳, *Yingzhi quanji*, 5.14b.

14. Meng's son and daughter-in-law committed suicide upon learning about his martyrdom. Sun Chengze, *Jifu renwu zhi*, 462; Gu Yanwu, *Ming ji shi lu*, 1.19; Xiong Wenju, "Bo zhen diao Meng Xiaoxing laoshi" 泊鎮弔孟肖形老師, *Xuetang xiansheng wenji*, 466.

15. Xiong Wenju, "Bo zhen diao Meng Xiaoxing laoshi," *Xuetang xiansheng wenji*, 466.

16. See, e.g., Zhu Zhongmei朱中楣, preface to *Suicao shi yu* 隨草詩餘, in Li Yuanding, *Shiyuan quanji*, 92.

17. Xiong Wenju, "Huai Lansheng shi" 懷蘭生詩 (475) , "Wang er Dinghua xunyi zhi" 亡兒鼎華殉義志 (522–24), "Nan huan Hanshang yu tongxiang zhulao shu" 南還邗上與同鄉諸老書 (534–35), "Yu menren Han Shengqiu zhonghan" 與門人韓聖秋中翰 (535), and "Tu dazhongcheng zhuanlue" 涂大中丞傳略 (543), in *Xuetang xiansheng wenji.* However, according to Xiong's former secretary Xu Yingfen, Xiong's close friend Tu Bihong claimed Xiong had no intention of committing suicide. Xu Yingfen, "Yu bian ji lue" 遇變紀略, in Gu Gongxie, *Danwu biji,* 35.

18. Gong Dingzi, "Qishou baoan shu" 祈壽保安疏 and "Luanhou de jiashu wei shuangqin qifo shu" 亂後得家書為雙親祈佛疏, in *Dingshantang guwen xiaopin*, 1.5a–5b and 1.7a; "Huanyuan lifo shu" 還願禮佛疏, "Qizi shu" 祈子疏, and "Qisi wen" 祈嗣文, in *Dingshantang xiaopin xuji,* 31a–32b,

33a–b, and 37a–38b. Xiong Wenju's commemorative essay of 1668 recalls that Gu Mei fearlessly followed her husband and jumped into a well upon the fall of Beijing. Xiong Wenju, "Ji Xu furen wen" 祭徐夫人文, *Lüouge jin ji*, 116.

19. See Ho Koon-piu's extensive study of the question of death and loyalty during the Ming-Qing transition, in "Ming-Qing zhiji shengsi nanyi shuo," "Should We Die as Martyrs?" and *Sheng yu si.*

20. Fang Yizhi, "Ji Li Shuzhang" 寄李舒章, *Lingwai gao* 嶺外稿, in *Fushan wenji,* qian ji, 584.

21. Fang Yizhi, "Ji Zhang Ergong" 寄張爾公, *Lingwai gao*, in *Fushan wenji,* qian ji, 606.

22. Fang Yizhi, "Jinan" 紀難, *Fang Yizhi Mizhi shichao* 方以智密之詩鈔, cited in Ren, *Fang Yizhi nianpu*, 125.

23. Xiong Wenju, "Tu dazhongcheng zhuanlue," *Xuetang xiansheng wenji*, 543–44.

24. Gu Gongxie, *Danwu biji*, 39.

25. Feng Menglong heard about this from an official and documented it in *Shen zhi lue*, 24b–25b.

26. Gong Dingzi, "Huai Fang Mizhi shi" 懷方密之詩, *Gong Dingzi shi,* 545–47. According to some witnesses, servants of metropolitan officials quickly switched sides. When the rebel army took over the capital, these servants told the soldiers where the officials were hiding in order to get rewards. Zhang Yi, *Sou wen xu bi*; Feng Menglong, *Jiashen jiwen*, 5b.

27. Xiong Wenju, "Yu Menren Han Shengqiu zhonghan" and "Tu dazhongcheng zhuanlue," *Xuetang xiansheng wenji*, 535 and 543–44. The funeral for the late Chongzhen emperor was staged by the Qing as a means of tricking the officials into returning to the capital. See documentation in Peng Sundai, *Liukou zhi*, *juan* 12.

28. Wei Xuelian, who surrendered to the rebels but committed suicide later, is a good example. On the competing documentation and comments on his suicide, see Huang Yi-nong, "Zhongxiao paifang yu shizijia."

29. Kishimoto Mio has reconstructed the timeline for the dissemination of news of the Chongzhen emperor's suicide in Jiangnan. According to her study, the process took more than a month. Kishimoto, "Chongzhen shi qi nian de Jiangnan." But according to the Fushe literatus Chen Zhenhui's documentation, by Chongzhen 17/4/17 many in Nanjing had learned about the emperor's suicide. Chen Zhenhui, "Shu jiashen nanzhong shi" 書甲申南中事, *Shu shi qi ze*, 2a–3a.

30. Lang Xingwei 朗星偉, "Tao xiangzei zhuchen xi" 討降賊諸臣檄, in Feng Menglong, *Zhongxing shilu*, 595–97.

31. Ibid.

32. "Changshu xian taopan gongxi" 常熟縣討叛公檄, in Feng Menglong, *Zhongxing shilu*, 606–7.

33. In *the List of Notorious Donglin Fighters,* Chen was matched with a rebel character from *Water Margin* as the "Courageous Star among the Stars of Earth called The Eye of Heaven."

34. Qian Haiyue, *Nan Ming shi*, 4164–65.

35. Feng Menglong, *Shen zhi lue*, 14a.

36. Li Qing, *Nandu lu*, 224.

37. "Changshu xian taopan gongxi," in Feng Menglong, *Zhongxing shilu*, 606–7.

38. "Songjiang tao xian qi xiangzei xi" 嵩江討獻妻降賊檄, in Feng Menglong, *Zhongxing shilu*, 607–8.

39. Ibid.

40. Gu Yanwu, *Sheng an benji*, *juan* 1, annex to "Jiashen 5/11."

41. Feng Menglong mentioned this in his documentation of the charges against the above-mentioned Yang Rucheng in *Shen zhi lue*, 23b.

42. Ji Liuqi, notes to "Jiaxing fu shenjin gongtao wei hu zhengfu siwu xi" 嘉興府紳衿公討偽戶政府司務檄, *Ming ji bei lue*, 613.

43. Ying Zhang, "Confucian Principles."

44. The main author of the Wu County proclamation was Yuan Lianbi, a Fushe activist and Suzhou native. He had garnered quite some fame in the area and within the Fushe-Donglin community. "Wujun gongtao xiangzei weiguan" 吳郡公討降賊偽官, in Feng Menglong, *Zhongxing shilu*, 594–95.

45. Li Qing, *Nandu lu*, 177.

46. Xiong Wenju, "Wang er Dinghua xunyi zhi," *Xuetang xiansheng wenji*, 522–24.

47. For a good summary of the Hongguang regime, see Struve, *Southern Ming*, chap. 1.

48. A lot of under-the-table discussions and negotiations were happening at the time among various groups of officials in different locales. See Xia Xie, *Ming tongjian*, 2526.

49. For a review of the controversies, see Wakeman, *Great Enterprise*, vol. 1, 331–46.

50. See, e.g., Peng Ershu, *Mingshi duan lue*, 646.

51. Xia Xie, *Ming tongjian*, 2562.

52. Xu Zi, *Xiaotian jinian fu kao*, 157–58.

53. Gu Cheng, *Nan Ming shi*, chap. 2. Huang Daozhou documented this in "Xing yuan ji lue" 興元紀略, *Huang Zhangpu ji*, 32.1a–2b.

54. It has been argued that the Hongguang emperor was not as morally corrupt as the widespread image has suggested. Li Qing (*San yuan biji*) probably has provided the most important testimony in his account of the Southern Ming court. See Zhang Yuxing, "Nan Ming Hongguang di 'shide' boyi."

55. Whereas in political history, the term "pure element" often refers to officials who refused to overlook their colleagues' moral defects, in this particular context, "pure element" was not only a self-proclaimed label but, more importantly, a sarcastic usage applied to certain officials by their opponents.

56. Li Qing, *Nandu lu*, 165. *Shun* literally means "compliance," but it was also the name of the short-lived regime established by the rebels, the Shun.

57. "Qing zhu nichen shu" 請誅逆臣疏, in Li Qing, *Nandu lu*, 165. The same text is included in Huang Zongxi, *Hongguang shilu chao*, 209.

However, not all sources mention Gu Mei; see, for example, Feng Menglong, *Zhongxing shilu*, 648.

58. Gu Jingxing, "Xuezhong de dibao Hefei Gong gong chu xingbu shilang" 雪中得邸報合肥龔公除刑部侍郎, *Baimaotang ji*, 666. Gu notes that Ma Shiying entered Gong's name into the Donglin list. From a very different perspective, the literatus Lin Shidui documents that Gong was an evil figure within the Donglin faction. Lin Shidui, "Pengdang dalue" 朋黨大略, in *He cha dui tan*.

59. Li Qing, *Nandu lu*, 237; emphasis added.

60. Gu Yanwu, *Sheng an benji*, 2.14b.

61. Dennerline, *Chia-ting Loyalists*, 210–12.

62. These officials supposedly submitted the memorial at Ruan Dacheng's instruction. Lin Shidui, *He cha dui tan*, 4.16a–19a. Yu Huai's famous *Banqiao zaji* has recorded the Jiangs' sexual adventures.

63. Li Qing, *Nandu lu*, 224.

64. Huang Zongxi, *Hongguang shilu chao*, 204.

65. Wen Bing, *Jia-yi shian*, 544.

66. Ruan Dacheng, "Buzhong buxiao dani yuanxiong shu" 不忠不孝大逆元凶疏, in ibid., 543.

67. Li Shiqia et al., *Taihu xianzhi*, 7.14a. Taihu County was repeatedly attacked by rebels, in 1638, 1641, and 1643. The one in 1643 was especially brutal and cost a lot of lives. The Lei family lost many members, including Lei's sister-in-law. I was not able to consult the Lei family genealogy.

68. Ibid.

69. Chen Zhenhui, "Lei xianfu Yanzuo" 雷憲副演祚, *Shanyang lu*, 4a–b.

70. Yuan Kai's memorial, recorded in Huang Zongxi, *Hongguang shilu chao*, 211–12.

71. This is most obvious in the censor Xiong Rulin's comments on the impeachments of Jiang Yueguang and Lei Yanzuo. See Li Qing, *Nandu lu*, 224.

72. Tan Qian, *Zaolin zazu*, 129.

73. For example, in his documentation at the time, Feng Menglong acknowledged Madam Wang as Ni's concubine but not as his official wife. Feng Menglong, *Shen zhi lue*, 3b.

74. Tan Qian, *Zaolin zazu*, 129.

75. Xu Zi, *Xiaotian jinian fu kao*, 223. This categorization meant that the court needed more time to consider specific circumstances and determine the nature of cases such as Gong's.

CHAPTER 4: MORALIZING, THE QING WAY

1. Guo Chengkang, "Ye tan Manzu Hanhua," 89.

2. Li Wen, "Da fa ze wen" 答髮責文, *Liaozhai hou ji*, 690–91. In Chinese sources, the act of shaving the forehead to adopt the Manchu hairstyle is referred to as *tifa* and often translated as "head shaving" in English scholarship.

3. For a discussion of the question of "generation" during the Ming-Qing transition, see Struve, "Chimerical Early Modernity."

4. Chen Shengxi, *Ming-Qing yidai shi*, 262–80.

5. "Li Ruolin bei Zhao Kaixin can qiu bazhi ben" 李若琳被趙開心参求罷職本, *Zhanggu congbian*, vol. 3, no page number.

6. Jin Zhijun, "Qing le zhuchen sheng yilun xi fenxiao shu" 請勒諸臣省議論息紛囂疏, *Xizhai ji*, Shucao疏草, 1.17a–18b.

7. Ibid., Dorgon's response cited after the text of the memorial by Jin Zhijun.

8. "Zhu Tinghan chen san shi ben" 朱廷翰陳三事本, *Zhanggu congbian*, vol. 6, 28a–b.

9. Zhao Erxun, *Qing shi gao*, 9620.

10. Wakeman, *Great Enterprise*, vol. 2, 869–70.

11. Jiang Liangji, *Shi er chao Donghua lu*, 47.

12. Ibid., 48.

13. *Zhanggu congbian*, vol. 4, 14a.

14. Jiang Liangji, *Shi er chao Donghua lu*, 48.

15. Gong Dingzi, "Kou qi sheng ci zhaoli enxu yi guang quanrang shu" 叩乞聖慈照例恩恤以光泉壤疏, *Hefei Gong Duanyi gong zoushu*, 1.26a–27a.

16. Guoshiguan, *Erchen zhuan*, 806–7.

17. Gong Yunsu 龔允肅, "Xixuan gong zixu xinglue" 息軒公自敘行略, in Gong Zhaoxin et al., *Hefei Gong shi zongpu*, vol. 1, 1b.

18. *Qing shilu*, vol. 3, 221. Grand Secretary Feng Quan was one of the Grand Examiners that year and hence the junior Sun's official mentor. See Jiang Qingbo, *Qingchao jinshi timing lu*; *Zichuan xianzhi* (Qianlong 8 and Qianlong 41 eds.).

19. *Qing shilu*, vol. 3, 208.

20. Li Yuanding was the son of a locally prestigious family. It is not clear why Zhu Zhongmei's father, Prince Zhu Yiwen, let her become Li's concubine. I thank Grace Fong and Wang Yizheng for a very helpful discussion about this couple via e-mail in spring 2012.

21. The prince is also known as Zhu Yile. Yang Haiying, *Hong Chengchou*, 160–69. For Zhu Zhongmei and Li Yuanding's marriage, see Zhao Xuepei, "Qingshu kuangfang."

22. *Qing shilu*, vol. 3, 214. The instability in the region escalated into a full-fledged rebellion led by Jin Shenghuan, who had surrendered to the Qing. See Struve, *Southern Ming*, chap. 5. Jin was the most powerful official in the area in the years before he switched his allegiance and became an anti-Qing leader again. Sun Poling argued that Jin's impeachment of his father cost the latter his job. See the junior Sun's memorial (Shunzhi 9/7), Zhongyang yanjiuyuan lishi yuyan yanjiusuo shuwei diancang yu shuwei xuexi lianhe mulu 中央研究院歷史語言研究所數位典藏與數位學習聯合目錄, http://catalog.digitalarchives.tw/Exhibition/Detail.jsp?OID=2598707 (accessed Nov. 8, 2011). For a discussion of Sun's death in Shandong, see Chang and Chang, *Redefining History*, esp. 11–22.

23. Scholars have pointed out the prominent presence of turncoats of Shandong origin—the Suns among them—at court during these years.

Wakeman, *Great Enterprise*, vol. 2, 865–68, esp. n. 43. Before this, Gong's closest Jiangxi friends at court, Xiong Wenju and Li Yuanding, both encountered political frustrations as a result of factionalism. Zhao Erxun, *Qing shi gao*, 6324; Xiong Wenju, "Ci mian libu shilang shu" 辭免吏部侍郎疏, "Gaobing liqing nanhuan shu" 告病力請南還疏, and "Cheng zhongtang gaoxiu shi bu kan ren yuanyou" 呈冢堂告休十不堪任緣由, and "Tu da zhongcheng zhuanlue," *Xuetang xiansheng wenji*, 531–33 and 543.

24. *Qing shilu*, vol. 3, 232; Luo Xiujin 羅繡錦, "Huguang Sichuan zongdu wei gong cu anchen ji chu shishi" 湖廣四川總督為公促按臣即出視事 (Shunzhi 3/8 [1646]), in Zhongyang yanjiuyuan lishi yuyan yanjiusuo shuwei diancang yu shuwei xuexi lianhe mulu 中央研究院歷史語言研究所數位典藏與數位學習聯合目錄, http://catalog.digitalarchives.tw/item/00/26/67/a3.html (accessed Nov. 18, 2011).

25. *Qing shilu*, vol. 3, 232.

26. For instance, see "Like Tachiha deng guanhuashang deng jin jie wei zhai can furen weixian guanyuan shi" 吏科他赤哈等官花上等謹揭為摘參赴任違限官員事, *ZYYMQDA*, vol. 8, A8–40 (4-1) –(4-4).

27. See Luo Xiujin's memorial cited in n. 24.

28. *Qing shilu*, vol. 3, 233, 505; Guoshiguan, *Erchen zhuan*, 486–87. On the marginalization of Jiagalang, see, e.g., Yang Zhen, *Qingchao huangwei jicheng zhidu*, 59; Yang Haiying, *Hong Chengchou*, 258.

29. *Qing shilu*, vol. 3, 233, 505; Guoshiguan, *Erchen zhuan*, 486–87.

30. "Chen Diaoyuan ti wei zhai can Song Quan suo chen san kuan zhishi hanhu ben" 陳調元題為摘參宋權所陳三款支飾含糊本, *QDDASLCB*, vol. 13, 111–12.

31. "Wang Tingjian ti wei Song Quan shi ci yan zui qing ci bachi ben" 王庭諫題為宋權飾詞掩罪請賜罷斥本, *QDDASLCB*, vol. 13, 112–13.

32. "Mandahai deng ti wei huiyi kechen can kuan shushi ying zhun Song Quan zhishi ben" 滿達海等題為會議科臣參款屬實應准宋權致仕本 (Shunzhi 3/16), *QDDASLCB*, vol. 13, 114–16.

33. *Qing shilu*, vol. 3, 334.

34. The Shunzhi emperor's strong desire to claim authority was explicitly reported by the Korean mission to Beijing in Shunzhi 8/2 (1651). Wu Han, *Chaoxian Li chao shilu*, vol. 9, 3809.

35. Yao Nianci, *Qingchu zhengzhi shi tanwei*, esp. part 2, chap. 2.

36. Song Luo, "Wenkang gong jiazhuan" 文康公家傳, in Song Quan, *Wenkang gong yiji*, 36b–37a, and Song Luo, *Mantang nianpu* 漫堂年譜, in *Xibei leigao*, 47.7a. See also imperial mourning edicts in Song Luo, *Shangqiu Song shi jiasheng*, 1.50a–52a.

37. "Mandahai deng ti wei huiyi Zhang Xuan jiucan Chen Mingxia bushi ben" 滿達海等題為會議張煊糾參陳名夏不實本 (Shunzhi 8/5/23), in *QDDASLCB*, vol. 13, 116–22.

38. Ibid.

39. Ibid.

40. *Qing shilu*, vol. 3, 485. For the opinions written by Tantai and other Manchu officials on the board, see "Mandahai deng ti wei huiyi Zhang Xuan jiucan Chen Mingxia bushi ben," *QDDASLCB*, vol. 13, 121–22.

41. "Shaanxi dao jiancha yushi Luo Guoshi ti wei libu Han guan xunsi wangfa qing chi bu yanjiu ben" 陕西道監察御史羅國士題為吏部漢官徇私枉法請敕部嚴究本, *QDDASLCB*, vol. 13, 133–34. The two cases mentioned here—those of Gong Dingzi and Hao Jie—took place during Chen Mingxia's term as president of this board. The current president Gao Eryan had only recently replaced Chen and had all along been a close friend to both Hao and Gong. See Zhao Erxun, *Qing shi gao*, 6333.

42. Gong Dingzi, "Wu Xuehang zhao tong Jin Qifan sima yin Luo Qinzhan shiyu yuyuan shi Qinzhan yi yanshi zhe" 吳雪航招同金豈凡司馬飲羅欽瞻侍御寓園時欽瞻以言事謫, *Gong Dingzi shi*, 708–9. See also Yang Haiying, *Hong Chengchou*, 267.

43. This particular observation draws upon Ning Wanwo's report to the emperor that Chen had told him the only way to ensure a peaceful dynastic transition would be to drop the head shaving policy and allow the Han to resume their traditional dress code. But it is not clear when this conversation occurred. Chen could have said this at the very beginning of the Shunzhi reign, when the Manchus did not fully enforce the head shaving policy anyway.

44. Miller, *State versus Gentry in Early Qing Dynasty China*, esp. 56–63.

45. *Qing shilu*, vol. 3, 640.

46. Ding Yizhuang, *Manzhou de funü*, 331.

47. Ibid., 326.

48. Yang Haiying, *Hong Chengchou*, 100–102; Ding Yizhuang, *Manzhou de funü*, 326–27.

49. Ding Yizhuang, *Manzhou de funü*. Hu Shi'an's poems congratulating this marriage contain a note indicating the ceremony took place around the time of the fifteenth of the first month. Hu Shi'an, "He yuanfu Feng Lu'an xiansheng cihun er shou" 賀元輔馮鹿庵先生賜婚二首, *Xiuyan ji*, 513. See also Yang Haiying, "Hong Chengchou Liu shi furen kao," 262–71.

50. Yang Haiying, *Hong Chengchou*, 100–102.

51. Wang Dafeng, "Feng Quan nianpu" (entry Shunzhi 2), in "Jidu fengyun," 269. It is not clear if this woman was given the title of "secondary wife" (*ciqi*), or if at the time she was considered to be one. I was not able to consult the Feng family genealogy, which is in the possession of the National Library of Beijing but is currently unavailable.

52. Tan Qian, *Beiyou lu*, 381.

53. Mann, *Precious Records*, chap. 2.

54. Kutcher, *Mourning in Late Imperial China*, esp. 79–119.

55. Yang Haiying, *Hong Chengchou*, 64–65.

56. Yang Haiying examines Hong's complicated relationships with other military personnel, turncoats, and Ming loyalists in *Hong Chengchou*, chap. 4. Miller discusses Hong's complicated relationship with local literati during the pacification campaign in *State versus Gentry in Early Qing Dynasty China*, 68–77.

57. Yang Haiying, *Hong Chengchou*, chap. 4.

58. "Hong Chengchou qing shouzhi ben" 洪承疇請守制本, *Zhanggu congbian*, vol. 4, 7b–8b.

59. For more analysis of the Manchu woman, Madam Liu, and Hong's Han wife, Madam Li, see Yang Haiying, *Hong Chengchou*, 95–102. Yang Haiying points out that Madam Li did not go to Nanjing probably because of this, and that careful planning must have be done beforehand by Hong and his family.

60. The imperial order is attached to Hong Chengchou's memorial in this collection of documents.

61. *Qing shilu*, vol. 3, 272.

62. Later he signed as *jin hou dai shouzhi* 今候代守制 and *jin jiaodai shouzhi* 今交代守制 when he was transferring the job to his successor. Hong Chengchou, "Jiangnan zhaofu Hong Chengchou jietie" 江南招撫洪承疇揭貼 on Shunzhi 4/6/22, 8/6, 9/14, 9/27, 10/23, and 11/18, Shunzhi 5/1/14 and 1/28 (dates indicate when they were received in Beijing) and "Jiangnan zhaofu Hong Chengchou tiben" 江南招撫洪承疇題本 (Shunzhi 5/2/26 and 2/29). Memorials in *Ming Qing shiliao*, bing bian, vol. 2., 113–29.

63. Yang Haiying, *Hong Chengchou*, 310.

64. *Qing shilu*, vol. 3, 507.

65. Ibid., 429; Guoshiguan, *Erchen zhuan*, 599.

66. Wang Dafeng, "Feng Quan nianpu," in "Jidu fengyun," 271.

67. A sample celebratory essay can be found in Tan Qian, "Rong ming chi shou xu" 榮命馳壽序, *Beiyou lu*, 232–33. The essay praises the spirit of "governing by filial piety" in Feng Quan's request for leave and the emperor's approval.

68. Feng Quan's memorial submitted on Shunzhi 12/2/16 (1655), "Jiebao mu shi qing zhaoli chagei jizang" 揭報母逝請照例察給祭葬, in Zhongyang yanjiuyuan lishi yuyan yanjiusuo shuwei diancang yu shuwei xuexi lianhe mulu 中央研究院歷史語言研究所數位典藏與數位學習聯合目錄, http://catalog.digitalarchives.tw/Exhibition/Detail.jsp?OID=2547612 (accessed Nov. 18, 2011).

69. *Qing shilu*, vol. 3, 703.

70. Feng Quan retired in Shunzhi 13/2 (1656). Zhao Erxun, *Qing shi gao*, 144–45.

71. Tan Qian, "Rong ming chi shou xu," *Beiyou lu*, 232–33. Tan notes that this essay was written on behalf of someone else but eventually was not adopted.

72. The term *qifu* in earlier periods referred to the practice of officials resuming office without completing the mourning term. But in Ming-Qing times, it also meant returning to office after a full mourning term. Tan Qian in this case uses it to refer to *duoqing*, which is reflected in this translation.

73. Tan Qian, *Beiyou lu*, 412. Interestingly, the "book project" might have been a commentary on the *Classic of Filial Piety*, which was made an officially commissioned work by the Shunzhi emperor but put aside when Feng Quan retired. The project, titled *Yuzhi Xiaojing yanyi*, was commissioned in Shunzhi 13/1 (1656) but was not finished until Kangxi 21 (1682). It took the court another few years to officially publicize it throughout the empire (in Kangxi 29 [1690]). See Lu Miaw-fen, *Xiaozhi tianxia*, 216–17.

74. Miller discusses this question in chapter 1 of *State versus Gentry in Early Qing Dynasty China*, though not through examining officials' personal virtues.

75. *Qing shilu*, vol. 3, 210; emphasis added.

76. Yang Nianqun has discussed similar moves on the part of the Kangxi and Qianlong emperors but still emphasizes the Han literati-officials' attempt to "educate and transform" the Shunzhi emperor. Yang Nianqun, *Hechu shi Jiangnan?*, 80–102.

77. Elliott, *The Manchu Way*.

78. The first mention of this concept by the Shunzhi emperor occurred in Shunzhi 11/11 (1654). Yao Nianci, *Qing chu zhengzhi shi*, 411–14. Yao suggests that the emperor "proposed" this term.

79. Wakeman, *Great Enterprise*, vol. 2, 865–68, esp. n. 43.

80. Deng Zhicheng, *Qing shi jishi chu bian*, 490.

81. Yang Haiying, *Hong Chengchou*, esp. 266–69; Yao Nianci, *Qing chu zhengzhi shi*, esp. 408–19.

82. The Jesuit missionary Johann Adam Schall von Bell expressed persistent, moralistic concerns about the Shunzhi emperor's interest in sex. Alfons Väth, S. J., *Tang Ruowang zhuan*, 282–83, 321.

83. *Qing shilu*, vol. 3, 616.

84. Ibid.

85. The Shunzhi emperor's response to Ji's memorial claimed that the eunuchs were not sent out to recruit Han girls from Jiangnan for the palaces but for other buying missions. Kan Hongliu suggests Ji Kaisheng believed the rumors passed on by his family and analyzes his severe punishment in the context of the early Qing regime's attempt to control rumors. Kan Hongliu, "Qing chu shehui chuanwen."

86. That the censor Li Senxian was severely punished for petitioning for leniency on behalf of Ji Kaisheng in Shunzhi 15 (1658) clearly reveals how deeply Ji's rather conventional Confucian moral remonstration had annoyed the emperor.

87. Yang Zhen, *Qingchao huangwei jicheng zhidu*, 76; Michael G. Chang, *A Court on Horseback*, 380–91, 403–9.

88. Wang Yongji, *Yuzhi renchen jingxin lu*, 761–72, and Shunzhi's preface to the book, 761–62. The most severely prosecuted and politicized cases include the Case of Ren Zhen (Shunzhi 10 [1653]) and the Case of Gu Ren (Shunzhi 12 [1655]). For a good discussion about these cases, see Yao Nianci, *Qing chu zhengzhi shi tanwei*, 404–17.

89. *Qing shilu*, vol. 3, 729.

90. Ibid., 809.

91. Yang Xin, *Cheng Zhengkui*, 7–8; Cheng Dagao, "Qimeng lu" 奇夢録, cited in Cheng Zhengkui, *Qingxi yigao*, 375.

92. *Qing shilu*, vol. 3, 851.

93. For a summary of this case, see Elman, *A Cultural History of Civil Examinations*, 204–5; Wakeman, *Great Enterprise*, vol. 2, 1004–5, esp. nn. 38–39.

94. *Qing shilu*, vol. 3, *juan* 121.

95. Ibid., *juan* 117. This proposal was accepted.

96. Ibid., 1038. For a biography of Dai Mingyue, see Guoshiguan, *Erchen zhuan*, 743.

97. Yao Nianci, *Qing chu zhengzhi shi*, 413–14.

98. Wakeman, *Great Enterprise*, vol. 2, 967.

99. *Qing shilu*, vol. 3, 688.

100. Ibid., 1038.

101. Ibid., 1037–39.

102. Ibid., 1038.

103. Miller, *State versus Gentry in Early Qing Dynasty China*, 63–68.

104. Guy, *Qing Governors*, 330–31. One example Guy analyzes is how, in the sensitive environment during the years leading up to the Three Feudatories Rebellion, the emperor allowed Bian Sanyuan to remove himself from the governor's position using his mother's illness and old age as an excuse.

105. Here I focus only on Wu Sangui and Geng Jingzhong because the Shangs' case was much more complicated and Shang surrendered early.

106. *Qing shilu*, vol. 4, 588.

107. Ibid., 605–6.

108. Ye Mengzhu, *Yue shi bian*, 260–62. The fact that this was not printed or circulated much in manuscript suggests that the author personally believed in that image of Wu Sangui.

109. Luan Xing, *Jiashen shi shang*, 279–81. Luan gives a careful account of the various editions of this novel (*Xinbian jiao Chuang tongsu xiaoshuo*) and their differences.

110. These lines appear in a song in this play: 報父書甘為忤逆兒／受王封哪識存亡義. Jiang Shiquan, *Jiang Shiquan xiqu ji*, 132.

111. *Qing shilu*, vol. 4, 624–25.

112. Ibid., 627.

113. Crossley, *Translucent Mirror*, 123–28.

114. Wakeman, *Great Enterprise*, vol. 2, 1113–17. For a review of Fan's exemplary image from the seventeenth to the nineteenth century, see Guy, *Qing Governors*, 264–66.

115. *Qing shilu*, vol. 4, 586. For a study of the Manchu practice of observing the mourning term, see Huang Lijun, "Qing chu manren shouzhi." This was by no means a top-down policy. Some Manchu literati had been observing the twenty-seven-month mourning period since the early Shunzhi reign. The Manchu rulers had issued an imperial edict demanding that the Eight Banners identify and honor filial sons and chaste wives in the same way as did the Han. The censor Chen Jitai, a Han-bannerman official, memorialized and asked the emperor to consider requiring Manchu bureaucrats to follow the same norms, that is, resigning for twenty-seven months to mourn a deceased parent. What is striking here is that Chen Jitai's memorial confirms the impression that most Han officials were expected to follow the rule and that they indeed conformed to it. Chen Jitai, "Qing xing tongzhi yi zhong dalun shu" 請行通制以重大倫疏 (Shunzhi 10 [1653]), in *Huang Qing zouyi*, 6.9a–10a.

116. For a critique of this moral contrast, see Kahn, "The Politics of Filiality." Guo Chengkang offers a balanced and concise overview of how the Manchu rulers "criticized, rebuilt, and modified" Han practices in "Ye tan Manzu Hanhua."

117. For discussion of the Shunzhi emperor as a "passive figure" in the state-versus-gentry struggles over sovereignty, see Miller, *State versus Gentry in Early Qing Dynasty China*, chap. 2.

118. Ibid., chap. 4.

119. Yang Nianqun, *Hechu shi Jiangnan?*, 97–98.

CHAPTER 5: CONQUEST, CONTINUITY, AND THE LOYAL TURNCOAT

1. Hu Shi'an, "He xiangguo Feng Lu'an yugao guixing xu," 賀相國馮鹿菴予告歸省序, *Xiuyan ji*, 599. Based on this essay and the one composed by Tan Qian on behalf of his official patron (see chap. 4 in this book), we can tell that many metropolitan officials were involved in the celebration.

2. Ibid., 598; Tan Qian, *Beiyou lu*, 412.

3. Cited in Zhang Sheng, "Feng Quan," 92.

4. Definition of "ethno-dynastic rule" from Michael G. Chang, introduction to *A Court on Horseback*.

5. Zhang Sheng, "Lun Chen Mingxia yu Fang Yizhi." See also Wakeman, *Great Enterprise*, vol. 2, 866.

6. Cao Rong, "Tongshe guoji er shou" 同社過集二首, *Jingtitang shiji*, 265.

7. Li Wen, "Baishi zi nan lai beixi jiaoji er fu" 百史自南來悲喜交集而賦, *Liaozhai hou ji*, 672–73.

8. Xiong Wenju, "Chen Shaozai jixing shi xu" 陳少宰紀行詩序, *Xuetang xiansheng wenji*, 513–14.

9. Ibid.

10. Ibid., 514.

11. Feng Menglong, *Shen zhi lue*, 25b.

12. For a brief review of Gong's and Cao's official careers in the early Qing, see Guoshiguan, *Erchen zhuan*, *juan* 6 and 12.

13. Gong Dingzi, "Ti hua yu Cao Qiuyue" 題畫與曹秋岳, *DSTWJ*, 6.33a.

14. The orchid as a metaphor for loyalty has a long history, probably since the time of Qu Yuan (ca. 343–277 BCE). In his *chuci*-style poems, the orchid symbolizes gender- and status-specific manly virtues. Geng, *The Fragile Scholar*, chap. 2.

15. Yu Xin was an official in the Liang (502–57) and was sent to the Western Wei (535–56) as an envoy but retained there against his will. During this time, the Western Wei conquered the Liang. He was forced to serve the new ruler and given high positions, but he was ashamed of having served two dynasties and lamented that he could not return to the south. See Graham, "*The Lament for the South.*"

16. For example, Xie Zhengguang, "Qing chu erchen Cao Rong jiqi yimin menke" 清初貳臣曹溶及其遺民門客, *Qing chu shiwen*, 261.

17. Liu Li, "Lun Qing chu erchen shiren shige."

18. For instance, see Jiang Cai's poem cited in ibid., 19.

19. The loyalist Gu Jingxing's documentation, cited in Zhao Yu, "Gong Dingzi jiaoyou," 18.

20. "Chrysanthemum of the East Bamboo Fence" is an allusion to Tao Qian of the Eastern Jin dynasty. "Thornferns of the Western Mountains" refers to Bo Yi and Shu Qi, who upon the fall of their state, protested against the succeeding regime (the Zhou) and refused to serve.

21. Gong Dingzi, "Ti hua yu Cao Qiuyue," *DSTWJ*, 33a.

22. Ibid.

23. Ibid.

24. Wakeman, *Great Enterprise*, vol. 2, 867.

25. Zhang Sheng, "Chen Mingxia yu Gong Dingzi, Yan Ermei."

26. See, e.g., *Qing shilu*, vol. 3, 781–84, 791, 800–801.

27. Song Quan, preface to *Baihuatang shi*, 2a–b; Song Quan, "Ding taifuren xingshi" 丁太夫人行實, *Wenkang gong yiji*, 26b–32b; Song Luo, "Wenkang gong jiazhuan" 文康公家傳, 33a–37b, and "Wenkang gong nianpu" 文康公年譜, appendix 8b, in Song Quan, *Wenkang gong yiji*; Song Luo, "Ji renwu tuonan shimo" 記壬午脫難始末, *Xibei leigao*, 26.1a–3a.

28. Song Quan, preface to *Baihuatang shi*, 2a, and "Ding taifuren xingshi," *Wenkang gong yiji*, 29a–b; Song Luo, "Wenkang gong jiazhuan," in Song Quan, *Wenkang gong yiji*, 33a. The three memorials are included in Song Quan, *Wenkang gong yiji*, *juan* 2.

29. Song Quan, preface to *Baihuatang shi*, 2a.

30. Ibid.

31. Ibid., 2a–b.

32. Song Luo, an earlier preface to *Shangqiu Song shi jiasheng*, 7a.

33. "Daxueshi nianbiao" 大學士年表, *MS*, 6093.

34. Song Quan, "Ding taifuren xingshi," *Wenkang gong yiji*, 30a–b; *MS*, 9494. Also see Song Luo, "Ji Wenkang gong Zunhua ping wei shimo" 記文康公遵化平偽始末, *Xibei leigao*, 3a–6a. The turncoat Wu Weiye includes this event in "Tongcheng ji" 通城擊 in his historical work *Sui kou jilue*, 268–69. It is very similar to Song Luo's documentation, with a few differences. Some historical records show that Song Quan surrendered to Li Zicheng's rebel regime. Duan Yubin, "Ming-Qing shiqi Shangqiu Song shi," 17–18.

35. Zhao Erxun, *Qing shi gao*, 9494.

36. Song Quan, "Ding taifuren xingshi," *Wenkang gong yiji*, 30b.

37. Ibid., 27a.

38. Ibid.

39. "Yu ji Ding taifuren wen" 諭祭丁太夫人文, included in Song Luo, *Shangqiu Song shi jiasheng*, 3.49a–b. A year later the court granted Song Quan a six-month leave to go back to his hometown and properly bury his mother. Song Luo, "Wenkang gong nianpu," in Song Quan, *Wenkang gong yiji*, appendix 18b.

40. Song Quan, "Ding taifuren xingshi," *Wenkang gong yiji*, 31a; Song Luo, "Wenkang gong nianpu," in Song Quan, *Wenkang gong yiji*, appendix 17b–18b; Liu Yuyou 劉餘祐, "Huang Qing taizi taibao nei Hanlin

Guoshiyuan daxueshi zeng shaobao jian taizi taibao guanglu dafu shi Wenkang Song gong muzhiming" 皇清太子太保內翰林國史院大學士贈少保兼太子太保光祿大夫謚文康宋公墓誌銘, in Song Luo, *Shangqiu Song shi jiasheng*, 11.25b.

41. Song Luo, "Wenkang gong jiazhuan," in Song Quan, *Wenkang gong yiji*, 36a.

42. Feng Quan and Song Quan, "Ti wei zhi jiu beiluan fangke yi zheng renxin shi" 題為直糾悖亂坊刻以正人心事 (Shunzhi 5/3 [1648]), *ZYYMQDA*, vol. 8, A8-5 (2-1)–(2-2).

43. For a discussion of this resemblance, see Shelley Hsue-lun Chang, *History and Legend*, 34.

44. Liu Yuyou, "Huang Qing taizi taibao nei Hanlin Guoshiyuan daxueshi zeng shaobao jian taizi taibao guanglu dafu shi Wenkang Song gong muzhiming," in Song Luo, *Shangqiu Song shi jiasheng*, 11.27a.

45. Ibid., 11.25b.

46. Tang Bin, "Song Wenkang gong shendaobei ming" 宋文康公神道碑銘, in Song Luo, *Shangqiu Song shi jiasheng*, 11.38a–42b.

47. "Gaozeng Wenkang gong guanglu dafu ji Liu furen yi pin furen yi dao" 誥贈文康公光祿大夫暨劉夫人一品夫人一道 and "Chifeng Zhao tai ruren yi dao" 敕封趙太孺人一道, in Song Luo, *Shangqiu Song shi jiasheng*, 1.2a–3a. Both were issued on Kangxi 6/11/26 (1667).

48. Liu Wanhua, "*Shangqiu Song shi jiasheng* bianzuan."

49. Song Quan, "Miyun shu zhong" 密雲署中, *Baihuatang shi*, 14b.

50. Liu Wanhua, "*Shangqiu Song shi jiasheng* bianzuan." The earliest print was made in Kangxi 14 (1675).

51. Song Luo, the earlier preface to *Shangqiu Song shi jiasheng*, 7a.

52. Song Luo, "Ding furen zhuan" 丁夫人傳, *Shangqiu Song shi jiasheng*, 6.2a–b.

53. The traditional Chinese way of counting age includes the year of birth.

54. Song Luo, *Mantang nianpu* 漫堂年譜, in *Xibei leigao*, 47.3b–4a.

55. Michael G. Chang, *A Court on Horseback*, chap. 2.

56. Ibid., 77–78.

57. *Qing shilu*, vol. 4, 1194.

58. Wang Shizhen, "*Huizhong ji* xu" 回中集序, in Song Luo, *Xibei leigao*, jiu xu ("earlier prefaces"), 10a. See also Wang's documentation of this event in Wang Shizhen, *Chi bei ou tan*, 70.

59. Wang Shizhen, "*Huizhong ji* xu," in Song Luo, *Xibei leigao*, jiu xu, 10a–11b.

60. Zhang Zilie, "*Jialetang gao* xu" 嘉樂堂稿序, in Song Luo, *Xibei leigao*, jiu xu, 3a–4a. For a brief account of the Song men's political careers in the late Ming and early Qing, see Des Forges, *Cultural Centrality and Political Change*, 80–85.

61. Wei Xi 魏禧, "Shu *Shangqiu Song shi jiasheng* hou" 書商丘宋氏家乘後, in Song Luo, *Shangqiu Song shi jiasheng*, 14.5b.

62. Gong Dingzi, "Wen jing yi Xiaoji yong Shaoling de shedi xiaoxi yun zizhu" 聞警憶弟孝積用少陵得舍弟消息韻自注, *DSTSJ*, 119.

63. Gong Dingzi, "Ti hualan yu Xiaoji di" 題畫蘭與孝積弟, *DSTWJ*, 6.35b.

64. Ibid.

65. Yan Ermei, "Xuzhou xiaolian Yan Gugu ming Ermei yi Wu Su shi" 徐州孝廉閻古古名爾梅貽武愫詩, in Gu Yanwu, *Ming ji shi lu*, 1. Another rejection letter, from Yan to Qing governor Zhao Fuxing, that circulated in the early Qing literati community sounded very similar to one that had been written by the loyalist Xia Yunyi. It might have resulted partly from literati imagination. Yan Ermei's reproach of Zhao Fuxing is recorded in multiple sources as well. For example, Zhang Xiangwen, Baida shanren nianpu, in Yan Ermei, *Yan Gugu quanji*, 9a (entry Shunzhi 2 [1645]). See also Yan Ermei's own poetic documentation, "Man caofu Zhao Fuxing jianzhao que zhi" 滿漕撫趙福星見招卻之, Nan Zhili ji 南直隸集, in *Baida shanren shi* 白耷山人詩, in Yan Ermei, *Yan Gugu quanji*, vol. 3, 1.5a. The poems were written in Shunzhi 2/run 6.

66. Zhang Xiangwen, *Baida shanren nianpu*, in Yan Ermei, *Yan Gugu quanji*, entries Shunzhi 3 (1646) and Shunzhi 4 (1647).

67. Ibid., 6a, 14a.

68. Yan Ermei, "Da Gong Xiaosheng wu shou" 答龔孝升五首, *Nan Zhili ji*, in *Yan Gugu quanji*, 1.5a–b.

69. Ibid.

70. See chap. 4 in this book.

71. This account of Gong Dingzi's career draws on Dong Qian, *Gong Zhilu nianpu*.

72. For a concise description of these attacks on gentry interests, see Wakeman, *Great Enterprise*, vol. 2, 1067–73.

73. See Gong's memorial cited in Dong Qian, *Gong Zhilu nianpu*, 31.

74. Zhao Yu, "Gong Dingzi jiaoyou," 51.

75. See Yan Ermei's notes to his poem, "Gong sikou wei yu tishu de yun xiji yi shi bao yu yu yiyun da zhi" 龔司寇為余題疏得允喜極以詩報余余依韻答之, *Bei zhili ji* 北直隸集, in *Baida shanren shi*, in *Yan Gugu quanji*,, vol. 4, 2.3a. Wei Yijie, then grand secretary, and a couple of friends also made efforts. For a careful discussion of Gong's role in this case, see Zhao Yu, "Gong Dingzi jiaoyou," 23–27.

76. See, e.g., Bai Qianshen, *Fu Shan de shijie*, chap. 2; Xie Zhengguang, *Qing chu shiwen*.

77. Zhao Yu mentions many of Gong Dingzi's contemporaries—inside and outside the government, including Buddhist masters—who praised Gong's public virtues. Zhao Yu, "Gong Dingzi jiaoyou."

78. Yan Ermei, "Lian shiren Zhang shi Fan shi yu Nanzhuang" 殮室人張氏樊氏於南莊, *Baida shanren shiji shi juan wenji er juan*, 428–29.

79. Yan Ermei, "Wen liang shiren lie si ku zhi" 聞兩室人烈死哭誌, ibid., 428. Yan's meaning in using the word *zhong* in this poem is ambiguous. It could refer to the women's devotion to him, which supported his loyal commitment, or perhaps he is implying these women were "loyal" to the fallen Ming. For a careful examination of Wen Tianxiang, masculinity, and political culture in the Southern Song, see Davis, *Wind against the Mountain*.

80. Zhuo Erkan was considered one of the few who held very strict criteria for the category *yimin* (Ming loyalist). For a detailed analysis of Zhuo and the *yimin* poetry collection he compiled, see Pan Chengyu, *Qing chu shitan*. The compiling of this book and its gradual publication took place in Kangxi 20s–30s. Many contemporaries had heard about its earlier partial, gradual publication and sought to see a copy.

81. Zhuo Erkan, *Yimin shi*, 464.

82. For the details, see Ying Zhang, "Politics and Morality," chap. 6.

83. Yan Ermei's poem to Fang Wen contains a line that describes the scene. "Taohuacheng ye zeng Fang Erzhi chushi" 桃花城夜贈方爾止處士, *Baida shanren shiji* shi *juan wenji er juan*, 401.

84. Meng Sen draws on Yu Huai's *Banqiao zaji* in "Hengbo furen kao" 橫波夫人考, *Xinshi congkan*, 123–63.

85. The Gong family genealogy records that Madam Tong was given the honor of the first rank; so was Gong Dingzi's second official wife, Madam Shi. This took place in Kangxi 7 (1668). Gong Zhaoxin, *Hefei Gong shi zongpu*, juan ci, "fengzeng biao" 封贈表. For sources that mention her different names, see Meng Sen, "Hengbo furen kao."

86. Many years ago, Gong Dingzi's father was buried in a new family cemetery here. Later Gong and his brothers were all buried nearby. Gong Zhaoxin, *Hefei Gong shi zongpu*, *juan* 1.

87. Yan Zhengju, "Ji Gong dasikou yuanpei Tong furen wen" 祭龔大司寇元配童夫人文, *Sheyuan ji*, 25.18b–20b. Gu Mei died in the seventh month of the same year (Kangxi 3 [1664]).

88. Gong Zhaoxin, *Hefei Gong shi zongpu*, 1.21b.

89. Yan Ermei, "Lujun xia qiu shi san shi shou wei Gong Xiaosheng zuo" (no. 2) 廬郡夏秋詩三十首為龔孝升作, *Baida shanren shiji shi juan wenji er juan*, 429–31.

90. Ibid.

91. Yan wrote these lines for Gong: "President of the Board (Gong Dingzi) can be seen as the Big Dipper / Lujun (Gong's hometown) is the Donglin." Yan Ermei, "Lujun xia qiu shi san shi shou wei Gong Xiaosheng zuo" (no. 25), *Baida shanren shiji shi juan wenji er juan*, 432.

92. Yan Ermei, "Lujun xia qiu shi san shi shou wei Gong Xiaosheng zuo." This set of poems contains a note explaining that Yan came to mourn Gong Dingzi's wife, Madam Wang, But this appears to be an error. According to the historical allusions in this poem, Yan meant to write "Dingzi's mother, Madam Wang."

93. Ibid..

94. See, e.g., Meyer-Fong, *Building Culture*; Xie Zhengguang, *Qing chu shiwen*.

95. Early Qing literati created an extremely complicated discourse surrounding the *yimin* identity. See Zhao Yuan, *Zhidu, Yanlun, Xintai*; Pan Chengyu, *Qing chu shitan*; Struve, *Ming-Qing Conflict*; Wai-yee Li, introduction to *Trauma and Transcendence*, ed. Idema, Li, and Widmer.

96. In contrast to my analysis, Wing-ming Chan argues the turncoats' self-justification and their moral claims did not have much effect on the early-Qing discourse of loyalty. Chan, "Early-Qing Discourse on Loyalty."

CONCLUSION

1. For a discussion of contemporary multimedia image politics, see Khatib, *Image Politics in the Middle East*, 7.

2. Chow, *Publishing, Culture, and Power*; Clunas, *Superfluous Things*.

3. Fei, "Writing for Justice."

4. See, e.g., Volpp, "Classifying Lust"; Clunas, *Superfluous Things;* Fei, "Writing for Justice" and *Negotiating Urban Space*, chap. 4; and Brook, *Praying for Power.*

5. I thank Robert Hymes for his insightful comments and questions when I presented part of this research as "Friendship in the Shadow of Factionalism and Loyalism in the Early Qing," at AAS 2013 in San Diego.

6. Wei Shang, *Rulin Waishi and Cultural Transformation.* The Chinese edition of Shang's book further elucidates this point.

7. Hanan, *The Chinese Vernacular Story*, chap. 9; Zhang Yongwei, "*Doupeng xianhua.*"

8. Jiang Wu, conclusion to *Leaving for the Rising Sun.*

9. Theiss, *Disgraceful Matters*, 48.

10. Ibid., esp. chaps. 1–2. See also Thorton, *Disciplining the State*, esp. chaps. 1–3.

11. Theiss, *Disgraceful Matters*, 212.

12. De Bary, "Chen Te-Hsiu and Statecraft."

13. Ko, *Teachers of the Inner Chambers*, 24–25.

14. Ng, "The Epochal Concept of 'Early Modernity.'"

15. For a good example, see Kevin Sharpe's analysis of early modern England and monarchs' image-making efforts in *Selling the Tudor Monarchy.* Parker's *Global Crisis* looks at the phenomenon of the "public sphere" in various parts of the world, including China. The similar tendencies pointed out by Parker were indeed the conditions for the emergence of image politics in China and elsewhere.

16. Hunt, *The Family Romance of the French Revolution.*

17. Liang, *Ming-Qing jiazu xiaoshuo.*

18. Goldman, "Coda," in *Opera and the City.*

19. Qin Jitang 秦際堂, "Ti Yu Danxin *Banqiao zaji*" 題余澹心板橋雜記, quoted in preface to Yu Huai, *Banqiao zaji*, 7.

20. Wai-yee Li offers an excellent analysis of the early Qing construction of late-Ming courtesans as heroes. She asserts that the literati imagined the late-Ming courtesan figure to express their mixed feelings of self-reproach and self-justification. Wai-yee Li, "Heroic Transformations." For a discussion of the early Qing literati's invention of the courtesan as a cultural ideal, see Wai-yee Li, "The Late Ming Courtesan."

21. For discussion of historical reflections on the late Ming, see Qin, *Qing mo Min chu de wan Ming xiangxiang*; Chen, Wang, and Shang, *Wan Ming yu Wan Qing*; Idema, Li, and Widmer, *Trauma and Transcendence*; and Wai-yee Li, *Women and National Trauma.*

BIBLIOGRAPHY

PRIMARY SOURCES

Cao Rong 曹溶. *Jingtitang shiji* 靜惕堂詩集 (*SKCM*-ji 198).

Chen Zhenhui 陳貞慧. *Shanyang lu* 山陽錄. Shanghai: Wenming Shuju, 1915.

———. *Shu shi qi ze* 書事七則. Shanghai: Wenming Shuju, 1915.

Chen Zilong 陳子龍. *Chen Zilong shiji* 陳子龍詩集. Edited by Shi Zhecun 施蟄存 and Ma Zuxi 馬祖熙. Shanghai: Shanghai Guji Chubanshe, 2006.

———. *Chen Zilong zizhuan nianpu* 陳子龍自撰年譜. In Chen Zilong陳子龍, *Chen Zilong shiji* 陳子龍詩集, edited by Shi Zhecun 施蟄存 and Ma Zuxi馬祖熙. Shanghai: Shanghai Guji Chubanshe, 2006.

Cheng Zhengkui 程正揆. *Qingxi yigao* 青溪遺稿 (*SKCM*-ji 197).

Du Dengchun 杜登春. *She shi shimo* 社事始末. In *Donglin shimo* 東林始末. Beijing: Zhonghua Shuju, 1991.

Du Fu 杜甫. *Du gongbu shiji* 杜工部詩集. Hong Kong: Zhonghua Shuju, 1972.

Du Jun 杜濬. *Bianyatang quanji* 變雅堂全集. In *Huanggang Du Yuhuang shiwen quanji* 黄岡杜于皇詩文全集. Daoguang 23 ed. National Library of China.

Fan Ye 范曄. *Hou Hanshu* 後漢書. Beijing: Zhonghua Shuju, 1965.

Fang Wen 方文. *Tushan ji* 嵞山集. Shanghai: Shanghai Guji Chubanshe, 1979.

Fang Yizhi 方以智. *Fangzi liuyu cao* 方子流寓草 (*SKJH*-ji 50).

———. *Fushan wenji* 浮山文集 (*SKJH*-ji 113).

Feng Menglong 馮夢龍. *Gujin tan'gai* 古今譚概. In *Feng Menglong quanji* 馮夢龍全集, edited by Wei Tongxian 魏同賢. Shanghai: Shanghai Guji Chubanshe, 1993.

———. *Jiashen jiwen* 甲申紀聞. In *Jiashen jishi* 甲申紀事, compiled by Feng Menglong. Hand-copied manuscript, Republican period. National Library of China.

———. *Shen zhi lue* 紳志略. In *Jiashen jishi* 甲申紀事, compiled by Feng

Menglong. Hand-copied manuscript, Republican period. National Library of China.

———. *Zhongxing shilu* 中興實錄. In *Nan Ming shiliao ba zhong*, edited by Huang Zongxi 黃宗羲. Nanjing: Jiangsu Guji Chubanshe, 1997.

Gao Tingzhen 高廷珍 et al. *Donglin shu yuan zhi* 東林書院志. Taipei: Guangwen Shuju, 1968.

Gong Dingzi 龔鼎孳. *Dingshantang guwen xiaopin* 定山堂古文小品. Qingyutang 慶餘堂. Daoguang 14 ed. National Library of China.

———. *Dingshantang shiji* 定山堂詩集 (*SKJH*-ji 117).

———. *Dingshantang wenji* 定山堂文集. Gong shi Zhanluzhai 龔氏瞻麓齋, 1924. National Library of China.

———. *Dingshantang xiaopin xuji* 定山堂小品續集. Qingyutang 慶餘堂. Daoguang 14 ed. National Library of China.

———. *Gong Dingzi shi* 龔鼎孳詩. Edited by Chen Minjie 陳敏杰. Yangzhou: Guangling Shushe, 2006.

———. *Hefei Gong Duanyi gong zongshu* 合肥龔端毅公奏疏. Qingyutang 慶餘堂. Daoguang 14 ed. National Library of China.

———. *Xichuan zheng pu* 浠川政譜. Baojintang 寶謹堂. Daoguang 15 ed. Reprint, Guangxu 7. National Library of China.

Gong Zhaoxin 龔照昕 et al. *Hefei Gong shi zongpu* 合肥龔氏宗譜. Guangxu 16 ed. Anhui Provincial Library.

Gu Gongxie 顧公燮, comp. *Danwu biji* 丹午筆記. Suzhou: Jiangsu Guji Chubanshe, 1985.

Gu Jingxing 顧景星. *Baimaotang ji* 白茅堂集 (*SKCM*-ji 205–6).

Gu Yanwu 顧炎武. *Gu Tinglin shiji* 顧亭林詩集彙注. Edited by Wang Quchang 王蘧常. Shanghai: Shanghai guji Chubanshe, 2006.

———. *Ming ji shi lu* 明季寔錄 (*SKWS* 2.21).

———. *Sheng an benji* 聖安本紀. In *Jingtuo yishi* 荊駝逸史, vols. 9–11. Beijing: Zhongguo Tushuguan, 1911.

Guoshiguan 國史館. *Erchen zhuan* 貳臣傳. In *Qing dai zhuanji congkan* 清代傳記叢刊, compiled by Zhou Junfu 周駿富. Taipei: Mingwen Shuju, 1985.

He Canran 賀燦然. *Bo Bo Manlu pingzheng*驳驳漫録评正. In *Beijing tushuguan guji zhenben congkan* 北京图书馆古籍珍本丛刊. Beijing: Shumu Wenxian Chubanshe, 1998.

———. *Manlu pingzheng* 漫錄评正. *Beijing tushuguan guji zhenben congkan* 北京图书馆古籍珍本丛刊. Beijing: Shumu Wenxian Chubanshe, 1998.

———. *Manlu pingzheng* 漫錄评正. Wanli ed. National Library of China.

Hu Shi'an 胡世安. *Xiuyan ji* 秀巖集 (*SKCM*-ji 196).

Huang Daozhou 黃道周. *Huang Daozhou Xiaojing* 黃道周孝經. Shanghai: Shanghai Shuhua Chubanshe. 2011.

———. *Huang Shizhai xiansheng chidu* 黃石齋先生尺牘. Shanghai: Shangwu Yinshuguan, Republican period.

———. *Huang Shizhai xiansheng wenji* 黃石齋先生文集 (*SKXX*-ji 1384).

———. *Huang Zhangpu ji* 黃漳浦集. Edited by Chen Shouqi 陳壽祺. Reprint, 1875–1911. National Library of China.

———. *Huang Zhangpu wenxuan* 黃漳浦文選 (*TWWXCK* 137).

———. *Xiaojing ji zhuan* 孝經集傳. In *Meiguo Hafo daxue Hafo-Yanjing tushuguan cang zhongwen shanben huikan* 美國哈佛大學哈佛燕京圖書館藏中文善本彙刊, vol. 1. Beijing and Guilin: Shangwu Yinshuguan and Guangxi Shifan Daxue Chubanshe, 2003.

Huang Daozhou and Cai Yuqing 蔡玉卿. *Huang Shizhai gong kangli wei ke gao* 黃石齋公伉儷未刻稿. Taipei: Guoli Zhongyang Tushuguan, 1973.

Huang Qing zhouyi 皇清奏議. Lushun: Guji Zhenglichu, 1936.

Huang Zongxi 黃宗羲. *Hongguang shilu chao* 弘光實錄鈔. In *Mingdai yeshi congshu* 明代野史叢書. Beijing: Beijing Guji Chubanshe, 2002.

———, ed. *Nan Ming shiliao ba zhong* 南明史料八種. Nanjing: Jiangsu Guji Chubanshe, 1997.

———. *Nanlei wen ding* 南雷文定 (*SBBY*).

Ji Liuqi 計六奇. *Ming ji bei lue* 明季北略. Edited by Wei Deliang 魏得良 and Ren Daobin 任道斌. Beijing: Zhonghua Shuju, 2006.

Jiang Liangji 蔣良騏. *Shi er chao Donghua lu* 十二朝東華錄. Taipei: Wenhai Chubanshe, 1963.

Jiang Shiquan 蔣士銓. *Jiang Shiquan xiqu ji* 蔣士銓戲曲集. Edited by Zhou Miaozhong 周妙中. Beijing: Zhonghua Shuju, 1993.

Jin Risheng 金日升. *Song tian lu bi* 頌天臚筆 (*SKJH*-shi 5–6).

Jin Zhijun 金之俊. *Jin Wentonggong ji* 金文通公集. Huaitiantang 懷天堂. Kangxi 25 ed. National Library of China.

———. *Xizhai ji shi juan Zuo shu shucao wu juan fulu yi juan* 息齋集十卷佐樞疏草五卷附錄一卷. Shunzhi-Kangxi ed. National Library of China.

Li Guangzuo 李光祚. *Changzhou xianzhi* 長洲縣志. Qianlong 18 ed. In *Zhongguo difangzhi jicheng: Jiangsu sheng difangzhi* 13 中國地方志集成: 江蘇省地方志. Nanjing: Jiangsu Guji Chubanshe, 1991.

Li Qing 李清. *Nandu lu* 南渡錄. In *Nan Ming shiliao ba zhong*, edited by Huang Zongxi 黃宗羲. Nanjing: Jiangsu Guji Chubanshe, 1997.

———. *San yuan biji* 三垣筆記. Beijing: Zhonghua Shuju, 1997.

Li Shiqia 李世洽 et al. *Taihu xianzhi* 太湖縣志. Shunzhi 10 ed. National Library of China.

Li Wen 李雯. *Liaozhai houji* 蓼齋後集 (*SKJH*-ji 111).

———. *Liaozhai ji* 蓼齋集 (*SKJH*-ji 111).

Li Xinchuan 李心傳. *Dao ming lu* 道命錄. In *Congshu jicheng chu bian* 叢

書集成初編, edited by Wang Yunwu 王雲五. Shanghai: Shangwu Yinshuguan, 1936.

Li Xunzhi 李遜之. *Chongzhen chao jishi*崇禎朝記事 (*SKJH*-shi 6).

Li Yuanding 李元鼎. *Shiyuan quanji* 石園全集 (*SKCM*-ji 196).

Li Yuanmei 黎元美. *Lianxuge ji* 蓮鬚閣集 (*SKJH*-ji 183).

Lin Shidui 林時對. *He zha cong tan*荷鍤叢談. In *Qingdai gaoben baizhong huikan* 清代稿本百種彙刊, vol. 26. Yangzhou: Jiangsu Guangling Guji Keyinshe, 1990.

Liu Zongzhou 劉宗周. *Liu Zongzhou quanji* 劉宗周全集. Taipei: Zhongyang Yanjiuyuan Zhongguo Wenshi Yanjiusuo, 1997.

———. *Renpu leiji* 人譜類記. In *Zhenben shanshu* 珍本善書. Shanghai: Shanghai Dazhong Shuju, Republican period.

Lu Shiyi 陸世儀. *Fushe jilue* 復社紀略. In *Donglin yu Fushe* 東林與復社, edited by Taiwan Yinhang Jingji Yanjiushi 臺灣銀行經濟研究室. Taipei: Taiwan Yinhang Jingji Yanjiushi, 1968.

Lu Tenglong 盧騰龍. *Suzhou fuzhi* 蘇州府志. Kangxi 20 ed. National Library of China.

Ma Shiqi 馬世奇. *Danningju wenji* 澹寧居文集 (*SKJH*-ji 113).

Mao Xiang 冒襄. *Tongren ji* 同人集 (*SKCM*-ji 385).

Ming Huidian 明會典. Wanli ed. Beijing: Zhonghua Shuju, 2007.

Ming Qing shiliao 明清史料. 10 vols. Edited by Guoli Zhongyang Yanjiuyuan Lishi Yuyan Yanjiusuo 國立中央研究院歷史語言研究所. Shanghai: Shangwu Yinshuguan, 1936.

Ming Shenzong shilu 明神宗實錄. Taipei: Zhongyang Yanjiuyuan Lishi Yuyan Yanjiusuo, 1966.

Ni Huiding 倪會鼎, comp. *Ni Yuanlu nianpu* 倪元璐年譜, edited by Li Shangying 李尚英. Beijing: Zhonghua Shuju, 1994.

Peng Ershu 彭而述. *Mingshi duan lue* 明史斷略 (*SKWS* 1.2).

Peng Sunyi 彭孫貽. *Liukou zhi* 流寇志. Hangzhou: Zhejiang Renmin Chubanshe, 1983.

Qian Fen 錢棻. *Xiaolin chu ji* 蕭林初集 (*SKWS* 6.23).

Qian Qianyi 錢謙益. *Chu xue ji* 初學集, edited by Qian Zeng 錢曾 and Qian Zhonglian 錢仲聯. In *Qian Muzhai quanji* 錢牧齋全集. Shanghai: Shanghai Guji Chubanshe, 2003.

———. *You xue ji* 有學集, edited by Qian Zeng 錢曾 and Qian Zhonglian 錢仲聯. In *Qian Muzhai quanji* 錢牧齋全集. Shanghai: Shanghai Guji Chubanshe, 2003.

Qian Renlin 錢人麟. *Donglin biesheng* 東林別乘. Guangzhou: Guangdong Sheng Zhongshan Tushuguan. 1958.

Qian Shisheng 錢士升. *Ciyutang ji* 賜餘堂集 (*SKJH*-ji 10).

Qian Yiji 錢儀吉, comp. *Bei zhuan ji* 碑傳集. Beijing: Zhonghua Shuju, 1993.

Qing shilu 清實錄. Vol. 3. *Shizu zhang huangdi shilu* 世祖章皇帝實錄. Beijing: Zhongguo Shuju, 1985.

Qing shilu 清實錄. Vol. 4. *Shengzu ren huangdi shilu* 聖祖仁皇帝實錄. Beijing: Zhongguo Shuju, 1985.

Shen Defu 沈德符. *Wanli ye huo bian* 萬曆野獲編. Beijing: Zhonghua Shuju, 2004.

Shen Shoumin 沈壽民. *Gushan yiji* 姑山遺集 (*SKJH-ji* 119).

Sima Qian 司馬遷. *Shiji* 史記. Beijing: Zhonghua Shuju, 1959.

Song Luo 宋犖. *Shangqiu Song shi jiasheng* 商丘宋氏家乘. Kangxi ed. National Library of China.

———, comp. *Shangqiu Song shi san shi yiji* 商丘宋氏三世遺集. Kangxi ed. National Library of China.

———. *Xibei leigao* 西陂類稿. Kangxi ed. National Library of China.

Song Quan 宋權. *Baihuatang shi* 白華堂詩. Kangxi 6 ed. In *Shangqiu Song shi san shi yiji* 商丘宋氏三世遺集, compiled by Song Luo. Kangxi ed. National Library of China.

———. *Wenkang gong yiji* 文康公遺集. In *Shangqiu Song shi san shi yiji* 商丘宋氏三世遺集, compiled by Song Luo. Kangxi ed. National Library of China.

Sun Chengze 孫承澤. *Chunming meng yu lu* 春明夢餘錄. Hong Kong: Longmen Shudian, 1976.

———. *Jifu renwu zhi* 畿輔人物志 (*SKCM*-shi 119).

———. *Tianfu guangji* 天府廣記. Beijing: Bejing Chubanshe, 1962.

Sun Chuanting 孫傳庭. *Jianlao lu* 鑒勞錄 (*SKCM*-shi 128).

Suzhou fuzhi 蘇州府志. Kangxi 20 ed. National Library of China.

Tan Qian 談遷. *Beiyou lu* 北遊錄. Beijing: Zhonghua Shuju, 1981.

———. *Zaolin zazu* 棗林雜俎. Beijing: Zhonghua Shuju, 2006.

Tang Juanshi 湯狷石. *Zheng Man shiji* 鄭鄤事蹟 (1–5). In *Guxue huikan* 古學彙刊, vol. 1, no. 6. Shanghai: Shanghai Guocui Xuebaoshe, 1912.

Tang Xiuye 湯修業. *Zheng an chuanxin lu yuangao* 鄭案傳信録原稿. Hand-copied manuscript. National Library of Beijing.

Wan Shihua 萬時華. *Gaiyuan chu ji er juan er ji san juan* 溉園初集二卷二集三卷 (*SKJH*-ji 144).

Wang Shaohui 王紹徽. *Donglin dianjiang lu* 東林點將錄 (*MDZJCK*-xuelin lei 5, appendix 1).

Wang Shizhen 王士禛. *Chi bei ou tan* 池北偶談. Beijing: Zhonghua Shuju, 2006.

Wang Yongji 王永吉. *Yuzhi renchen jingxin lu* 御制人臣儆心録. In *Wenyuange*

Siku quanshu 文淵閣四庫全書. Taipei: Taiwan Shangwu Yinshuguan, 1983.

Wei Xueyi 魏學洢. *Maozhan ji* 茅簷集. In *Siku quanshu zhenben* 四庫全書珍本 4, edited by Wang Yunwu 王雲五. Shanghai: Shangwu Yinshuguan, Republican period.

———. *Wei Zijing yiji* 魏子敬遺集. Edited by Qian Fen 錢棻. Chongzhen ed. National Library of China.

Wen Bing 文秉. *Jia-yi shian* 甲乙事案. In *Nan Ming shiliao ba zhong* 南明史料八種, edited by Huang Zongxi 黃宗羲. Nanjing: Jiangsu Guji Chubanshe, 1997.

Wen Zhenmeng 文震孟. *Wen Wensu gong riji* 文文肅公日記. National Library of China.

Wenyuange Siku quanshu 文淵閣四庫全書. Reprint. Taipei: Taiwan Shangwu Yinshuguan, 1983.

Wu Liang 吳亮. *Wanli shuchao* 萬歷疏鈔 (*SKJH*-shi 58).

———. *Zhiyuan ji* 止園集. Tianqi ed. National Library of China.

Wu Shanjia 吳山嘉. *Fu She xingshi zhuanlue* 復社姓氏傳略. Nangaitang 南陔堂, Daoguang 11.

Wu Weiye 吳偉業. *Sui kou jilue* 綏寇紀略. Edited by Li Xueying 李學穎. Shanghai: Shanghai Guji Chubanshe, 1992.

Wu Yifeng 吳易峰 et al. *Taihu xianzhi* 太湖縣志. Qianlong 26 ed. *Zhongguo difangzhi congshu* 中國地方誌叢書. Taipei: Chengwen Chubanshe, 1985.

Wu Yuancui 伍袁萃. *Bo Manlu pingzheng*驳漫錄评正. In *Beijing tushuguan guji zhenben congkan* 北京图书馆古籍珍本丛刊. Beijing: Shumu Wenxian Chubanshe, 1998.

———. *Linju manlu* 林居漫録. Wanli ed. National Library of China.

———. *Linju manlu* 林居漫録. Reprinted hand-copied ms. (*SKCM*-zi 242).

———. *Linju manlu* 林居漫録. In *Beijing tushuguan guji zhenben congkan* 北京图书馆古籍珍本丛刊. Beijing: Shumu Wenxian Chubanshe, 1998.

———. *Tanyuan zazhi* 彈園雜志 (*SKJH*-ji 35).

———. *Yi'antang gao* 貽安堂稿. Wanli ed. Shanghai Library.

Wuyue Caomang Chen 吳越草莽臣. *Wei Zhongxian xiaoshuo chijian shu* 魏忠賢小說斥奸書 (*GBXSJC*).

Xia Xie 夏燮. *Ming tongjian* 明通鑒. Changsha: Yuelu Shushe, 1998.

Xiao Mu 蕭穆. *Jingfu leigao* 敬孚類稿. Hefei: Huangshan Shushe, 1992.

Xiong Wenju 熊文舉. *Lüouge jin ji* 侶鷗閣近集 (*SKJH*-ji 120).

———. *Xuetang xiansheng wenji* 雪堂先生文集. In *Beijing tushuguan guji zhenben congkan* 北京圖書館古籍珍本叢刊. Beijing: Beijing Tushuguan Chubanshe, 1998.

Xu Yingfen 徐應芬. *Yu bian jilue* 遇變紀略. In *Danwu biji* 丹午筆記, edited by Gu Gongxie 顧公燮. Suzhou: Jiangsu Guji Chubanshe, 1985.

Xu Zi 徐鼒. *Xiaotian jinian fu kao* 小腆紀年附考. Beijing: Zhonghua Shuju, 2006.

Yan Ermei 閻爾梅. *Baida shanren shiji* shi *juan wenji er juan* 白耷山人詩集十卷文集二卷 (*SKJH*-ji 119).

———. *Yan Gugu quanji* 閻古古全集. Edited by Zhang Xiangwen 張相文. Beijing: Zhongguo Dixuesuo, 1922.

Yan Zhengju 嚴正矩. *Sheyuan ji* 涉園集. Kangxi ed. National Library of China.

Yang Sichang 楊嗣昌. *Yang Sichang ji* 楊嗣昌集. Edited by Liang Songcheng 梁頌成. Changsha: Yuelu Shushe, 2005.

Yang Wenfeng 楊文峰 et al. *Xinchang xianzhi* 新昌縣志. Qianlong 58 ed. In *Zhongguo difangzhi huikan* 中國地方志匯刊 27. Beijing: Zhongguo Shudian, 1992.

Ye Mengzhu 葉夢珠. *Yue shi bian* 閱世編. Beijing: Zhonghua Shuju, 2007.

Ye Xianggao 葉向高. *Qu bian* 蘧編. Taipei: Weiwen Tushu Chubanshe Youxian Gongsi, 1977.

Yu Huai 余懷. *Banqiao zaji* 板橋雜記. Edited by Xue Bing 薛冰. Nanjing: Nanjing Chubanshe, 2007.

Zhang Mingbi 張明弼. *Yingzhi quanji* 瑩芝全集. Daoguang ed. National Library of China.

Zhang Pu 張溥. *Qiluzhai shiwen heji* 七録齋詩文合集. Taipei: Weiwen Tushu Gongsi, 1977.

Zhang Shiwei 張世偉. *Zhang Yidu xiansheng Ziguangzhai ji shi liu juan fu Zhou libu jishi yi juan* 張異度先生自廣齋集十六卷附周吏部紀事一卷 (*SKJH*-ji 162).

Zhang Tingyu 張廷玉 et al. *Ming shi* 明史. Beijing: Zhonghua Shuju, 1974.

Zhang Xia 張夏, comp. *Yuqiao hua* 漁樵話. Hand-copied ms. National Library of China.

Zhang Yi 張怡. *Sou wen xu bi* 謏聞續筆. In *Ming mo shishi zachao san zhong* 明末史事雜鈔三種. Hand-copied ms. National Library of China.

Zhang Zilie 張自烈. *Qishan wenji* 芑山文集 (*SKJH*-ji 166).

———. *Qishan wenji* 芑山文集. In *Yuzhang congshu* 豫章叢書. Nanchang: Hu Sijing Tuilu 胡思敬退廬, Republican period.

Zhanggu congbian 掌故叢編. 10 vols. Reprint. Yangzhou: Guangling Guji Shushe, 1990.

Zhao Erxun 趙爾巽. *Qing shi gao* 清史稿. Beijing: Qingshiguan, 1927.

Zheng Man 鄭鄤. *Miyang caotang shiji* 峚陽草堂詩集 (*SKJH*-ji 126).

———. *Miyang caotang wenji* 峚陽草堂文集 (*SKJH-jibu* 126).

———. *Tianshan zixu nianpu* 天山自敘年譜. In Zheng Man鄭鄤, *Miyang caotang wenji* 峚陽草堂文集 (*SKJH*-ji 126).

Zheng Xuan 鄭瑄. *Zuofei'an ri zuan* 昨非菴日纂. Beijing: Beijing Tushuguan Chubanshe, 1996.

Zhongyang yangjiuyuan lishi yuyan yanjiusuo xiancun Qingdai neige daku yuancang Ming Qing dang'an 中央研究院歷史語言研究所現存清代內閣大庫原藏明清檔案. Edited by Zhang Weiren 張偉仁. Taipei: Zhongyang Yanjiuyuan Lishi Yuyan Yanjiusuo, 1986.

Zhou Zhikui 周之夔. *Qi cao shiji qi juan wenji ba juan Qi cao er ji* 棄草詩集七卷文集 八卷棄草二集 (*SKJH*-ji 112–13).

Zhu Changzuo 朱長祚. *Yujing xin tan* 玉鏡新譚. Beijing: Zhonghua Shuju, 1997.

Zhuang Qichou 莊起儔. *Zhangpu Huang xiansheng nianpu* 漳浦黃先生年譜. In Huang Daozhou 黃道周, *Huang Zhangpu wenxuan* 黃漳浦文選 (*TWWXCK* 137).

Zhuo Erkan 卓爾堪. *Yimin Shi* 遺民詩 (*SKJH*-ji 21).

Zichuan xianzhiu 淄川縣志. Kangxi 26 ed. and Qianlong 8 ed. National Library of China.

Zichuan xianzhiu 淄川縣志. Qianlong 41 ed. In *Zhongguo difangzhi jicheng: Shandong fu xian zhi* 中國地方志集成: 山東府縣志 6. Nanjing: Fenghuang Chubanshe, 2004.

Zuo Fu 左輔 et al. *Hefei xianzhi* 合肥縣志. Jiaqing 8 ed. Reprint, 1920. In *Zhongguo difangzhi congshu: Huazhong difang* 中國地方志叢書: 華中地方 628. Taipei: Chengwen Chubanshe, 1985.

SECONDARY SOURCES

Allen, Sarah M. "Oral Sources and Written Accounts: Authority in Tang Tales." In *Idle Talk: Gossip and Anecdote in Traditional China*, edited by Jack W. Chen and David Schaberg, 71–87. Berkeley: University of California Press, 2014.

Atwell, William S. "From Education to Politics: The Fu She." In *The Unfolding of Neo-Confucianism*, edited by W. T. de Bary, 333–67. New York: Columbia University Press, 1975.

Bai, Qianshen 白謙慎. *Fu Shan de shijie: Shi qi shiji zhongguo shufa de shanbian* 傅山的世界：十七世紀中國書法的嬗變. Beijing: Sanlian Shudian, 2006.

Birge, Bettine. "Women and Confucianism from Song to Ming: The Institutionalization of Patrilineality." In *The Song-Yuan-Ming Transition in Chinese History*, edited by Paul Jakov Smith and Richard von Glahn, 212–40. Cambridge, MA: Harvard University Asia Center, 2003.

Bossler, Beverly. *Courtesans, Concubines, and the Cult of Female Fidelity.* Cambridge, MA: Harvard University Asia Center, 2013.

Brokaw, Cynthia J. *The Ledgers of Merit and Demerit: Social Change and Moral Order in Late Imperial China.* Princeton: Princeton University Press, 1991.

Brook, Timothy. *The Confusions of Pleasure: Commerce and Culture in Ming China.* Berkeley: University of California Press, 1998.

———. *Praying for Power: Buddhism and the Formation of Gentry Society in Late-Ming China.* Cambridge, MA: Harvard University Press, 1993.

Brown, Miranda. *The Politics of Mourning in Early China.* Albany, NY: SUNY Press, 2007.

Buck, Pearl S. *All Men Are Brothers.* London: Methuen & Co., 1937.

Chaffee, John. "The Historian as Critic: Li Hsin-ch'uan and the Dilemmas of Statecraft in Southern Sung China." In *Ordering the World: Approaches to State and Society in Sung Dynasty China*, edited by Conrad Schriokauer and Robert Hymes, 310–35. Berkeley: University of California Press, 1993.

Chan, Alan K. L., and Sor-hoon Tan, eds. *Filial Piety in Chinese Thought and History.* London: RoutledgeCurzon, 2004.

Chan, Wing-ming. "The Early Qing Discourse on Loyalty." *East Asian History* 19 (2000): 27–52.

Chang, Chun-shu, and Shelley Hsueh-lun Chang. *Crisis and Transformation in Seventeenth-Century China: Society, Culture, and Modernity in Li Yü's World.* Ann Arbor: University of Michigan Press, 1992.

———. *Redefining History: Ghosts, Spirits, and Human Society in P'u Sung-ling's World, 1640–1715.* Ann Arbor: University of Michigan Press, 1998.

Chang, Kang-i Sun. *The Late-Ming Poet Ch'en Tzu-lung: Crises of Love and Loyalism.* New Haven: Yale University Press, 1991.

Chang, Michael G. *A Court on Horseback: Imperial Touring and Construction of Qing Rule, 1680–1785.* Cambridge, MA: Harvard University Asia Center, 2007.

Chang, Shelley Hsue-lun. *History and Legend: Ideas and Images in the Ming Historical Novels.* Ann Arbor: University of Michigan Press, 1990.

Chen Baoliang 陳寶良. "Wan Ming rujia chuantong de benghuai yu xin dianfan de chongjian" 晚明儒家傳統的崩壞與新典範的重建. *Shehui kexue jikan* no. 4 (2012): 163–73.

———. *Zhongguo liumang shi* 中國流氓史. Beijing: Zhongguo Shehui Kexue Chubanshe, 1993.

Chen, Jack W., and David Schaberg, eds. *Idle Talk: Gossip and Anecdote in Traditional China.* Berkeley: University of California Press, 2014.

Chen Pingyuan 陳平原, Wang Dewei 王德威, and Shang Wei 商偉, eds. *Wan Ming yu wan Qing: Lishi chuancheng yu wenhua chuangxin* 晚明與晚清：歷史傳承與文化創新. Wuhan: Hubei Jiaoyu Chubanshe, 2002.

Chen Shengxi 陳生璽. *Ming-Qing yidai shi dujian* 明清易代史獨見. Shanghai: Shanghai Shiji Chuban and Shanghai Guji Chubanshe, 2006.

Chen Wanyi 陳萬益. *Wan Ming xiaopin yu Mingji wenren shenghuo* 晚明小品與明季文人生活. Taipei: Da'an Chubanshe, 1988.

Chen Xushan 陳緒山. "Lichao wu bai tian: Huang Daozhou di san ci ruchao weiguan pingshu" 立朝五百天：黃道周第三次入朝為官評述. In *Haixia liang'an Huang Daozhou xueshu yantaohui lunwen ji* 海峽兩岸黃道周學術研討會論文集, 249–55. Dongshan, 2011.

Chen Yinke 陳寅恪. *Liu Rushi biezhuan* 柳如是別傳. Beijing: Sanlian Shudian, 2001.

Chen Yongming 陳永明. "Xiang Qing Mingchen yu Qing chu yulun" 降清明臣與清初初輿論. *Hanxue yanjiu* 27: 4 (Dec. 2009): 197–228.

Cheng Junying 程俊英 and Jiang Jianyuan 蔣見元, comps. *Lunyu jishi* 論語集釋. Beijing: Zhonghua Shuju, 1990.

Cheng Shude 程樹德. *Lunyu jishi* 論語集釋. Taipei: Yiwen Yinshuguan, 1965.

Chia, Lucille. "The Use of Print in Ming Dynasty China: A Very Brief Survey." In *Books in Numbers: Seventy-fifth Anniversary of the Harvard-Yenching Library Conference Papers*, edited by Wilt L. Idema, 143–96. Cambridge, MA: Harvard Yenching Library, Harvard University, 2007.

Chow, Kai-wing. *Publishing, Culture, and Power in Early Modern China*. Stanford: Stanford University Press, 2004.

———. *The Rise of Confucian Ritualism in Late Imperial China: Ethics, Classics, and Lineage Discourse*. Stanford: Stanford University Press, 1994.

Clunas, Craig. *Elegant Debts: The Social Art of Wen Zhenming, 1470–1559*. Honolulu: University of Hawai'i Press, 2004.

———. *The Superfluous Things: Material Culture and Social Status in Early Modern China*. Honolulu: University of Hawai'i Press, 1991.

Coady, C.A.J., ed. *What's Wrong with Moralism?* New York: Blackwell, 2006.

Crossley, Pamela. *Translucent Mirror: History and Identity in Qing Imperial Ideology*. Berkeley: University of California Press, 1999.

Dardess, John. *Blood and History in China: The Donglin Faction and Its Repression, 1620–1627*. Honolulu: University of Hawai'i Press, 2002.

Davis, Richard. *Wind against the Mountain: The Crisis of Politics and Culture in Thirteenth-Century China*. Cambridge, MA: Council on East Asia Studies, Harvard University, 1996.

de Bary, William Theodore. "Chen Te-Hsiu and Statecraft." In *Ordering the World: Approaches to State and Society in Sung China*, edited by Robert P. Hymes and Conrad Schirokauer, 349–79. Berkeley: University of California Press, 1993.

Deng Zhicheng 鄧之誠. *Qing shi jishi chu bian* 清詩紀事初編. In *Qingdai zhuanji congkan* 清代傳記叢刊, compiled by Zhou Junfu 周駿富. Taipei: Mingwen Shuju, 1985.

———. *Sangyuan dushu ji* 桑園讀書記. Shenyang: Liaoning Jiaoyu Chubanshe, 1998.

Dennerline, Jerry. *The Chia-ting Loyalists: Confucian Leadership and Social Change in Seventeenth-Century China*. New Haven: Yale University Press, 1981.

Des Forges, Roger. *Cultural Centrality and Political Change in Chinese History: Northeast Henan in the Fall of the Ming*. Stanford: Stanford University Press, 2003.

Ding Guoxiang 丁國祥. *Fushe yanjiu* 復社研究. Nanjing: Fenghuang Chubanshe, 2011.

Ding Yizhuang 定宜莊. *Manzhou de funü shenghuo yu hunyin zhidu yanjiu* 滿洲的婦女與婚姻制度研究. Beijing: Beijing Daxue Chubanshe, 1999.

———. "Reflections on the 'New Qing History' School in the United States." *Chinese Studies in History*, vol. 43, no. 2 (Winter 2009–10): 92–96.

Dong Qian 董遷. *Gong Zhilu nianpu* 龔芝麓年譜. Taipei: Guangwen Shuju, 1971.

Duan Jiangli 段江麗. *Lifa yu renqing—Ming-Qing jiating xiaoshuo de jiating zhuti yanjiu* 禮法與人情—明清家庭小說的家庭主題研究. Beijing: Zhonghua Shuju, 2006.

Duan Yubin 段雨彬. "Ming-Qing shiqi Shangqiu Song shi jiazu yanjiu" 明清時期商丘宋氏家族研究. MA thesis, Beijing Shifan Daxue, 2010.

Ebrey, Patricia. *Women and the Family in China*. London: Routledge, 2002.

Elliott, Mark. *Emperor Qianlong: Son of Heaven, Man of the World*. New York: Pearson, 2009.

———. *The Manchu Way: The Eight Banners and Ethnic Identity in Late Imperial China*. Stanford: Stanford University Press, 2001.

Elman, Benjamin A. *A Cultural History of Civil Examinations in Late Imperial China*. Berkeley: University of California Press, 2000.

Elvin, Mark. *The Retreat of the Elephants: The Environmental History of China*. New Haven: Yale University Press, 2006.

Epstein, Maram. *Competing Discourses: Orthodoxy, Authenticity, and Engendered Meanings in Late Imperial Chinese Fiction*. Cambridge, MA: Harvard University Asia Center, 2001.

Fan Shuzhi 樊樹志. "Dangzheng yuanwo zhong de Zheng Zhenxian Zheng Man fuzi" 黨爭漩渦中的鄭振先鄭鄤父子. *Wenshi zhishi* 12 (2003): 68–76.

———. "Donglin shuyuan de shitai fenxi: 'Donglin dang' lun zhiyi" 東林書院的實態析:'東林黨'論質疑. *Zhongguo shehui kexue* no. 2 (2001): 188–208.

———. *Wang Ming shi* 晚明史. Shanghai: Fudan Daxue Chubanshe, 2003.

Fei, Siyen. *Negotiating Urban Space: Urbanization and Late Ming Nanjing.* Cambridge, MA: Harvard University Asia Center, 2010.

———. "Writing for Justice: An Activist Beginning of the Cult of Female Chastity in Late Imperial China." *Journal of Asian Studies* 71 (2012): 991–1012.

Fu Hongzhan 傅紅展. "Cai Yuqing jiqi xiaokai *Xiaojing*" 蔡玉卿及其小楷孝經. In *Zhongguo shufa quanji: Mingdai bian Huang Daozhou juan (fu Cai Yuqing)* 中國書法全集: 明代編黃道周卷(附蔡玉卿), vol. 56, edited by Liu Zhengcheng 劉正成, 27–31. Beijing: Rongbaozhai, 1994.

———. "Zuopin kaoshi" 作品考釋. In *Zhongguo shufa quanji: Mingdai bian Huang Daozhou juan (fu Cai Yuqing)* 中國書法全集: 明代編黃道周卷(附蔡玉卿), vol. 56, edited by Liu Zhengcheng 劉正成, 298–99. Beijing: Rongbaozhai, 1994.

Fukumoto Masakazu 福本雅一. "Wu Changshi to Zhou Yanru" 呉昌時と周延儒. In *Yamane Yukio kyōju taikyū kinen Mindaishi ronsō*山根幸夫教授退休紀念明代史論叢, edited by Mindaishi kenkyūkai Mindaishi ronsō henshu iinkai 明代史研究會明代史論叢編集委員會, 283–306. Tokyo: Kyuko Shoyin, 1990.

Ge Rongjin 葛榮晉 and Wang Juncai 王俊才. *Lu Shiyi pingzhuan* 陸世儀評傳. Nanjing: Nanjing Daxue Chubanshe, 1996.

Geng, Song. *The Fragile Scholar: Power and Masculinity in Chinese Culture.* Hong Kong: Hong Kong University Press, 2004.

Goldman, Andrea. *Opera and the City: The Politics of Culture in Beijing, 1770–1900.* Stanford: Stanford University Press, 2012.

Graham, William T., Jr. *"The Lament for the South": Yü Hsin's "Ai Chiang-nan Fu."* London: Cambridge University Press, 1980.

Greenbaum, Jamie. *Chen Jiru (1558–1639): The Background to Development and Subsequent Uses of Literary Personae.* Leiden: Brill, 2007.

Gu Cheng 顧誠. *Nan Ming shi* 南明史. Beijing: Zhongguo Qingnian Chubanshe, 1997.

Guo Chengkang 郭成康. "Ye tan Manzu Hanhua" 也談滿族漢化. In *Qingchao de guojia rentong: "Xin Qingshi" yanjiu yu zhengming* 清朝的國家認同——"新清史"研究與爭鳴, edited by Liu Fengyun 劉鳳雲 and Liu Wenpeng 劉文鵬, 71–92. Beijing: Zhongguo Renmin Daxue Chubanshe, 2010.

Guo Jianpin 郭建萍. "*Gujin tan'gai* xiaohua yanjiu" 古今談概笑話研究. MA thesis, Shandong Shifan Daxue, 2014.

Guy, R. Kent. *Qing Governors and Their Provinces: The Evolution of Territorial Administration in China, 1644–1796*. Seattle: University of Washington Press, 2010.

Hanan, Patrick. *The Chinese Vernacular Story*. Cambridge, MA: Harvard University Press, 1981.

Handlin-Smith, Joanna. *Action in Late Ming Thought: The Reorientation of Lu K'un and Other Scholar-Officials*. Berkeley: University of California Press, 1983.

———. *The Art of Doing Good: Charity in Late Ming China*. Berkeley: University of California Press, 2009.

Hartman, Charles. "Li Hsin-ch'an and the Historical Image of Late Sung *Tao-hsueh*." *Harvard Journal of Asiatic Studies* 61:2 (2001): 317–58.

He Zongmei 何宗美. *Ming mo Qing chu wenren jieshe yanjiu* 明末清初文人結社研究. Tianjin: Nankai Daxue Chubanshe, 2003.

Hershatter, Gail, and Wang Zheng. "Chinese History: A Useful Category of Gender Analysis." *American Historical Review* 113:5 (Dec. 2008): 1404–21.

Hinsch, Bret. "The Emotional Underpinnings of Male Fidelity in Imperial China." *Journal of Family History* 32 (2007): 392–412.

Ho Koon-piu 何冠彪. "Ming-Qing zhiji shengsi nanyi shuo tantao" 明清之際生死難易說探討. *Xin shixue* 4:2 (June 1993): 61–93.

———. *Sheng yu si: Mingji shidafu de jueze* 生與死：明季士大夫的抉擇. Taipei: Lianjing Chuban, 1997.

———. "Should We Die as Martyrs to the Ming Cause?: Scholar-Officials' Views on Martyrdom during the Ming-Qing Transition." *Oriens Extremus* 37:2 (1994): 123–51.

Ho, Ping-ti. "In Defense of Sinicization: A Rebuttal of Evelyn Rawski's 'Reenvisioning the Qing.'" *Journal of Asian Studies* 57:1 (Feb. 1998): 123–55.

Holzman, Donald. "The Place of Filial Piety in Ancient China." *Journal of the American Oriental Society* 118:2 (Apr.–June 1998): 185–99.

Huang Lijun 黃麗君. "Qing chu manren shouzhi kaoshi" 清初滿人守制考實. *Zhongzheng lishi xuekan* 8 (2006): 249–69.

Huang, Martin. "Male Friendship and Jiangxue (Philosophical Debates) in Sixteenth-Century China." *Nan Nü: Men, Women and Gender in China* 9:1 (2007): 146–78.

———. "Male Friendship in Ming China: An Introduction." *Nan Nü: Men, Women and Gender in China* 9:1 (2007): 2–33.

———. *Negotiating Masculinities in Late Imperial China*. Honolulu: University of Hawai'i Press, 2006.

Huang, Ray. *1587, a Year of No Significance: The Ming Dynasty in Decline*. New Haven: Yale University Press, 1981.

Huang Yi-nong 黃一農. "*Zhongxiao* paifang yu Shizijia" 忠孝牌坊與十字架. *Xin shixue* 8:3 (1997): 43–94.

Hucker, Charles O. *The Censorial System of Ming China*. Stanford: Stanford University Press, 1966.

———. "The Tung-lin Movement of the Late Ming Period." In *Chinese Thought and Institutions*, edited by J. K. Fairbank, 132–62. Chicago: University of Chicago Press, 1957.

Hunt, Lynn. *The Family Romance of the French Revolution*. Berkeley: University of California Press, 1993.

Idema, Wilt L., Wai-yee Li, and Ellen Widmer, eds. *Trauma and Transcendence in Early Qing Literature*. Cambridge, MA: Harvard University Asia Center, 2006.

Jian Ruiyao 簡瑞瑤. *Mingdai funu fojiao xinyang yu shehui guifan* 明代婦女佛教信仰與社會規範. Taipei: Daoxiang Chubanshe, 2007.

Jiang Qingbo 江慶柏. *Qingchao jinshi timing lu* 清朝進士題名錄. Beijing: Zhonghua Shuju, 2007.

Jiang Yixue 蔣逸雪. *Zhang Pu nianpu* 張溥年譜. Jinan: Qilu Shushe, 1982.

Ju Mingku 鞠明庫. *Zaihai yu Mingdai zhengzhi* 災害與明代政治. Beijing: Zhongguo Shehui Kexue Chubanshe, 2011.

Kahn, Harold. *Monarchy in the Emperor's Eye: Image and Reality in the Ch'ien-lung Reign*. Cambridge, MA: Harvard University Press, 1971.

———. "The Politics of Filiality: Justification for Imperial Action in Eighteenth Century China." *Journal of Asian Studies* 26:2 (Feb. 1967): 197–203.

Kan Hongliu 闞紅柳. "Qing chu shehui chuanwen yu huangquan ganyu" 清初社會傳聞與皇權干預. In *Qingdai zhengzhi yu guojia rentong* 清代政治與國家認同, edited by Liu Fengyun 劉鳳雲, Dong Jianzhong 董建中, and Liu Wenpeng 劉文鵬, 392–403. Beijing: Shehui Kexue Wenxian Chubanshe, 2012.

———. "Qing chu shixue shang de erchen" 清初史學上的貳臣. *Xueshu yanjiu* 8 (2009): 108–12.

Khatib, Lina. *Image Politics in the Middle East: The Role of the Visual in Political Struggle*. London and New York: I.B. Tauris, 2013.

Kieschnick, John. *The Impact of Buddhism on Chinese Material Culture*. Princeton: Princeton University Press, 2003.

Kishimoto Mio 岸本美緒. "Chongzhen shi qi nian de Jiangnan shehui yu guanyu Beijing de xinxi" 崇禎十七年的江南社會與關於北京的信息. *Qing shi yanjiu*, no. 2 (1999): 25–32.

Knapp, Keith. *Selfless Offspring: Filial Children and Social Order in Medieval China*. Honolulu: University of Hawai'i Press, 2005.

Knoblock, John, and Jeffrey Riegel, trans. *The Annals of Lü Buwei: A Complete Translation and Study*. Stanford: Stanford University Press, 2000.

Ko, Dorothy. "Pursuing Talent and Virtue: Education and Women's Culture in Seventeenth- and Eighteenth-Century China." *Late Imperial China* 13:1 (June 1992): 9–39.

———. *Teachers of the Inner Chambers: Women and Culture in Seventeenth-Century China*. Stanford: Stanford University Press, 1994.

Kutcher, Norman. "The Fifth Relationship: Dangerous Friendships in the Confucian Context." *AHR* 105:5 (Dec. 2000): 1615–29.

———. *Mourning in Late Imperial China: Filial Piety and the State*. Cambridge: Cambridge University Press, 1999.

Lai Xiaoyun 賴曉雲. "Cong Huang Daozhou shu *Xiaojing* lun qi shufa yishu" 從黃道周書〈孝經〉論其書法藝術. MA thesis, National Taiwan University, 2004.

Lee, Cheung Yin. "Emperor Chengzu and Imperial Filial Piety of the Ming Dynasty: From the *Classic of Filial Piety* to the *Biographical Accounts of Filial Piety*." In *Filial Piety in Chinese Thought and History*, edited by Alan K. L. Chan and Sorhoon Tan, 141–53. London: RoutledgeCurzon, 2004.

Lee, Pauline. *Li Zhi: Confucianism and the Virtue of Desire*. New York: SUNY Press, 2012.

Levine, Ari Daniel. *Divided by a Common Language: Factional Conflict in Late Northern Song China*. Honolulu: University of Hawai'i Press, 2008.

———. "Public Good and Partisan Gain: Political Languags of Faction in Late Imperial China and Eighteenth-Century England." *Journal of World History* 23:4 (2012): 841–82.

Li, Han. "News, Public Opinions, and History: Fiction on Current Events in Seventeenth-Century China." PhD diss., University of California, Irvine, 2009.

Li, Wai-yee. "Heroic Transformations: Women and National Trauma in Early Qing Literature." *Harvard Journal of Asiatic Studies* 59:2 (Dec. 1999): 363–443.

———. "The Late Ming Courtesan: Invention of a Cultural Ideal." In *Writing Women in Late Imperial China,* edited by Ellen Widmer and Kang-i Sun Chang, 46–73. Stanford: Stanford University Press, 1997.

———. *Women and National Trauma in Late Imperial Chinese Literature*. Cambridge, MA: Harvard University Asia Center, 2014.

———. "Women as Emblems of Dynastic Fall in Qing Literature." In *Dynastic Crisis and Cultural Innovation: From the Late Ming to the Late Qing and Beyond*, edited by David Der-wei Wang and Shang Wei, 93–150. Cambridge, MA: Harvard University Asia Center, 2005.

Liang Xiaoping 梁曉萍. *Ming-Qing jiazu xiaoshuo de wenhua yu xushi* 明清家族小說的文化與敘事. Tianjin: Nankai Daxue Chubanshe, 2008.

Lin Zhiying 林芷瑩. "Yi ju wei ge: Chuanqi *Lü mudan* de xiezuo yu Wu Bing de gaibian" 以劇為戈——傳奇《綠牡丹》的寫作與吳炳的改編. *Qinghua xuebao* 42:4 (2012): 669–731.

Liu, Adam Y. C. *Chinese Censors and the Alien Emperor, 1644–1660*. Hong Kong: Center of Asian Studies, University of Hong Kong, 1978.

Liu Fengyun 劉鳳雲, Dong Jianzhong 董建中, and Liu Wenpeng 劉文鵬, eds. *Qingdai zhengzhi yu guojia rentong* 清代政治與國家認同. Beijing: Shehui Kexue Wenxian Chubanshe, 2012.

Liu Fengyun 劉鳳雲 and Liu Wenpeng 劉文鵬, eds. *Qingchao de guojia rentong: "Xin Qingshi" yanjiu yu zhengming* 清朝的國家認同——"新清史"研究與爭鳴. Beijing: Zhongguo Renmin Daxue Chubanshe, 2010.

Liu Li 劉麗. "Lun Qing chu erchen shiren shige zhong de Yu Xin yixiang" 論清初貳臣詩人詩歌中的庾信意象. *Hainan shifan daxue xuebao* no. 3 (2013): 18–21.

Liu, Lydia H., Rebecca E. Karl, and Dorothy Ko, eds. *The Birth of Chinese Feminism: Essential Texts in Transnational Theory*. New York: Columbia University Press, 2013.

Liu Wanhua 劉萬華. "*Shangqiu Song shi jiasheng* bianzuan liuchuan kao" 《商丘宋氏 家乘》編纂流傳考. *Yindu xuekan* no. 2 (2013): 38–42.

Liu Wenpeng 劉文鵬. "Qingdai kedao 'fengwen zou shi' quanli de ruohua jiqi zhengzhi yingxiang" 清代科道"風聞奏事"權力的弱化及其政治影響. In *Qingchao de guojia renting: "Xin Qingshi" yanjiu yu zhengming* 清朝的國家認 同——"新清史"研究與爭鳴, edited by Liu Fengyun 劉鳳雲 and Liu Wenpeng 劉文鵬, 299–313. Beijing: Zhongguo Renmin Daxue Chubanshe, 2010.

Liu Yongqiang 劉勇強. "Xiaoshuo qiyuan wenti de san chong hanyi" 小說起源問題的 三重含義. *Ming-Qing xiaoshuo yanjiu* no. 1 (2006), page number unavailable.

Liu Zhengcheng 劉正成. *Zhongguo shufa quanji: Mingdai bian Huang Daozhou juan (fu Cai Yuqing)* 中國書法全集: 明代編黃道周卷 (附蔡玉卿). Vol. 56. Beijing: Rongbaozhai, 1994.

Liu Zhigang 劉志剛. *Tianren zhiji: Zaihai, shengtai yu Ming-Qing yidai* 天人之際: 災害, 生態與明清易代. Changsha: Zhongnan Daxue Chubanshe, 2013.

Liu Zhongxing 劉中興. "Jietie yu Mingdai gonggong yulun" 揭貼與明代公共輿論. MA thesis, Huazhong Shifan Daxue, 2008.

Louie, Kam. *Theorizing Chinese Masculinity: Society and Gender in China.* Cambridge: Cambridge University Press, 2002.

Lu Miaw-fen 呂妙芬. "Religious Dimensions of Filial Piety as Developed in Late Ming Interpretations of the *Xiaojing*." *Late Imperial China* 27:2 (Dec. 2006): 1–37.

———. "Wan Ming shiren lun *Xiaojing* yu zhengzhi jiaohua" 晚明士人論孝經與政治教化. *Taida wenshi zhexue bao* 61 (2004): 223–60.

———. *Xiaozhi tianxia: Xiaojing yu jinshi zhongguo de zhengzhi yu wenhua* 孝治天下—孝經與近世中國的政治與文化. Taipei: Zhongyang Yanjiuyuan, 2011.

———. *Yangming xue shiren shequn* 陽明學士人社群. Taipei: Zhongyang Yanjiuyuan Lishi Yanjiusuo, 2003.

———. "Zuowei yishixing wenben de *Xiaojing*: Ming-Qing shiren *Xiaojing* shijian de ge'an yanjiu" 作為儀式性文本的孝經：明清士人孝經實踐的個案研究. *Zhongyang yanjiuyuan jindai shi yanjiusuo jikan* 60 (2008): 1–42.

Lu, Weijing. "Reviving an Ancient Filial Ideal: The 17th-Century Practice of *Lumu*." *China Historical Review* (forthcoming).

———. *True to Her Word: The Faithful Maiden Cult in Late Imperial China*. Stanford: Stanford University Press, 2008.

Luan Xing 欒星. *Jiashen shi shang* 甲申史商. Zhengzhou: Zhongzhou Guji Chubanshe, 1997.

Luo Jizu 羅繼祖. "Sun Lin *Siya ji*" 孫臨《肆雅集》. *Wenxian* (1981): 199–201.

Mann, Susan. *Precious Records: Women in China's Long Eighteenth Century*. Stanford: Stanford University Press, 1997.

McDermott, Joseph P. "Friendship and Its Friends in the Late Ming." In *Jinshi jiazu yu zhengzhi bijiao lishi lunwen ji* 近世家族政治比較歷史論文集, edited by the Institute of Modern History of Academia Sinica, 67–96. Taipei: Institute of Modern History of Academia Sinica, 1992.

McMorran, Ian. "The Patriot and the Partisans: Wang Fu-chih's Involvement in the Politics of the Yong-li Court." In *From Ming to Ch'ing: Conquest, Region, and Continuity in Seventeenth-Century China*, edited by Jonanthan D. Spence and John E. Wills, Jr., 133–66. New Haven: Yale University Press, 1979.

Meng Sen 孟森. *Xinshi congkan* 心史叢刊. Beijing: Zhonghua Shuju, 2006.

Meyer-Fong, Toby. *Building Culture in Early Qing Yangzhou*. Stanford: Stanford University Press, 2003.

Miller, Harry. "Newly Discovered Source Sheds Light on Late Ming Faction: Reading Li Sancai's *Fu Huai xiao cao*." *Ming Studies*, vol. 47 (Spring 2003): 126–40.

———. "Opposition to the Donglin Faction in the Late Ming Dynasty: The Case of Tang Binyin." *Late Imperial China* 27: 2 (2006): 38–66.

———. *State versus Gentry in Early Qing Dynasty China, 1644–1699*. New York: Palgrave Macmillan, 2013.

———. *State versus Gentry in Late Ming Dynasty China, 1572–1644*. New York: Palgrave Macmillan, 2009.

Mitchell, W. J. T. *Picture Theory: Essays on Verbal and Visual Representation*. Chicago: University of Chicago Press, 1994.

Ng, On-cho. "The Epochal Concept of 'Early Modernity' and the Intellectual History of Late Imperial China." *Journal of World History* 14:1 (Mar. 2003): 37–61.

Nuyen, A. T. "Filial Piety as Respect for Tradition." In *Filial Piety in Chinese Thought and History*, edited by Alan K. L. Chan and Sor-hoon Tan, 203–14. London: RoutledgeCurzon, 2004.

Ōki Yasushi 大木康. "Mao Xiang and Yu Huai: Early Qing Romantic *Yimin*." In *Trauma and Transcendence in Early Qing Literature*, edited by Wilt L. Idema, Wai-yee Li, and Ellen Widmer, 231–48. Cambridge, MA: Harvard University Asia Center, 2006.

———. *Ming mo Jiangnan de chuban wenhua* 明末江南的出版文化. Translated by Zhou Baoxiong 周保雄. Shanghai: Shanghai Guji Chubanshe, 2014.

Ono Kazuko 小野和子. *Mingji dangshe kao* 明季黨社考. Translated by Li Qing 李慶 and Zhang Rongmei 張榮湄. Shanghai: Shanghai Guji Chubanshe, 2006.

Owen, Stephen. "I Don't Want to Act as Emperor Any More: Finding the Genuine in *Peach Blossom Fan*." In *Trauma and Transcendence in Early Qing Literature*, edited by Wilt L. Idema, Wai-yee Li, and Ellen Widmer, 488–510. Cambridge, MA: Harvard University Asia Center, 2006.

———. "Postface: Believe It or Not." In *Idle Talk: Gossip and Anecdote in Traditional China*, edited by Jack W. Chen and David Schaberg, 217–24. Berkeley: University of California Press, 2014.

Pan Chengyu 潘承玉. *Qing chu shitan: Zhuo Erkan yu Yimin shi yanjiu* 清初詩壇：卓爾堪與《遺民詩》研究. Beijing: Zhonghua Shuju, 2004.

Parker, Geoffrey. *Global Crisis: War, Climate Change, and Catastrophe in the Seventeenth Century*. New Haven: Yale University Press, 2013.

Peterson, Williard. *Bitter Gourd: Fang I-chih and the Impetus for Intellectual Change*. New Haven: Yale University Press, 1979.

Qian Haiyue 錢海岳. *Nan Ming shi* 南明史. Beijing: Zhonghua Shuju, 2006.

Qin Yanchun 秦燕春. *Ming mo Min chu de wan Ming xiangxiang* 清末民初的晚明想像. Beijing: Beijing Daxue Chubanshe, 2008.

Raphals, Lisa. *Sharing the Light: Representations of Women and Virtue in Early China*. Albany, NY: SUNY Press, 1998.

Rawski, Evelyn S. *The Last Emperors: A Social History of Qing Imperial Institutions*. Berkeley: University of California Press, 2001.

———. "Presidential Address: Reenvisioning the Qing: The Significance of the Qing Period in Chinese History." *Journal of Asian Studies* 55:4 (Nov. 1996): 829–50.

———. "Was the Early Qing 'Early Modern? The Qing Formation and the Early Modern Period.'" In *The Qing Formation in World-Historical Time*, edited by Lynn A. Struve. Cambridge, MA: Harvard University Asia Center, 2004.

Ren Daobin 任道斌. *Fang Yizhi nianpu* 方以智年譜. Hefei: Anhui Jiaoyu Chubanshe, 1983.

Rolston, David, ed. *How to Read the Chinese Novel.* Princeton: Princeton University Press, 1990.

Rosemont, Henry, and Roger T. Ames. *The Chinese Classic of Family Reverence: A Philosophical Translation of the Xiaojing.* Honolulu: University of Hawai'i Press, 2009.

Sanders, Graham. "I Read They Said What He Wrote: Orality, Writing, and Gossip in Tang Poetry Anecdote." In *Idle Talk: Gossip and Anecdote in Traditional China*, edited by Jack W. Chen and David Schaberg, 88–106. Berkeley: University of California Press, 2014.

Sato Masayuki 佐藤將之. *Zhongguo gudai de zhong lun yanjiu* 中國古代的忠論研究. Taipei: Guoli Taiwan Daxue Chuban Zhongxin, 2010.

Schaberg, David. "Word of Mouth and the Sources of Western Han History." In *Idle Talk: Gossip and Anecdote in Traditional China*, edited by Jack W. Chen and David Schaberg, 38–54. Berkeley: University of California Press, 2014.

Shang Wei 商偉. *Li yu shi ba shiji de wenhua zhuanzhe: Rulin waishi yanjiu* 禮與十八世 紀的文化轉折：《儒林外史》研究. Beijing: Sanlian Shudian, 2012.

Shang, Wei. *Rulin Waishi and Cultural Transformation in Late Imperial China*. Cambridge, MA: Harvard University Asia Center, 2003.

Shanghai Shuhua Chubanshe 上海書畫出版社, ed. *Huang Daozhou Xiaojing* 黃道周孝 經. Shanghai: Shanghai Shuhua Chubanshe, 2011.

Sharpe, Kevin. *Image Wars: Promoting Kings and Commonwealths in England, 1603–1660*. New Haven: Yale University Press, 2010.

———. *Selling the Tudor Monarchy: Authority and Image in Sixteenth-Century England*. New Haven: Yale University Press, 2009.

Shiroi Takashi 城井隆志. "Minmatsu no yichi han Toulin ha seiryoku ni tsuite—Gu Tenshun o megutte" 明末の一反東林派勢力について一 顧天峻をめぐて. In *Yamane Yukio kyōju taikyū kinen Mindaishi ronsō* 山根幸夫教授退休記念明代史論叢, edited by Mindaishi kenkyūkai Mindaishi ronsō henshu iinkai 明代史研究會明代史論叢編集委員會, 263–82. Tokyo: Kyuko Shoin, 1990.

Shyles, Leonard. "Defining Images of Presidential Candidates from Televised Political Spot Advertisements." *Political Behavior* 6:2 (1984): 171–81.

Sieber, Patricia. *Theaters of Desire: Authors, Readers, and the Reproduction of Early Chinese Song-Drama, 1300–2000*. New York: Palgrave Macmillan, 2003.

Smith, Judith G., ed. *Tradition and Transformation: Studies in Chinese Art in Honor of Chu-Tsing Li*. Seattle: Spencer Museum of Art at the University of Kansas in association with the University of Washington Press, 2005.

Sommer, Matthew. *Sex, Law, and Society in Late Imperial China*. Stanford: Stanford University Press, 2000.

Spence, Jonanthan D. *Treason by the Book*. New York: Penguin Books, 2002.

Struve, Lynn A. "Chimerical Early Modernity: The Case of 'Conquest Generation' Memoirs." In *The Qing Formation in World-Historical Time*, edited by Lynn A. Struve, 335–80. Cambridge, MA: Harvard University Asia Center, 2004.

———. *The Ming-Qing Conflict, 1619–1683: A Historiography and Source Guide*. Association of Asian Studies Monograph and Occasional Paper Series no. 56. Ann Arbor, MI: AAS, 1998.

———, ed. *The Qing Formation in World-Historical Time*. Cambridge, MA: Harvard University Asia Center, 2004.

———. *The Southern Ming: 1644–1662*. New Haven: Yale University Press, 1984.

Sun Kaidi 孫楷第. *Zhongguo tongsu xiaoshuo shumu* 中國通俗小說書目. Beijing: Guoli Beiping Tushuguan, 1933.

Swope, Kenneth. "All Men Are Not Brothers: Ethnic Identity and Dynastic Loyalty in the Ningxia Mutiny of 1592." *Late Imperial China* 24:1 (2003): 79–129.

Theiss, Janet. *Disgraceful Matters: The Politics of Chastity in Eighteenth-Century China*. Berkeley: University of California Press, 2004.

Thorton, Patricia M. *Disciplining the State: Virtue, Violence, and State-Making in Modern China*. Cambridge, MA: Harvard University Asia Center, 2007.

Turner, James Grantham. "'Romance' and the Novel in Restoration England." *Review of English Studies*, n.s., vol. 63, no. 258 (2012): 58–65.

Väth, Alfons, S. J. *Tang Ruowang zhuan* 湯若望傳. Translated by Yang Bingchen 楊丙辰. Taipei: Shangwu Yinshuguan, 1960.

Vitiello, Giovanni. *The Libertine's Friend: Homosexuality & Masculinity in Late Imperial China*. Chicago: University of Chicago Press, 2011.

Volpp, Sophie. "Classifying Lust: The Seventeenth-Century Vogue for Male Love." *Harvard Journal of Asiastic Studies* 61:1 (June 2001): 77–117.

Wakeman, Frederic, Jr. "Boundaries of the Public Sphere in Ming and Qing China." *Daedalus* 127:3, Early Modernities (Summer 1998): 167–89.

———. *The Great Enterprise: The Manchu Reconstruction of Imperial Order in Seventeenth-Century China.* 2 vols. Berkeley: University of California Press, 1985.

———. "Romantics, Stoics, and Martyrs in Seventeenth-Century China." *Journal of Asian Studies* 43:4 (Aug. 1984): 631–65.

Wang, Chen-main. "Claiming Dynastic Legitimacy: Qing Strategies during the Dorgon Era." In *The Scholar's Mind: Essays in Honor of Frederick W. Mote*, edited by Perry Link, 147–80. Hong Kong: The Chinese University of Hong Kong, 2009.

———. *The Life and Career of Hung Ch'eng-ch'ou (1593–1665).* Association for Asian Studies Monograph and Occasional Paper Series 59. Ann Arbor, MI: Association for Asian Studies, 1999.

Wang Dafeng 王大鋒. "Jidu fengyun hua Feng Quan: Zhuozhou 'Kuaixuetang Feng shi' cu kao" 幾度風雲話馮銓——涿州'快雪堂馮氏'粗考. In *Zhuozhou wenshi ziliao*: *Zhuozhou renwu lu xuji* 涿州文史資料：涿州人物録續集, *Wenshi ziliao* 文史資料, vol. 5, edited by Zhengxie Zhuozhou Shi *Wenshi Ziliao* Weiyuanhui 政協涿州市文史資料委員會, 261–77. Beijing: Zhengxie Zhuozhou Shi Wenshi Ziliao Weiyuanhui, 1997.

Wang Enjun 王恩俊. "Fushe chengyuan de jiashi jiqi yingxiang" 復社成員的家世及其影響. *Shixue jikan*, no. 1 (Jan. 2007): 83–87.

———. *Fushe yu Ming mo Qing chu zhengzhi xueshu liubian* 復社與明末清初政治學術流變. Shenyang: Liaoning Renmin Chubanshe, 2013.

———. "Shilun Fushe neibu de zhengzhi fenqi" 試論復社內部的政治分歧. *Dongbei shida xuebao* 205 (issue 1, 2007): 21–25.

Wang Fansen 王汎森. *Wan Ming Qing chu sixiang shi lun* 晚明清初思想十論. Shanghai: Fudan Daxue Chubanshe, 2004.

Wang Hung-tai 王鴻泰. "Ming-Qing de zixun chuanbo, shehui xiangxiang yu gongzhong shehui" 明清的資訊傳播，社會想像與公眾社會. *Mingdai yanjiu* [Taipei] 12 (June 2009): 41–92.

———. "Qinglou mingji yu qingyi shenghuo: Ming-Qing jian de jinü yu wenren" 青樓名妓與情藝生活–明清間的妓女與文人. In *Lijiao yu qingyu: Qian jin dai Zhongguo wenhua zhong de hou/xiandai xing* 禮教與情慾——前近代中國文化中的後／現代性, edited by Hsiung Ping-chen 熊秉真 and Lu Miaw-fen 呂妙芬. Taipei: Zhongyang Yanjiuyuan Jindaishi Yanjiusuo, 1999.

———. "Shehui de xiangxiang yu xiangxiang de shehui" 社會的想像與想像的社會. In *Wan Ming yu Wan Qing: Lishi chuancheng yu wenhua chuangxin* 晚明與晚清：歷史傳承與文化創新, edited by Chen Pingyuan, Wang Dewei, and Shang Wei, 133–47. Wuhan: Hubei Jiaoyu Chubanshe, 2001.

Wang Jian 王劍. *Mingdai mishu yanjiu* 明代密疏研究. Beijing: Zhongguo Shehui Kexue Chubanshe, 2005.

Wang, Richard. *Ming Erotic Novellas: Genre, Consumption, and Religiosity in Cultural Practice.* Hong Kong: The Chinese University Press, 2001.

Wang Zijin 王子今. *"Zhong" guannian yanjiu—yizhong zhengzhi daode de wenhua yanjiu yu lishi yanbian* "忠"觀念研究——種政治道德的文化研究與歷史演變. Changchun: Jilin Jiaoyu Chubanshe, 1999.

Wright, Arthur F., ed. *Confucianism and Chinese Civilization.* New York: Atheneum, 1964.

Wu Chengxue 吳承學. *Wan Ming xiaopin yanjiu* 晚明小品研究. Nanjing: Jiangsu Guji Chubanshe, 1998.

Wu Chucai 吳楚才 and Wu Diaohou 吳調侯, comps. *Guwen guanzhi* 古文觀止. Beijing: Zhonghua Shuju, 1959.

Wu, H. Laura. "Corpses on Display: Representations of Torture and Pain in the Wei Zhongxian Novels." *Ming Studies* 59 (May 2009): 42–55.

Wu Han 吳晗, comp. *Chaoxian Li chao shilu zhong de Zhongguo shiliao* 朝鮮李朝實錄 中的中國史料. Vol. 9. Beijing: Zhonghua Shuju, 1980.

Wu, Jiang. *Enlightenment in Dispute: The Reinvention of Chan Buddhism in Seventeenth-Century China.* London: Oxford University Press, 2011.

———. *Leaving for the Rising Sun: Chinese Zen Master Yinyuan & the Authenticity Crisis in Early Modern East Asia.* London: Oxford University Press, 2014.

Wu, Silas. *Communication and Imperial Control in China: Evolution of the Palace Memorial System, 1693–1735.* Cambridge, MA: Harvard University Asia Center, 1970.

Xie Canglin 謝蒼霖. "*Yuzhang congshu* ben *Qishan wenji* dianjiao houji" 豫章叢書 本《芑山文集》點校後記. *Journal of Jiangxi Institute of Education* (Social Sciences) 26:2 (2005): 60–63.

Xie Guozhen 謝國禎. *Ming-Qing zhiji dangshe yundong kao* 明清之際黨社運動考. Shanghai: Shanghai Shudian, 2004.

Xie Zhengguang 謝正光. *Qing chu shiwen yu shiren jiaoyou kao* 清初詩文與士人交遊 考. Nanjing: Nanjing Daxue Chubanshe, 2001.

Xie Zhengguang 謝正光 and Fan Jinmin范金民, eds. *Ming yimin lu huiji* 明遺民錄彙輯. Nanjing: Nanjing Daxue Chubanshe, 1995.

Xin Deyong 辛德勇. "Ji Nan Ming keben *Xicao qiu si*" 記南明刻本西曹秋思. *Yanjing xuebao* [Yenching journal of Chinese studies] 18 (2005): 69–109.

Yan Liqun 閻立群. "Qingrun xiuya, yunwei duju: Gu Mei he ta de *Lanshi tu*" 清潤秀 雅，韻味獨具-顧眉和她的《蘭石圖》. *Shoucang jie* 66 (June 2007): 60.

Yang Haiying 楊海英. "Hong Chengchou Liu shi furen kao" 洪承疇劉氏夫人考. In *Qingshi lunji: Qinghe Wang Zhonghan jiaoshou jiu shi huadan* 清史論集：慶賀王鐘翰教授九十華誕, edited by Zhu Chengru 朱誠如, 262–71. Beijing: Zijincheng Chubanshe, 2003.

———. *Hong Chengchou yu Ming-Qing yidai yanjiu* 洪承疇與明清易代研究. Beijing: Shangwu Yinshuguan, 2006.

———. "Longwu zhengquan de zhongxing zhanlue jiqi pomie—guanyu Longwu 'bing fa wu lu' shoufu Nanjing jihua de yanjiu" 隆武政權的中興戰略及其破滅--關於隆武"兵發五路"收復南京計劃的研究. In *Gushi wencun* 古史文存*: Ming-Qing juan* 2, edited by Zhongguo Shehui Kexue Yanjiuyuan 中國社會科學研究院. Beijing: Shehui Kexue Wenxian Chubanshe, 2006.

———. *Yuwai Changcheng: Wanli yuanchao kangwo Yiwu bing kaoshi* 域外長城：萬曆援朝抗倭義烏兵考實. Shanghai: Shanghai Renmin Chubanshe, 2014.

Yang Nianqun 楊念群. *Hechu shi Jiangnan?: Qingchao zhengtong guan de queli yu shilin jingshen shijie de bianyi* 何處是江南？—清朝正統觀的確立與士林精神世界的變異. Beijing: Sanlian Shudian, 2010.

Yang Xin 楊新. *Cheng Zhengkui* 程正揆. Shanghai: Shanghai Meishu Chubanshe, 1982.

Yang Zhen 楊珍. *Qingchao huangwei jicheng zhidu* 清朝皇位繼承制度. Beijing: Xueyuan Chubanshe, 2009.

Yao Nianci 姚念慈. *Qing chu zhengzhi shi tanwei* 清初政治史探微. Shenyang: Liaoning Minzu Chubanshe, 2008.

Ye Gaoshu 葉高樹. *Qingchao qianqi de wenhua zhengce* 清朝前期的文化政策. Taipei: Daoxiang Chubanshe, 2006.

Ye Jun 葉軍. "Zheng Man yanjiu: Jianlun Mingdai houqi dangzheng" 鄭鄤研究：兼論 明代後期黨爭. PhD diss., Fudan Daxue, 2002.

Yü, Chun-fang. *The Renewal of Buddhism in China: Chu-hung and the Late Ming Synthesis*. New York: Columbia University Press, 1981.

Yu, Jimmy. *Sanctity and Self-Inflicted Violence in Chinese Religions, 1500–1700*. London: Oxford University Press, 2012.

Zhang Jue 張覺. *Han Feizi jiaoshu* 韓非子校疏. Shanghai: Shanghai Guji Chubanshe, 2010.

Zhang Sheng 張升. "Chen Mingxia yu Gong Dingzi, Yan Ermei 'juejiao' kao" 陳名夏 與龔鼎孳、閻爾梅"絕交"考. In *Gu Cheng xiansheng jinian ji Ming-Qing shi yanjiu wenji* 顧誠先生紀念暨明清史研究文集, 157–67. Zhengzhou: Zhongzhou Guji Chubanshe, 2005.

———. "Feng Quan shishi zakao" 馮銓史事雜攷. *Dushi zhaji* (1998): 89–96.

———. "Lun Chen Mingxia yu Fang Yizhi de jiaowang" 論陳名夏與方以智的交往. *Anhui shixue* 2 (2000).

Zhang Xianbo 張憲博. "Fushe de zhengdaohua quxiang" 復社的政黨化趨向. *Mingshi luncong* 6 (2004): 414–43.

Zhang, Yimin. "The Role of Literati in Military Action during the Ming-Qing Transition Perioid." PhD diss., McGill University, 2006.

Zhang, Ying. "Confucian Principles and Representations of a Scandal: Writing about Zheng Man in the Seventeenth and Eighteenth Centuries." *Intellectual History* [Sixiang shi] (Taipei). Forthcoming.

———. "Li Zhi's Image Trouble." Paper presented at the "Writing, Virtues, and the Social World: Li Zhi and 16th-Century China" workshop at the University of Chicago, October 18–19, 2013.

———. "Politics and Morality during the Ming-Qing Transition, 1570–1670." PhD diss., University of Michigan, 2010.

———. "The Politics and Practice of Moral Rectitude." *Late Imperial China* 34:2 (Dec. 2013): 52–83.

Zhang Yongwei 張永葳. "*Doupeng xianhua* zhi lishi xushi guankui" 《豆棚閒話》之歷 史敘事管窺. *Jiangnan daxue xuebao* no. 2 (2007): 75–78.

Zhang Yuxing 張玉興. "Nan Ming Hongguang di 'shide' boyi" 南明弘光帝"失德"駁 議. *Wenhua xuekan* issue 3 (2008): 40–57.

Zhao, Jie. "A Decade of Considerable Significance: Late-Ming Factionalism in the Making, 1583–1593." *T'oung Pao*, 2nd ser., vol. 88, fasc. 1/3 (2002): 112–50.

Zhao Xuepei 趙雪沛. "Qingshu kuangfang de linxia fengzhi: Ming zongshi nü ciren Zhu Zhongmei chutan" 清疏曠放的林下風致—明宗室女詞人朱中楣初探. *Beijing daxue xuebao* (zhexue shehui kexue ban) no. 4 (2004): 132–41.

Zhao Yu 趙羽. "Gong Dingzi jiaoyou shiji kaolue" 龔鼎孳交遊事跡考略. MA thesis, Nankai Daxue, 2005.

Zhao Yuan 趙園. *Ming-Qing zhiji shidafu yanjiu* 明清之際士大夫研究. Beijing: Beijing Daxue Chubanshe, 1999.

———. *Zhidu, yanlun, xintai: Ming-Qing zhiji shidafu yanjiu xubian* 制度·言論·心態——《明清之際士大夫研究》續編. Beijing: Beijing Daxue Chubanshe, 2006.

Zheng Chenyin 鄭晨寅. *Huang Daozhou lungao* 黃道周論稿. Zhengzhou: Henan Renmin Chubanshe, 2014.

———. "Huang Daozhou xiaoti shixing kao" 黃道周孝悌實行考. *Min-Tai wenhua jiaoliu* no. 2 (2010): 49–57.

———. "Shiguan yishi yu zhijian fanshi: Huang Daozhou zoushu yong *Yi* lunxi" 史官意識與智諫范式：黃道周奏疏用《易》論析. *Jimei daxue xuebao* (shehui kexue ban) no. 4 (2010): 75–85.

———. "*Xiaojing* 'yi xiao wei zhong' shuo de kunjing yu chaoyue: yi Ming mo daru Huang Daozhou wei ge'an" 《孝經》"移孝為忠"說的困境與超越–以明末大儒黃道周為個案. *Xinan jiaotong daxue xuebao* (shehui kexue ban) 13:3 (May 2012): 57–63.

Zheng Chenyin and Tang Yunzhu 湯雲珠. "Huang Daozhou yu *Xiaojing* de lishi yuhe" 黃道周與《孝經》的歷史遇合. *Xiaogan xueyuan xuebao* no. 5 (2010): 26–31.

Zheng Wei 鄭威. *Huang Daozhou moji daguan* 黃道周墨跡大觀. Shanghai: Shanghai Renmin Meishu Chubanshe, 1992.

Zhou, Yiqun. "The Hearth and the Temple: Mapping Female Religiosity in Late Imperial China, 1550–1900." *Late Imperial China* 24:2 (Dec. 2003): 109–55.

Zito, Angela. *Of Body and Brush: Grand Sacrifice as Text/Performance in Eighteenth-Century China*. Chicago: University of Chicago Press, 1997.

INDEX